More critical acclaim for ANTHEM...

"Brilliant...a passionately written book.
I couldn't put it down."
—Bobbie Battista, CNN

"A highly personal if raw portrait of 'the unpublicized America.' "
—*Elle*

"Gabel and Hahn let the subjects speak for themselves.
In allowing the individual voices to combine on the'
they let us hear the symphony."
—*Huntsville Times*

D1517438

...and for ANTHEM, the documentary film, winner of the 1997 Fipresci Jury Prize

"One of the most charming and thought-provoking
documentaries of 1997!...
a road movie that takes your heart and mind cross-country."
—*Chicago Tribune*

"Four stars!...A stunning documentary...
Vital and unique!"
—*Box Office Magazine*

"Funny and immensely thought-provoking."
—*Seattle Post-Intelligencer*

"Delightful...humorous, yet thoughtful...
a refreshing lack of cynicism [with] a great deal of wisdom."
—*Los Angeles Times*

"Essential viewing...an uplifting ode to all that's still great!"
—*Variety*

"Memorable...illuminating...
Anthem offers several remarkable and thought-provoking moments...
A rousing success!"
—*Hollywood Reporter*

ANTHEM

AN AMERICAN ROAD STORY

SHAINEE GABEL AND KRISTIN HAHN

AVON BOOKS ◆ NEW YORK

"Nigger Song: An Odyssey," from Rita Dove, *Selected Poems*, Pantheon Books, copyright © 1980, 1993 by Rita Dove. Used by permission of the author.

"Oppression" by Jimmy Santiago Baca from *Jimmy Santiago Baca: Immigrants in Our Own Land.* Copyright © 1982 by Jimmy Santiago Baca. Reprinted by permission of New Direction Pub. Corp.

AVON BOOKS, INC.
1350 Avenue of the Americas
New York, New York 10019

Copyright © 1997 by Shainee Gabel and Kristin Hahn
Front cover art supplied by Zeitgeist Pictures
Interior design by Stanley S. Drate/Folio Graphics Co., Inc.
Visit our website at **http://www.AvonBooks.com**
ISBN: 0-380-79014-9

Library of Congress Cataloging in Publication Data:

Gabel, Shainee.
    Anthem : an American road story / Shainee Gabel and Kristin Hahn.
    p.   cm.
1. United States—Description and travel. 2. Gabel, Shainee—Journeys—United States. 3. Hahn, Kristin—Journeys—United States. 4. Interviews—United States. 5. United States—Social conditions—1980-   6. Anthem (Motion picture) I. Hahn, Kristin. II. Anthem (Motion picture) III. Title
E169.04.G33   1997   97-3239
917.304'929—dc21   CIP

First Avon Books Trade Paperback Printing: October 1998
First Avon Books Hardcover Printing: August 1997

AVON TRADEMARK REG. U.S. PAT. OFF. AND IN OTHER COUNTRIES, MARCA REGISTRADA, HECHO EN U.S.A.

Printed in the U.S.A.

OPM 10 9 8 7 6 5 4 3 2 1

THIS BOOK IS DEDICATED TO
ALL OF THE PEOPLE WHO LENT US THEIR VOICES,
AND TO OUR MOTHERS—WHO GAVE US OURS.

ACKNOWLEDGMENTS

This book (journey) would not have been possible without the support of our families (especially Jennifer Gabel, Charlotte Brookstein, Jeanne Gabel and Col. H. B. Norton), friends, and friends of friends who gave us their couches, their Rolodexes, their two cents, and their faith.

To all of the assistants, publicists, agents, receptionists, and lawyers who returned our calls and, in turn, added dots to the map of our itinerary.

For reading and reading and reading, we'd like to thank Jo Ann G., Nick D., Christopher B., J. C., and Michael K.

Thanks to Renee Zuckerbrot for your eyes, your ears, and Reeses pick–me-ups.

To Todd Komarnicki: Thanks for nothing? Thanks for everything?

People who stuck their necks way out and are greatly appreciated for it: Amy Nesbitt and her indefatigable New Orleans transcribers, Carol Dean, Julie Yaeger, Lynn Harris, Joe Berlinger, Bruce Sinofsky, RJ Cutler, Bob Hawk, Lee Keele, Emily Russo, and Nancy Gerstman.

All of our love and gratitude to our patron saint, Doug Brinkley.

To Jennifer Rudolph Walsh, Jay Mandel, and the Virginia Barber Agency: Thank you for the fuel, the fire, and the endless stoking.

To our production team: the tireless Lucas Platt, the fearless Bill Brown, and the relentless Andrea Buchanan and Edet Belzberg.

Our love to our parents: Gary Brookstein (Net Guru), Nancy Erskine, Dianne Lauf and Howard Hahn for trusting that we would actually make it. And an extra hug and kiss to Jo Ann Gabel for being there every step of the way, making sure we would.

To Ed Woll and Joey Slotnick, for loving us ever more, no matter how far away.

To everyone at Avon Books, thanks to all of you who helped create this book. Of course our special thanks to Kristin Cortright.

To Jennifer Hershey, our editor extraordinaire, we salute you for your vision, your confidence, your pushing and prodding and boosting. Thank you for seeing a book.

CONTENTS

INTRODUCTION
· 1 ·

THE ROAD
· 7 ·

CONTENTS

THE END OF THE ROAD

• 387 •

A journey is a person in itself; no two are alike.
And all plans, safeguards, policing, and coercion are fruitless.
We find after years of struggle that we do not take a trip;
a trip takes us.

—JOHN STEINBECK,
Travels with Charley: In Search of America

Dear _____:

We are writing to invite you to be interviewed for our independent documentary film: *Anthem*.

Anthem will explore the power of inspiration as captured in a series of interviews with contemporary American visionaries, attempting to humanize and demystify the process of ascension into prominence in American society through the stories of those who are forecasting and shaping how Americans think, believe, and live.

The interviewees are demographically diverse, span all generations, and include well-known faces alongside unknown faces. By asking each participant to tell the story of his/her own journey, *Anthem* examines the modern relevance of the American legacy that says the "American dream" grants every citizen the gift of equal and unrestricted opportunities. *Anthem* will look at the question of the "dream's" gradual demise versus its ability to reincarnate itself in the next millennium.

The goal of the film is to compose an "anthem" about the promise and sickness of this country, comprised of voices from all regions and generations; a new American Anthem that can serve as a time capsule for the America that enters the twenty-first century. In the spirit of Studs Terkel's *Working* and John Steinbeck's *Travels with Charley*, we believe the story will be woven by the mythology of the American on the road, the people encountered along the way, and the opinions of Americans on America.

The interview will be conducted informally at a location and time that is convenient for you, with a very small crew (us). We ask that the setting illustrate an aspect of your life that is personal and organic to your nature. The interview will require thirty to forty-five minutes.

In an age associated with reckless media, desensitization to violence, and an ill planet, we believe that *Anthem* will find a voice that speaks of hope, faith, and volition. We would be honored if you would join us.

Best regards,
Shainee Gabel and Kristin Hahn

INTRODUCTION

anthem: **1** a sacred vocal composition **2** a hymn of praise or loyalty

We introduced ourselves over Oreos while standing around the catering table. We were both working for the director of an independent film called *Ed and His Dead Mother.* By the time Ed's mother had sucked the blood of her fourth or fifth victim, we had become inseparable on the set, finding a kinship that quickly became friendship.

The idea began as one of those fantasies you have when things get too claustrophobic or predictable, which in Los Angeles can be pretty often. We were both working in different arenas of the film and television worlds. Neither of us was doing exactly what we had come for. But in our minds we were preparing—as it seems most Los Angeles transplants are—for something more fulfilling. We wanted to make a film of our own. We wanted to work together. We wanted to get out of Los Angeles. We wanted to see the country. It wasn't long before we discovered that we shared a dream. We named it *Anthem.*

Over the next two years, the notion grew and changed and took on a life of its own. We didn't go out one night and decide over a beer to make a time capsule road movie about the American dream, the American hero, the land, and the lingering influence of the founders of the country. Many ostensibly unrelated factors—including a handsome Englishman, Kristin's recurring dreams of Wyoming, a school in South Central, and a few job changes—conspired with perfect synchronicity to bring us to the right place at the right time.

However, the most fundamental impetus came from the city we were living in, a city that generates most of the images that have come to define America. We grew tired of the broadcast version of this country—government gridlock, ubiquitous violence, intolerance, and disenfranchisement. We were not convinced that ours is a time defined only by political apathy, declining opportunities, and the general malaise that has become synonymous with our generation—a generation identified only by a letter, nondescript and clandestine. There had to be more.

We felt compelled to explore another possibility—the idea that America is the land of dreams, a place where things can happen. The idea was to ask a diverse group of Americans a series of questions in hopes of getting a more accurate picture of the country. We thought: If we could distill America into one collective voice, a song, a composition, what might it sound like and what would it tell us? If we could tell the story of the American dream—by living our own—how many voices would we meet along the way? How many versions of the dream would they speak of and who would say the dream is still alive? Maybe we do still live it. Maybe there would be something out there that binds even the seemingly most disparate of us. Maybe it depends on who you ask.

Inevitably, at the age of twenty-six, we were consumed by the promise of absolute liberation—just us, a car, a camera, and a lot of people to meet—the ultimate road trip. We quit our jobs and holed up at a friend's in Lake Tahoe, where we planned, talked, schemed, and typed. Constructing the interviewee list for *Anthem* was part research, part instinct. It was an unscientific process—we selected a lot of people who we simply felt personally drawn to—but we did try to include a representative voice from as many sections of American culture as we could manage: education, conservation, science and medicine, entertainment, literature, politics, religion, and so on. We weren't necessarily looking for the most well-known figure in each field; instead we sought out the maverick. We also planned to talk to people that we'd meet along the way in gas stations and diners: our intention was to ask the politician, the farmer, the rock star, and the waitress the same list of questions.

We left Lake Tahoe with a stack of invitations, dropping them in a mailbox on the way out of town. A couple of weeks later we received our first reply, a yes from Ben Cohen and Jerry Greenfield, the ice cream moguls. A second acceptance from George Stephanopoulos soon followed—two firm dates for the otherwise empty *Anthem* itinerary. Suddenly we had exactly four weeks to sublet our apartments, pack for a life on the road, prepare a mobile production unit, and schedule a host of other interviews.

We had no viable car, no camera, no sound equipment, no lights, no tripod, no sleeping bags, no real technical experience, no other confirmed interviews, and no financial backing. We did have faith, however. And hope. And trust. And so we made long lists of our needs—both personal and production—and split them up for the most challenging scavenger hunt of our lives.

Before we could get on the road, we needed to recruit a third member of our team. We planned to shoot the majority of the trip ourselves, but we needed a cinematographer who could follow behind us, capturing unconventionally emblematic images of Americana that we could later combine with our own footage. This talented enthusiast must also be so lured by the romantic notion of the open road that he'd find his own equipment (we couldn't afford to rent any), provide his own transportation (not minding the extra 20,000 miles on his odometer), and be willing to work for free. Enter Bill Brown, part twenty-five-year-old disillusioned film school student, part angel. After a one-hour meeting, he agreed to appear in towns a few weeks after we had left, to shoot images based on long voice mail messages we'd leave for him describing our experiences with each place and person.

In addition to Bill, two of our friends, Andrea Buchanan and Edet Belzberg, agreed to be our stationary associate producers in L.A. They would help with some research and scheduling. Shainee's father volunteered as our Internet guide, and we were officially staffed.

The following book is the story of our trip; its telling was guided by our collective (now-fermented) memory, nearly two hundred hours of video and audio recordings, and our journal entries. With two separate voices to tell the story, our hope is to take the reader along with us on our journey—to see some of what we saw and hear some of what we heard. Our goal was not to critique what people had to say but to listen and observe, letting the readers decide for themselves where the voices of America overlap, contradict, and echo one another. However, please keep in mind that the group of participants is not intended to be a representative sampling of the country. The makeup of this project was self-determined: in order to include a given perspective, someone, of course, would need to agree to an interview. Despite this, we worked hard to achieve a balance of genders and ethnicities. Where we didn't, it wasn't for lack of trying.

We are not trained historians, sociologists, or journalists. We are not attempting to uncover any new or startling conclusions about the state of the nation and its origins. We know that different people on a different trip with a different purpose might tell a different story. What we hope to offer is simply a snapshot of America—at one moment in time shortly before the dawn of a new millennium—as witnessed by two young women who took a long road trip one summer.

—Kristin Hahn and Shainee Gabel, 1997

[America] is truly the home of all nations and in [its citizens'] veins flows the blood of every people on the globe. Patriotism, in the exclusive meaning, is surely not made for America. Mischievous everywhere, it were here both mischievous and absurd. The very origin of the people is opposed to it. The institutions, in their principle, militate against it. The day we are celebrating (July 4th) protests against it. It is for Americans, more especially, to nourish a nobler sentiment; one more consistent with their origin, and more conducive to their future improvement. It is for them more especially to know why they love their country; and to *feel* that they love it, not because it *is* their country, but because it is the palladium of human liberty—the favored scene of human improvement.

—Fanny Wright, social reformer,
Fourth of July oration, 1828

THE ROAD

LEAVING LOS ANGELES 6/6

(Shainee)

When the day came to leave Los Angeles, we were overwhelmed by such a mixture of opposing emotions and anxieties that they all seemed to cancel one another out. I truly felt nothing: no anticipation, no apprehension. I remember sitting down on the plane and wondering whether I was experiencing a state of mind somehow remotely akin to the goal of Zen Buddhism. Several years earlier I had read a book called *Zen for Beginners*, which described a way to achieve inner calm through counting exercises. The idea was to try to clear your mind of all thoughts and focus on a number, beginning with one and eventually reaching ten. If any other thought popped into your brain, you were supposed to start over. I never got past three.

Now, after weeks of frantic preparation, without any counting, I had suddenly reached a sacred state of perfect senselessness.

I slept on the plane to Tampa, Florida, where Kris and I had arranged to pick up the car we'd borrowed for the first stretch of our trip. The airport was the usual nightmare, especially with our trunks of camera equipment, clothes, and provisions for the next three months. That's how long we thought we'd be gone— three months, not twelve. That belief, along with pretty much every other notion of how our project would progress, was shattered and reshaped again and again over the course of the next year.

When we arrived at the motel in Tampa, we immediately dug into our trunks. We pulled out boxes upon boxes of gadgets—and gadgets for the gadgets, all wrapped in bubble paper—and began the task of unraveling the mystery that was our equipment. I liked how compact it all was, how it could be packed up and swung over our shoulders, keeping us mobile and spontaneous. We were a unit, a family; Kris, myself, our two Sony VX3s (which were soon christened "the twins"), and our Sony DAT Man, the only male in the group.

Our goal was to become the specialists that were absent from our equation: the crew. It seemed important that we have some extra stuff to fiddle with, since that's what crew people do: fiddle. So before we got on the road, we stopped at a local camera shop and bought even more lens attachments, cleaners, and cases to add to our collection—the more stuff we had, the more it would look like we knew what we were doing. I thought of musicians tuning their instruments—the twist of a guitar string, the rosin on a bow, and the way they look up and squint at something no one else can see while they listen for the improved note. All the fiddling communicates a special secret knowledge. In our case, I hoped fiddling would communicate pure technical skill.

The next morning we packed up the car and drove our inaugural few hundred miles. Our destination was New Orleans, and the trip would take us north on I-75 toward Jacksonville, and then west on I-10 along the Gulf Coast through Alabama and Mississippi to Louisiana, a total of 653 miles. Neither one of us had ever driven that stretch, nor had we ever set foot in the states of Mississippi or Louisiana.

We got off the highway around Biloxi to see what remained of the old Gulf Coast South. That early in the trip I still had fantasies of driving cross-country on winding back roads, byways lined with the colorful sights and sounds of small-town America.

Biloxi would be our first official venture off the beaten six-lane path. It was our first official brush with disappointment, too. I was expecting grand old Southern antebellum mansions with sumptuous lawns and gardens sprawled out along the water, complete with a riverboat's pipe organ soundtrack. In actuality, what greeted us was a tourist trap: the flashing lights of casinos, food stands, and souvenir and T-shirt shops. There was a pipe organ, but the music repeated on a seven-minute loop that would have driven even the most grounded person mildly batty. After about five miles of what looked like Disney World's version of the South, we lost interest in the scenery and switched our attentions to our new best friend—the radio.

Mississippi riverboats

We found National Public Radio's ubiquitous *All Things Considered* on the local station and were greeted with commentator Andrei Codrescu's observations on the garish realities of the typical American family vacation—high entrance fees, ostentatious billboards, motels with free HBO, and so on. He chastised the "McDonaldized Americans" who leave junk food in national parks and get the deer addicted to McEverything. There was an eerie synchronicity between Andrei's commentary and what we were seeing.

Eventually, we returned to the interstate not terribly discouraged. It was, after all, only our first day on the road. And before we knew it, we had crossed the Louisiana sunset into Slidell and were about to experience one of the most enchanted cities in the country for the first time in our lives.

DOUG BRINKLEY

HISTORIAN

NEW ORLEANS, LOUISIANA

(Shainee)

We were meeting Dr. Doug Brinkley at the Howling Wolf, a bar in the warehouse district of New Orleans, at 9 P.M. Although this was technically the beginning of our journey, it had in actuality begun a couple of months before, with an article from a magazine and a trip to Kent State. Earlier that spring, when we'd been drawing up our wish list of interviewees for the trip, I had read an article on Doug in *Spin*. Although we would find out later that Doug is one of the most well-respected young writer/professor/historians in the country, the article focused on a program that Doug had started called the Majic Bus. Later, when we actually interviewed Doug, he explained the inspiration for the project.

"I was a history professor at Hofstra University in New York," he said. "I had turned thirty and had just written a biography of Dean Acheson and one of James Forrestal, but I was tired of teaching in a stodgy classroom atmosphere. So I decided to take to the open road, using cross-country family vacations I had taken as a boy as inspiration. I also drew from the books *On the Road* and *The Electric Kool-Aid Acid Test*.

"Ralph Waldo Emerson once said, 'There is no truth but in transit,' and I've always liked that saying. I like the idea of seeing the country by getting out, escaping the classroom. So I hooked up with a trucker named Frank Perugi who had an old New York City Transit bus. We gutted it, made it into a moving classroom, and I started teaching on the road."

Doug's mission to experience history as a living, breathing entity by traveling across the country was quite similar to our goal, so we put Doug on our initial wish list. The article had mentioned how busy Doug was with other commitments, but he responded to our request very quickly. I remember getting the call. I was sitting in my living room surrounded with all the paraphernalia involved in planning our trip—books, magazines, and endless pieces of paper covered with endless lists. When the phone rang, I couldn't even find it. I finally unearthed it and heard Doug Brinkley's enthusiastic voice, coming from what sounded like a noisy airport. Doug spoke quickly and loudly, trying to be heard over the flight announcements. Not only did he want to participate but he wanted to help us get more people involved. By the way, did we think we could possibly make it out to Kent State for the twenty-five-year commemoration of the student killings—less than three weeks away—so that he could meet us and maybe introduce us to some people?

Kent State?

In Ohio?

Doug's enthusiasm hit me like a stun gun. He was the first person to give our project the very simple but imperative response of "Do this. It's a great idea. I will help you." I held the phone tightly as Doug rattled off the impressive list of Americans that the Majic Bus had visited over the prior three years, people he could help us contact.

He and his students had visited Dr. Martin Luther King, Jr.'s, home in Atlanta and Carl Sandburg's home in North Carolina, and had discussed Tennessee Williams while strolling through the French Quarter in New Orleans. In addition to studying and reading novels and historical texts that correlated with each stop on the Majic Bus road, Doug sought out people that his students would find inspiring. They had discussed *Death of a Salesman* with Arthur Miller in Miller's Connecticut backyard. They had traveled to New York City and shared their thoughts about *Beloved* with Toni Morrison. They even met with the ailing William Burroughs in Lawrence, Kansas, after studying *Naked Lunch* on the bus.

I myself had attended a very expansive northeastern state college with an enormous choice of curricula, but I had never even dreamed of a class this good. Kris and I were soon to learn for ourselves just how vast a difference there was between thinking you know something about a person or a place and seeing and hearing things firsthand.

Doug wrapped up his thumbnail sketch of himself by mentioning some of his other projects: fiction, television shows, guest lectures, a radio show on American poets, and a two-volume biography on President Jimmy Carter, researched by accompanying the former President on trips all over the world. Later, when Doug had become a friend, he would intrigue us with anecdotes about peace talks in Haiti with Carter and intimate dinners with Yasir Arafat, where the yogurt sauce was served by an Uzi-toting butler.

Doug continued to speak very fast. He didn't have a lot of time to talk and no time to take a breath. I just listened. Doug quoted Thomas Wolfe, saying that "there are a billion forms of America," and suggested that we were both trying to peek in on all of these subcultures. I was beginning to suspect that this man had been sent to Kris and me as a guide, a kindred spirit.

He wanted to meet us as soon as possible. We had been insanely busy, trying to prepare for the trip, and there was no time to spare for such a meeting. But so far our itinerary began and ended with Ben and Jerry, our lone confirmed interview, and Kent State was the only other offer on the table. We decided to go.

KENT STATE, OHIO 5/5

(Shainee)

Doug Brinkley had felt compelled to take us under his wing and we couldn't have asked for a more inspiring mentor. We decided that we would make Kent State a trial run—we'd get used to driving distances, talking to strangers, and running equipment. We called and got a press pass for the weekend-long event whose speakers included former Senator Eugene McCarthy, Senator George McGovern, and journalist Charlayne Hunter-Gault. We flew to the East Coast, borrowed a car from my family, and drove the 420 miles from my family's home in New Jersey to Kent State. It was on this trip that we got our very first and very last flat tire. It was on this trip that we met our first scary truck stop where nothing looked appetizing—except the seventeen flavors of pies. It was on this trip that we would meet three people who we would eventually interview. And it was on this trip that we discovered that we were really about to take a journey of our own making.

Doug gave a speech at the conference about American pop culture and how it reflects history. He was witty and irreverent, and I remember noting how anomalous he was in this otherwise somber memorial weekend.

At one point Doug went on a riff about tracking American trends through popular music. There was an old woman sitting in front of us who looked like she had stepped out of *American Gothic*. She was apparently offended by Doug's inclusion of such topics as Bob Dylan and Chuck Berry in a serious gathering about a time in history that killed off a president, his brother, a pacifist civil rights leader, 55,000 American soldiers, untold Vietnamese, and five college students who were at the wrong place at the wrong time. The woman actually got up and left the room with a most audible gasp when Doug explained that the band Steely Dan had lifted their name from a dildo in *Naked Lunch*. We had just dived headfirst into the deep end with this singular man.

After Doug's speech, we introduced ourselves. He is a thirty-four-year-old with the face and energy of a teenager—to describe him as boyish is an understatement. He always wears jeans, a button-down shirt, and a sports jacket that is usually a little too big. And he always talks a mile a minute. He told us how excited he was to see McGovern and McCarthy speak—two presidential hopefuls from that infamous time in political history—and that he'd known Senator McGovern for a while and wanted to introduce us to him that night.

We gave Doug a lift back to his hotel. He had a mandatory conference dinner, but we would meet later for a drink. On the way, we told Doug about our infant plan for *Anthem*: the subject matter, the themes, the targeted interviewees, our backgrounds, and so on. It seemed that we were passing the test because he began to list all the people that he could help us contact. By the time we reached the hotel,

Kristin was madly scratching on a stray napkin. As we pulled up to the hotel door, Doug nimbly gathered up his blossoming pile of books and papers, stepped half-way out of the car and said, "I have calls to make, the dinner, a run, and a shower—meet me back here in two hours." And he slammed the car door shut. Kris and I watched the man/boy disappear into the hotel in silence. She turned to me with an expression on her face that said exactly what I was thinking: "What *is* he?"

We went to our own motel to change and on the way back to Doug's hotel, we talked about the impact of a figure like George McGovern—how he would be discussed in history classes for centuries to come as the man who spoke out against the Vietnam War, spoke up for black people and for women, and whose campaign was the target of Nixon's Watergate conspiracy. Our conversation moved from the mark of the Vietnam War on my parents' generation and the generations to follow to the horror of the Kennedy and King assassinations, and the radical changes in mores during the 1960s. We were about to meet George McGovern, a man who personified a legendary period of time in this country, and I wondered what it would feel like to come face-to-face with a real live chapter in history. I was nervous.

We met in the hotel lobby where Doug was sitting with the senator over drinks. They stood up when we approached and Doug made introductions. Senator McGovern pumped our hands and said, "So I hear you're making a movie!" Exactly what a grandpa would say. He looked more like a sweet older man than the elder statesman that I had pictured in my mind's eye. We had seen pictures of Senator McGovern smiling radiantly during his nomination acceptance, marching with Dr. Martin Luther King, Jr. But now he was older and looked . . . fragile. Doug said that they needed to finish talking and he would meet us in the bar downstairs. McGovern offered that he'd be happy to consider participating in *Anthem* and we said our good-byes.

Kris and I spent the next fifteen minutes picking the cashews out of the mixed nuts before Doug joined us. We hadn't known him for more than a couple of hours, but when he sat down, we could tell he was upset. Kris asked him what was wrong. He told us that Senator McGovern's daughter had been unsuccessfully battling alcoholism for many years. She had been walking home one night about six months earlier and had passed out in a snowbank. She froze to death, leaving her two little girls behind.

Doug had not seen the senator since it happened. When they were parting, he'd felt that he must acknowledge the tragedy and had given Senator McGovern his condolences. The senator broke into sobs and Doug was stunned by the depth of his grief. He consoled Senator McGovern as best he could and walked him to the elevator.

After telling us this, Doug was still visibly shaken and we were left speechless, feeling like voyeurs looking head-on into the lump lodged firmly in the grandpa's throat and seeing firsthand what he carried with him, so close to his spirited surface, every moment of the day. It was devastating.

We returned to the conference the next day and watched Senator McGovern speak. He was eloquent and seemed kind, standing tall and strong behind the podium. I understood for the first time why my parents had believed in him so deeply. He spoke of the tragedy of Kent State, of the grief of the entire country, and of the collective shock of disbelief as everyone watched their televisions and looked to one another with questions of "What happened? What have we done?" Senator McGovern told the story of one man in particular whose daughter had been killed in the shooting. He was a steel worker from Pennsylvania who had written to the senator asking one simple question: "Why?" Apparently, McGovern had stayed in touch with him for several years. On more than one occasion, the man would show up at the senator's office unannounced and just cry. Senator McGovern went on to speak of the anguish of losing a child, whether they are eight or eighteen or forty. We listened, knowing how well he understood.

On our way out of the auditorium, I looked closely at the artless buildings and the symmetrical lines of cement sidewalks marked intermittently with nondescript street lamps. The students walked slowly between the buildings, balancing books, papers, and cups of coffee. There was nothing extraordinary about this place. I continued to stare into the face of the homely campus, trying to re-create in my mind the events of that fateful day. But it was incomprehensible. Even though I had seen footage of the incident, I couldn't imagine the forces that conspired to result in the death of five students. I thought about the countless demonstrations and rallies against apartheid during my own college years and it seemed impossible to me that the vigor and righteousness of youth could be so gruesomely misconstrued as threatening. The irony is that the dead and injured were not even involved in the demonstration. They just happened to be walking by, maybe trying to balance *their* books, papers, and cups of coffee. Kris and I didn't know then that the American government has never made any official apologies or reparations to the families of the victims—even to this day, more than twenty-five years later.

The entire weekend was an incredible journey back to a time and place that until then had only been the stuff of textbooks and tests. I had known about Kent State, but I had never truly felt the impact of what the American public must have experienced during those years of upheaval, protest, war, and political scandal. It was the first of several times in the months to come when we would be thrust into someone else's shoes—to see, hear, and feel as they did—if only for a moment. It struck me then, while Kris and I were still in preparation for our journey, that we were embarking on a trek that would be far different from anything we could ever imagine. Our trip was something that we would live and come to understand only through actual experience. It was a distinction that Doug knew well and we were grateful for the early introduction to a simple truth.

NEW ORLEANS, LOUISIANA   6/8

(Shainee)

Before we left Los Angeles, I had purchased a discount motel card that was supposed to make booking a room in advance easier and cheaper. I tried it out for the
first time when I called to get us a room at a Quality Inn in Louisiana. The person
on the other end of the 800 number said that everything in New Orleans was either
occupied or too expensive for us, so at their suggestion and with the assurance of
proximity to New Orleans, we unloaded in nearby Harvey.

We would not be staying in the thumping heart of the Crescent City, but we
were glad just to be somewhere with running water. That night, for the first time,
it occurred to Kris and me that we would have to lug all of our clothes and all of
the equipment—including the computers, television, and mini-VCR—into our
motel every night. And we did, sometimes up several flights of stairs, every single
night for the next six months.

The motel was dingy, with beds like the swayback mares of summer camp,
covered in shades of orange and brown. We showered and hurried and tried not to
look road-weary. We wouldn't have time to eat if we were going get to the Howling Wolf by nine o'clock, so we went without dinner, which was also the beginning
of a trend. When we arrived at the bar at nine-fifteen, Alex Chilton, a friend of
Doug's, was playing. Doug had already filled us in on the legendary singer/song-
writer whose number-one hit with the Box Tops, *(I'm Going Home, My Baby Done
Wrote Me) The Letter*, is a classic.

The warehouse district of New Orleans has been gentrified over the last ten
years, so what used to be nineteenth-century storage for the "wares" that would
come up and down the Mississippi is now largely upscale apartments and restaurants. The buildings are painted in every color of the spectrum—as is most of
New Orleans—and the streets are largely still paved with cobblestones. Doug didn't
show up until way after ten o'clock. By the time he arrived, I had already decided
that he had forgotten us.

The hour we spent waiting for him was one of the most difficult *Anthem* tests
that I had endured so far. Since his phone call, our itinerary had become more
crowded, and I thought of how we had scheduled everything around meeting
Doug, on time, in New Orleans, on this particular Friday night. I began to have
thoughts of failure. What if people just didn't show for interviews? We had maybe
eight or nine tentative acceptances so far and we had simply made the decision to
go, picked up, and promptly left. We had left our homes, our jobs, our friends, and
our boyfriends, we had borrowed a ridiculous sum of money, and we were now
sitting in some bar in New Orleans waiting for a man who we had talked to for
two hours once in Ohio. I began to think that maybe we had made some obscene

mistake. Just when my blood sugar finally crashed and Kris had reassured me for the one hundred seventeenth time that Doug would show, he did.

I stole a handful of olives from the bartender's garnish selection to satisfy my plummeting glucose and ordered a Scotch. The last time I'd had a drink was the last time I had seen Doug. I began to see a pattern forming. We watched the band and screamed a polite conversation over the blaring speakers, nodding and smiling at each other, even though we couldn't hear a word of what anyone was saying. At the end of the show Doug went backstage to talk to Alex while Kris and I waited outside, bleary-eyed and happy and a little tipsy. There was music coming from the bar next door and the whole scene was very sultry and Tennessee Williams-esque. When Doug finally emerged he said, "Time for the tour." We had thought we'd be going back to our Harvey hovel for some desperately needed sleep, but we were soon to learn that Doug did not understand the concept of rest.

We got into Doug's Jeep and drove to the French Quarter. One of our friends had dubbed New Orleans "a theme park of itself," and she was undoubtedly referring to the surreal movie-set quality of the French Quarter. Even though we were exhausted, we were still enchanted as Doug recounted the history of the Cajuns, the Creoles, and the Indians who all intersected in one city to create a world that is a unique mix. In fact, the entire state of Louisiana is arguably its own little universe with its own notoriously proud codes and laws, bearing little relationship to any other part of the country. It is beautiful and mystical and old.

Coming from Philadelphia, I have always been partial to the historical cities of America. It was one of the things I missed the most when I lived in Los Angeles—a sense of past. Kris grew up amidst the southwestern clash of ancient adobe and prefab strip malls and marveled at the rows of balconied apartment buildings and shotgun houses that lined streets only wide enough for a horse and carriage.

We arrived at Café du Monde and stepped into another century and another continent. The café's interior was a salmon color and flanked on all sides by pillars and high arches. There were no actual walls in the open-aired main seating area, only railings of black iron lattice supporting massive green ceiling-to-floor canvas shades that could be rolled down in the case of rain or cold. Awnings with broad green and white stripes jutted out onto the street. The ceilings were about forty feet tall, with enormous fans that whirl always. Row upon row of small tables with iron chairs filled the floor, and along the far wall the staff sat and relaxed between customers.

There were at least ten waiters, even at that hour, and they were all dressed in a uniform that resembled that of the Good Humor man who used to come tinkling into the cul-de-sac of my childhood neighborhood every afternoon at five-fifteen. The staff consisted of white, black, and Asian men and women of all ages. Some sat alone and sipped coffee, some smoked, some stared off toward the dark Mississippi River. A few Vietnamese waitresses huddled together over Tupperware containers of rice and chatted in their native tongue. Doug explained to us that the café positions were a favored job for recent immigrants to New Orleans.

Local legend has it that since the café opened almost 100 years ago, it has never closed, except during one hurricane. It is always open and always willing to serve. The café's late-night clientele was a bustling cross section that included "gutter punks" (the New Orleanian term for runaway teens with Day-Glo hair who live in the streets and parks), a group of middle-aged men in suits (no doubt a contingent from the ever-popular New Orleans convention package), young daters, and tourists.

Best beignets this side of the Atlantic

Café du Monde has a very limited menu. There is chicory coffee, chicory coffee with milk, fresh-squeezed orange juice, and these remarkable fried pieces of dough drowned in powdered sugar called *beignets*. Doug ordered two plates for us and a round of café au laits and I guess we finally had dinner. Everything cost a dollar and tasted like France.

We stayed at the café late into the balmy night. Doug was thrilled that we were so impressed with his home city and told us stories about the great Mississippi Delta, the Louisiana Purchase, and the origins of jazz. He spoke so lovingly of New Orleans. We were rapt.

Eventually, Doug dropped us off at our car and suggested that we interview him the next morning at his usual morning haunt, a coffee bar called True Brew. We said, "Sure, what time?" He thought for a second about what he needed to accomplish before he flew to Washington the next afternoon and said, "Well, how about you meet me after my run at . . . let's say eight?" We smiled wearily in agreement. It was 4 A.M.

As of this writing, I'm still not sure how we managed to drag our asses to the café that morning. Doug was already halfway through his second double latte when we arrived. We got our coffees and started the interview. Doug began by describing his childhood in Atlanta and later in Toledo, Ohio. His father had clearly planted the seed of the Majic Bus with the family trips he planned for the Brinkleys every summer.

"We had a twenty-four-foot Coachman trailer and we would drive everywhere. By the time I was sixteen, I had already visited forty-eight states, getting to see Yellowstone, Yosemite, the Grand Canyon, the Mississippi River, the Painted

Desert. Reading my American folklore, plus all of these travels, made me decide that I wanted to be an American historian.''

Doug told us that working in a record store during college opened up his view of America even more; he found his first inspirations among singers like Woody Guthrie and Hank Williams.

''I remember sitting at a coffeehouse and reading, over about a two-day period, Woody Guthrie's book *Bound for Glory*, which I loved, because he talked about his life as a folksinger traveling the country. And of course Guthrie wrote *This Land Is Your Land.* But they cut out the verse I like the best, the one that talks about the other side of the 'no trespassing' sign, the blank side that 'was made for you and me.' I always liked that idea of ultimate freedom . . . and I don't like fences.''

Later, at Georgetown, Doug wrote his doctoral dissertation on Dean Acheson, Harry Truman's secretary of state, who was famous for his role in the Korean War and his China policy during Mao Tse-tung's Cultural Revolution.

Doug said, ''Acheson was a very influential person, very conservative, a pragmatic sort. I always had romantic inclinations, but doing the dissertation on somebody who was the ultimate pragmatist was good for me.'' He paused. ''After that, I was able to balance the two, instead of being all wild-eyed and looking at life like a thundercloud.'' The Acheson piece was later published by Yale University Press and was the beginning of Doug's writing career, which has since included a volume of poetry, countless historical biographies, and a forthcoming novel.

Doug Brinkley

''I'm writing a biography of Jimmy Carter,'' Doug continued. ''The first volume, *Jimmy Carter: Citizen for Peace*, looks at what President Carter has done since he left the White House on January 20, 1981.''

The filming of Doug's interview at the café was interrupted several times by the clanging of dishes and a perturbed woman speaking very loudly to her boyfriend on the pay phone at the door. Soon after we had officially begun shooting our very first interview, we made our very first official decision to change locations to eliminate ambient noise. We went to Doug's apartment a few blocks away and we got another false start when Kris stopped me in midquestion to flatten Doug's cowlick. He smiled like an embarrassed kid, saying he never could control the lawless locks, and helped her by licking his own hand and pressing it to his head. That taken care of, he continued to speak about how he had first been bitten by the teaching bug while coaching a Little League T-ball team.

"I always liked the idea of passing on what I knew to others. The key to teaching is just pointing to the door and letting students kick it open themselves. Kerouac had a line about young people: 'They're all angels of pure future.' I always liked that line." He smiled. "I would like to think that when all the Majic Bus students grow old and gray, and they look back at the sweep of their lives, the moments they spent on the Majic Bus will be one of their highlights.

"So I look at the whole Majic Bus with a little bit of wildness; I think learning should be wild, too. There's a little bit of anarchy involved with just splitting, taking off, and meeting all these writers. I try to keep that rough edge to it."

With this, Doug had articulated exactly how we hoped to feel in looking back on our own trip. We went on to talk about the fact that each generation experienced this country differently.

"Kurt Vonnegut once told me, when I mentioned Generation X, 'Look, you're all Generation A. Everybody's starting new. You're facing life new, you're facing different sets of problems.' It doesn't make sense to say today's generation has a more bogus deal than a generation that had to barrel through the Great Depression or had to pioneer out west with endless disease. Does this generation face a unique set of problems? Absolutely. You're growing up in a time when love or sex can equal death from AIDS, there's a five-trillion-dollar debt, and environmental degradation . . . but there are also advantages.

"With that said, what is true about generations is that people living within an age difference of five or six years are gonna go through America at this moment in time together. And in old age, they will have seen the transformation of American culture through a similar lens. A certain moment of time is a very shared kind of experience among the people who lived through it together."

Doug had just made a pertinent point, one that would also define the time capsule goal of our project. This same trip, taken even one year later, would be completely different—and Doug was prepping us to take in as much as we could and to recognize it as a connecting experience. We moved on to asking Doug about his own influences. Who did he admire?

He answered, "Ken Kesey, who wrote *One Flew Over the Cuckoo's Nest*, talks about warriors, the people who are fighting for things. One is Morris Dees, at the Southern Poverty Law Center in Montgomery, Alabama. Morris started his career doing mail-order catalogs, made a lot of money. But he put quite a bit back into fighting hate crimes. Through the Southern Poverty Law Center, he's tackled skinheads, taken on the KKK, White Citizens Councils . . . and Morris has been in the forefront of using the law to shut these groups down."

Doug went on to name some other personal heroes. "Coretta Scott King, the widow of Dr. Martin Luther King, Jr., because of the dignity she carries with her. Millard Fuller, a minister and reverend in Marietta, Georgia, who's created Habitat for Humanity, where they build low-income housing for people. Jimmy Carter is somebody I admire immensely.

"And somebody else—Chuck Berry. It's the 1950s, Eisenhower's President, the remnants of McCarthyism are still with us, and for an African-American to come out and sing *Roll Over, Beethoven* was a revolution. Rock 'n' roll was slapping European culture in the face. The song was an affirmation not only of African-American culture but of American culture.

"I'm also a great admirer of Franklin Roosevelt, who was elected president four times. A man with polio, whose legs were like strands of spaghetti, who had to be lifted and moved places. A man who was able to lead the country through some of our most traumatic times by saying, 'You have nothing to fear but fear itself.' That's optimism. If I have a philosophy, it's one of optimism. And FDR had that."

From the beginning of our trip, we were curious about whether we would be able to find common links between seemingly disparate people by looking to whom they cited as influential. Doug's list was eclectic, but he was the first to mention the name that would emerge as the most-oft-mentioned inspiration: Thomas Jefferson.

"I know, Jefferson had slaves, but he just stood so tall. John Kennedy had that great line when he had a group of Nobel Prize winners in the White House and he went up to make a toast. Kennedy said, 'Never has there been so much genius sitting and eating around the table at one time in the White House, except when Thomas Jefferson dined alone.' "

I asked Doug if he felt that we were living up to the founding principles of the country. He smiled wide and said, "Well, I think that we're trying. The founding principles were flawed. The Constitution was made for white, male, land-owning aristocrats of that time. But by having enough flexibility in the Constitution and in the Bill of Rights, we've been able to end slavery and grant women and African-Americans the right to vote. Progress has constantly been made on the great ideal of democracy."

We asked Doug how he defined the American dream. He responded by calling it "one of those all-pervasive clichés that hangs over our heads like a black storm cloud. It used to have a positive connotation," he said, "but now it seems too much like it's something you have to live up to. If you don't . . . Look out! I love the book *Fear and Loathing in Las Vegas* by a friend of mine, Dr. Hunter Thompson, where he's dealing with the American dream after Vietnam and Watergate. He asks a guy at a taco stand in Las Vegas, 'Have you seen the American dream? What happened to the American dream?' The guy answers, 'Oh, the American dream is down the road, about four miles. But it's been condemned.' This guy's taking it literally, talking about some old hotel or something. I think that kind of captures the notion that the American dream doesn't exist. It's a shut-down concept. However, the idea of having your own personal dream in America is very real and it's something that people should pursue."

Later we would find that what Doug defined as a personal dream—or rather the *freedom* to pursue a personal dream—is indeed how many people define the

American dream. I was curious about where the term came from and asked Doug about its origin. "It became an immigrant term. It's a variation on 'In America, the streets are paved with gold.' Andrei Codrescu, a Romanian poet friend of mine who lives in New Orleans, says that in Romania they used to say, 'In America, dogs have pretzels on their tails.' It's such an odd kind of image, but it meant that there was extra wealth here."

Doug went on, suggesting that the term "American dream" was really just propaganda. "America was never paved with gold. It was paved with the sweat of slaves from Africa and coolie labor from Asia and with the decimation of Native Americans. There was a lot of violence and slaughter going on for this American dream. I don't think it's a good concept to hold on to. And maybe one of the things that we need to do is just get beyond it."

It was interesting that Doug cited propaganda as the origin of the concept of American dream. As one would expect regarding propaganda, we would find that most people we interviewed were either offended if they recognized the American dream as such or completely bought into it. Everyone seemed to have very strong opinions one way or the other. Doug spoke next about another topic that would resurface regularly on our trip—the experience of movement.

"One thing I always was interested in," he said, "was the movement westward, the settling of the country, the 'sea to shining sea' idea. The historian Frederick Jackson Turner has this frontier thesis where he says, 'Americans have a frontier valve that's psychological.' And what he means is you might be from St. Louis, Missouri, and never leave, but in your mind you know you could pick up tomorrow, move to Phoenix, change your name, and take on a new identity. That psychologically, we have space and movement and the one shared thing that everybody in the United States has—except for the Native American people—is this movement experience. Whether you were escaping from the Irish potato famine in the 1840s, whether you were escaping poverty in Poland in the 1920s, whether you were from Asia, coming over from Vietnam in boats, coming up from Mexico, or coming from Africa and being forced through slavery to move here. We've all had a shared movement experience. It defines the American character in many ways."

Though Kristin and I had been traveling only a short time, I knew that Doug was citing a prevalent truth, one that would come up again and again. Kris and I were craving this very movement ourselves. Later, John Perry Barlow would say that the idea of movement is in our genes, Studs Terkel would discuss the nomadic America as part of the birth of the country, and Willie Nelson would speak lovingly of the Gypsy living inside of him. For myself, it was the luxury of autonomy coupled with the endless space that comes with traveling that struck a chord. What Doug already knew—and what we were about to find out—were the advantages of never being stationary.

Doug continued the thought, saying, "I never know how much of an American I am until I'm abroad. I'll go to a city like Amsterdam and I'll be thinking, 'Isn't this great.' Then, after about a week, I start getting claustrophobic. Everything seems small. I don't feel the space.

"I might be here in downtown New Orleans right now, but believe me, I feel the river, and I feel this vastness, that if I just get on I-10 heading west, I'm in the Texas plains or I'm along the Red River, if I head north. There's just this vast space in America that's really liberating. So I can relax here. I don't feel cramped because I can always take off. The escape valve in the twentieth century is the automobile."

The glaring difference between the frontier days and now is that we have nowhere new to go. We've settled as far west as we can, and I wondered if Doug had an opinion on whether reaching the end of Manifest Destiny had had an impact on the country's sense of boundlessness.

"That's a good question. There were two big intertwined issues in nineteenth-century America: slavery, which was resolved with the Civil War, and western expansion. But by 1898, at the time of the Spanish-American War, the United States had settled the country as far westward as possible. People were sitting in San Francisco and Seattle and Los Angeles and they were still looking westward and finding only the Pacific Ocean. The United States became an imperial power and started acquiring empires—Hawaii, Cuba, Puerto Rico, Guam, the Philippines. We couldn't stop ourselves. That's why we have this whole theme in twentieth-century America of becoming global, trading everywhere, going everywhere. 'Go to the moon!' John F. Kennedy called his program the New Frontier—it was his general slogan for his administration."

As Kristin and I set out to look for an American identity, we decided early on to ask people to tell us a story that would begin or end: "Only in America." It eventually became *Anthem*'s $25,000 question. Doug laughed, saying it sounded like the beginning of a poem, but answered, "Only in America would a professor of history be allowed to teach a university class living on a bus—and have the students get college credit for it. Only in America can you go into a place like the French Quarter and hear cowboy singers from El Paso, zydeco singers from Lafayette, and jazz musicians from right here. Nowhere but in America can you find the diversity of landscape: the great redwood trees, two thousand years old; the Mojave, the world's second-largest desert; the Rocky Mountains. I think also only in America do you have New York City, which is *the* city; every other city in the world pales compared to New York."

Doug also said that the one book you needed to read to understand America was Walt Whitman's *Leaves of Grass*. Whitman's was another name that would surface repeatedly, especially when we talked with writers. We spoke a little bit about Walt Whitman and his personification of the hope that the country was founded on, which got Doug on a roll about the unique qualities of America and how they are being misdirected.

"I love this country just a huge amount. I became an American historian because of it. But it's because I love it so much that I'm going to have to get the strength—as a writer, teacher, citizen—to confront things that I don't like. So often people who are more toward the left, where I would put myself, just don't get out there and fight. Rush Limbaugh could just be swatted away like a fly. He's historically wrong about everything he talks about and he's going to go down in history as just another cheap demagogue. He's teaching and preaching to the masses division, hate, mockery, ridicule, everything that Whitman would have disliked. And Walt Whitman stands *huge*, he's gigantic! He's like Paul Bunyan, while Rush is this little shrimp of a figure. Yet we lose track of that sometimes."

Doug went on: "And I think that people who are progressive need to get out and be a little more combative and *not* be so critical of other people. Whitman used to say, 'I contradict myself. I am large, I contain multitudes.' We *all* contradict ourselves."

We talked a little bit about the criticism of politicians in particular and the fact that government leadership is no longer allowed any contradictions. Then the phone rang and Doug jumped very quickly to get it. His body language said, "Please don't make me sit here any longer." I looked at my watch and saw that we had been asking him questions for over an hour. Doug was our first interview and we had wanted to test *all* of our proposed questions on him. I think, at that point, we were moving into the realm of torture. We decided to stop. When Doug returned, he made no move to sit back down. We told him we were done and he breathed deeply and said, laughing, "I think you guys probably got it."

The night before, at Café du Monde, we had asked Doug if we could cap the interview with some footage of him speaking by the river and repeating some of the lore around the flowing legend. But he suggested going to his office first so he could make some calls for us and give us some contact information for potential *Anthem* interviewees. We followed Doug into the neighboring room. He had a huge folk portrait of President Carter hanging over his desk. There were also citations, photographs, framed Majic Bus articles, and a poster with an old photo of Jack Kerouac and his poem *Tangiers* printed on it. The office was cluttered in a cozy kind of way. There was a huge calendar on one wall with all of Doug's appointments and trips; every daily square had at least two commitments scrawled on it.

Doug began flipping through his enormous Rolodex and shooting suggestions out as it whirled. First he called his friend Andrei Codrescu—by coincidence the same commentator we'd heard the day before on NPR—who was indeed home and agreed to let us come over that afternoon. Doug also called his pal Dr. Hunter S. Thompson while we were there and explained to Hunter's machine that there was a "high fun factor" involved in allowing us to come and interview him. Apparently, "fun" was the secret password needed for entrance into Dr. Thompson's world. Doug gave us profuse warnings about Hunter when he hung up the phone. He said he was happy to try to get Hunter to be in *Anthem*, but he couldn't be held responsible for anything that happened as a result. Doug said it was unlikely that we'd ever even get Hunter to answer the phone, that we might just have to show up at Hunter's home in Colorado and hope for the best. We assured Doug that we could take care of ourselves, wrote down a few more numbers, and then we all left for the river.

We drove down to the waterfront in Doug's Cherokee and thanked him profusely for all of his help. It was quite clear that he had been officially installed as our patron saint, and he would play the role with great skill over the year to come.

We weren't quite sure why Doug had taken us on, in addition to all of his other missions. Over a beer in New York a year later, we would ask him why he cared so much. He would reply with a sincere smile that he saw himself in us and that a lot of people had helped him for no apparent reason; he wanted to do the same. It was the beginning of a series of random acts of kindness by virtual strangers that would provide us with the ability to continue our trip.

We arrived at the river and parked the Jeep. At this point it was getting late and Doug had to catch a plane, so we had to make it quick. He walked very fast and Kris and I almost tripped over each other, trying to keep up. Doug started to talk about the Mississippi cutting through the Crescent City and I noticed Kris playing with our ''brand-new'' used camera. The battery had gone dead and the only thing she had recorded was Doug's explanation of T. S. Eliot naming the river ''the great brown god.'' Kris saw me looking at the camera as Doug continued to discuss the Mississippi. She knew that I knew it wasn't recording, but neither of us wanted to tell Doug that we had dragged him down to the river for no reason. So we just listened and enjoyed him for ourselves.

When Doug was finished with his abridged lecture, *The Mississippi River 101*, we all walked back to his Jeep. Doug was in front of us with his too-big sports coat, on this terrifically hot day, strolling alongside his beloved Mississippi, and just then the riverboats began to play *When the Saints Go Marching In*. It was a wonderfully gratuitous moment of schmaltz that made us both smile.

Doug drove us back to our car and we said our farewells with a round of hugs. He said he enjoyed the interview and called us ''earnest.'' Kris and I climbed out of the Jeep and Doug called out his open window to say that we'd all have to travel together sometime. We promised to meet him in Mexico for margaritas with a day's notice. He gave us a thumbs-up and drove away.

ANDREI CODRESCU

AUTHOR • POET • NPR COMMENTATOR

NEW ORLEANS, LOUISIANA

(Kristin)

New Orleans is the smallest big town in America. In our few short days there, we realized that everyone knows just about everyone else. Thanks to Doug, soon after our farewell by the river, we were headed toward the garden district and climbing the stairs to a pale yellow stained-glass antebellum home that belonged to a man who had recently intrigued us with his report about summer tourism on National Public Radio (NPR). Andrei is a regular commentator on the station, as well as an author, poet, and fellow independent filmmaker.

Andrei opened the door and greeted us with his head slightly drooping. He seemed overly tired or maybe hung over. With few words, he led us into his kitchen, and we all sat at his dining table, just kind of politely smiling at each other. Andrei is about fifty with a significant mustache, graying black hair, and a thick Romanian accent. He immigrated from Transylvania in the late 1960s; thirty years later, he is a prominent American writer.

Andrei explained he had just returned from Los Angeles, where he had attended the Digital World Conference as a panelist, and was jet-lagged. We asked him how the conference was. "It was an interesting combination of hippies, who now rule cyberspace, and business types, who are worried about where their millions of dollars are going," he said flatly. Andrei said most things flatly. I figured he probably knew they were funnier that way, or else he just couldn't—in his exhaustion—muster the energy to inflect.

We sat for a while at the kitchen table and talked about life on the road, New Orleans food, the insanity required to make a movie, how peculiar this America is, and the exquisite art covering his walls, all painted by his wife.

Andrei loved the food in New Orleans and spoke of it as a jeweler does the Hope Diamond. "Coops is tremendous—go there!" he urged. "They have this hot seafood dish that comes with all kinds of sea creatures that are perfectly made for late-night alcohol. It's got so much spice, it cuts right through the fog." I could tell he wished he knew us better so he could convince us to head to Coops for Dixie beers and generous bowls of sea creatures and blow off the interview. As exhausted as we were, I think Shainee and I would have preferred his idea to ours, but the fact that we were strangers seemed to preclude informality and helped us stay focused on why we had come.

"Have you read my book *Road Scholar?*" Andrei inquired. Shainee had seen the film version that Andrei had also directed, but neither of us had read the book. "The book is interesting because it has more stuff in it. They had to cut a lot out of the film, as you can imagine. There were about forty-five hours of film." Shainee and I had no idea, as we attentively nodded our heads, that we would soon be in a similar situation ourselves, cutting down almost 200 hours of our own footage into two, and then writing a book, which would indeed have more stuff in it.

We talked about where we could do the interview; Doug had suggested a nearby cemetery—a well-known favorite spot of Andrei's. I figured it reminded Andrei of his homeland. The tombstones in New Orleans were all above ground, as the city is built on a swampland. The ground literally swallows the graves just a little each day, so instead of underground caskets, large mausoleum-type structures huddle together like miniature medieval villages. "The cemetery is closed," Andrei said, seeming as disappointed as a vampire might be at the same news. "I went by it last night and I could not get in," he confirmed. So we opted for Andrei's heavily foliaged backyard as the interview spot.

Lafayette Cemetery, New Orleans

Andrei sat down on a bench surrounded by gardenias, crape myrtles, and a banana tree. Shainee asked Andrei what had inspired him most to become a writer. He spoke of his childhood in Transylvania and his teenage immigration to the United States. "I always knew I was a poet. I started writing poems when I was twelve, and I figured that was the thing I knew how to do. The chief source of inspiration for me was the town where I grew up because it was a very medieval place filled with ghosts who told their stories to me. And a host of old Romanian poets got me fired up as well. I believed—and still do—that poets were important to society because they carried, in a mysterious way, all the burdens of the world, and I couldn't think of anything better to be.

"Then later on," he continued, "my inspiration was simply being alive in the

United States, which was such an incredible thrill and miracle after the deadness of the fifties and early sixties in my home country . . . the fact of being alive, suddenly, in a Technicolor world, because I grew up in a monochromatic world where there was one color and it was gray. Even the simple contrast of having left this world where photos of old party secretaries hung on the walls and coming to a place where there were advertisements of . . . hundred-foot-tall women eating chocolates. The difference was between an image that upbraided and punished you versus one that cajoled and seduced and enticed. And all of a sudden, the world had exploded into color, and the pleasure of that is . . . still here.'' Andrei pointed to his chest.

Fresh from Doug's apartment and the idea of the movement gene, I couldn't help but think of Andrei as another variation on that theme—the commonality of all Americans coming from some other place, recently or otherwise. Andrei did not descend from the restlessness of the frontiersmen, but rather had escaped from behind an Iron Curtain to a new land where he was able to offer a fresh perspective on things the rest of us had just simply gotten used to.

''Luckily, my exile coincided with my wanderlust—that time in one's teens when an intense need for freedom just hits you,'' Andrei explained. ''I wanted to come to America because this was where the sound was coming from—rock 'n' roll. This is where the Beatles were landing. There was no question that America was the hippest place in the world and that's where everyone wanted to go. I listened to smuggled tapes of the Rolling Stones, Bob Dylan, and the Beatles, and it was like the Pied Piper—their music brought people out of their shells and we became awake to something new.

''I feel a certain liberty in speaking here that is satisfying to me,'' Andrei said. ''And I like the casualness of American society and the fact that we're not terribly bound by manners, rules, and mores here as Europe is, for example. We don't have the kind of strict social codes that dictate behavior. Americans are rather idiosyncratic and essentially friendly. Even in these days of paranoia about immigration and foreigners, I think there is a basic streak of openness in Americans.''

Andrei sat silent for a beat, apparently considering his last comment, and then added, ''We are bound by our laws inspired by the founding principles to be a multiethnic, multicultural society. I think places like Wyoming could use a few Pakistani restaurants.'' Andrei paused for a chuckle.

Because of Andrei's perspective on America, we were especially curious how he would define an iconic concept such as the American dream. ''Well,'' he responded, ''I'm not sure I believe in that American dream notion. I have plenty of dreams at night, and I think dreams should stay in the nocturnal realm, but I would say that the American dream for immigrants is a question of an identity switch. You can come here and be someone else—literally be born again.'' I thought of Doug's statement about Americans having the unique freedom to be able to go to another state, change their name, and take on a new identity. Andrei seemed to be happily rooted in a place where his personal identity was flexible, not absolute.

He reminded me of how comforting it was to be in control of that aspect of one's life.

"There have been periods in America," Andrei said, "when there has been a negative reaction to the idea of changing and picking up and starting over, and I think this is one of those times. I think we are now concerned about roots and defending our little patch, which seems to be more important than moving and changing and being free."

More people we would later meet on our trip would speak of a turning cultural tide toward establishing roots. But it contradicted what Shainee and I had already observed in everyone from the friends we'd left behind, to strangers we'd meet in small-town diners—a hunger to leave, to move. I think most Americans exist in a state of constant inner conflict—to root or to roam, both instincts equally strong. I thought of Doug's reference to the psychological release valve of the frontier, something that we have all inherited. But we came as wanderers seeking roots. I wondered which was the stronger legacy. Which was the more profound psychological and biological need?

Shainee asked Andrei, in terms of the shift toward establishing and defending roots, if he thought we were progressing or regressing as a culture. "Well, I don't think we're regressing," Andrei replied. "I don't think there is such a thing as going back on consciousness. I think we are now more clearly and more starkly divided in this country than we were when we were more inchoate in our differences. There is a lot more of everything in the world right now.

"It used to be you could go into a store and there would be a hundred things. Now there are a hundred thousand things, and they're all smaller, more colorful, and more interesting than ever before. It's as if our consciousness is creating a river of products and ideas that flows in every direction, and I don't think consensus is quite as easy as it used to be. So to live consciously right now is to be able to live with paradox—and not one, but many, because it's a tremendously paradoxical reality."

Given Andrei's idea about the impossibility of consensus in a society that is characterized by a river of choices and ideas, Shainee asked Andrei how he felt about the cohesion and modern interpretation of our civil liberties.

"Well," he began, "clearly, the Bill of Rights and the Constitution are fundamental to anybody who comes to this country from somewhere else, because the first thing that you gain is the freedom of speech and that's a liberty not specified anywhere else. I think the pursuit of happiness is a great notion but one that has unfortunately become the relentless pursuit of happiness—which is to say an obsessive immersion in material values—and that just can't bring about any kind of real happiness. It always moves it just out of reach. There's the kind of happiness that advertising promises you, but it's never quite satisfied because you need to buy the next product. So there will be no satisfaction.

"I also believe," he continued, "that there is a need to rewrite the document, making it what the poet Gary Snyder called 'The Declaration of Interdependence.'

While we clearly would assert our independence, we would also recognize our kinship to the land and to the animals and to the natural world, which is not defended anywhere in that original document. Maybe because the founding writers didn't know—it didn't seem necessary then, even though Jefferson, for one, was a great lover of the natural world.

"We ignore the fact that landscape creates us," Andrei said. "It makes us who we are. It's wonderful that Southerners are different from New Englanders, that they speak differently, that they tell different stories, that they have different daily experiences. The more we acknowledge the landscape and what the land does to us, the clearer we think—the better we are. In that sense, you know, your great travelers—Jack Kerouac, Whitman, Henry Miller . . . people who celebrated the variety and the differences of this country—are very important to everybody. It is important to be provincial, but it is also important to see that as part of a bigger spectacle."

We asked Andrei what he valued most about his landscape here in America. "I certainly have a sense of spaciousness. Usually after two months of being in Europe, I run right back because I somehow feel closed in, claustrophobic. I like to come here because I feel I have the space to stretch out," he said with a great sweep of his arms.

I found it curious that both Andrei and Doug had expressed the same sense of spaciousness—both while sitting in tightly knit neighborhoods in a heavily populated, boisterous city. They both seemed to feel that space was at their fingertips—just knowing it was there gave them peace of mind.

We then asked Andrei our "Only in America" question . . .

"Only in America," Andrei repeated, slowly rolling his words through his accent, "can you open a telephone book in New Mexico and find six pages of psychic healers—people who read your aura, regress you to a past life, see what's in the stars, and heal you through photons. Only in America can you drive and see so many cartoon versions of our country." Because Andrei had traveled the freeways and blue highways of America, and we were just beginning, we didn't yet know firsthand the road show that is America. But after experiencing the Lisa Presley airplane exhibit at Graceland, Dollywood, America's

Largest Cow, and an assortment of wax museums, we would become officially indoctrinated into America's cartoon tourist hall of fame. Hype is something that Americans seem to do better than anyone else.

Finally Shainee gave Andrei the opportunity to be president for a day . . .

Andrei laughed loudly at the absurdity of such a proposition, but he bit anyway. "If I were president—which I certainly don't want to be!—I would decree an end to boredom. I don't know if you can do that by edict, but I would mandate that everyone be tremendously amused for at least five minutes every day. And I think our collective spirits would be buoyed. I believe crankiness is at the source of all the horror we see. I mean people don't just shoot each other because they're poor, but also because they're cranky," Andrei declared, perfectly deadpan.

The sun was setting quickly behind us, reflecting its last colors into Andrei's sunglasses—this man who had come to this country so relatively recently but who had already become so essentially American through the shared values, liberties, and experiences of life in this country. It seemed clear at that moment that being American was a state of mind.

Suddenly I realized we had been sitting outside for quite some time. "Are we torturing you?" I asked Andrei, half-serious.

"Not yet," he said, laughing. "I'm just starting to enjoy this. You're the one who has to stand up and hold the camera."

Good point, I thought. I appreciated his concern and then wished we knew Andrei well enough to immediately head for Coops and continue the conversation over the sweating bottleneck of a cold Dixie beer.

We asked Andrei one last question about his opinion of the future of the American experiment. He jumped right in. "Well, the future of the American experiment is the future of the world, because the American experiment is *the*

twentieth-century experiment. The millennium will happen as a result of where we go from here—this place. That's just a fact. The languages of science, the languages of technologies, the languages of the imagination are all, in fact, driven by America right now."

His words evoked such a sense of possibility—accompanied by the risk of not living up to one's potential—that I wondered if America wasn't like the popular kid in high school. Things are easy when you're young and charismatic, but so often long-term success—an exceptional adulthood—comes out of some different kind of character that doesn't manifest itself early on. Would our still-young country live up to its promise in middle age?

We all walked in soft shadow toward Andrei's back door and through his house. We gathered up our things in the available early evening light as Andrei disappeared into his library near the foyer.

Shainee and I moved toward the front door ready to leave as Andrei emerged from his study with an armful of books, written mostly by him. "Here, this is for road reading," he said, piling them into our arms. We thanked Andrei for his time and his road ethics—we were just beginning to learn the ways of the road and accept our reliance on total strangers. I wasn't used to relying on anyone, so for me, this part of the trip was an act of surrender. Shainee and I had to begin to accept that as we traversed the landscape we would need to depend on people—for their suggestions, their support, their lemonade, their books, their understanding, their insight, their couches.

As I shook Andrei's hand, I noticed something behind him near an umbrella rack, something I had somehow missed when we first walked in—a blow-up doll of Edvard Munch's *The Scream*. It stood about four feet tall, a silent, agonized howl escaping its mouth, holding the sides of its melting face. Andrei was right, he was indeed a part of this world called America—a spectacle, as he had defined it—where seminal Expressionist art is mass-marketed as weeble-wobble inflatable dolls and Romanian nocturnal dreamers can speak their minds in the light of day.

It was time for some of that Southern food Andrei had extolled when we first arrived. Shainee and I drove down the lamp-lined streets toward the French Quarter. Along the sidewalks, street mimes made balloon animals for children; young tappers gave it their all for gazing tourists—bottle caps nailed to the bottoms of their shoes—and the jazz spilled out from clubs as we passed them, onto the road and into our open windows. We found Coops and, sure enough, the distinct aroma of sea creatures. For the first and probably last time in my life, I ate fried alligator—one sea creature I'm now pretty certain is not intended to be eaten by humans.

Shainee and I made a toast. "To Andrei for the restaurant recommendation and to each other," we said, the trip ahead still a mystery yet to be unraveled. We both had a palpable sense that we were on the road—together—for a reason, but the only thing we were sure of at this point was each other. We had a binding trust and a shared dream, and I was holding tightly on to a silent faith that those two things would fill our deficient itinerary and carry us far.

LEONARD BLAIR

SAXOPHONIST

NEW ORLEANS, LOUISIANA

(Shainee)

After twenty-four hours in the city, I decided that I wanted to have an affair with the whole of New Orleans: the pungent smells, the music, the moist heat, the lolling "sugar babies" and "y'alls," the iron balconies with flowerpots of night-blooming jasmine, the people, and the river. It was a city of spellbinding color and inspiration, and I couldn't think of a better place for our road trip to begin.

On our second night in the city, we ate in a restaurant that Andrei had suggested, where we ordered alligator nuggets, but Kris wrinkled her nose at the idea of sucking crawfish heads. We discussed the completion of our first two interviews and agreed that their content was promising. We had been worried that our questions might be limiting by design because we wanted to dissect several clichés that might not elicit anything but blank stares. We happily acknowledged that the opposite had been true and ate enough to make up for the deprivation of the prior two days. Exhausted, sated, and quite pleased with ourselves, we found our way back over the river to our Quality home.

Our last day in New Orleans was the crown jewel. We returned to Café du Monde for creamy iced coffees and more *beignets*. It was crowded with tourists during the day and was a much different place than we had seen at 3 A.M. As we sipped our drinks, we watched a man play saxophone in front of the main seating area. Tourists were throwing money in his case as they filed past this man, who stood out among the bevy of musicians that blanketed the streets and parks of New Orleans. He wore a bittersweet expression that managed to convey both his love for playing and his ambivalence about the venue. His repertoire included everything from *Winter Wonderland* (I guess to trick the tourists into forgetting the ninety-degree weather) to the *Pink Panther Theme*.

We approached him with our camera and were surprised that he didn't balk. It was the first of many times that we thought we would have to cajole people into ignoring a camera in their face, only to realize that they were quite comfortable with it—even welcomed it. Leonard actually knew the make and model of our Steadycam. He opened up to us immediately, not even bothering to ask what we were interviewing him for. We asked him to talk about New Orleans, what he loved about it and why he lived there.

Leonard—a day at work

Leonard proudly bragged about the food, the music, and the people. He claimed that you could walk down the street and say ''Good mornin' '' to someone and they would undoubtedly say ''Good mornin' '' back. "It's always been very culturally and ethnically diverse,'' he added. ''People living in the same neighborhood together . . . pulling together in times of strife and looking out for each other's kids.''

Doug had already filled us in on the diversity of New Orleans. Now Leonard was suggesting that there was more harmony in New Orleans than in other Southern cities, specifically between blacks and whites. We did know that the Creole population—a mixture of Caribbean and Spanish blood—had at one time been the ruling class, so the tradition of multiculturalism ran deep. We also suspected that the music might be what bound people together in this town. Leonard went on to talk of the modern New Orleans music scene.

''Jazz is America's gift to the world—culturally. Before that, pretty much any- and everything else was copied from Europe and various other countries. Jazz was started right here in New Orleans. So there are lots of local musicians that I look up to and these are cats who are not that well known, but hell, they're really great musicians, I've learned a lot from them. I only started getting really serious about music as a career—even though I have a degree in music—about four years ago when I started hanging in a community called the Tremé. It's a historical district right outside the quarter and there's a lot of music there. I started sitting in, learning tunes, getting back to my roots. These musicians helped me along. They're older cats, just incredible.

''Here I am now. I play out here just about every day in front of the Café du Monde and that's really good supplemental money. Two years ago I was able to quit my day job. Music's all I do now. I was waiting tables and bartending for fifteen years—and in this town that's a very good living because of our tourism—however, I'd say that I make at least 50 percent more than my best days as a waiter or bartender just about every day.''

Leonard was the embodiment of the American dream as defined by the music community of his hometown. He was doing what he wanted when he wanted and loving the life that he had created for himself by pursuing his passion. We asked him if he would say that he was living his dream. Without missing a beat, he said, "Definitely."

When Kris asked Leonard what he valued most about living in America, he looked straight into the camera and said, "The freedoms that are afforded. That's it—we're free people, we're not dictated to. This is a country that was built and then developed into a place where if you have the means or if you just have a thought and can find support, then you can obtain your dream. A lot of what is wrong about America is that people who were born here, for whatever reason, sometimes think that they're basically owed something. You're not owed anything. For instance, you see foreigners coming over here all the time, and they seem to climb the ladder a lot faster than most Americans do. The reason why is that they see the opportunity. And that's just what I'm doin'. I'd like to see this country through the eyes of a foreigner, coming over here to realize the dream."

Leonard had articulated what many people we met on our trip would echo: that many Americans seem to misconstrue opportunity as a guarantee. It was interesting to see the threads of patterns emerging so early in the trip. We had already heard from Doug about the responsibility of a generation to not get bogged down by thinking that their obstacles are any bigger than any other generation's and from Andrei discussing America from the perspective of someone from behind the Iron Curtain. On first glance, these three men had not had anything in common but a zip code, but they all seemed to embrace similar ideas about what this country had to offer.

Leonard told us that his band would be playing in the Tremé later that afternoon. He gave us directions to a place called Joe's Cozy Corner and said to drop in around five. We spent the rest of the day catching up on our research for upcoming interviews and then we headed to Joe's.

We drove down narrow streets that were lined with brightly colored cottages adorned with lattice ironwork and with floor-to-ceiling shutters painted in contrasting colors. Leonard had told us that the Tremé was largely a black neighborhood and we could see that we were far from invisible as people stared at us unabashedly as we drove by. This was a very close, very old community; in fact, Doug had told us that it was the oldest black urban community in the country. It was beautiful at that time of day, with late-afternoon gold casting its lanky shafts across the roofs and into the eyes of the groups of children that played around grandparent feet on the porches and stoops.

We asked for directions a couple of times and it seemed that Joe's Cozy Corner was indeed cozy because no one knew where it was. Not even the seemingly oldest woman in New Orleans, who, upon realizing that we were looking for a bar, responded, "Sugar, I been a teetotaler since the Prohibition, so Lord knows I wouldn't know of such a place." We thanked her anyway. It was reassuring to me that we—two white girls—could be lost in a Southern black urban neighborhood, a stereotypically precarious situation, and the stereotypical reaction—fear—was absent. I was not as hyperconscious of my skin color as I had been in South Central Los Angeles or parts of the Bronx in the past. At first I thought that it was because Leonard had affected our expectations, but then I realized the instinct was my own. In my gut I felt an acceptance and tolerance that was specific to this city.

Our entrance into Joe's Cozy Corner confirmed, however, that there was still trepidation about outsiders in the Tremé. People looked at us quickly, then self-consciously ignored us. But the waitress, a bastion of the Southern feminine hospitality we had already come to love, didn't even give us time to question whether or not it was appropriate for us to be there. Her smile told us not to feel shy or uncomfortable. She took us both by the hand and led us to a table where a man in his sixties was stirring a whiskey, took our drink order, and left us there. The man who shared our table did not return our smiles and shifted uncomfortably when Kris and I sat down.

What followed was a Lite beer in a time warp. Leonard's huge brass band wailed in the smoke-filled literal hole-in-the-wall, a space without a single window to give away the time of day. It was packed. The patrons were mostly middle-aged and older, very few young people. There was a particularly outstanding group of large women in cat's-eye glasses, dressed in tight, incandescently colored matching ensembles and high heels, dancing by the stage with absolute abandon. The music was powerful, the kind you can feel pounding in your sternum. The musicians were passionate and sweaty, and everyone in the room seemed to swing simultaneously in a common rhythm. It was gorgeous and I knew as I sat there listening, opening, that I was living what would become a wonderful memory. I felt privileged and wanted desperately to preserve the moment, but this was one of the rare times that we could not record anything. The bandleader did not want us to shoot inside because he thought it would disrupt the happening for everyone. He was probably right.

Leonard, now in his element, had shed his tourist persona and was freely gyrating, smoking, winking, and playing. He was home and this music was his being. I was glad that he didn't have to play any more Christmas carols that day. His playing had taken on the passion that I had seen in his eyes earlier when he had said that jazz was America's first gift to the world. Here, with his fellow brass, he ripped, and we were there, and so grateful that he had invited us.

We joined Leonard outside at their break. He introduced us around and one of the younger band members apologized that we couldn't shoot inside, but he suggested we go to a jazz funeral that would be happening the next day if we wanted to get some good footage. We got the time and address as Leonard kissed us and asked us to stay in touch. As the second set started, we went back inside, although we could stay for only a few more songs. When we got up to go, our tablemate looked at us and spoke for the first time. ''You girls be careful now,'' he said with a toothless smile.

JAMES REDFIELD

AUTHOR OF *THE CELESTINE PROPHECY*

HOOVER, ALABAMA

(Kristin)

I have to admit that I had some preconceived notions and a great curiosity about this man, this avatar, James Redfield, whose name I had seen on every fiction bestseller list for many months. The months, at this writing, have become years. On our trip, we'd wanted to interview people whose ideas were shaping the country. Certainly, in considering people who were shaping the country at that moment, we could not ignore Redfield's influence.

Everyone I knew had read the "little green book," including me. Yes, I read it—cover to cover. It is the story of a middle-aged man's journey to Peru in search of an ancient manuscript whose nine Insights are transforming the collective consciousness of mankind. *The Celestine Prophecy* is a kind of New Age *Raiders of the Lost Ark* with some awkward dialogue. But the story kept me on the page, and I think even Redfield might be the first to say that the communication of the ideas—not elegant writing—was the driving force behind his book.

The story's subtext is that all things are living, even things most people would typically consider inanimate. The main character gradually becomes able to recognize energy fields around people and objects in the natural world and grows to understand that the energy and intention we put out into the world is ultimately the cause and effect of what we get back. Via nine discovered "Insights," Redfield encourages a heightened sense of being and of living—a greater sense of awareness of all that is around us and our individual significance in the bigger picture.

At least that seems to be what he's getting at. The question is what makes this book—written by a first-time writer—so compelling. Exactly what chord has Redfield struck with this little green book that he had originally sold out of the trunk of his car? The most unexpected readers have been drawn to it—people on Wall Street, conservative grandparents, Harvard grads, and people in small towns in Iowa.

I couldn't help but wonder what this meant about America and what need these diverse people had in common. Were we having a coming-of-age as a more spiritual culture? Or was it just a backlash against the go-go eighties, mass penance for two decades of buying diamonds and furs with stock market winnings? Why are we all starving for meaning and morality in 200 pages or less? We wanted to meet Redfield and find out what *he* thought the obsession with his book signified for America.

We arrived around 10 P.M in the one-road town of Alabaster, Alabama, a teeny dot on the map just south of Birmingham. It was probably the most prosaic Wal-mart town America had ever given birth to. How does Redfield manage to eke out inspiration here? I wondered. I felt bad for its residents and could only hope that the darkness shrouded the town's hidden treasures.

There was only one motel, and we drove to it, praying for a room for our weary bodies. We weren't yet used to the demands of being on the road or the hairy schedule we had unwittingly boxed ourselves into.

Registering for the last available room, we noticed a group of construction workers standing around their truck watching us. We self-consciously walked to our room, lugging all of our belongings from the car, and turned the key to our luxury suite. We stood a few feet inside the room, again stunned. Speechless.

Lying on the bed were two men clothed only in briefs and big boots. They stared back at us and for a moment no one spoke; there were too many thoughts to process at once. We spun around and quickly shut the door behind us with a meek "Sorry." We saw, on second glance, that the number on the door did not actually match the one on our key, and we ran, horrified, to Room 14. We rushed inside, slammed the door, and locked it. After we recovered from the embarrassment, we looked around and noticed that Room 14 hadn't been cleaned in about fourteen years. Not only that, we now possessed the alarming knowledge that our key opened other people's doors. Did *everyone* have a master key or were we just the lucky one-millionth customer?

Shainee ventured outside after a while to get a soda from the machine, and one of the ogling construction workers struck up a conversation. She later said he was nice and explained that he and the other guys—who happened to be occupying *all* of the other rooms in the motel—built Shoney restaurants across America. "You only build *Shoneys*?" Shainee had asked him. "Yeah," he'd replied. "We're in and out in six days, eight if it's a deluxe job. And then we travel to the next town." Shainee was intrigued by the idea that a major restaurant could be constructed from top to bottom, including a full kitchen, in less than a week. That's where the conversation ended, however, because I had gotten paranoid and come out to retrieve her.

Early the next morning we drove to Redfield's office just down the road. We waited in what turned out to be the *Celestine* clearinghouse. Four women sat in a room answering thousands of phone calls, letters, and faxes, all requesting more of the phenomenon that is James Redfield. Although the *Celestine* women had computers, there was nothing high-tech about their setup. The scene looked more like an insurance office from the early eighties than the headquarters of a million-dollar industry. Redfield came through the door.

Our physical encounter was nothing extraordinary. In short, Redfield was pleasant and prepared. I wondered if all the attention he had gotten from the book had made him apprehensive—even paranoid—of "cynical media people" who take great delight in crushing sweet-natured dreamers who try to usher in spiritual messages to the hungry masses. After the formality of our hellos, without wasting a breath, Redfield asked to see our interviewee release form. No one had yet asked us that, particularly before ten words had been exchanged.

It was clear he had been taken advantage of by *Celestine* poachers. But despite his anxiousness, he was quite a gentle, soft-spoken man with nondescript features, except for his penetrating sea-colored eyes. What he didn't yet believe was that we weren't the enemy, we weren't the establishment, and we weren't undercover *New York Times* book critics. We were just curious.

Redfield suggested we follow him out to his house near Hoover, a neighboring town. We soon saw that Alabaster was prettier in the daylight, once you veered off the main road, and as we got closer to Redfield's lake house, the greenery and grandeur grew. We drove down a long private road past a lake and then onto an even smaller, more private road to a sign that designated the area as REDFIELD. I recognized spots of natural beauty reminiscent of those in his novel as we headed down a winding picture-book road, tree-lined on either side, that dead-ended at the door of a discreet lake cabin. It sat right on the water, with no other houses, roads, or even power lines in sight. I thought of how rare that was—undisturbed landscape as a 360-degree view. Redfield had land, a dock, a beached canoe, and a screened-in porch overlooking the water. I envied him. He had managed to find the naturalistic Peruvian descriptives from his novel right here in small-town Alabama.

Early on, Shainee and I had decided that she would handle most of the Q&As, and I would manage most of the visuals. But occasionally we would switch roles for one reason or another, and this became one of those times. Regardless of who played interviewer and who played chronicler, there was a freedom for both to interject at any given time. If one of us saw a window for a question, she would ask it, or if the interview wasn't staying on track, it would be just as much the other's responsibility to guide it back.

I did find great satisfaction in my role as primary camera person, being able to simultaneously keep my eyes on both Shainee and the person we were with, like an omnipresent fly on the wall. And there's a phenomenon about cameras that I noticed while having one in front of my face for six consecutive months. When a camera, particularly a video camera, is being pointed at someone, they tend to forget there's a person attached to the apparatus. They are more focused on the camera itself, so in a sense, the operator can disappear and observe the subject almost invisibly. I also loved watching Shainee weave the questions, rephrasing some of the more personal ones we had written the night before each interview. She is one of the great inquisitors, instinctively turning every stone.

We set up near Redfield's canoe on the lakeshore. James smoothed his hair, crossed his legs, and began to explain his upbringing in a rural community outside of Birmingham, a community with ''joint barn raisings.''

''There was a lot of centering around a particular church where spiritual ideas were talked about, but mainly in vague, routine Methodist ways,'' Redfield said. ''But I think my early religious experiences really sensitized me to two things. One being the importance of a sense of community and the other a sense of needing more tangibility and clarity of spirituality. As far back as I can remember, I wanted more of a sense of the experience of spirituality.''

I wasted no time, asking James the most pressing question: ''Why did you write *The Celestine Prophecy* and what do you hope the Insights offer to people?''

''The book is really an adventure parable about what is possible,'' James said, his piercing eyes unblinking. ''It's my view that the Insights are all coming to us at the same time. They are archetypal in nature, they're sort of destined. I believe we're all shifting in the same way worldwide in this moment in history. And I think the book puts some of that into words. It's not creating it, it's not even leading it, because it's already happening,'' he said with typical Southern modesty.

Redfield had this idiosyncratic habit of visually punctuating his thoughts with hand and arm gestures, forming a globe with his palms, or a crescent shape with one hand, or miming an open book or Bible—always a circular shape in motion. If you couldn't hear what he was saying, you would think he was signing his interview because his body movements were choreographed to the intention of his words. Everything was coming together, opening up, or coming full circle.

James went on to talk about a country-wide cultural movement focused on living one's dream. I asked him how he would personally define his idea in the context of the American dream.

''Well, I think that the American dream is ultimately the human dream. I think the collective dream is a direct result of the Founding Fathers, who believed in the evolution of human beings, believed that they were creating this new ideal culture in which everyone could participate—a culture in which more and more people feel empowered and feel part of the overall system. I think that we have a long way to go, but that dream and goal are still very much alive. I think that our current dialogue out there is: How do we get to that place? And out of that dialogue, I believe, will come our path.''

"Speaking of paths, do you have a personal definition of inspiration?" I asked.

"I think that inspiration is an experience that is very definable. It's a sense of inner knowing that there is something that we want to do. There's something that we want to create, there's something that we want to explore. I think that one of the important shifts happening right now in human culture is the shift toward finding our niche, finding our mission, finding our contribution to the world, and not being content with anything less than that."

The concept of having a mission and being aligned with it would surface throughout the trip at a reassuring rate. I was constantly surprised that across the board, people used the specific word "mission" to identify their job or personal interest, always in the context of being impassioned by a daily purpose. Eventually, I noticed that the people I would identify as thoughtful idealists were always the ones who acknowledged, without being prodded, that they had a "mission."

The Celestine Prophecy has a hopeful sensibility, portraying our collective consciousness as a mission that is bound to move in a more constructive and spiritual direction. I wondered how Redfield felt about the future of America.

"I'm actually optimistic. I look at it this way—a lot of problems seem to be coming to a head. The environmental problems are coming dramatically into public consciousness, the problem of children without role models, the polarization between the affluent and those who have been left behind are coming to light. From one angle, things look like they're getting much worse—crime and the rest. But I think, at the same time, underneath all this, there is this bubbling empowerment and, interestingly enough, an explosion of creativity and spiritual mission—a movement toward the best of our tradition. I think we'll turn the corner early in the next century."

At this point, the audio recorder suddenly shut off and we had to stop and change batteries. As I loaded in four new batteries, I jammed the case and couldn't unstick it. Shainee and I pulled at it for five minutes, then James tried. He decided to go to his house for some tools to pry it open. All Shainee and I could do was laugh at the absurdity of this scene—two bumbling production flunkies waiting for James Redfield, spiritual guide to millions, to get his tool set to liberate our batteries. By the time he returned, we had jimmied it open. We thanked him, embarrassed, and moved on.

I asked James why he had chosen Birmingham as his home. "Well, there's something valuable about roots. This is where I began. The South is, in its own way, more receptive to spiritual ideas than many other parts of the country that one would think of as more liberal. The South can be fundamental—and dogmatic in certain ways—but most of the people in the South believe in a divine guidance. Most people in the South believe that we live in not just a physical world but in a spiritual world. And," he added as a separate appreciation, "it's beautiful wooded country."

The conversation led to the uniqueness of America, and I sprung the "Only in America" question on James. "I think that only in America"—he paused—"can so many creative ideas that are recognized as valid and contributory come from so many individuals who were previously unheard of. It's one of our strongest and most important traditions. If we can continue to avoid a ruling intellectual elite, we will continue to enjoy the fruits of diverse labor and diverse voices. I think that's an essential element to the founding principles of our country.''

Coming from a man whose bestselling book had originally been rejected by a dozen or more publishing houses before he self-published it, I could see why Redfield felt it important that the cultural and intellectual power centers of this country have their own checks and balances. Ironically, one of the biggest publishing conglomerates eventually paid a lot of money to take over the rights to *The Celestine Prophecy* after Redfield had sold thousands of copies on his own, purely by word of mouth.

I knew that Redfield believed there was a significant link between the coming of the new millennium and the phenomenal worldwide success of *The Celestine Prophecy*. ''Here in North America,'' Redfield began, ''we've reached a materialistic plateau. And I think people are realizing they have this ability to create and to feel intuitively guided toward certain directions in their life . . . Once we find the shape of our dreams, the universe is designed to open up, so that our dreams manifest, particularly if it is to contribute in any way to make the world a better place. That knowledge is out. And it's that knowledge that's creating a whole different worldview and approach to life as we finish up this century and we go on.''

James may be right in saying we've reached a materialistic plateau, but I was skeptical about what came next. Were we really on the verge of a massive paradigm shift where we'd evolve into a more enlightened, humanistic culture? Or would the pendulum just swing back to a collective disenchantment with spiritualism? I knew that unfortunately, neither we nor James had an answer to this one, so we called it a day.

We took a walk around Redfield's land. He had relaxed since our very formal greeting in his Alabaster office. I guess he realized we weren't out to call him the Second Coming and then crucify him. Just for fun, I squinted my eyes at him, wondering if I could see his aura. Everyone in *The Ce-*

Kristin and James

lestine Prophecy had an ''invisible'' color that encircled them in an ethereal cloud. James stared right back at me, not squinting. ''Can you see my aura?'' I queried. ''Do I have a color?''

James paused and then looked at the periphery of my body. ''Blue,'' he said resolutely. "Blue with some green flecks. Blue is the color of inspiration, so I guess it's probable that you and Shainee are on to something with this."

"Huh," I said, feeling a bit abashed, but hoping his vision was accurate.

We left soon after. James pointed us back to the main road, saying, "Give me a call if you're ever in this part of the country again." We returned his wave, heading away from his little piece of paradise down the storybook drive toward Alabaster.

We had penetrated the camp of a cultural phenomenon and a New Age guru and found a man—a rather ordinary, unassuming man—at its helm. His success and the connective tissue between himself and millions of total strangers seemed as surprising to James as it was to us, although he had had some time to get used to it. And although *The Celestine Prophecy* was—and continues to be—an easy target for critics and cynics alike, Shainee and I both knew that Redfield was right about one thing: the undeniable and unexplainable connection between us and the people we were bound to meet.

A MOTEL IN ROANOKE, VIRGINIA   6/14

(Shainee)

Today was surreal. We spent the night outside of Chattanooga, a quiet micropolis. Kris and I treated ourselves to a decent dinner and even had a glass of wine. After we dined, we went for a walk along the water park by the Tennessee River and talked. I've been studying the maps again and I'm sad that we don't have time to check out the Smokies or hike a little along the Appalachian Trail. Even though it is early in our trip, I fear that we may not be able to really see America in the way that we fantasized. Everything's just so hectic and hurried all the time. Here's hoping things calm down a little.

I can only imagine what the towns heading up toward Knoxville might have been like if we'd had time to explore. Such inviting names: Spring City, Sweetwater (a Southern favorite), Strawberry Plains, and my favorite, Soddy-Daisy. We'll miss them all on this trip. We are blazing northeast to make it back to Philadelphia in time for my cousin's wedding.

The best we could do was drive up to the top of Lookout Mountain. It was a magnificent view of green and clouds as far as we could see, but also an appalling tourist trap. Tennessee boasts several natural wonders, but one of the really good ones seems to have been co-opted by the same people who've taken over Coney Island. I wonder what the Grand Canyon would look like if Universal Studios built a "Canyon Coaster" as an added attraction. The worst part was the food. There was absolutely nothing for quasi-veggie Kris to eat. While I, the carnivore, gave in to the hunger with a hot dog, Kris was irritable with only a Diet Coke. Our turn at tourism was less than successful.

Neither of our moods was helped when we stopped for gas on our way out of town and were approached by two toothless young men with unfortunate haircuts and tobacco-stained T-shirts who inquired if we were traveling alone. Kris kept her eyes on the gas pump's handle when she answered, "Yep, just us and our dead boyfriends there in the trunk." They went away.

In spite of our high irritability factor, Kris could not let go of the need to do a little exploring. This afternoon, around mile 150, she was shooting signage out the window and shrieked as one that delighted her whizzed by in the viewfinder. There was no discussion, she made us go.

Dollywood is something that could truly only happen in America. There are signs for the park as far as forty miles away, and every 100 feet, you are bombarded with mammoth pictures of Dolly, her teeth, her breasts, and her hair. She's like a never-ending Rose Bowl float. We drove past more signs like BIBLE FACTORY OUTLET and then a string of various Elvis attractions. The first sign said ELVIS MUSEUM and had a picture of Elvis in his white jumpsuit, titled simply MEMORIES. '50s & '60s.

EXCITING! in lights. Farther down the road there was a place called THE MUSIC MANSION advertising a much-younger Elvis with a cowboy hat and six-string acoustic. A visit to the mansion promised to be SENSATIONAL and EMOTIONAL. It seems that the road to Dollywood is trying to capitalize on one of Tennessee's other claims to fame by breaking his life into chapters and giving them each their own venue for A-list impersonators.

Various forms of clean American fun—including bowling alleys, video arcades, miniature golf, and waterslides—dot the way to Gatlinburg, home of Dollywood. Of course the destination vacation is not complete without a deluxe Americana clutter of Pizza Huts, free-HBO motels, Long John Silvers, and fully stocked gas stations. Andrei's prophetic words during our first few hundred miles have begun to haunt us.

We turned left when the DOLLYWOOD sign told us to, and were immediately whisked away from the torpor of the highway. It was replaced by a winding tree-lined street revealing three consecutive white archways kindly leading us to the sweet temptation of Dollywood. Each archway announced our imminent approach with the park signature of a yellow butterfly surrounded by pink and yellow roses. Dolly smiled down on us at every bend. The butterfly morphed into the logo W of DOLLYWOOD as we passed under the final archway, which proudly stated: WELCOME TO DOLLYWOOD, ENTERTAINMENT CAPITAL OF THE SMOKIES. I didn't doubt it for a second.

We blazed right past the empty booth requesting three of our dollars to park. We decided early on that we could not contribute any of our precious little money to this place, which turned out to be quite prohibitive, because even though the park was scheduled to close in less than two hours, they wanted thirty-two of our dollars to enter it. No way. That was about 750 miles in gas money. We walked around outside of the entrance, which was a plaster of paris interpretation of a Southern mansion, certainly built by the same company who makes Santa's villages for malls all over the country. On each side of the park entrance there were red-and-green trolleys that boasted GATLINBURG, GATEWAY TO THE SMOKIES. People were boarding for tours of the park, but wouldn't let us on—no tickets. Dolly classics blared in every direction from massive bullhorn speakers on thirty-foot poles.

Dollywood is a foreign planet to us, so we were determined to tap in, start expanding our obviously limited horizons, and do a successful "person on the street" interview. We began to case the entrance to the park with our camera and DAT machine in hand. First we tried the employees—ladies in long petticoat skirts who took tickets and men in caps and blue uniforms who drove trolleys, but they all said we would have to clear it with the press office first, and they didn't care that it was a video project "for school," either.

We did marginally better with the patrons of the park. We talked to a middle-aged couple who told us that the American dream of being good to your neighbors has been beaten out by greed and Teenage Mutant Ninja Turtles. An old man in a South Carolina baseball hat and mysterious massive gauze bandage taped around his throat told us, "As long as we got America, we got nothing to worry about." And finally two rather large girls with plastic containers of nachos suggested that we all band together to abolish taxes. I guess it was obvious that we were outsiders, because no one was at all that interested in talking to us. In fact, everyone we encountered seemed to be unfazed by the

spectacle that they were participating in, but they all thought *we* were really weird.

Dollywood was an *Anthem* bust, but it is still a testament, in some ways, to how far one person can go in this country if they have the guts and the money. In spite of the uneasiness that I feel about hype being sold as family fun, I have a strong sense of respect for Dolly. She is a woman who came from quintessentially humble beginnings and, by reaching for the brass ring and turning it into Grand Ole Opry platinum, has reached a level of Grade-A super American stardom. She has used it to create the ultimate American homage—one's own theme park. The people we talked to that day were certainly happy to pay their sixteen dollars to help Dolly celebrate that fact. Only in America.

RITA DOVE

POET • FORMER U.S. POET LAUREATE

CHARLOTTESVILLE, VIRGINIA

(Kristin)

We were trying to make it to Philadelphia in a hurry so Shainee could attend her cousin's wedding, and we could interview Bill Siemering, a visionary of public radio in America and abroad. It was particularly heavy driving from Gatlinburg to Roanoke, Virginia. We pulled into the small town, checked into a Howard Johnson's, and fell into bed. In those few minutes of silence before we fell asleep, we remembered that Doug Brinkley had told us that Rita Dove, our recent U.S. Poet Laureate, lived in Charlottesville. We had wanted to interview her but had not yet contacted her office.

In a panic, realizing Charlottesville was a neighboring town, we jumped out of bed and grabbed the phone book. After many midnight calls to the University of Virginia, we finally got an ultrafeminine automated voice system that allowed us to punch in the first three letters of ''Dove'' and then transferred us to the corresponding voice mail. Technology was actually working in our favor, it seemed.

We left a long and frantic message explaining who we were, what *Anthem* was, that we were in the area from midnight until the following afternoon, and would there be any way on God's green earth that she could see us? *Please?* We hung up knowing it was an insane proposition and a suspicious kind of message to leave on a stranger's machine in the middle of the night, but we went to sleep in peace, knowing that we had at least tried.

At 9 A.M. the next morning, the phone startled us. Shainee answered, and I overheard half a conversation between her and Rita Dove's assistant. Looking a bit addled, Shainee hung up and said, ''We have to be there in two hours. Her assistant said that today is the first day Rita has been in her office in six months. She says Rita thinks it must be kismet that we called her with such an outrageous request at an equally

outrageous hour, so she wants to do it.'' I stood still at the bathroom door, tooth-
paste foaming in my mouth, and slowly nodded my head to Shainee.

We had just enough time to dress, pack up, clean the cameras, and write
questions for Ms. Dove in the car. Luckily, we had picked up two of her books—one
short stories, one poetry—a couple of weeks earlier. We had learned that she had
published more than eight books, mostly poetry; she was only the second African-
American poet to win the Pulitzer Prize (for *Thomas and Beulah*); and she was the
Commonwealth Professor of English at the University of Virginia. But just recently I read that President Clinton bestowed the Charles Frankel Prize of the National Endowment for the Humanities upon her in January 1997.

We drove around the University of Virginia campus, trying to find Rita's office and bemoaning the mazelike nature of all college campuses. A student pointed
us to a building that looked jarringly new
compared with the nineteenth-century
Jeffersonian architecture of the rest of the
UVA grounds.

I heard Shainee's back snap as we
rounded the corner to Rita's office. She
held on to her side and kept walking.
Shainee has scoliosis, although you would
hardly know it with her superhuman
threshold for discomfort. Her tolerance of
physical pain during our trip always
seemed rather heroic to me, and I thought
of all the intrepid exploring duos who had
come before us. Lewis and Clark, Living-
stone and Stanley . . . although they had
it just a bit rougher than we did, I liked
thinking of us in the same brave tradition.

The "Grounds" of UVA

We were perspiring from the Virginia
summer as Rita opened her door and cooled us with her warm smile. She was everything I *hadn't* expected—extremely young, buoyant, welcoming, and funny. Most
intriguing, her fingernails were each painted a different color of the rainbow. Not
exactly cast from the academic Poet Laureate mold. And speaking of casts, she was
sporting one on her left arm that started at her palm, wrapped around her thumb,
and covered her arm up to her elbow. It was like her own white wand, colors shower-
ing from its tip as she gestured with her words.

Rita showed us around some of the perfectly manicured campus, past a monu-
mental outdoor amphitheater and a multitude of neoclassic columns and archways.
The grounds were designed by Thomas Jefferson and, according to Rita, are a mani-
festation of Jefferson's philosophy of melding environment with education.

''All the buildings you see here were built in Jefferson's time,'' Rita said, pointing
in all directions (but away from her own building). ''He died before it was completely

finished. He used to sit at Monticello with a telescope and supervise the construction from there.''

We decided to plant ourselves on the grassy knoll that Rita said was Jefferson's favorite spot—a green park framed by housing that Jefferson designed as an ''academical village'' where students and teachers would live together and learn together.

Rita Dove

Rita told us that of all Jefferson's accomplishments—in fields as diverse as architecture, education, farming, politics, design, horticulture, philosophy, and elocution—the three things he most wanted to be remembered for were as the writer of the Declaration of Independence, for his writings establishing religious freedoms, and as the founder and designer of the University of Virginia. Conspicuously absent from the list was his presidency. Knowing that definitely gave me pause as I scanned the grounds. (Traditionally, the students and faculty of UVA never use the word ''campus,'' but rather the word ''grounds.'') Jefferson was a genius at imbuing architecture with meaning, always attentive to infusing form with a sensitivity to function. We had stumbled upon a living metaphor for Jefferson's ideas for the foundation of the country itself—meaning and function.

''Jefferson went to France,'' explained Rita, ''and came back with all these notions of architecture as something that can inspire you to higher things. So his notion applied to a university was that students could come here to be uplifted . . . aspire to the stars.''

She continued: ''When you think about it, the grounds of UVA really set the tone for education as being something that contains the entire person and not just something that you rack up like points. It's an entire way of being.''

Rita sat on the ridge directly in front of Thomas Jefferson's Rotunda, a neoclassical building, domed and anchored with yet more white columns. The students milling about seemed to respect the area, being careful not to step on even the concrete surrounding the structure, as if it were young, delicate grass.

Neither Shainee nor I knew very much about the history of the position of Poet Laureate. I later found out that it is an honorary position established by Congress in 1985, but is thought of, for the most part, as a titular honor, more than a job description. Rita, however, seemed to take the position more seriously.

''Well,'' Rita explained, ''the job was actually conceived to be a lightning rod for literature in the country. Originally, the Poet Laureate was asked to consult with the Librarian of Congress to make sure that the poetry and literature of their time was adequately represented there. The job, though, has expanded to be kind of a consciousness for literature—and for culture—in the country. So for me, I think what that meant was to raise the awareness about poetry in this country.''

As with many of the other people we had interviewed and would interview, Rita used her specific, particular talent to carve a life of tremendous scope and cultural impact. I was inspired to see someone take a personal and honorable thing and turn it into something substantial, and accessible to everyone. While poetry may seem to be a narrow, esoteric pursuit, it represented a rather epic responsibility to Rita as a repository of culture for her people and her time. As she put it, ''I use it as a bully pulpit to talk about why culture is important in our lives. It's the memory of our country. All of our history books, they give us the facts. But the heartbeat is in the culture.''

Rita paused and stared over our heads. For some reason, I had a sensation that she was reading cartoon bubble thoughts above us. But maybe she was just seeing suspended words . . .

''To me, a poem is almost like someone whispering to another person, or you hear the whispering in your head. I hope with my own poems that the reader feels a connection, soul to soul, that'll help us all feel a little less alone on the planet. And it does have the power to direct change. A writer can make the word 'dark' be something positive. You can relieve a word like 'hysterical' of its misogynistic implications. You can make the language your own. That's what poetry is about.''

The little bit of Rita's poetry that I had been able to read before meeting her certainly emerged from that place of making the language her own. She anchored sobering words in whimsical stories that would take root in your gut and beg you to read again. One poem I had read on the way to her office lingered:

Nigger Song: An Odyssey

We six pile in, the engine churning ink:
We ride into the night.
Past factories, past graveyards
And the broken eyes of windows, we ride
Into the gray-green of nigger night.

We sweep past excavation sites; the pits
Of gravel gleam like mounds of ice.
Weeds clutch at the wheels;
We laugh and swerve away, veering
Into the black entrails of the earth,
The green smoke sizzling on our tongues . . .

In the nigger night, thick with the smell of cabbages,
Nothing can catch us.
Laughter spills like gin from glasses,
And ''yeah'' we whisper, ''yeah''
We croon, ''yeah.''

For Rita, the act of reading and writing poetry seemed to represent one of the most basic of all human endeavors—shattering the isolation that many are born into because of the nature of fear in dichotomized, estranged communities. Rita believed that creating windows into each other's minds and souls would be the only way to keep our communities and our civilization connected and alive. In one way or another, Rita made a correlation between understanding each other and living up to the founding parents' ideals. "I do believe," she said, "if we can at least acknowledge that no matter how different we are as people, that we have the same kinds of emotions—that we all fear, dream, wish, all those things—it will be a little more difficult for us to reject or kill each other. I think at a base level that's what literature, what poetry does, and what I hope that my poems do."

A large group of people who were absorbed in a campus tour walked closely by us. Rita momentarily stopped speaking, and we all watched the group's movement with the same rapt curiosity as they clearly had for their tour guide. They were a group of men, middle-aged, of the well-suited, business variety. As they moved in unison like a jellyfish with great tentacles, we spotted a woman at its heart. The three of us, still watching, simultaneously broke our stillness to comment on this asymmetrical visual equation.

Shainee and I would soon discover that this tour group would be indicative of future experiences. At this point in our trip, many of the interview requests we had sent to the women on our list remained unanswered. About a month after our encouraging meeting with Rita Dove, we would have to accept the hard fact that Rita's spontaneity and accessibility would be the exception, not the rule. For every ten men we would find at the center of a professional or artistic universe, statistically, one or—at best—two women would excel, rather unobtrusively, at its core. And of these women, many seemed so overextended that I imagine they could hardly balance the daily demands, much less obscure requests for interviews. Their male counterparts, however, seemed to be able to spread themselves much thinner; if one man said no to an interview, there was always another to fall back on.

From Governor Ann Richards to the astronaut Dr. Mae Jemison to the musician Melissa Etheridge to the poet Dr. Maya Angelou, we found it more challenging to penetrate women's camps of schedulers, assistants, agents, and publicists. At first we took it rather personally; now we accept the void as cause and effect of a culture in midshift. As Geraldine Ferarro would later explain to us as we neared the end of our journey: "Women are not prominent in those circles . . . [At the time of this interview] We have eight female United States senators. We have one woman governor. That's not a huge universe." Ferraro spoke specifically of politics, but we found it true for "the circles" of most fields we probed.

We told Rita of our dilemma, and she had some of her own thoughts, drawing from personal experience. "When I was growing up," she said, "as a woman—a black woman—I assumed I would have to be a hundred and fifty percent better than anyone else in order to be given the same chance. This is something that I just assumed. Now my daughter thinks that if she does her best, she'll be judged as an equal. It's uncertain if she will be or not."

As the group and their tour guide drifted away, Rita reclaimed the thread of our earlier conversation about her path to becoming Poet Laureate. "Two years ago, I was asked to be Poet Laureate of the United States," she said, beginning to laugh, "which was certainly not something I expected in *my* life! I am the youngest one they've ever had, and it seemed to me that the message they were sending out was that I should be a *hands-on* kind of laureate and do something.

"Suddenly," Rita continued, "I had cameras in my face and people asking, 'What are you going to do for poetry?' What I decided to do was just explain how I felt about poetry, how I had always felt—why poetry moved me and what I hoped it could do for other people. To my surprise, people began to write in and give me their ideas. I discovered there are so many people out there who used to love to write poetry or stories, and read, and somehow feel vaguely ashamed that they had this period in their life. So I began to ask myself, 'Why is it that in this country, culture is something shameful, has become something that is somehow not viable or valuable?' I wanted to help change that. So, as Poet Laureate, what I tried to do was bring poetry back to the people, not let it exist on Mount Olympus at the universities."

Shainee asked Rita how she'd ended up where she was today. Rita, in return, described a childhood in which education was presented as the way to overcome the hurdles and the backlash of racism. This would be a theme we would come across over and over again in our travels. Charlayne Hunter-Gault, Jimmy Santiago Baca, and Studs Terkel, among others, would express similar experiences of rising above the fray through education and the art of communication. The belief that with education, anything becomes possible seems to define our country as much as any other aspect of our culture. How apropos, I thought, that we were sitting here on Jefferson's college grounds.

Shainee asked Rita if she had a personal definition for inspiration, and she replied by calling it "the bolt-out-of-the-blue thing that comes down and strikes you. You don't know where it comes from and you take it and run. I think, though, there is another kind of inspiration—the inspiration of hard work. I really believe that the muse does not visit you unless you're at work. If she's going by and you're in your tree, just kind of dreaming, she thinks, 'Well that's not gonna yield anything.' But if you're working, she might drop it down and see what you can do with it.

"The word 'inspiration' comes from the root 'to inspire,' to take a breath. So in a certain way, inspiration is taking things in, being attentive, breathing in all of life."

Talking about inspiration led us to the idea of dreaming. We asked Rita what the American dream meant to her. "I think the definition in the Declaration of Independence is a pretty good one: 'life, liberty, and the pursuit of happiness.' It doesn't guarantee that you're gonna get it, but that you at least have the freedom to *pursue* it. It seems that many people think the American dream is a promise, that this is what you're going to get and you just sit back and take it in. I really feel that when they made this nation, they thought of it as something that is ongoing, something that we must continually redefine and continually struggle for."

The idea of struggle in America was another common theme that emerged early in our search. Many people would speak of the struggles of those who had come before them—those seeking and working toward the most civilized version of our foundation. Rita was concerned that many people viewed our young nation as something that was "complete"—something to take advantage of as a mature, full-grown entity. Rita, among others, defended the idea of *process* as a necessary approach to the potential continued growth of America.

We talked with Rita about other countries' societal norms and asked her if she felt that growing up in America—even in the context of civil rights—had afforded her the choice of what to do with her life. "I think it is specifically American that we feel doors are open—or if they aren't open, that we should open them and walk through them." Doug Brinkley's words echoed in my mind's eye: "The key to teaching is just pointing to the door and letting kids kick it open themselves." A specifically American theory of education, too?

Just then a student, oblivious to us and the camera, passed by on his way to class, whistling the theme song to *The Andy Griffith Show*. On that note, we asked Rita how she felt about our social and cultural progress toward embracing American fundamentals like "All men are created equal." "In 1952 when I was born," she recalled, "it was inconceivable that there could be a black Poet Laureate, especially a black Poet Laureate who could talk equally about both Walt Whitman and Langston Hughes. It would have been assumed that a black person could only talk about black poets. So we have made immense progress on that level. But I do think that it's a pendulum swing, and we go back and forth. At the moment, I think we're swinging back: there's presently a backlash against gender and race. It's part of the whole way that history swings back and forth in a cyclical nature. At least I hope so."

Rita was America's first official black female Poet Laureate. Talking a bit about role models and heroism, Rita had this to say: "It's all right to have role models as long as they're diverse and some of them are close to home. The tendency to pick, as a role model, someone on television is not only unrealistic, but it can really depress a young person as they try to reach that unattainable goal. They lose context for understanding all the sacrifices and struggles along the way. That's why I believe some role models should be your parents and neighbors and people that you grow up with. I would say our concept of heroism has become—as we become more of a global village—much more superficial. The celebrity craze that we have in this country encourages a kind of cartoon sense of reality. It can only lead to frustration and, in the end, to violence."

We wouldn't hear anyone label heroism as specifically as a "cartoon sense of reality" until the end of our journey. Robert Redford, an iconoclast hero himself, would repeat Rita's sentiments exactly. And Studs Terkel and John Waters would also join the ongoing discussion—all alarmed by the legacy that media was leaving behind.

We wondered who Rita had been influenced by, besides Thomas Jefferson and other authors and poets. "Of course, Thomas Jefferson was a great conflict of character," she acknowledged. "He had slaves—and other contradictions. But in terms of someone who really inspired me, I would say Rosa Parks. Because what she did was show how one single, ordinary person could change the course of history by simply saying, 'I'm tired, I'm not doing it anymore.' She showed us that a small act can change the world. I think we often get discouraged because we feel like we have to sacrifice in a superhuman way in order to impact or change history. Sometimes one person's small act, like not sitting down in the back of a bus, can set the ball rolling.''

I thought the idea of one small act changing the course of history was an insightful way of looking at heroism—like those little, hardly noticeable forks in the road that you look back on, realizing they quietly changed your life. Sometimes the way the media defines heroism seems to be merely smoke and mirrors compared to the small acts of kindness and justice that are in actuality shaping the country—whispers that have shouting implications.

As we walked her back to her office, passing more Jeffersonian architecture, she told us how much she loved the landscape of Virginia.

''I believe it matters to the human heart what kind of space it moves through. I believe we are what we perceive. We take in this world, this land that we travel. It becomes a part of our conscience. If what's out there is ugly because we've damaged or destroyed it, then what does that do to our consciousness? What ugliness are we taking in?''

As we approached Rita's door, we asked her one last question about her thoughts on freedom in America. Rita jumped right in, saying, ''I think the impulse of the Founding Fathers was to encourage people not to be afraid of freedom. It takes an immense amount of courage to allow freedom in others, especially if you don't like what they're saying, or if you don't like the way they're living, or if you feel it threatens you. It takes an immense amount of confidence in one's self. I think at this moment''—Rita paused—''in this country, we're exhibiting a lot of juvenile behavior—a lot of fear of the other and the tendency is to want to smash down that which is different . . . But I do think that the Constitution is a sturdy document; it has so many built-in checks and balances. It's very difficult to change it irrevocably. That's what I'm basing my hope on today.''

Rita opened her door. ''I'm so glad this worked out,'' she said as she waved her hat and rainbow nails in an arch above her head as a farewell. And she was gone.

Rita's evaluation of America's promise was clearly influenced and inspired by Thomas Jefferson, the greatest irony being that, during his time, Jefferson wasn't truly able to apply his enlightened thoughts to the well-being of ''all men.'' And yet, here was a successful black woman standing before Jefferson's proud design, quoting him and being influenced in a positive way by his lingering ideas, and now adapting them to apply to all people in a way he could not. Rita was right. It really was—and would continue to be—an ''ongoing process.''

I think, more than anyone in the early part of the trip, Rita gave us the security that we were on *some* kind of right track. Which direction the track led still wasn't clear, but around Virginia, something settled into feeling ''right.''

BILL SIEMERING

CO-FOUNDER OF NATIONAL PUBLIC RADIO

PHILADELPHIA, PENNSYLVANIA

(Shainee)

After we left Rita, we drove five hours to my family's home in New Jersey for the wedding in nearby Philadelphia. Rita had informed us that our route toward Washington, U.S. 29, was the same route that Jefferson had taken every week from Monticello. She said that it was a road that she always enjoyed traveling, thinking of Jefferson going back and forth by carriage along the pastures of Virginia. It was still rural enough for us to pretend that we could see what he had seen. We drove quietly, took a cue from Rita, and tried to reflect on what our Founding Father had wrought as we wound through the summer greens of Thomas Jefferson's Virginia.

The wedding came and went that weekend with my mind whizzing in and around the disposable cameras and cake cutting. I managed to concentrate on the ceremony and then returned to planning the next leg of our trip in my head. Seeing my boyfriend and my family was a welcome respite and it would soon become clear that Kris and I would occasionally have to step out of our mobile cocoon to reconnect with our real lives.

After we unpacked, we began to watch the footage of the prior ten days. It did not look very good. We had not been so naive as to think that the two of us alone could operate the equipment as well as a crew of trained professionals, but we hadn't been prepared for *this*. There were blown-out faces, inaudible words, and a lot of unintentional jerking and moving. It seems our Steadycam was not willing to do its namesake job of steadying without some help from us. Kris and I stared at the screen stunned and didn't speak for hours afterward.

That night I lay in bed worrying about the life-or-death status of our child, the film we so wanted to make. My stomach churned with dread, my mind raced with questions of whether we had begun something that would ever mean anything, and sleep was nowhere in the room. What were we *thinking*? How arrogant of us to think that we could proficiently accomplish the work of skilled technicians who did nothing but shoot and record for a living, in addition to handling all of the duties of the director, the writer, the producer, and the research staff. We were running two cameras, sound, writing interviews, researching interviewees, scheduling around the agendas of some of the busiest people in the country, navigating thousands of miles, searching for cheap places to stay, and then last—and, at that end-of-the-day moment, certainly least—we were trying to find *Anthem*'s voice. We were attempting to say something in a language that we had not yet learned, and there was no time to be reflective. On top of everything, we had not foreseen the exhaustion factor, which was kicking our ass already. These and many other whinings and whimperings poured out from the dark room that night.

The next day we looked each other squarely in the eye and vowed to make it better. We consoled each other—of course there would be a learning curve—and reminisced fondly about our prior experiences in film and television, when we had had the luxury of a crew to back us up. We knew exactly what we wanted the movie to look like and we could not be discouraged by technology. Our mission was bigger than "the twins" and together we could figure it out. Certainly, Lewis and Clark had encountered much heartier setbacks during their discovery of America. All we were doing was *re*discovering the country. We just chose to bring along a couple of cameras.

After two days of dubbing and viewing and interminably tedious camera and sound tests, it was time for our interview with Bill Siemering, co-founder and first program director of National Public Radio. Bill was a recent MacArthur genius grant recipient, a grant that is bestowed, not applied for. He was about to leave for South Africa for six months, where he would help to create a national public radio of their own. Bill lived outside of Philadelphia, only twenty miles from my family's home, so the stress of traveling would not be an issue for this interview. Just the stress of wondering whether this was a movie we were making, or a really well-meaning interpretive video experiment.

On the morning of the interview, Kris and I went through our preinterview ritual: labeling the stock, cleaning the cameras, checking for all lens attachments, making sure all of the batteries had charged sufficiently, and then printing out the interview. We loaded up and—with stiff upper lips—drove to the home of Bill Siemering in Chestnut Hill. We were both hopeful, although the previous two days had left us feeling fragile. Kris tentatively suggested that maybe our audience would find our neophyte cinematography "kind of . . . charming." We laughed, and the mood was broken.

We were excited about the prospect of spending time with Bill Siemering, who had given us some of our most cherished on-the-road entertainment staples: *All Things Considered*, *Morning Edition*, and *Fresh Air*. No matter what state we traveled through, we could always count on NPR to be there to comfort us with voices that had begun to feel like close friends: Noah Adams, Cory Flintoff, Linda Wertheimer, and the rest of the NPR family.

Bill was a tall man in his fifties, slender and balding, with white hair. He lived on a quiet residential street between Chestnut Hill proper and Wissahickon Creek, one of the several streams and rivers that run through Greater Philadelphia. We knew that he was a little uncomfortable with the idea of speaking to a device that was recording more than just his radio voice, because he had asked us weeks earlier if he could see the questions we were planning to ask. He wanted to prepare and had mentioned more than once that he wasn't sure how interesting the visual would be.

Bill asked if we would like to do the interview in Fairmount Park, right by the Wissahickon. He said it would require a bit of a walk, but he thought it was a

Shainee and Bill

nice setting. We agreed. I hadn't walked through Fairmount Park since I was a kid and I thought the calm of the forest surrounding the creek would do us good that day. The park was still as beautiful as I had remembered, but unfortunately, it was a terribly hot day. My romantic visions of Bill, Kris, and I waxing lyrical about the inception of NPR in the woods turned out to be not so realistic. There were swarms of awful stinging gnats, the "short walk" was actually pretty long, and I thought Kris was going to keel over from the weight of our equipment.

From the beginning, Kris reasoned that she would have to bear the physical brunt of carrying the bulk of our stuff, as I have a meddling curvature of the spine. As a result, she never let me carry very much, while she played the role of human mule. I always felt terribly guilty, but she was unwaveringly magnanimous about it and would not let me dwell on my inadequacy. In spite of her good nature, we did spend an inordinate amount of time maneuvering around the issue of accommodating my cramped back behind a steering wheel for hundreds of miles, sleeping on floors and cardboard beds, finding no chiropractors at any truck stop, and very little time or place to go for a good long walk. Once in a while I would feel rebellious, grab the heaviest suitcase when Kris wasn't looking, and try to break out of my invalid status, only to regret it later on. Eventually, with the help of a family-sized bottle of Advil, an orthopedic car seat, two sets of luggage wheels, and a promise to take up the practice of walking around motel parking lots in the morning, we found a rhythm of carrying, packing, and moving our stuff every day. We accepted our fate early on, although we occasionally wished we had a boyfriend or two around to lug things *for* us. An ugly, unfeminist longing, but one to which we readily subscribed.

When we started our journey to the interview spot, Bill offered to carry some of our stuff and smiled when he saw the apprehension on our faces at burdening him. "He *is* a man," I cajoled Kris, and he agreed, smiling, "I *am* a man." Kris remained a trooper throughout, but this was one of those rare days when we actually had someone offering to pick up the slack. We gave in. And I made a mental note to utilize the "weighted-down damsel" scenario at every opportunity.

We made our way down the bank of the creek, Bill telling us how this was his wife's and his favorite trail. The heat was almost unbearable, little bugs were in our eyes, ears, and mouth, and there was no food in our bellies. Bill led us into a clearing, and we set up the equipment.

I began the interview in the usual way, asking Bill how he got started. He explained that he had been teaching at SUNY Buffalo in 1962, which gave him a lot of freedom to experiment with the university radio station. As a founding member of the board of directors of the fledgling National Public Radio, he was asked to write the mission statement. "We wanted to be natural and conversational in style. We wanted to use the radio medium in imaginative ways, to use the sound of being out of a studio to help tell the story, to go where people are comfortable, where they're living their lives, and not just view the world through the perspective of experts that write *about* somebody. We wanted to hear the human voices of people.

"So the very first voice on the very first *All Things Considered* was a black nurse talking about drug addiction. We were making an intentional statement: 'We're going to primary sources, people talking about their very own lives.' Also on that very first *All Things Considered* was May Day, the largest demonstration of the antiwar movement in Washington; over five thousand people were arrested. And we had a same-day documentary about that. Which still stands, I think, as one of the best records of that day. Anyway, as a result of writing this mission statement, I was asked to become the first program director."

Given that we all know what was in store for NPR, I asked Bill what the mission statement meant for him at that time.

"It said that we would speak with many voices and many dialects and reflect the diversity that is America. Another objective was to celebrate the human experience with joy. I was aware of how we didn't celebrate our differences positively. People were labeled and were thinking in stereotypical ways. And I think that's a shorthand the media perpetuates, specifically the commercial media, and I was trying to get beyond that. I wanted NPR to be an agent for change. We would give people positive tools to become active citizens and not just passive receivers of information. That's what democracy is about."

I thought about what Bill was saying and realized that I had never thought about broadcast media as a fundamental ingredient of democracy. Of course, freedom of speech is an idea that is ingrained in us all as an entitlement. I had always thought of NPR as a palatable and provocative alternative to the silliness of talk radio or the barking of Top 40 deejays. It had never occurred to me that during its inception, NPR actually provided a voice to those who had none. I asked Bill what he envisioned would become of NPR.

"One of my influences was Frank Lloyd Wright, who talked about things growing organically, being natural, the absence of artifice. And those are qualities that I wanted to bring to this. I thought NPR would prevail against the kind of phoniness and hype and superficiality of the commercial media.

"About two weeks after we were on the air, we had the first public radio conference and I was barraged with complaints. 'Well, it doesn't sound like CBS. Who are these people?' 'You've got too many women—you know women's voices don't transmit well.' And 'Bill, you know women just don't have the authority that men do.' The idea was that a woman could do soft features but not hard news. Really sexist, but that's the way people thought back then. And they really did say that women's voice frequencies, the higher frequencies, just make a mess of the meters and don't transmit well."

Bill saw the incredulous expression on my face at the absurdity of not having women commentators. He laughed and finished my thought. "The higher frequencies do affect things, but we all know it's possible to have women on the air. They were used to hearing a male white voice of authority from New York reading copy and telling them, 'That's the way it is.' "

In our minds, NPR was a seminal source of information, not only for news but to hear from the rest of the country in their own words. In many ways, NPR programs were an inspiration for us to go out and gather seemingly disparate voices for ourselves. I asked Bill what he had hoped NPR would contribute to its listeners and if NPR had changed or lived up to his ideal.

"It's certainly even exceeded what I envisioned. But first of all, our shows had to be solid journalistically. Because if it wasn't credible—if it was viewed as simply a liberal or conservative mouthpiece—then it wouldn't succeed. I feel very strongly about the importance of accuracy, fairness, and balance in news presentation. It's like sterile instruments for a surgeon; it's a requirement for credibility. So I envisioned that it really would be regarded as some of the most valuable time people spent with their media.

"I also hoped it would break down stereotypes. I know this has happened. While I was manager of WHYY in Philadelphia, we broadcast a documentary on the Pink Triangle, the persecution of homosexuals in Nazi Germany. And I got a letter from a listener that said this program opened her up to viewing homosexuals in a different way. After I had been named program director of NPR, somebody asked, 'What criteria will you have for success?' I said, 'If when somebody who is different, who is marginalized in our society, goes and knocks on a door for a room or a job, and the door is open to them because the person on the inside has heard something on National Public Radio, that would be one measure of success.'

"The other part is it has become very influential beyond the NPR listeners. I think eight out of ten newspaper editors—and certainly all the network television news anchors and producers—listen to public radio as a resource for story ideas. So the influence is far greater than the number of people who listen to it every week."

It sounded like Bill had taken the long-lost idea of the town hall meeting and translated it into radio waves. It hadn't occurred to me until that moment how limited the media must have been back then. Our next interviewee, John Waters, would allude to the 8 million magazines available now. I asked Bill if he remembered a moment when his idea of populist radio crystallized for him.

"I remember covering a civil rights organization called *Build* in Buffalo. I would go to their press conferences, where they explained some problem about schools. They usually had a prepared presentation that might take about three minutes or something. And after the cameras went off, the journalists said, 'Look, we can only use about forty-five seconds of this, so why don't you edit it down and give us something shorter.' And I thought, 'Some of these problems have taken us three hundred years to solve. It's not asking too much to explore something for three minutes. They're pretty complex things we're talking about here.' I realized the great distortion and disservice that was being done to people who were in protest, who were trying to make life better for themselves.

"Reverend Martin Luther King had said, 'We have to write our essays in the streets.' That's a factor of television. In television, it's frequently: 'What's the picture?' They covered people marching and they covered people breaking windows. But what's behind all this? What's behind the anger? What are the needs here? That was never really explored. So that was one of the turning points."

Bill Siemering

Bill went on to say that, in addition to providing a forum and giving enough time to explain the issues, they tried to demystify and deformalize the news-gathering process. They thought that by having the reporters talk about what was going on in the studio—what was coming up next and how they would cover it—that it would become a little bit more accessible. It seemed obvious to us that these practices are now pretty much standard across the board. "Coming up next" is now a phrase that defines news time. I found it interesting, though, that even then, the media was interested mostly in sound bites. It makes it that much more surprising that NPR has survived all these years.

We talked to Bill a little bit about the precarious situation of NPR at that time and the threat that its potential dissolution could pose. "There's so much cynicism that people are tuning out government and I think that's a real danger. I mean in other countries—and I probably wouldn't be as sensitive to this if I hadn't been overseas and seeing how it is in fresh democracies, where they're still struggling with these issues—but you see how totalitarian regimes silence independent media in a variety of ways. It seems like the attempt to silence public broadcasting in this country is clearly an ideological one, not a cost issue. It costs the equivalent of a postage stamp per person to keep public radio going."

I asked Bill about what *was* lacking in our current media in his opinion. He replied, "There was a piece in *Newsweek* on South Africa titled *No News Is Good News*, and it was about the fact that since the violence has stopped there's not much news coming out of South Africa. That's a deplorable state of affairs—if the only thing worth reporting is violence, it's no wonder it feeds itself. Imagine if the discovery of the Salk vaccine was not made known because it was good news, and people were still getting paralyzed by polio. In South Africa, they have done an extraordinary job going from one of the most racist societies in the world to one that is trying to be inclusive. South Africans may have come up with a cure for our body politic that we need to know about, that can be replicated elsewhere."

Bill's point was well taken. More than once during our trip, irresponsible or excitable media would be cited as a source of the demise of the American dream. But as Bill had pointed out, responsible media was also an avenue for free speech and therefore a fundamental element of the dream as well.

I asked Bill if he could expound on what he would be doing next and he explained that he was presently working for the Soros Foundation, which was helping to develop community radio in South Africa. In the past the radio had been a tool for the proponents of apartheid, and the people had never had a chance to speak for themselves. He was gearing the new broadcasting corporation toward being a tool of empowerment, education, improved health care, and providing a forum for the South African choirs and other cultural voices that had never been heard before.

Bill's license plate

He likened being in South Africa at this moment to what our hometown, Philadelphia, might have felt like when Thomas Jefferson was writing the Declaration of Independence. He talked of early beginnings and a reinvention of self. "To be part of the excitement of innovative ideas bubbling forth, of both the boldness of it and its fragility as well. And if I can make some small contribution to that, it's wonderful. I feel it's a gift for me to be able to be there and provide some small assistance."

Bill had reiterated the definition of democracy and access for us early in our trip. He was a gentle, soft-spoken man who had given a rather loud and pervasive voice to the American community at large and was planning on extending his vision across the continents. In addition to the questions surrounding the freedom of the press and how it can enrich or soil, depending on who is interpreting the gift, Bill was one of the first people to communicate a quality that we would find very often in those who we were drawn to: compassion. He had successfully taken his own observations and grievances and funneled them into a concrete solution. We wrapped up his interview with one of our staple questions, asking him who he admired and had found influential.

''I think of Walt Whitman and his celebration of the country—and of the individual. There's a short thing of his I might like to read if I could, a very personal thing. I think that this expresses in a very intimate way what is extended out for all of us.''

Apparently Bill had prepared for this question because he then, very carefully and a little self-consciously, pulled out a sheet of notebook paper that he had evidently typed himself. ''Walt Whitman wrote:

> 'The soul reaching, throwing out for love
> As the spider from some little promontory,
> Throwing out filament after filament,
> Tirelessly out of itself that one at least may catch
> And form a link, a bridge, a connection.'

''And I think we all do that individually in our lives. We're reaching out for some connection and I think we do that in our work in any kind of media. That's quite an American kind of thing to do.''

JOHN WATERS

FILMMAKER

BALTIMORE, MARYLAND

(Shainee)

I met John Waters for the first time in the spring of 1994. I was working as the director of programming for a nonprofit independent film organization in Los Angeles and my job included scheduling and running screenings and seminars. I had planned a screening of John's film *Serial Mom*, with a discussion following, to be moderated by Quentin Tarantino. Apparently, the two had met a year or two earlier, gotten drunk together one night in a bar, and bonded. Quentin was a big fan of John's films and a pretty big draw himself, so the evening looked promising—standing room only, in fact.

One of the perks of my job was spending time with filmmakers I admire. The plan that night was that I would meet John for dinner before the screening with a couple of other pertinent people and then we would all go to the screening together. John insisted that we meet at Musso & Frank's, a legendary Hollywood steak house, for dinner and martinis. The waiters were all over sixty-five and, as a group, below average in height. They wore red coats and black slacks. Most of them had been working there for twenty years or more. They spoke softly, cajoling you into any number of luscious cuts of beef.

We sat in a round leather booth and ordered cocktails. I remember John being surprised that I drank Scotch and I hoped I hadn't ruined his scenario by refusing his offer of a martini. He looked exactly like I had pictured, impeccable in a fabulous suit and his immaculately manicured, pencil-thin mustache. The conversation was easy and effusive and I was taken by how clever John was. He told us stories of how Orson Welles, who had a regular table at Musso & Frank's, usually dined alone. John made him sound at once tragic and superior.

Preparing for a John Waters event was notably more fun than others. John had provided his home number in Baltimore early in the planning process and we spoke frequently. It was gratifying to be able to call a film-maker directly and not have to go through a series of agents, managers, and assistants. When the time came for Kristin and me to draft our original wish list of interviewees for *Anthem*, we took many factors into consideration. John's accessibility and gregarious good nature, not to mention nonconformist repertoire, had stuck with me and we sent him one of our first-round invitations.

I thought for sure he would be one of our first positive responses. I had no doubt that he would remember our merry evening together and invite us to come see him on our way through Baltimore. As the weeks ticked on toward our departure from Los Angeles, however, we heard nothing. I called and I called but got no response. I was actually a little embarrassed because I had assured Kris that we would at least get a direct answer from John—us being so chummy now and everything—and all she ever heard was me being blown off by his assistant. As the number of unreturned messages to John piled up, his assistant began to get very short and almost nasty with me when I called. I was mortified.

One day I told Kris that we should give up. She urged me to try one more time and John's assistant proceeded to tell me, without the use of euphemisms, not to call again. I was hurt and bewildered as to why this man, who had seemed so open and affable, was now rebuffing me. We left Los Angeles planning to try to concentrate on one of the other filmmakers that we had targeted. It wasn't until we were in my family's home in New Jersey, between interviews, that I got a message from John on my voice mail in Los Angeles: Would I please call him immediately?

When I called his number in Baltimore, John got on the phone right away and apologized profusely. Apparently, he had confused me with a woman who had essentially been stalking him. Ever since John had put Patty Hearst in his film *Cry Baby*, people all over the country had been badgering him to put them into one of his films. John has a very devout following and is forever fending off quasi-freaks and crackpots who want some kind of validation from him. The woman's name was something close to Shannon, and she was an FBI informant, a Mafia witness, or an ex-con—or all of the above. John said he hated her, she was driving him crazy, and he had given his assistant explicit instructions to get rid of me (Shannon) at any cost. Weeks later he happened to be flipping through his phone book, saw my name and phone number in it, and realized that he was giving the cold shoulder to the wrong woman. He continued to apologize, saying he didn't usually do interviews and he didn't even know what our film was about, but he felt so bad that he would do it—no questions asked. So we were invited to his house in Baltimore.

The day after our interview with Bill Siemering we drove the 110 miles to John's neighborhood, which was within the city limits of Baltimore, but looked very suburban. I was not surprised to find that John was still living in his home-town among those he revered and reviled in his work: suburbanites. From the man who created such cult classics as *Mondo Trasho*, *Pink Flamingos*, and *Hairspray*, and helped give birth to a range of celebrities that includes Johnny Depp, Ricki Lake, and the almighty Divine, we expected the unpredictable. Later, John would fill us in about his love/hate relationship with his very own neighborhood.

"I grew up in middle-class suburbia, upper-middle-class, kind of, and those are always the people that are attacked in my movies. And they always lose. And the people that win in my movies are always the outsiders. No matter if they're fat, gay, drag queens, black, uh, Communists. Subversive always wins and suburbia loses. And I think that I still root for outsiders to win, you know. All my movies are about people that take what is a disadvantage in society, proudly turn it into a style, and win.

"And I love Baltimore because it's an extreme city. There's rich and poor, there's not much in the middle. Debutantes hang out with bank robbers here. It's my kind of town. *Serial Mom* was shot in the neighborhood I grew up in. It was great! The people were lovely to us.

"The difference is, their parents had hated me when I first started making films here. They're in nursing homes and now my generation *lives* in the houses. It's funny, you know, my age group *is* the establishment now, which is the final irony in my life of ironies, really. The people I hate are the people that judge other people, and they will always be my target, really, and I think they deserve to be hacked to pieces with a chain saw and eaten by Divine."

We arrived in John's neighborhood on a bright, perfect summer day that matched the bright and perfect sunny houses and green lawns that make up John's cinematic world. In John's films most things happy and shiny on the surface ultimately elicit suspicion about the depravity that lurks beneath. It was with this suspicion in mind that we began our search for one of Baltimore's local celebrities.

Kristin and I were slightly confused about the address. Some of the streets seemed to have similar names and the numbers would go up and then down. We came upon a house that matched the address we had been given, but keeping in mind the Waters rule that nothing is ever as it seems, we were still thrown off by this quintessentially suburban house, which was not distinctive or appealing in any way. Scariest of all, there was a metallic sky-blue Ford Tempo in the driveway, circa 1986. John is notoriously retro and campy, but there was nothing even mildly cool about that car. It just *couldn't* be his.

We unpacked our equipment anyway and went to the door with some hesitation. A man in his late sixties answered, wearing chinos and a short-sleeved wash-

and-wear yellow workshirt. He seemed unfazed to find two young women carrying cameras. We told him that we were there to see John, that we had an appointment. He responded, "John Waters does not live here anymore, but people like
yourselves always seem to be looking for him." Hmmm.

Kris tried to get a little more information out of the man, while out of the
corner of my eye I saw a long, sleek, late-model black Buick swerve around the
corner. I could hear the man telling Kris that some of the neighborhood street
names were similar, and that we had to be careful about "street" versus "avenue"
versus "road," and so on. I knew all we needed to do was follow that Buick, which
stuck out like a sore thumb in this neighborhood, but shone like a beacon for us,
the lost ones.

We got back in the car, Kris mumbling, "What did that man mean he doesn't
live here *anymore*?" We barreled down the street, now on the verge of late, and
found the exact same address a few blocks away. This house, however, was splen-
did and intriguing—surprisingly Hansel and Gretelish—and I felt much better
about the prospect of actually finding John inside.

We got out and went to the door, where we were met with a sign that said
PLEASE RING DOORBELL. WE CANNOT HEAR IF YOU KNOCK. We rang obediently and then

waited. Finally we heard John's voice approaching. He answered the door while
speaking into a portable phone, introduced himself quickly, told us to come in
as he headed back up the stairs still talking, and then disappeared with a faint "I'll
be right back down." Kris and I both had
our mouths open to say something when
we heard John shut the door upstairs and
continue his now muffled conversation.

John came down a little while later.
He had changed into a crisp white shirt
and looked very fresh. We decided to set up
outside in the backyard. It was a beautiful
yard, lush and large, with stone benches
and big leafy trees. When we were ready,
I began by asking John how he became a
filmmaker.

John says "Hello" after a quick change

John took the deep breath of a man who has told the same story too many
times and answered, "I made my first movie when I was sixteen. It was a logical
progression from when I was a puppeteer for children's birthday parties. I had
started to take drugs and get in trouble, so my grandmother gave me a movie
camera, which in an odd way got me in movie trouble, but it kept me out of *real*
trouble. And I made an 8-mm black-and-white movie called *Hag in a Black Leather
Jacket*, and that's how it began. I was greatly influenced at the time by under-

ground movies. I went to the drive-in every single night, so I saw *Blood Feast* and all the exploitation films that were very, very big in Baltimore. Sadly, today, they don't exist anymore; all those theaters are gone.''

I asked John if he or his grandmother knew that he wanted to make films at such a young age when she gave him that camera.

''No, I mean, who knows what they want to be at twelve? I wasn't that much of an obsessional neurotic. I knew there was going to be show business in some way. Basically, I wanted to be Captain Hook, then Elvis Presley, then I decided that I maybe should try something a little more down-to-earth like . . . film director.''

We all laughed and I saw Kris catch herself from enjoying John too much in fear of shaking John's picture framing up and down. John was among the majority of the people that we would meet who would cite some knowledge of a direction at an early age. I pressed him about the influence that his family had on him.

''I would've never said that there was any philosophy in my family then, but now when I think about it, it did seep in. My father lent me the money to make those early movies, even though they were against every possible thing he believed in. He was Republican, my mother's brother was Undersecretary of the Interior for Nixon. So they were very, very straight. But they were loving, and they figured this was better than prison, which they were worried about. So they backed the early movies, and I paid them back. I think they were so shocked when they got their money back that they kept lending me double the amount until finally my father, after *Pink Flamingos*, said, 'Okay, this time don't pay me back. Set yourself up in business.' I didn't go to college.

''So they were incredibly supportive, but at the time I didn't realize that. I thought, 'Well, of course. He's my father. Why shouldn't he?' But I was making movies that attacked every belief he ever had. To this day he's never seen *Pink Flamingos*, and why should he? I'm not going to, when he's almost eighty years old, make him sit down and watch a movie that he would very much hate. But his hatred of it is maybe the fuel I ran on at the time. And the reason people liked that movie was because they thought, 'God, could you imagine if my parents saw this?' Now I meet people all the time, kids your age, at schools, who say, 'My mother turned me on to your movies,' and I think, 'Boy, have times changed!' ''

John was living proof that the American dream was alive. He had taken the support of his parents and turned it into his own film genre, his own subculture. I found it ironic and comforting that a man who had built his body of work on the debasement of the fundamentals of one popular version of the American dream (the nuclear family, the white Republican, Formica counters, and so on) was actually born and bred in it. His success even paid homage to it, in a strange way. I asked John what kept him going.

''I wonder sometimes what makes me want to keep making these films . . . It's the ritual of making them, it's what I do. And I never wake up and think, 'Oh, God, I hate what I do for a living,' which is, I think, the difference between insanity and sanity.''

His words sunk in. How many people would we pass by on the highways of America who could say the same? John reminded us that we too were lucky enough, at least for that day, to be on the positive side of his equation. We moved on to the question of how filmmaking influences and contributes to American culture.

"I think the one great thing that film has done has been to improve the sense of humor of Americans. When I went to film school, you couldn't have made *Mondo Trasho*. They would have said, 'You've failed. Get out of school. You can't do this kind of movie.' I've gotten, in this last month, two theses that were written about me from major colleges. That's the difference in thirty years, that bad taste is now a legitimate study." John laughed heartily and continued. "I'm not so sure I'm for that, either, to tell you the truth. I think it may have gone too far the other way, but people can laugh at everything that's terrible now. I'm not saying I changed it, but maybe I made it a tiny bit easier to laugh at things that you might have been embarrassed to laugh about thirty years ago."

I asked John if he thought that a change in our political climate had contributed to our ability to laugh at ourselves.

"Oh, God, certainly. I mean, Watergate made it safe to never ever trust your leaders again. Then there was Vietnam. I didn't know one person who died in Vietnam, not one. Which is kind of amazing, considering my generation was there at the height of when everybody was dying. But my Vietnam is AIDS. I guess every generation gets paid back in some way: I didn't know anybody who died then, but half the people I know are now dead from AIDS. That's a sobering thing that makes you realize every day is what counts and all that kind of corny stuff, which is very, very true."

John stopped to take a breath. His air conditioner was being fixed that day and the repairman kept turning it on intermittently to test it. He would roll his eyes and shrug at us every time it happened, knowing that it could screw up our sound. Kristin took the opportunity to adjust the arm of the Steadycam; she definitely must have been tired by that point. John watched her, fascinated, and jerked when the arm cracked into position.

"It's like a gun the way she cocks that thing," he said coyly, with admiration. Kris smiled confidently—we were getting comfortable with our "stuff"—and we continued, asking John's opinion on how the American hero has changed.

"The main way it's changed is that notoriety and fame are exactly the same, there's no difference. I've said this before: Manson and Madonna; Manson would get the better table. I'm staggered by these people who go onto Oprah's or Ricki's show, that go on and tell things that I might talk to my shrink about, my closest friends, but they just think it's being in show business! And I'm not really interested in it, to be honest. I look away. I think it's a kind of taste that doesn't delight me. It's *bad* bad taste.

"There's so much media now. When I was a kid, *Life* magazine, which is twenty magazines today, was *the* influence. It's what made Jackson Pollock famous, it's what made the Zapruder film famous, it was *the* magazine. If you were in *Life*, you were known all over America. Now there's eight million magazines and you have to read all of them, if you're a hooked media junkie, which I am. So they have to fill those pages, they have to find so many things to write about that they've actually gotten down to people's personal problems. That your entire family raped you under the Christmas tree. And they forget that that's not the same as writing a novel. But in America it's the same.''

John Waters was not the obvious critic of bad taste in the media. But the criticism was weightier coming from him, certainly, a man who seemingly has no boundaries. And his words would resonate throughout our trip and be reiterated often, particularly by those who had gained some sort of notoriety.

At that moment the air conditioner went on again and John stopped to ask us if we were okay with the sound problem. Before we could answer, his neighbor answered for us by turning on his lawn mower. John leaned in and cupped his mouth, ''I can't do anything to stop him. We're suing that neighbor. At least he's cutting the lawn—*finally*—after months. Maybe we should go inside.'' We agreed to go inside and John jumped up to make a couple of calls while we packed up to move into his living room. Kris asked if we could shoot some b-roll while he was on the phone and John said sure, but we should know that his electric chair had been shot *so* many times. He suggested, filmmaker to filmmaker, that we skip it. Electric chair?

We went inside the cool house. It felt like an English castle with its heavy walls, winding staircases, and gothic furniture. We found a parlor toward the back of the house in which to set up for the remainder of the interview. John would sit on a plush scarlet settee with imposing bookcases on both sides.

When we had finished putting the cameras back together, John had not yet returned, so we decided to wander and found the electric chair sitting in a hallway. Kris asked me if I wanted to sit in it and I looked at her as if she had asked me if I wanted to have my toenails pulled out. Kris, however—knowing it was only a replica made for one of John's films—jumped at the chance for a moment of rest and happily plunked herself down. After we shot some of John's movie posters in the hallway, we returned to the living room to wait for John.

After a few minutes, John entered, holding an Instamatic camera and muttering something about scaring the air conditioner man. He explained that he had to take a picture of every person that entered his house, it was just something that he routinely did. He apparently had upset the air conditioner man by asking him to pose for the required portrait on his way into the house. John got himself settled on the couch and then pointed the camera at Kris and me. We both must have frozen because he paused for a second, taking his eye away from the viewfinder, and said, ''It's not a sex thing.'' We laughed and I winced as the flash went off— because, of course, I had blinked. Great, I'll be recorded in the annals of John Waters history with my eyes half-cocked and my mouth wide open. Then we continued with a discussion of the people and events that John had found influential.

"I had influences, people I looked up to: Walt Disney, Ingmar Bergman, Russ Meyer, Fellini—off the top of my head. Andy Warhol, certainly. William Castle, he was an influence. You know, one good thing about doing this for so long is that I meet most of the people I've wanted to meet my whole life. Of those people I named before, I've met almost every one of them. I regret that I'll never meet Tennessee Williams, somebody who was a huge influence on me when I was a teenager. I never met him."

John had put his finger on one of the many fringe benefits of this trip, the opportunity for Kristin and me to meet a bunch of fascinating people—face-to-face. It was what John Perry Barlow would later call "an excellent scam." Another fringe benefit was discovering America firsthand—our awesome road trip. John had some experiences driving cross-country as well.

Kris and one of the twins

"I've driven across the country on all five interstate routes. It was a wonderful experience. I did it when I was younger. It's the last thing I want to do right now, but I'm glad I did it. It was really an eye-opening thing to realize there's plenty of room for a lot more people. You know, they're all in a tight little area," he said, scrunching his body into a ball on the couch. "Then there's all this space! There's room for billions of movie theaters and shopping malls." He laughed.

I asked John, "What do you see in the future as we approach a new millennium change?"

"Well, it's going to be the worst New Year's Eve ever. Don't go out! That night is a night to lock your doors and stay in. Every asshole in the universe will go out that night!" John continued, now seriously. "I've certainly led my life as a guarded optimist. I hope for the best but know the worst can happen. Seems like a fairly healthy way to live." We all nodded in agreement and I asked him if he believed in the American dream.

"Well, I think the American dream is a very fifties kind of thing—the American flag, Mom and apple pie—and I think everybody knows that it doesn't work, really, it's kind of old-fashioned. I think people do believe that you have a chance here. The class thing isn't so important here as it is in Europe, where you're born into a class and you can't ever escape that.

"But anyway, is there an American dream? I'm not sure that I have one. At least the one you're talking about, the thing that says the common man, every person, has the same dream. I value the freedom that I've had in my life. And that is the American dream, I think. Certainly a nineties, or eighties, or seventies version of it.

"I think the sixties changed our idea of the American dream. We knew all this stuff we were brought up with was really impossible. I never understood anyone who wanted to be like everyone else. I still don't. I never wanted to be. My dream is certainly not a house in suburbia and a good-paying job with a pension. That is not my dream at all. That would be my American nightmare."

It was funny that John was talking about suburbia as part of his "American nightmare" when from our perspective, his house looked to be very close to suburban. Even though he lived within the city limits of Baltimore, there were still single-family homes with lawns, complete with neighbors who don't mow them. But John definitely had taken his self-defined kryptonite and managed to twist it into a fortress of strength. He finished his thought, and it was time for us to go.

"My dream is, really, I always said I just wanted a Xerox machine and a black Buick. And I've achieved that."

Aha.

BEN COHEN AND
JERRY GREENFIELD

FOUNDERS OF BEN & JERRY'S ICE CREAM

SUGARBUSH, VERMONT

(Kristin)

We left the home of John Waters and headed toward two other iconoclasts known for blazing a dairy trail that had turned ice cream into a socially conscious and compassionate food group, while successfully redefining the responsibilities of business toward the community. We were drawn to the duo because they had managed to implement and sustain an unorthodox vision that challenged the self-interest of capitalism. In the spirit of "life, liberty, and the pursuit of happiness," Ben and Jerry were exercising their right to place as much importance on giving something back as they did on the bottom line.

The other thing that we found interesting about their Vermont operation is that Ben and Jerry's idea of supporting their community was not limited to the pastoral hills of Vermont but actually spanned the country with a variety of social contributions. The Ben and Jerry philosophy seemed right at home in Vermont, where communities are still very much intact and the Vermont ethos of *know thy neighbor* thrived in this world within a world.

Ben and Jerry were the first people to say yes to our interview request. I found it mildly amusing that as the catalyst responsible for putting us on the road in the first place, they were suddenly itching to blow us off. Jerry's eyes darted from left to right, distracted by the festival backstage action, while Ben attempted—fighting the noise of the live zydeco band ten feet away—to answer a few simple questions about the meaning of life in America. We were, after all, sitting together at Ben & Jerry's annual One World, One Heart Festival.

Sitting face-to-face with them, we realized that our initial call from Ben, in which he so kindly offered his advice and encouragement—inviting us to the festival to do an interview—would be valuable for not much else than the much-needed jump start. Having finally made it to Vermont, and being far enough down the road to never look back, we realized that Ben and his compadre Jerry were actually a mirage that had thankfully led us to water.

Last-minute research

Thousands of people milled around the ski mountain that had been transformed into a mini-Woodstock: multiple stages featuring bands from all over the world, hemp merchandise booths, and—of course—all-you-can-eat ice cream stands. It was an ambitious office party designed to thank their local community for its support. Although our time with Ben and Jerry was distracted and brief, they did respond positively to the questions we were asking, and they did confirm some of the ideas that we were exploring. That—and free Chunky Monkey—made the trip worth the effort.

The idea of community was one of the themes that had already surfaced in other interviews, in which people addressed the need for individual responsibility in order to sustain community. Ben stressed the importance of taking accountability out to the public sector, saying that he felt we weren't, as a culture, living out our values. He acknowledged that the eighties were so focused on increasing personal wealth that a lot of people are now looking at their lives and sensing that something is missing. I thought again about the phenomenal success of *The Celestine Prophecy*.

Ben and Jerry both believed, as did many others we met, that it was indeed possible to balance equality and capitalism if capitalism had its own system of checks and balances and if there was individual and community participation. It was apparent by the way they talked about themselves and their business that they didn't consider their approach to be extraordinary, just necessary. Ben outlined the historical progression of influences on our civilization, explaining that it used to be religion, then it was government, and then it was business. He went on to argue that when religion and government were the most powerful forces, they had the purpose—the purported purpose—of working to improve the quality of life for everyone. But business has never had that purpose, operating within its own narrow self-interest. Ben believed business was going to have to start taking more responsibility for the society as a whole if we were indeed going to evolve. "If it doesn't happen," he said, "then I think there will be a revolution. And there should be."

I asked Ben and Jerry what Vermont—the landscape—gave to them personally.

Ben said that one of the big draws was the cows. "Cows are very mellow creatures," he explained. Ben, a very mellow creature himself, went on to point out that the biggest things around Vermont and many other rural places were mountains. He felt that natural surroundings allowed people to see themselves realistically in proportion to the world and universe while maintaining a personal relationship to the land. In cities, he argued, the biggest things around are monstrous buildings that are man-made. "I think you can start to get the erroneous impression," Ben explained, "that people are a bigger part of the universe than they really are."

After a heartfelt handshake, the two practically skipped away. We left the festival grounds exhausted from our day in the mountain sun and crashing from the pints of heavy cream and sugar we had dutifully consumed.

Ben Cohen

Sugar crash

JOHN IRVING

NOVELIST

DORSET, VERMONT

(Kristin)

Getting a confirmation from John Irving's office was a literal surprise. We had put out "a call to arms" to several American novelists. But we had not so much as heard a decline from most of them, the exceptions being Norman Mailer and Arthur Miller, who both politely refused via their assistants and book publishers. Mr. Mailer's secretary called and offered a consolation message in a thick Brooklyn accent: "Mr. Mailer regrets he cannot participate in *Anthem*, although he thinks your project is very interesting. He is himself working on a similar topic as we speak. I guess great minds think alike." We appreciated the overly complimentary blow-off.

So the yes from Mr. Irving's agent was welcomed. It was a short, to-the-point message—so short that I didn't believe it was true. I called to confirm his interest. "Yes, he'd like to do it," said his agent, "but you'll have to come to Vermont, to our house." It turns out his agent is his wife.

I said that coming to Vermont was no problem and set a date for the day after Ben and Jerry. We'd already realized how rare it was to catch two interviewees in the same area at the same time.

Shainee and I were thrilled by the idea of meeting the man behind *The Cider House Rules, The World According to Garp, A Prayer for Owen Meany*, and other novels we'd loved. Reading through his bio and research materials that we had downloaded from the net, Shainee said, "Well, I'm not going to talk literature with him, that's for sure. He's too well read."

Shainee and I had never pretended to be experts on any subject, but we were sometimes apprehensive that our interviewee would start interviewing us about our knowledge of their work or field of expertise. Research brush-ups—often while we drove—go only so far.

We pulled over to a pay phone just a few hours before we were scheduled to arrive at the Irvings'. I dialed their number to confirm our imminent arrival with the assistant, with whom I'd been talking regularly. A man's voice gruffly greeted me on the other side of the receiver, and I asked with a sneaking suspicion, "Is this *John?*" As it rolled off my tongue, I kicked myself, wishing I had said, "Mr. Irving."

The disembodied voice paused and then responded with some wariness, "Yes." I explained who I was and that I was calling to confirm that Shainee and I were on our way for the interview. My explanation was met with utter silence. Not certain if I had stunned him or if he had hung up, I too sat silently and then decided to add, "We've been speaking to your wife and your assistant for the last month, and they said to come today at two o'clock."

Again, utter silence.

Having too much at stake to give him an out, I offered, "We can certainly come at three or four—whatever is good for you."

"Why don't you come at three," the voice finally offered. I'm not sure if either of us said good-bye. The awkwardness of the conversation made it seem like it was the first time either of us had used a telephone.

"But at least he did say, 'Come at three'—he did say '*come*,'" I assured Shainee as we followed the directions to his house, which was gorgeous and remote and sprawled on top of its own hill.

We knocked on his large glass front door. "Hi, can we live here with you and your family?" Shainee joked, seeing John in his spacious living room, coming toward the door.

Then he was there, inarguably handsome, holding his door open, not really saying much, but at least smiling. He showed us into the living room and, skipping over idle chitchat, asked us where we would like to do the interview. We all decided on his office, where the large windows overlooked an extraordinary natural landscape. There was indeed the famous red typewriter that I had read about and

John Irving

near it, an enormous dictionary that was perched on its own handcrafted stand like a Fabergé egg.

John informed us that he really had only an *hour*, so we got started.

He spoke about his prep school education and of being a bit of a loner, often on the "outside." A dedicated wrestler during the drug culture of the sixties, he avoided the Vietnam draft in his early twenties by virtue of the fact that he had already married and birthed a son. So, John explained, he never really felt a shared experience with his generation. "I grew up in a hurry," he admitted. John did seem serious and old-fashioned, but not "conservative."

Writing was a discipline to John, just as competitive wrestling and fatherhood had been. "I started writing and wrestling at the same time, when I was fourteen. Writing is not a career choice. It's a habit," he declared.

Shainee asked John what kind of impact he felt fiction writers today were having on American culture.

"The impact of one's writing," he began, "has largely deteriorated. I don't think that a writer of literary fiction today, especially in this country, is a person of any real influence on the society. We're not a reading country. The last statistic I saw was, I think, fewer than one percent of the adult population of this country reads hardcover books. Who are you actually making an impact on? English majors? Maybe. I think the only people I'm influencing are largely people who would generally agree with me in the first place. And the only way you change a society or really influence a culture is to be of influence on those people who are *not* of your opinion.

"Over time, the four or five million paperback copies of *Garp* that were sold in America are not nearly as impressive to me as the fact that the hardcover of *Son of the Circus* sold forty thousand copies in Norway. Now, the Norwegians are readers. Maybe, per capita, I have some influence on the Norwegians!"

John went on to discuss the empirical value of the novel and the modern American writer. As I watched him continue a long monologue, I realized the interview had run off-track. Shainee and I both tried a number of times to elicit responses on subjects as diverse as the American dream, the American hero, American politics, and the landscape. But what we got instead was John Irving, the prominent, though humble, novelist and a privileged one-on-two literature seminar.

Shainee and I both realized halfway through John's thirty-minute monologue on how to create a character and develop a story that he didn't know anything about *Anthem*; his wife—who was out running an errand—had probably forgotten to tell him why we were coming or show him our faxed materials, and he had obviously assumed that we were coming to interview him on the usual subject of writing.

Don't get me wrong. The literature seminar was interesting and educational and partial blame for the unsuccessful interview fell on us, for not knowing how to gracefully or respectfully stop someone who takes a sharp left onto Tangent Row.

After the interview, I asked John if I could take some shots of his wrestling photos. I wasn't exactly sure how we'd use the footage, but Shainee and I were just trying to cover all bases. John didn't really respond but instead walked down the hallway toward an oversized door. I got the feeling he was expecting me to follow. He led me into a room that was a dead ringer for my junior high school gym. It was enormous and took me back to children's yelps and hollers in a game of dodgeball. The expansive floor was covered in an apple red wrestling mat—the exact color of John's typewriter—and there were photos, wall to wall, of John at all ages and his sons at all ages in tight jumpers and in various compromising positions.

Shortly thereafter, John guided us back to the front door, sending us on our way with a friendly good-bye.

Shainee and I were both kind of stunned by the experience, realizing as we pulled away that we had just *not* crafted a successful interview about America. We both knew we had failed, but at least we had learned something about interviewing technique. And as John said to me in his gym, when I commented on his wrestling record: "You win some, you lose some."

CONCORD, MASSACHUSETTS 6/25

(Shainee)

As we drove through the lush green hills of southeastern Vermont into New Hampshire and then down toward Boston, Kris stayed glued behind the camera. It was the first time, in a series of many, that she would be taken over by the landscape and forget that we might not need an entire hour of Vermont's beauty on tape. But it *was* exquisite—the land was in full bloom and the towns and their buildings spoke of a different century. I wished that either I could take a turn shooting or that she would stop, because I had no one to talk to when she was overcome like this.

Our destination was Concord, Massachusetts, where over two centuries before, on April 19, 1775, someone had fired the "shot heard round the world," to which someone else had responded with the cry, "Let it begin here!" And so it did, when twenty-one days later the Second Continental Congress met in my beloved Philadelphia to nominate a Virginian by the name of George Washington to command the Continental Army and fight for democracy.

Our schedule dictated that we would be staying in Concord for a few days to visit with a man named Michael Kellett. Michael had founded an organization called RESTORE: The North Woods, which was dedicated to the restoration and preservation of the forests that extend from Portland, Oregon, to Portland, Maine. He lives near Walden Pond and many of his beliefs are predicated on those of Henry David Thoreau.

Michael had arranged time to take us hiking through Walden Woods and he had enlisted the help of his friend Rudy Engholme, a member of the Environmental Air Force, to take us flying over Walden Pond and possibly up over the Maine Woods as well. Michael warned us ahead of time that the ever-present possibility of bad weather could keep us from flying, so we had left a few days open in order to stay flexible.

We arrived in Concord on a Sunday evening. We drove the streets of the colonial town looking for an inn and found several reminders of the Revolution, including the Old North Bridge (the first Revolutionary battle site), the Grave of the British Soldiers, and the Minuteman Statue. We got out of the car to read the

Battle Monument, which is engraved with Ralph Waldo Emerson's famous *Concord Hymn*:

Concord Hymn

(Sung at the completion of the Battle Monument, April 19, 1886)

By the rude bridge that arched the flood,
    Their flag to April's breeze unfurled,
Here once the embattled farmers stood,
    And fired the shot heard round the world . . .

After we found that we could not afford any of the charming inns adorned with images of Paul Revere and Redcoats, we settled on the suggestion of a cheery man at work in his garden and found a motel just outside of town. From there we called Michael Kellett, who told us that they were expecting a storm and that we probably would not accomplish either of the goals planned for the next day in the rain. We agreed to wait it out for twenty-four hours and decided to wander around the area the next afternoon.

I had been telling Kris about the fishing communities north of Boston and how much I wanted her to see them. She had never been in that part of the country, so I viewed the rain as an opportunity to introduce her to the mystical gray of the northeastern coast. We agreed that a fisherman's voice would be a good one to add to our infant chorus and what better place to begin than America's oldest fishing community: Gloucester, Massachusetts? I tried to prepare Kris by recalling the Gorton's of Gloucester fish sticks commercial, singing, "Trust the Gorton's fisherman . . ." in my own stab at a warbling baritone. But she had no idea what I was warbling about. Yet another testament to the regional differences between a desert girl and a girl raised by the ocean.

MICHAEL SPINOLA

FISHERMAN

GLOUCESTER, MASSACHUSETTS

(Shainee)

They have lobster and . . . What are littlenecks?" Kris asked me, looking directly into the camera lens.

"Clams," I responded and panned around to shoot a sign that said BOULEVARD OCEANVIEW, SPECIALIZING IN PORTUGUESE & SEAFOOD.

Kris grimaced. "That doesn't sound very good," she said, continuing to peruse the chalkboard menu. Eventually she acknowledged the skinny middle-aged woman standing at the take-out window, saying, apologetically, "I'm not sure what we want yet."

The woman stood behind the screen with her arms folded and answered, "Take your time. I'm here till three." She pushed the screen open with her elbow in order to give herself somewhere to lean while Kris continued to ponder the coastal fare, confused. I suggested that maybe she should stick with a grilled cheese and ordered a crab cake sandwich for myself. While Kris paid, I zoomed in on the Historic Gloucester Fishermen's Memorial Statue before turning the camera off to sit down and eat.

It was a misty, overcast, unseasonably cold afternoon for June, even that far north. We had stopped for our first meal of the day at a small seafood shack facing the water. Rows of streets with wooden houses painted in muted colors and divided by stone fences make up the town of Gloucester. A prototypical Eastern seaside town, signs of Gloucester's biggest industry are everywhere. The waterfront looks industrial with its tankers, trolling boats, and huge warehouse docks. There are mountains of lobster traps, nets, and businesses devoted to the craft—Gloucester Marine Railways Corp., Cape Pond Ice House, Three Lanterns Ship Supply, and Fairtry Fisheries, with a FOR SALE sign. It is a quiet town, except for the piping cries of the numerous seagulls, a nice atmospheric touch.

We finished eating and piled back into the car to begin our search for a real live fisherman. It was very quiet—almost desolate—as we drove back and forth along the waterfront looking for some sign of fishing activity. The streets had names like FRIEND and HOPE and I wondered if the town had Quaker origins. We crossed in front of the sturdy statue of the fisherman in rain gear at the wheel of his threatened ship, went past a road sign that said ELDERLY XING, and headed toward the water.

We parked near a landing where people could look out through those big binoculars that cost a quarter and scanned the docks for bodies in mid-fish. There were very few, but we spotted a large rusting ship bobbing in the distance and decided to check it out.

Kris held the camera tightly as we walked around the boat, which was docked for repairs. Her name, in clear block letters on her stern, was SAINT MARY. Kris and I looked around for her captain, wandering around another ship and into a shed before we finally found a man in a white undershirt and jeans who was coiling a thick rope around his arm. He looked up when we approached, and this time Kris explained that we were making a short film about the area and the fishing industry and asked if he would mind answering a couple of questions. He pushed the rope coil up his arm with the elegance of a woman pulling on long black satin gloves, poising himself to remove the cigarette dangling from his mouth, and told us that we should talk to the owner. The man pointed to a wiry man in a blue T-shirt who looked busy on the deck of the ship and shouted, "Mike! Mike!"—but Mike could not hear him. Kris offered to climb the twenty-foot ladder onto the deck to get Mike's attention. The first man looked at her with a crooked amused smile and said, "You would?" She nodded. "Then go ahead." So she did.

One thing I knew about Kris before we entered into this partnership was that she was not big on caution. I had learned not to waste energy on worrying about her decisions to endanger her own physical well-being, because she was always fine. She once told me that she had been worked on by a massage therapist who told her that she was "built for speed." I'd come to believe that "Godspeed" was part of that build.

My eyes followed her up the thin rickety ladder through the camera lens, laughing to myself as she called out with all familiarity to this stranger, "Mike? Mike, are you up here?" Soon after she was climbing back over the ship's railing, and Mike was putting down his arc welder to follow her. Apparently, he had agreed to be interviewed.

Mike was a slight middle-aged man with grey-streaked thick black hair and a thin face. His smile was wide but he was shy in front of the camera. We stood in front of his *Saint Mary*, the wind blowing and someone's transistor radio faintly touting "Boston's classic rock" in the background.

Kris began by asking, "You're a real fisherman, right?" He smiled and nodded and we made introductions all around. Kris verified with Michael that Gloucester was actually the oldest American fishing community and, satisfied, settled in behind the camera.

Michael said he had been living in Gloucester for his whole life. I asked him how long he'd been fishing and he proudly answered, "Thirty years." He said he had brothers and they'd had the family boat for fifty years.

He was not having an easy time opening up to us. He seemed like a very kind man, though, and it was obvious that he wanted to oblige us. I watched his face while I tried to relax him, recognizing the discomfort of answering the questions of strangers. I saw something in his eyes at the mention of his family and the legacy of their boat. From the looks of *Saint Mary*, she had seen some rough times. She was rusted and there were several patched holes in her bow. She looked her age and it showed in Michael's face.

I asked him why he chose to stay in Gloucester and why he kept fishing. He answered simply, "It's my home—the ocean, I mean."

"Was your family always here in America?"

"No, my dad was born in Italy, came to this country in 1924 as a boy, a thirteen-year-old. He started fishing on a boat and then he bought into a boat, then bought his own boat, then he got married and had three boys, and the three boys carried on in his line of work."

I was curious if Michael's father had ever told him why he left Italy.

"The only thing he told me was, in the old country, in Italy, there was starvation. It was to better himself. There it was bad, really bad. He lived here most of his life. He fished for fifty-four years before he passed away."

Kris asked Michael what he thought America had given his father personally. "Prosperity," he answered. "A future. There was no future in the old country, it's different today. Had he stayed there, he would have never been able to accomplish what he did by coming to America."

I asked him if he believed there was an American dream and, knowing what it meant to his father, what did it mean to him now? "Yes, there is an American dream." He nodded. "What does it mean to me? Being happy in what you are doing. I think that means more to me than anything."

He looked up to his boat and to the men busy working on it and said, "For me, I don't need so much. Some people need a lot, but I don't."

"Will your kids eventually take over the boat?" I asked.

"No. Life in the fishing industry is going downhill. I have two girls, thank God," he said, nervously kicking the ground. "If I had a son, I would keep him from fishing."

"Why is that?" I asked.

"All the reasons I've wanted to be on the water—they've all disappeared. The fish counts are down, it's very hard to make a living, and I don't think it's going to get any better. Nobody wants to pass it down anymore. The young kids should do whatever they want. Send them off to school or to college or whatever—anything. But keep them away from fishing."

Michael was obviously disturbed by the state of his profession and I felt a bit like we were pouring salt on an open wound simply by asking him about it. But he didn't sound like a man who felt that he had been wronged. He was instead simply resigned to the sad truth of the situation and was still out on this foggy day patching up his Lady Mary. I was sad, too, at the thought of this place losing its identity. I knew that I was not the only outsider

Saint Mary

who found this town so mesmerizing and mysteriously gray. Gloucester had inspired the writing of both Henry Wadsworth Longfellow and Rudyard Kipling. I thought there must be more to the equation of why this quiet town and its ancient fishing community were suffering, so I asked Michael his opinion.

"Well, years ago there were big boats and we were fishing by hand. Then you got into the nets and now you've got technology that's gonna wipe out the fish pretty fast. It only takes a few years to deplete the stocks. And that's what's happened here. I don't know how to stop it. The government doesn't, either. The politicians, they come to us for advice and some input and then they go back to Washington. They don't use one word we've said. They put someone in charge of the fisherman's commission from *Nebraska*!" Michael exclaimed in disbelief, his hand flying toward a direction that I could only assume was Nebraska. "A thousand miles from the ocean! What do *they* know about fishing?"

There was the fire of anger and loss in Michael's voice. I wasn't sure if it was a good thing that we had gotten this quiet man riled up, and there was a bit of an awkward silence. Michael was staring past us, his arms rising and falling in an attempt to communicate something—anything. He did not know what to do, now that he had blown off the steam, and we sensed his frustration. Kris tried to console him, coaxing, "So you don't feel represented?"

"No. Exactly." He breathed deeply and looked down at the paint on his sneakers. He continued calmly, "It's over, fishing. I think the fishing's down everywhere. I think it's the whole coast—East Coast, West Coast, down South. The technology today depleted the fish stocks."

Michael sighed and his quiet disposition returned with a smile as he looked to the bright side. "We're under a good conservation program right now, to try to bring them back. But it's going to take maybe eight to ten years and meanwhile it's very bad."

I asked Michael if the demise of the fishing communities was already having a direct effect on Gloucester's way of life.

"What's happened here now is, Gloucester is a fishing community, and the rules and regulations that they've put on us will put forty percent of the city out of business. Everything in Gloucester is related to fisheries. There are ice companies, there are the people who go to unload the fish off the boats—they're called 'lumpers.' It affects everybody. If I prosper, everybody prospers. It's like a chain reaction.

"If I don't make a living, the railway doesn't make a living, I don't buy a few extra groceries, I don't go to the movies, I don't go buy a car. What happens in a case like this is that guy"—Michael pointed to the Fairtry Fisheries—"will sell his fish plant and a condo will come in or it will become a yacht club or something like that. It happened down in Rhode Island. In Gloucester, when the fishing industry dies, everybody dies. And three hundred years of fishing have gone down the tubes."

We asked him what he would do himself if he could influence the government in their decision-making.

"What would I change?" he said. "I believe that charity starts at home. I think that we should help people in this country before we spend millions and billions abroad. There are people in this country who are starving. I don't know why, but the government has never helped the fisherman. They help the farmers, they've helped everybody else, but they've never—ever—subsidized the fisherman. And that's why we're in the predicament that we're in today. I feel like the government is stepping on the fisherman. We're so darn low right now, we're on our backs. We're not getting help."

"Do the environmentalists play a role?" I asked.

"A big part of it, yes. I'm a conservationist. I believe in it wholeheartedly. But when we can think more about a whale than our people, when you can spend three million dollars on a whale that's caught on the ice up in Alaska, then something is wrong.

"Nobody wants a free lunch, you know? We're fishermen, we work hard, but there are so many rules and regulations now that they're putting us out of business. Tell them don't go fishing for two years and that's the best way to start seeing the fish come back. In the meantime, help these guys out. You know, give them a couple hundred bucks a week, and they'll pump gas. I'll do something— whatever I have to—to get by. But at least help me out. But they don't."

I listened to Michael, remembering how he had spoken so proudly of his father and of the prosperity he had sought and found here. *Saint Mary* had much more to contend with now then she did fifty years ago. I asked Michael, reminding him of his earlier response, if he still believed in an American dream, in spite of all he had told us.

He looked at us directly and said confidently, "I still think that this is the greatest country in the world. Yes, definitely."

For Sale

Again he smiled wide and continued to while Kris thanked him for giving us his time and apologized for interrupting his work. He said he was happy to help out and wished us luck, turning to climb back up his ladder to *Saint Mary*'s deck. Michael kept looking back at us and smirking as he climbed. I guess it had finally sunk in that this was not an ordinary occurrence for him and with a mixture of excitement and apprehension he turned to us and asked, "All the way from the West Coast, huh?"

Kris chatted with him about where we were from and what we were doing. I packed up the camera, watching as he sat down on the ladder to listen to her. He was flattered by our interest and I was glad. When we finally made our way down the dock toward the car, I looked back at Michael as he stepped onto the deck of his ship, *Saint Mary*'s reflection rippling in the water and the lighthouse behind them. Except for the transistor radio, it could have been fifty years ago.

MICHAEL KELLETT

FOUNDER OF RESTORE: THE NORTH WOODS

CONCORD, MASSACHUSETTS

(Shainee)

Henry David Thoreau, a man forever associated with Walden Pond and the conservationist movement, accidentally set fire to the woods around the pond when he was twenty-six years old. More than 300 acres burned. Already known as something of an eccentric in Concord, Thoreau's fire did nothing to boost his reputation among his fellow citizens, nor did his subsequent publication of *Walden*. Yet today we imagine him as an environmental hero who interpreted the American dream on his own terms, paying homage to the land in *Walden* and exercising his individual rights in *Civil Disobedience*.

After the gloomy weather that had postponed our meeting with Michael Kellett, we were happy to awake the next morning to a crisp, radiant June day. The sun was vibrant and I was thrilled at the idea of spending the day in the woods. I love the blinding white flash of shimmer that summer sunlight brings to green leaves. We had planned on meeting Michael at his house and then following him to Walden Pond. Later we would be meeting his friend Rudy at the local airfield, to take a quick flight over the area.

Michael and a colleague began RESTORE a few years earlier, out of the extra bedroom of Michael's house. It is a small nonprofit organization with only a couple of part-time staff members and a few volunteers. Michael is a devout student of the writings and teachings of Henry David Thoreau, who, in Michael's opinion, paved the way for all American conservationists.

If one of our goals was to search out evidence of the influence of this country's forebears on today's visionaries. Michael was our holy grail. When Michael spoke, he sounded like an extension of Thoreau's spirit, living in and processing a contemporary world through the filter of Thoreau's sensibilities. One man, inspired, lays down a life of work and ideas for the next to pick up and run with it.

We arrived at Michael's house in the morning. He had a wonderful garden filled with wildflowers and unusual grasses and ferns. The garden led us to a screened-in porch where Michael was waiting for us. He was gentle-looking, with-sandy, almost strawberry hair, a full beard, and a slight build.

We sat on the porch and made our introductions, talking a little bit about the beginnings of RESTORE and Michael's longtime involvement in conservation movements. Prior to his environmental pursuits, Michael had worked in hospital administration. Kris asked him how he went from buying hospital syringes to joining the ranks of those who monitor how many wash up on coasts.

"Well, I was always interested. But there's a point where you just say, 'Some-body's got to take the first step.' You look around, and there aren't too many people doing it, so you think, 'Well, I guess I'm elected.' "

Kris asked him if we could actually conduct the interview in front of Tho-reau's cabin. Michael explained that there is a 370-acre state park surrounding Walden Pond that includes Thoreau's cabin site. He said our camera might pick up a lot of ambient noise, though, because the woods could get quite crowded with visitors. "And also, unfortunately, because of Route 2. They cut right through Walden Woods before anybody paid any attention. So, if you're not careful, you can hear the freeway."

Michael was so matter-of-fact about a freeway being built through the mid-dle of a historical forest that neither Kris nor I knew what to say. We had imagined Walden Pond as a bucolic oasis in the suburbanized octopus that surrounds Boston proper. I guess the incredulous look on our faces said what we were thinking.

"Oh, yeah, they were going to put the town dump across the street. They were going to build a big office complex kitty-corner from there, and they were going to build condos . . ."

"What were they thinking?" I asked, appalled.

"They weren't! They weren't thinking!" Michael almost shouted back. "People in Concord take it for granted. They have Louisa May Alcott's house, they have the Old North Bridge, they have Thoreau's house. The school he taught in with his brother is right up the street here. Somebody just lives in it, nobody even knows about it. I mean, Walden Pond—all this important stuff—and they just think . . ." Michael shrugged his shoulders and put a blank look on his face. "Oh, yeah."

Michael's cheeks had turned pink. The mild-mannered man had just roared. Passion. Just like the fisherman from the day before. It was a level of emotion that we would get used to encountering.

Kris still couldn't believe her ears. There had to be some explanation for peo-ple's disrespect for Walden Pond. She asked Michael again, "Why?"

"I think it's just human nature. In the Maine woods, they say, 'Oh, well, that's just a forest. It's nice, but nothing that special.' And I have to tell them, 'Believe me, this is special! Have you been anywhere else in the country and seen an ancient forest like this? This is different, folks!' And people in Alaska, I guess, say, 'Oh, it's just a bunch of tundra and caribou. Who cares?' "

''That's what is interesting about Henry Thoreau. He recognized the value of what was right in his own backyard. Most people don't seem to do that. It takes somebody from outside pointing it out.''

Apparently, the Walden Woods Project, which had involved Don Henley (a member of the band the Eagles) had raised the issue of Walden Pond's imminent destruction to a level of national awareness. Many supporters had jumped on the bandwagon and the woods had been saved from developers. In talking with Michael, we couldn't help noticing his unusual pronunciation of Thoreau's name. We felt kind of dumb repeating ourselves incorrectly, so we had begun to avoid saying his name until Kris finally brought it up.

''I've been saying Thoreau's name wrong for my whole life, how does he pronounce it?''

''THOR-oh, with the accent on 'Thor' '' (like I*gor*).

''THOR-oh,'' she repeated. ''Who knew?''

Kris thanked Michael for not correcting us. I made a mental note to try to remember to say it correctly. THOR-oh. It felt pretentious coming from my mouth.

We decided that it was time to get to the interview site, so we headed down the path toward our respective cars. As we walked past his garden, I commented on the tiny purple flowers that grazed our ankles. Michael explained that he was trying to restore his own property by slowly removing the species of plant life that weren't indigenous to the area. Including the grass.

''Nobody's lawn in the United States is an indigenous grass. It's all Asian species that were brought over. That's why they have to put all the poison and the fertilizer on it—it isn't meant to grow here. It's wimpy, and it needs all kinds of special help to keep it going. So I'm not helping ours. I'm letting it fade away.''

Michael pointed out the difference between the riot of color of the indigenous wildflowers and the measly ground cover that used to be a lawn. I myself was guilty of Michael's accusation of foliage ignorance. I never thought about where flowers came from or if they belonged here.

At that moment, I became particularly appreciative of what this trip was allowing us to do: enter a series of categorical worlds. Each person we met represented a different paradigm with its own set of rules, but all managed to fall under the umbrella of ''American.'' Would we find a common thread connecting the Romanian fables of Andrei Codrescu with the patrons of Dollywood? The man who founded NPR and the men who founded an ice cream empire? A man who defines his life by the sea and a man who defines his life by the wildflowers in his backyard? At that point, I didn't know. But I hoped that we would, and I looked forward to entering each person's world, learning their vocabulary, and seeing through the filter of their eyes.

We got into our respective cars and Kris and I followed Michael to the park. We pulled into a gravel lot surrounded completely by tall leafy trees. Michael asked us how and why we started our project as we applied the Siemering Law of Equipment Transportation, loading him up with our extra camera and tripod. I explained our trip as we began to trudge down a sandy path.

The park looked like most wooded areas in the Northeast, not extraordinary but pretty. Thoreau himself had described Walden's scenery as being "on a humble scale, and, though very beautiful, does not approach grandeur, nor can it much concern one who has not long frequented it or lived by its shore." The trees were peaceful and it was a little on the windy side. Kris turned the camera on while we were hiking to find a spot, and I asked Michael to begin by telling us a little more about his background.

Michael came from Detroit and his father worked for the Ford Motor Company most of his life. He described his childhood as average, middle-class. "I lived in a big city, surrounded by freeways, cars, and buildings. But in the summertime we would go on trips up to northern Michigan and to national parks and national forests. I found that I really liked everything that was missing from urban life. So when the opportunity came, it was very natural for me to get involved as a volunteer in conservation issues. I went to the University of Michigan and got a bachelor's degree in political science. Politics is mainly what determines the outcome in conservation and preservation of the environment."

We asked Michael to clarify the distinction between conservation and preservation. He explained that conservation is concerned with limiting the amount of resources that we squander. Preservation is a little more hard-core, wanting to keep what little we have left intact, while working toward restoring our resources to their prior state. Just then, we emerged on a sandy beach. There was a lovely glimmering, what I would call "Walden Lake" in front of us. "Wow . . . that's not a pond," I said.

"In New England, a pond can be what elsewhere may be called a small lake," Michael said. I nodded slowly, thinking about the puddles that in New Jersey we proudly labeled ponds. This place was a refuge of simple beauty. I quickly subtracted the freeway sounds and knew exactly why Thoreau had secluded himself here.

I remembered how Thoreau had capitalized the word "Nature" in *Walden*, much in the same way that most people capitalize the word "God." I commented that it was my understanding that Thoreau had written a lot about the idea of the environment as almost a religion or a greater spirituality.

"Right," Michael confirmed. "Thoreau said, 'The mass of men lead lives of quiet desperation.' And he was talking about people in the town of Concord who just go on, day after day after day, worrying about money, worrying about their job, worrying about all kinds of mundane concerns, and not thinking about the important things. Thoreau was able to cut through the layer that comes between us and the natural world.

"But it wasn't just nature, it was also social justice as well. He saw through all the hypocrisies of the way we treated Indians, and he was antislavery. He was a humanist *and* a naturalist, he saw the two as compatible. Today, we've got this schism that people think is people versus the environment or the economy versus the environment. Well, a hundred and fifty years ago Thoreau didn't see any incompatibility between people and nature. He saw them as part of the same continuum.''

We had climbed back up the embankment as Michael kept talking and I tried to clear the branches for him so they wouldn't get caught on his microphone cord. We came to a clearing in the midst of trees so tall that I had to crane my neck as far as it could go to see their tops. There was a sign that said HOUSE SITE. Michael explained that the area was called Thoreau's Cove because of the glimpse of shoreline that he could see from his cabin. ''This area was owned by Ralph Waldo Emerson. Thoreau knew Emerson and told him he wanted to go live in the woods someplace, so he asked if it would be all right to build a little cabin on his property. Emerson said, 'Sure.' ''

Kris and I looked around at the small patch of dirt, thinking about what living there must have been like. Kris asked where the actual cabin was. ''Shortly after Thoreau left, they tore it down and rebuilt it as a chicken coop. At that time it had no significance to anybody. There's a replica of the cabin near the parking lot, if you want to take a look later. People didn't even know where the cabin was until 1945, when Roland Robbins excavated the site.''

There were some granite posts connected by chains outlining a small rectangular space that looked barely big enough for a bed, let alone a whole house. I couldn't believe that anyone could live in a space so small, especially in the notoriously rough Massachusetts winters. Talk about cabin fever.

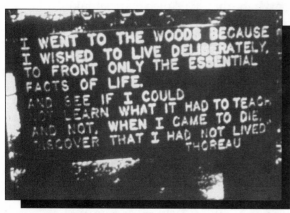

House site plaque

Michael continued, ''It was real small. Looking at it, though, it seems pretty comfortable to me. You see what you think when you see the replica. For one person, all you need are a table, a chair, a bed, and a stove.''

Michael turned to a pile of stones that allegedly included a few from Thoreau's original chimney. He told us that the pile was started by Bronson Alcott, Louisa May Alcott's father. ''He knew Thoreau and he came here, and this is where, from memory, he thought the cabin was when they came back twenty years later. He thought there should be some kind of a monument and threw a rock on the spot and other people with him threw a rock. After a while, it became a custom to throw a rock on the pile.

''And now people come here from all over the world. A Japanese school bought a former church not too far from here, and groups of kids from Japan come. Thoreau's really big in Japan. People all around the world have heard of Walden Pond, which is why we would like to see this become a national park.''

Michael explained that Walden is currently a state park. ''It's owned by the people of Massachusetts and there's very little money to maintain it. This is basically the extent of public education,'' Michael said, waving toward the pile of stones and a wooden plaque. ''Unless you already knew about the significance of this area, you'd come and go and never know. We'll see when we go down by the pond that this area's really degraded and the state is doing very little to truly restore it.'' Michael paused to look over toward a crowded man-made beach on the other side of the pond and continued, ''The National Park Service also controls crowds a lot better. If Yosemite were owned by the state, it would probably be overrun by people.''

We headed back toward the pond to set up for the bulk of the interview. Michael steered us to a beautiful little alcove barely big enough for all of us. Kris stepped over rocks and roots to try for a good establishing shot while I got Michael set up with sound. It was a windy day and I watched Kris maneuvering around a tree that hung over the water, using a branch as an anchor. She was definitely beginning to look like a rugged camera person, fearless and strong. I just hoped the branch didn't give way and send her and one of ''the twins'' into the water.

Michael continued, ''Thoreau was one of the first people to recognize the idea that wilderness was a good thing. 'In wildness is the preservation of the world' is what he said. Walden Woods is thought of by many people as the cradle of the conservation movement, because Thoreau was the first guy who realized that people are part of nature and nature is part of people and wrote it down in a way that even today, a hundred and fifty years later, people can understand and can relate to. In fact, I think that his work is even more important and relevant today, because our relationship with nature has gotten worse and worse.''

I wondered if working at his father's pencil factory had clued Thoreau in on the impending swell of industry and the havoc it would wreak. Michael said Thoreau was issuing a warning that we can appreciate only now.

''Conservationists are doing a lot of good work, but they're not getting the public excited and engaged and positive about where we're headed. Most of what you see is scary and negative—and largely true. We have to start looking toward big, positive visionary solutions, because the problems are big. We can't think small anymore. People care more than ever, but we in the conservation world are not providing the leadership. So RESTORE: The North Woods is meant to enunciate our vision in a simple way and ask people to help us. And it seems to be working.

''The other thing I should say about RESTORE is that our focus is not just on saving what's left of nature. We're trying to start reversing some of the destruction. We want to see the places restored to ecological health. We'd like to see more of the landscape as it looked several hundred years ago, not the way it looks today.''

I asked Michael to discuss the effects of Manifest Destiny—arguably the seed of the American Dream—on the land.

"I think Americans have been living without much thought about what we're doing, and it's catching up with us. People in Europe have lived with the land for a long time, and they've stabilized their existence somewhat. Unfortunately for them, they've stabilized in a situation where there is very little wilderness. It's not too late for Americans, because our population is still not that dense. There are still natural forests. Our rivers aren't beyond repair. Most of our native species are still here."

Michael went on to discuss the question of government versus private control of lands. Although he didn't consider the government a leading force in conservation, he cited the national parks as proof of some level of commitment. "Walden would not be protected if it were privately owned. It would be ringed by condominiums. It would be destroyed. So I don't have any patience for people who say, 'We just have to get used to not having any government involvement.' That won't work. There has to be private initiative, but that won't do the job alone.

"We ought to have a national goal to buy more public land and protect more lands and restore all of the different ecosystems in America so there are large areas protected all around the country. And we see, for example, our proposal for a Maine Woods National Park as just one little piece of a bigger picture, where we will start restoring the tallgrass prairie, the Great Lakes, more of the Everglades, and the southern Appalachians.

"There isn't leadership telling people why we should do this, why it's good for people. And I believe that preserving nature is good for people. I believe that. I don't make any apologies for creating big wilderness areas or restoring wolves. It's good for people, it's good for the planet, it's just a positive thing."

After a brief discussion about restoring wolves, the ubiquitous question of the spotted owl versus the timber industry came up. I asked Michael what he'd say to people who lost their jobs as a result of environmental efforts, and he said that environmental cleanup and restoration had become one of the largest sources of employment in Massachusetts. He also, however, expressed disregard for those who expect conservationists to provide statistics on the benefits of their plans in order to prove their worth. "It's pretty obvious that protecting the basis of life is good for the economy."

When asked about the public image of conservationists, Michael replied, "Unfortunately, conservation groups today are very competitive. There's a lot of turf, there's a lot of backbiting, there's competition for funding, for members, for issues. There's very little real cooperation. We depend more on grassroots activists or regular people helping us out.

"Rock Evans, who's on our board, who works for the National Audubon Society, and who's one of the people I do admire, says a lot of professional conservationists don't shed a tear when a tree is cut. They don't want to see the forest cut, but they won't fight tooth and nail for it. They won't, like Henry David Thoreau, spend a night in jail for not paying their taxes because they don't want their money to go to a war. We're basically trying to re-create a movement that has lost its fire and its vision.''

We began to pack up and walk back to our cars, as talked some more about the conservation movement of the seventies and its roots in a politically liberal atmosphere. Michael talked of one of his colleagues, Dave Foreman, one of the founders of the organization Earth First! Dave and Michael were working together on the restoration of our north woods, Michael overseeing the Northeast and Dave the Northwest. ''There's a lot more to Earth First! than the radical practices. That was just one old piece of it, the part the press liked,'' he said.

Kris and I followed Michael to the air terminal for our appointment with Rudy Engholme. Rudy is the New England director of the Environmental Air Force, which is a team of volunteer pilots who help with cleanups, forest fires, and surveying, donating their time, the use of their planes, and the fuel. Rudy had flown down from his home on the coast of Maine. He was a tall cheerful man in his forties with a toothy smile and a bull mustache to match his boyish thicket of brown hair.

Rudy explained that his plane was essentially a VW bug in the air, so we had to pack light. We discussed the easiest way to shoot out an open window of an airplane and Kris and I decided to bring only one camera, no Steadycam, and no sound system. When we got into the plane, Rudy got us wired to headsets so that we could hear each other in the air. It was very ''be all that you can be.''

There was a lot of discussion between Rudy and a woman named Doris in the tower who told us where we could go without bumping into another VW bug in the air. We began to taxi and everything

Michael and Shainee "geared" up

hushed as the plane lifted off. We ascended and began to glide around the pond that we had just hiked.

I felt a wave of queasiness as I looked down over the wing, to the bright blue splash surrounded by green trees and flanked by . . . housing developments and strip malls. I couldn't tell if my stomach was flip-flopping from the dipping of the little plane or from nausea at the disturbing sight. Spending the morning with Michael Kellett's gentle voice and philosophies, which echoed the legend of a man who will forever be associated with everything green, had lulled me, ironically, into a false sense of security about the situation. Looking down on Walden Woods from the air, I was slammed headfirst into the present, into the prefab, man-made modern Walden.

We flew for about an hour. Kris and I kept looking at each other as we listened while Michael pointed out various key spots. We each knew what the other was thinking. Disappointment. We had been sure that aerial shots of Walden Pond would stand out as one of the most beautiful in the film. If we hadn't experienced the peace of Walden from within, we would never know from surveying it from the air that it could be the place where conservation efforts had been born. It looked more like a good place for John Waters to make a movie.

We landed and went inside the terminal to have a coffee with Rudy. He was intrigued by our journey and was one of the first people to ask to take our camera and turn it on us. He seemed to enjoy operating it and did an impromptu interview of us on our impressions of Walden by air. We then, in turn, pointed the camera at Rudy and gave him a chance to talk about his work. "I think we have a limited amount of time left to save some really precious places. I love flying. It gives you a really different view than the way you see things on the ground," Rudy said. "The funny thing is, when you're flying, you don't see the boundaries that we usually think of. You don't see state lines, you don't see country lines. What you see are shores, woods, cities, schools, rivers, watersheds—terms that people don't often think in. Seeing things from the air really gives people a sense of how interconnected everyone is."

We thanked Rudy for his generosity and got back to Walden around four-thirty. Michael had promised to show us the replica of Thoreau's cabin, which was supposedly built for only eighteen dollars. It was small and simple and, as Michael had said, just big enough for a bed, a table, a chair, and a stove. Simplify, simplify—that was what we had all learned from Thoreau. There was a billboard near the entrance of the park where people could post some of their favorite Thoreau quotes. I focused on one in particular: ALL THINGS IN THE WORLD MUST BE SEEN WITH THE MINIMUM DEW ON THEM, MUST BE SEEN WITH YOUTHFUL, EARLY-OPENED HOPEFUL EYES.

Michael saw me reading the quote and said, "One thing I didn't say before is there's sort of an energy about this place. There's something focused on this pond, maybe in terms of all the years of people thinking about it and coming here. But you get this feeling about Walden that's more than just a pond and the trees around it. It's a symbol. Natural systems have a symmetry and an order. And I think there's something about that, that just hits down deep in people.

"All of us have a time or a place where we feel that energy and an excitement about either looking in the Grand Canyon or looking into a beautiful big old tree or looking at a pond or standing at a quiet place in natural surroundings. I think that's a throwback to our original genetic connection with nature. When we destroy natural areas we're really just putting a barrier between our feelings and our actions."

It was time for us to leave. We were expected at the home of old friends of Kristin's, who were living in the Berkshires with their new baby. We would stay one night there and head back down to Manhattan.

It had gotten to that lazy time on a summer afternoon where the light turns a shocking gold, reflected in prism specks on the pond. Before we called it a day, I asked Michael what he would ask people if he were making our trip across country with us.

"I'd ask people what they'd like America to be like a hundred years from now. What their vision is. I tell people about *my* vision of this place a hundred years from now. This freeway is not gonna be here. We're not gonna drive on concrete roads in internal combustion engine cars. This garbage dump will be reclaimed, and all the stuff will probably be recycled, and it will be refilled with clean fill and restored to a natural landscape. "I think my vision and reality are very compatible. I think it could go the way I want it to go. Somebody has to do it. It won't happen on its own.

"All of us who care to can evoke either the best in people or the worst. The people who founded this country were just people who wanted good things. I think it's up to us to decide what should happen. And right now, we're drifting as a country. But we've got it in us to do something great. We've done great things in the past. And we can do them in the future. The whole world is watching us. We generate sparks and the sparks are going to fly. And I think they're going to catch fire all over. All people need is a spark. They're ninety percent there, and that's the last little bit that brings them toward doing what they believe in, in achieving their vision.

"Maybe all some people need is to be told what they already know. That's what you two are trying to do, right?"

We nodded in affirmation and shook Michael's hand, thanking him for a wonderful day. I got back in the car, thinking about Michael's metaphor of generating sparks, and smiled to myself about the 300 acres of trees that the father of conservation had accidentally burned down.

WHILE IN NEW YORK CITY 6/28

(Kristin)

Passing the Manhattan Municipal Asphalt Plant, we made our way into the city, Shainee confidently guiding our course. Shainee has an unusually keen sense of direction, something that was neglected in my makeup at birth. While Shainee navigates like a salty dog on the open sea, I become frustrated, turning maps round and round in the hopes that a route will somehow appear in neon. When I drive alone, I usually convince myself that it will be somehow faster, easier, or better if I ignore the map and just follow my instincts. And if I get lost, I can always stop for directions.

Welcome to Manhattan

But sometimes I *feel* like getting lost, as does Shainee, and when the urge overcomes us, we veer off on back roads ignoring all maps—the dustier the road, the better. One good thing about America is you're never *that* far from help. And by exchanging navigational dialogue, you can uncover regional treasures that you surely would have missed otherwise. A recruited guide leaning into your window might throw in a tip on a garage sale nearby, or a teahouse along your route, or tell you not to miss the unmarked left turn to the old lighthouse.

I wonder if past explorers, like Lewis and Clark, sometimes "stumbled" upon some of their "discoveries" with the help of their era's direction-givers—never to be mentioned in their travel log back to Thomas Jefferson.

Surprisingly, sensing my way has often worked for me. But entering New York City, I realized that if it weren't for Shainee, I would probably be forced to take up permanent residence. I'd never find my way out.

CHARLAYNE HUNTER-GAULT

JOURNALIST • NATIONAL CORRESPONDENT FOR *THE NEWSHOUR WITH JIM LEHRER*

NEW YORK CITY

(Kristin)

We left the serenity of Thoreau's wooded stomping ground for the raucous stimulation of a metropolis. We parked the car in an overpriced twenty-four-hour Manhattan garage close to Charlayne Hunter-Gault's PBS office. (Well, at least Shainee *thought* it was close. Another *Anthem* "discovery": nobody's perfect.)

"How much farther?" I questioned, gasping for anything but humid air as we staggered down a number of streets, most of our weighty bags hanging about me like a busy bell captain. "Shai," I said, taking a breath, "I think I might die today." My body felt permanently crooked, and I was suddenly having visions of myself at thirty with chronic back problems.

"We're almost there," she encouraged more than once, and I could tell she was trying *not* to laugh. There were so many moments in the trip that only hearty laughter could properly punctuate, otherwise it would surely be tears. But we usually landed on the side of laughter; in this case, because we both had a keen, unspoken awareness of just how fantastic it was to be sweating, exhausted, hungry, crooked, lost, and heading for the office of a woman we had come to admire: Charlayne Hunter-Gault. This too, we would remind ourselves, is part of our dream.

In 1961, Charlayne and another black student desegregated the University of Georgia, which had been all-white for 176 years. When we first heard Charlayne speak at Kent State, she had talked about what it felt like to pull up to the Georgia campus with her mother on that first day, set upon by a crowd that shook their car until she and her mother fled. But Charlayne returned. In the middle of the night, a crowd of a thousand protestors surrounded her dormitory and someone heaved a brick through her window, shattering glass all around her. Charlayne was undaunted. This theme was repeated throughout her life and career: the more resistance she met, the stronger she became.

The transition from intolerance to integration was slow for Charlayne, but during our interview she shone with vivid personal optimism. She preferred to minimize her own triumphs, focusing instead on the long-term results: that because of what she and others endured, many could follow more easily, through doors that were previously closed.

"It just happened that my own high school graduation and aspirations coincided with the beginning of the civil rights revolution in the South," Charlayne explained. "Since I was about twelve, even younger, I had this dream of being a journalist. The University of Georgia was the only school in the state with a journalism school, and I wanted that education." That frequent refrain again: the American dream defined as access to education, and education defined as a catalyst for change in one's personal life—and in society.

"My grandfather and my father preached about the importance of education," said Charlayne. "Black people have always seen education as the key to their liberation. And while I grew up in a world within a world—a segregated world—my family and my community did their best to give us better than they had. I talk about the women who, in Zora Neale Hurston's words, 'have been in sorrow's kitchen and licked the pots clean.' And yet they had a vision that was based on the faith that the next generation would be better off.

"So when I told my mother that I wanted to be a journalist—this was in the forties in the Deep South, where there were no black journalists or women working for newspapers—my mother didn't say, 'Well, no, that's not really an option.' She said, 'If that's what you want to do.' And it was an extraordinary thing, because my mother couldn't, like the rest of the citizens within my narrow segregated world, give us first-class citizenship. But everything my parents did was geared toward giving us a first-class *sense* of ourselves.

"So when my mother said, 'If that's what you want to do,' she instinctively knew that dreams propel ambition and that even though I might not realize my ambition, she didn't want to thwart my dreams at an early age. Of course, as you grow older and enter the real world, there are always checks on your ambition. But if you have been given that suit of armor during your formative period, you figure out how to get over the challenges. Life's not always fair, but to get anywhere you've got to have ambition, and to have ambition, you have to have the capacity to dream and experience the passion of owning a personal vision."

Today, Charlayne is a leading American journalist, known to millions of television viewers for her evening reports on *The MacNeil-Lehrer NewsHour* and her current position as the national correspondent for *The NewsHour with Jim Lehrer*.

When we reached Charlayne's office, we found her immersed in paperwork. She set aside the work and gave us her full attention. Charlayne has piercing green eyes that lock on you like a tracking device while you talk with her, which we did while we set up. She explained that *The MacNeil–Lehrer NewsHour* was nearing the end of its run because Robert MacNeil was retiring. She sounded melancholy as she talked about the imminent farewell. Looking around her office, I could see why: there were mementos from ceiling to floor of the people she had interviewed and innumerable events she had covered over the course of nearly twenty years with *MacNeil-Lehrer.* Rows of mounted photographs of her with President Clinton, Nelson Mandela, Margaret Thatcher, Bill Cosby, and many others would soon be packed into the moving boxes that leaned against one wall. She was going with Jim Lehrer to Virginia, where they would now record the new program.

Charlayne had a busy schedule, so we plunged into the subject of how she had seen the American media evolve since the sixties. We were also curious about her impressions of where journalism was headed when so much enthusiasm was directed toward the "new media." "You can still walk into the vast majority of newsrooms in America," Charlayne began, "and not see any minority faces, not see any women in positions of power. In media centers like New York, and in places like *The Miami Herald,* where the editor, David Lawrence, is committed to having a newsroom that looks like America— certainly, that looks like Miami—you'll see some balance. But all American cities and towns are becoming multiethnic, and I think we need to step back from the daily grind and do a serious reassessment of exactly what our role and responsibility is as the media—as the chroniclers of our time. Particularly in this new information age, when there are those who believe that cyberspace is going to make what we know as 'media' today obsolete."

Charlayne invoked the patron saint of reporters, Edward R. Murrow, as she skeptically considered tabloid television. "Murrow, that late, great journalist of television, said, 'This instrument [television] can teach, it can illuminate, it can inspire, but it can only do so to the extent that human beings are willing to use it to those ends. Otherwise, it becomes merely lights and wires in a box.' And I think that vision of technology—he was talking about television in particular—is one that transcends his time. This technology has the potential to educate people who have not had access to education," she said, her green eyes intense. "To empower people who have been downtrodden and abused and oppressed by political systems and tyrannical governments, even"—and here she laughed—"democratic governments. Because as Michael O'Neill has said in his wonderful book *The Roar of the*

Crowd, a really important transformation takes place when citizens have access to information as it happens, because people then cannot be fooled and cannot be manipulated, since they know as much as the ruling elites.''

She paused to consider the implications. ''We're beginning to see concrete and positive results sprouting from our capacity to communicate with each other and disperse information in a timely way,'' she said. ''But there's still questions to be asked about the downside, the negative impact of some of this technology. This may sound simplistic, but I hope we are able to maintain some humanity as we use technology and try to keep the technology from using us. We see this in our political leaders today—'sound bite' city—which is going to increasingly affect the way we make decisions.'' As if acknowledging her own role in this process, she concluded, ''People now expect to be informed in a millisecond or two, and we seem to have lost appreciation for the kind of deliberation we have always employed in arriving at important decisions about how we live.''

I thought about NPR and Bill Siemering's foresight in sensing the need for an alternative information source that could explore issues in greater detail than the mass media could hope to do. Charlayne's frustration as a journalist—trying to offer in-depth stories to a television audience that expects grocery-list updates—was apparent. We shared her frustration, having been on the receiving end of each day's information packaged as if it were fast food: McNews.

In case there was any doubt about her own position, Charlayne stressed her optimism about the future of news and mass media in America, while echoing others before her. ''When I come back from other countries, I almost kiss the ground. Not that everything here is perfect,'' she hastened to add. ''Far from it. But our values—like freedom of the press—don't exist anywhere else the way they do here. We still have greater freedom to do what we do, to challenge our government, to challenge our leaders. And even though politics may be affecting some institutions that are supposed to be above politics, I still think, in the end, that there are principles that will transcend the politics of the moment, and Americans will rally around to preserve those principles.''

We never asked Charlayne about American heroism, but we now knew that she believed our country's principles would be preserved, not by a great and powerful leader, philosopher, or hero but, rather, by the people.

Charlayne had achieved what most people would consider the quintessential American dream, succeeding against all odds to attain a position of professional responsibility and prominence. Shainee asked how today's media sustains or diminishes the notion of an American dream.

Charlayne answered, ''I think one of the things that's causing so much anxiety today is that many parents are unable to see progress for their children beyond where they themselves have been. It creates a lot of conflict and resentment in our society.'' She considered this angle. ''I think we in the media need to step back from our instantaneous analysis. I think the social scientists need to throw away their old books and paradigms and bring some fresh thought to what is happening.

Because, indeed, what is America today? And who is an American? These definitions are all changing. Someone said to me recently—I think it was the late Ralph Ellison—that America was born as an experiment and continues to be."

There was one detail about our project that was positively eerie, and at this point we found it emerging in our conversation with Charlayne. It was as if the people we interviewed—and the people they quoted—had conferred on the variety of subjects we were presenting to them. Even at an early stage in our trip, strangers began to echo each other, sometimes even seeming to *hear* one another.

The idea that perhaps the country is still *being* founded—the American experiment continually evolving—was a bedrock of our discussions when Shainee and I first set out. But the crucial question was: If America was an experiment, what stage had it reached? And which way was it headed?

Charlayne continued, without a waver or doubt in her voice, "America is a country in transition. It is never any one thing. Now we have principles, democratic principles, and values that are more or less set in concrete and contained in documents that have survived all the ebbs and flows of the fickleness of the American public, the body politic. So what is an American today?" She paused to consider this. "Today's American *looks* different from an American of fifty years ago or a hundred years ago. How is the influx of people from different kinds of places—with different kinds of values—going to affect the American dream? I do think that's something we all need to look at. Zora Neale Hurston has another wonderful line: 'There are years that ask questions and years that give answers.'" Charlayne looked at us one by one, her stare piercing through the abstract notion, and said firmly, "I think this is, if not a question year, a question age."

I realized later that Charlayne had stumbled upon the answer to why Shainee and I were sitting in her office, nearly 3,000 miles from where our journey began: we were coming of age in a question age, not in the highly vaunted information age. We had been born into a generation inclined to question and examine the validity of most aspects of our lives, as well as those of our parents. Our generation's identity crisis seemed to have foundered on a critical question: Do we want to get lost or do we want to be found? Shainee and I were teetering somewhere between the extremes, as nomadic seekers attempting to understand this question age by asking our own.

After the interview, while we were packing up, Charlayne took the opportunity to ask us about our journey. "Oh! I just did Studs's radio show with him out there," she said upon hearing that we were going to interview Studs Terkel in Chicago. "He's wonderful. Tell him I said hi! I can't wait for his new book," she said while jotting down the address of an old church in Chicago she thought we might like to visit while there, and then we said our thank-yous and good-byes.

GEORGE McGOVERN

FORMER U.S. SENATOR • U.S. PRESIDENTIAL CANDIDATE IN 1972 •

DIRECTOR MIDDLE EAST POLICY COUNCIL

WASHINGTON, D.C.

(Shainee)

Coincidentally, our itinerary placed our two Kent State introductions back-to-back. We were scheduled to leave Charlayne and travel to see Senator George McGovern. So, after a couple of days of lugging equipment around New York and sleeping on the couches of friends and relatives, we were ready to head south again. A relatively short 233 miles on the spine of the Eastern Seaboard—I-95. Our destination was Washington, D.C.

Shortly after we had returned to Los Angeles from Kent State, we had quickly followed up our introduction to Senator George McGovern with a request for an interview. While we were driving through Alabama, on our way up to Virginia to see Rita Dove, we had stopped to make one of our pilgrimages to the pay phone, to check our messages. There was an old gas station on the side of the road that looked as though it had not fueled anyone's trips in a long time. But it did have a pair of phone booths. Kris and I stepped out of our car and into the dueling booths.

The phone ritual was one that would become tedious over the next few months. We used voice mail boxes in Los Angeles as an anchor phone number for friends, family, and prospective interviewees to get a hold of us while we were on the road. It got to the point where we both would have to call in at least three times a day.

The most irritating version of the phone ritual was when we stopped at a place with only one phone and Kris and I would have to wait and kill time while the other checked messages. I must have spent hours perusing convenience stores and studying road maps. The most luxurious version of the phone ritual was at a truck stop, where we could each sit down at a table, with a cup of coffee and our production notebooks, and make relaxed phone calls—without having to use the other's back as a desk to write down messages. The Alabama gas station rated about a six on a scale of one to ten.

I was punching in my retrieval code when I heard Kris scratching on the window that separated our booths. She leaned out of her booth, pushed the accordion door of mine open with her foot, and said, "Come here. You have to hear this." She pressed the button for replay and the following message came over the scratchy Alabama lines: "Hello there, Kristin and Shainee. This is George McGovern. It was such a pleasure receiving your invitation and the information on your project. It sounds wonderful and I love to hear about young people who are doing important work. I would be very honored to participate, but I am leaving the country for two months to teach in Austria, so it would have to be soon. I'll be in the Outer Banks at our family home over the Fourth of July weekend, so maybe we can get together before then." He left both his office and home phone numbers.

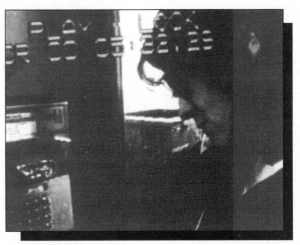

Phone ritual

His voice was reminiscent of Jimmy Stewart's, genuine and inviting, with thoughtful pauses. Again, I was reminded of any number of grandfathers. I laughed and handed the receiver back to Kris, who saved the message and hung up. "Can you believe he called us *himself* and left his home phone number?" she breathed. We had already discovered the added effort that assistants and publicists could require of us. They could either be our best ally or prove to be a brick wall. This was probably the first and the last time that someone who had "people" accepted an invitation personally. A former presidential candidate making his own phone calls was pure pleasure for us, especially in the early stages of the trip.

I jumped back on my phone to call my mother and father while Kris dialed Doug Brinkley in New Orleans to thank him for his help. As the phone rang, I turned and looked behind the gas station to a small pond where a man in his sixties was floating in a rowboat, his fishing line cast languorously over the side. His body language was that of a cat dozing in the afternoon sun of a window seat and we were sharing the warmth. I thought, this is it—right now—a moment that we will remember. A back road in Alabama, some wonderful news, all on a rosy-gold Southern afternoon.

My parents had both supported George McGovern when he ran for the presidency of the United States, and my father in particular was very emotional about the fact that his daughter had actually met the senator at Kent State. For them, Senator McGovern had represented a hope for change, for a more liberal, humanitarian approach to governing, for an end to violence at a time when everything seemed to be going to hell. My father had described him as being America's last chance to do the right thing. He said that he thought the Watergate scandal put the lid on the coffin of *his* idea of the American dream. His words were sadly echoed throughout the duration of our journey.

Later in our trip, we would find that Senator McGovern's name was mentioned very often in the same sentence as the words "honest," "human," "thoughtful," and "dreamer." Hunter S. Thompson would cite him as one of his only heroes, Studs Terkel would call him the "last living true democrat," and John Perry Barlow would agree. In some ways, I feel that it was better that we had not heard so much about George McGovern prior to meeting him, because it might have made our appointment more intimidating.

My mother was elated when I told her that we would be meeting with the senator. She spoke very quickly, saying that he certainly belonged in a film attempting to examine the current state of the American hero and that George McGovern had long been one of her own heroes. She finally took a breath, then continued, "Do you think you and Kristin would mind if I tagged along? I could be your photographer." My mother had a long-standing love of cameras. I

thought about it for a second, said it was fine with me, and told her I'd ask Kris what she thought.

At the time we had no intention of being characters in our own film, as we had leaned toward doing mostly everything on our own. There would be several people throughout the trip that would offer "help" in exchange for being allowed to accompany us on a given interview. My mother was the first person to whom we would say yes.

We picked my mom up on our way down from New York and arrived in Washington on a Friday afternoon. Senator McGovern was our thirteenth interview, so we had begun to develop a routine. But this day felt different from beginning to end. We were nervous about interviewing such an iconic figure and out of our element without our uniform of shorts and T-shirts. We had chosen instead to dig into our bag of "professional" clothes, which hadn't been touched since we quit our jobs in Los Angeles. My first mistake was taking off my Airwalks. Because of my back, shoes can make or break my whole day. But the consensus was that we had to look presentable. George McGovern was, after all, a former senator.

When we got to the senator's office at the Middle East Policy Council, the receptionist was expecting us and ushered us in. She explained that the McGoverns' granddaughters were visiting that day, and he was a little late returning from the Supreme Court, where he had taken them to meet a couple of his robed friends—such as Justice Ruth Bader Ginsburg. We set up the equipment and got my mother behind one of the video cameras. She was thrilled.

There was some time to kill until the senator returned, so we ran downstairs to get some extra batteries and a Diet Coke (we, of course, hadn't eaten anything). On the way back up, I noticed a man in a dark suit and short hair with a black earpiece walking behind us. I realized that I had seen another man with a similar earpiece walking on the street behind us earlier. I pulled Kris aside and told her that I thought maybe the Secret Service was following us. She laughed and said, "They don't waste their time on people like us." I pointed to his earpiece and said, "Don't be so sure." Kris enjoyed bringing up my James Bond paranoia as a steady subject of friendly mockery throughout the rest of the trip.

As we made our way back up to Senator McGovern's office, we acknowledged our trepidation to each other in the elevator. My mom looked nervous too, but she tried to be the good mom and said things like, "You'll be fine. Just relax." Things mothers say. I felt queasy thinking about how many experienced professional journalists had interviewed this man. What if I just froze? Kris and I were rarely nervous when we met people. It had just become accepted at a certain point that we were having once-in-a-lifetime experiences on a daily basis. Our whole trip made me feel like a child returning home after an enormously successful night of Halloween trick-or-treating, with a huge bag of candy. When separated, any piece would have been enough, but ingested all at once, it produced an odd feeling of absolute ecstasy tempered with a pinch of nausea and exhaustion. It was sensory overload all the time, so there were few spare moments to spend paralyzed by fearful respect. Once in a while, though, we would get anxious, and interviewing Senator George McGovern was to be one of those times.

Setting up

We looked at the walls and pictures that decorated the senator's office while we waited. He had portraits of Abraham Lincoln, Woodrow Wilson, and Thomas Jefferson. There was a picture of McGovern with President Clinton. The president had signed it: THANKS FOR GETTING ME INTO ALL OF THIS. One of Bill Clinton's first official political positions was as a state campaign leader during McGovern's presidential run.

My eyes hurried past several photographs of his family that were displayed on the bookshelf. I didn't want to know which one of the faces belonged to the woman who had died the year before. I also didn't want to know if the little girls visiting the senator belonged to her as well. I decided to run to the bathroom while I still had the chance and saw the girls coloring at the conference table as I passed by. They had not been there when we walked in, so I assumed the senator had returned and ran back to the office. He came in right behind me.

George McGovern is a tallish man with a square, lean build. He has a strong handshake and a face that you trust. He greeted us with familiarity and Kris and I introduced my mother, who took his hand with great pride. She was trying to play it cool, but I knew she was feeling a little shaky, overcome by years of admiration.

Senator McGovern asked if we had everything we needed and if it was okay if he called his wife before the interview. We told him that of course it was and he walked over to his desk, reaching for his glasses in his breast pocket. He peered through the thick lenses to see the numbers on the phone and dialed.

The senator's wife wasn't there, so we got him positioned in a chair in the corner. He asked how the project was going and we told him that it was starting to take shape. His wife called back and he got up to take the call. They talked about the girls and how they needed to get them to the airport on time, right after the interview. As he hung up the phone, the information made my stomach jump a little, knowing I'd have to be incredibly efficient.

Kris and my mother were behind cameras and there was nowhere for me to sit, except in the glaring emptiness of the senator's leather desk chair. I hesitated and Kris said, "Maybe you could sit in the senator's chair." I looked at him uneasily. He chuckled and said, "Well, no one else is sitting in it." So I pulled George McGovern's chair closer to George McGovern and we began.

"I was born in Mitchell, South Dakota, and went to Dakota Wesleyan University in that same town, primarily because I couldn't afford to go out of town to college. World War II came along, I enlisted in the war, became a bomber pilot, and used the G.I. Bill to go through graduate school at Northwestern. That really changed my life, because I went on to get my Ph.D. I studied American and European history, economics, and anthropology. It was during that period that I developed an interest in political and international affairs. I went back to teach at Dakota Wesleyan, and it was only a matter of time before I would get involved in politics.

"I began serving as the full-time organizer of the Democratic Party in South Dakota in 1953. After a couple of years of that, I ran for Congress and became the first Democrat in more than a quarter of a century to be elected to high office in South Dakota. And the rest of my career took off from there: the United States Senate and a run for the presidency, service at the White House for two years, a couple of terms as a delegate to the United Nations. Basically, that's my career."

I knew that McGovern had served in World War II from the research that we had done, but I didn't know that he had actually been a bomber pilot. I kept thinking of Newt Gingrich's favorite word of the moment: "McGovernik," a term he used pejoratively to describe a foe as an ultraliberal. The word certainly did not bring to mind someone who flew bomber planes over Europe. I asked the senator what kind of influence his family had had on him and he continued to fill us in on his background, saying that his father was a Methodist minister and a conservative Republican.

I asked Senator McGovern if he remembered a moment when he knew that he would go into politics. "It was listening to Adlai Stevenson's acceptance speech in the summer of 1952," he began. "Up until that point, I had viewed politics as kind of a seamy affair, although I had enormous admiration for some of the great historic figures, like Jefferson and Lincoln and Wilson and even Franklin Roosevelt in my own time.

"I didn't see it on television, I heard it on the radio," the senator added. "I was painting my apartment, probably at one or two o'clock in the morning, when he was introduced to speak. From that point on, I was hooked. I'd worked on the Stevenson campaign in '52, so when I had an opportunity a few months later to become the full-time executive director of the South Dakota Democratic Party, I seized on that chance. I guess you'd have to say that Adlai Stevenson inspired my political career."

I loved the image of a young George McGovern, alone, painting his walls, listening to a radio precariously perched on his stepladder, when he heard the words of an older man that changed his life. It was one of the most succinct descriptions of a crystallizing moment of inspiration that we would hear, but McGovern was only the first of many who could identify the exact moment they had made the choice that shaped the rest of their lives.

McGovern continued, "What struck me about Adlai Stevenson's approach to politics was that he saw it primarily as an educational process, in which you tell the people what the problems are and what you honestly believe are the most workable solutions. And you do that even if the chances of election are not all that great. He started off that campaign—and that great acceptance speech—by saying, 'Let's talk sense to the American people.' It's better to lose the election than to mislead the people, and that concept has guided me ever since.

"I also remember the late Wayne Morris, a senator from Oregon, saying about the same time that you're not really worth a damn as an elected official until you get over your fear of defeat. That inspired me. It made me see early on in my career that the important thing is to stake out your positions on public policy and then stay with those convictions, even though it may appear to be risky business to do so.

"I will say this. I later became one of the country's leading critics of the American policy in Vietnam. I think that I probably had as much to do with getting us out of Vietnam as any single member of the Senate. My whole presidential campaign was geared to mobilize the Democratic Party behind the decision to stop the war in Vietnam. We didn't win, but we mobilized almost thirty million people in that campaign. And when I started off on that issue eight of nine years earlier, before I became a presidential contender, I thought it would make me a one-term senator. The war was popular when I first began speaking out against it. But going back to the traditions of Stevenson and Wayne Morris and Abraham Lincoln and some of the great historic figures who stood by their convictions, I've always thought that that's the way to success and greatness in politics in the long run."

The concept that a politician would say what he or she believed and then simply fight for it, regardless of public opinion polls, is usually viewed as party line rhetoric. But I knew, looking into this man's eyes and watching his hands speak with his mouth as his passion rose, that he believed in it—absolutely. I asked the senator if he thought that his political philosophy was visible at all in today's political arena.

Senator McGovern replied, "I think one of the central weaknesses in our political situation today is that there are too many politicians with their finger up in the wind to see which way the latest public opinion poll indicates they should vote. I regret to say that that extends to very high levels in the government."

When I probed the senator by asking if he saw any remedy to our political leaders' obsequious response to anything named Gallup, he responded, "It's going to be difficult because of the use of modern media, advertising experts, campaign professionals, poll takers . . . All these devices are used to try to figure out how you can most cleverly reach the correct opinion to get yourself elected. I had a young man come to this office a while back and tell me he wanted to go into politics. He said that his plan was to spend two years studying poll taking, mass media, and advertising. He wanted to know if I thought that was a good way to launch a career. I said, 'Well, why do you want to go to Congress? What is it that you stand for, that makes you think that the rest of us ought to get behind you?' And he said, 'Well, I'll figure that out after I get there.' "

I couldn't help sneaking a glance over to the photo of George McGovern and President Clinton and wondering what the senator thought of the presidency now. I asked the senator what he thought about American heroes today.

He responded, "We don't have the kind of clearly defined heroes that I wish we had. I don't see anybody who does for politics what Magic Johnson or Michael Jordan or Patrick Ewing are doing for basketball. I don't see any Wilson or Roosevelt or Jefferson today. That doesn't mean we don't have some good people in politics. It just means that there seems to be a drought right now of political leaders of vision and inspiration."

Given that the senator had come from a conservative background, I asked him if he knew how he had become aligned with a liberal, "radical" movement, as it was labeled at the time.

"I've never thought of myself as a radical," McGovern explained. "I've never thought of myself as a left-winger or anything that those labels describe. But I do think of myself as a humane, liberal-minded, progressive political figure. And I came to that conclusion based on my study of American history. What I saw is that the great, progressive forward periods in American history came at times when there was a humane and liberal and imaginative leadership in charge. I think that if you just stop and consider the various public programs that are now generally supported by both conservatives and Republicans—whether you're talking about civil rights, women's rights, rural electrification, student loans, social security, you name it—almost any popular successful public program began as a liberal program over conservative opposition.

"Now, that doesn't mean the conservatives are evil," the senator continued. "It simply means they're more cautious; they're more critical of new ideas; they're more skeptical about government intervention in our lives; they're less inclined to propose sweeping public solutions to our problems."

I asked Senator McGovern why it seemed that "liberal" had become a bad word lately, if so many popular, politically fundamental programs were begun as liberal initiatives. He didn't pause before answering, "The conservatives were out of power for a long period of time. They were hungrier than the liberals and they got themselves better organized. I also think the Vietnam War split the liberals in this country right down the middle. We used to talk about the hawks and the doves. The Vietnam War was fought inside the Democratic Party and it literally tore the Democratic coalition in half. I don't think we've ever recovered from that.

"I also think that the civil rights movement ripped the Democratic Party in half. It alienated tens of millions of white voters who had been voting for liberal causes—especially in the South. We used to talk about the solid South, always voting Democratic. Now we talk about the solid South and we mean that it almost always votes Republican. That's in considerable part an outgrowth of the divisions of the civil rights movement.

"The party has suffered from becoming too fat and comfortable and complacent. And now it's suffering from still another evil: it's on the defensive. It's apologetic. You can't get a great many liberals today to even use the word. They'll say, 'No, I don't think of myself as a liberal, I'm a pragmatic progressive'—or some other high-falutin' term of that kind. So I think the liberal tradition today is left undefended. And that's dangerous, in terms of our hopes for future gains."

I asked the senator if he thought that the ills that he spoke of had affected the country in a deeper way. He answered that given his own experience, he feels that there is an unprecedented degree of skepticism about government and anger directed at Washington. He explained that he thinks it stems from the fact that we have been involved in some kind of war, including the Cold War, for over fifty years. He went on: "During the time I was in public life, the military budget was the biggest single sector of the federal budget. What that means is that for the last fifty years, a major part of every dollar that you pay in federal taxes went to the military, to fighting the Cold War. It also means that a high percentage of our scientific, industrial, and engineering talent was invested in the construction of the weapons of war. As a consequence, I think it created a psychology of militarism and war in the country that has not been healthy for the American spirit.

"The late President Eisenhower warned in his farewell address about what he referred to as 'the mounting power of the military-industrial complex.' And I think that's taken a heavy toll on the moral, spiritual, and political tone of American society and American politics. So that's had something to do with the increase of resentment toward government. People don't get an awful lot out of these military dollars. Nobody's in the market for a tank. Nobody goes to the store to buy a submarine or a missile that's buried out there on the prairie. Money that's marked for defense doesn't do much to enrich the quality of life. It may keep us alive in the event of a war, but it doesn't uplift our spirits or put food on the table or send us to college.''

Senator McGovern continued to share his thoughts about the rise in cynicism in the country by citing the assassinations of the 1960s. He said, ''In a great country like this when, in a few months' time, you strike down leaders of the caliber of John Kennedy and Martin Luther King and Robert Kennedy and Medgar Evers and others, you pay a big price. We may very well have changed the direction of America with those assassinations.

''Then along comes the Watergate scandal. President Nixon was elected with one of the biggest margins in American history, carried forty-nine states. I was on the receiving end of that in a very special way, since I was his opponent. But within a year of the election, the Watergate scandal drove this victorious president from office in disgrace. That has to be a shattering blow to the self-confidence of the American public who had just elected this man. So the same people that watched these great leaders shot down in the streets by assassins saw a man with an enormous landslide victory lead them into one of the worse scandals in American history. That was followed with the Irangate scandal, then the enormous S&L scandal. I don't think the country can take all those shocking blows without some increase in skepticism.''

The senator had mentioned the Watergate scandal, which led me to ask him what he thought about the way that Nixon's death was handled, the fact that he was given a commemorative stamp and all of the positive media coverage of his life.

He paused before responding, ''I think whenever a public figure dies, particularly one who's been on the scene as long as Nixon had, it's understandable that even his critics look for some positive thing they can say about him. Perhaps that was overdone at the time of President Nixon's death. I think it probably was. I went to his funeral, said some kind things about him; others did the same. I hope that students and teachers won't forget that there were serious constitutional violations carried out by President Nixon and his team that created one of the most serious political and constitutional crises this country has ever experienced.''

McGovern's firm but gracious response sequed into the question of what kind of impact he hoped that his own leadership had provided.

''I hope that people will look back on the sixties and seventies, when I was in national politics, and realize that I played a major part in ending a war we never should have gotten involved in,'' the senator said. ''I think the Vietnam War was the greatest single foreign policy disaster in our national history. There is nothing else that's been as costly and as big a blunder as that was. So the fact that I opposed it, in the United States Senate and as a presidential contender, I think is the way I'd like to have history remember me. In other words, I'd like to be remembered as somebody who at least sought the truth and tried to speak it."

Senator McGovern paused and looked at me. He asked if he was giving the kind of answers that we were looking for. He was concerned that they were too long and not appropriate for sound bites. I explained that we were aiming for an informal but informative type of answer and that I thought he was doing wonderfully. Kris added that we now knew firsthand why our parents had voted for him. We moved on to the American dream.

"Well, I think the American dream is still alive. For me, the American dream really begins with that great phrase: 'life, liberty, and the pursuit of happiness.' I still think that sums it up. In this country we do affirm life, we do affirm personal freedom, we do affirm the right of people to seek happiness. And I would hope that continues to be a guiding principle for the American people."

"What do you personally value most about living in America?" I asked. Without missing a beat, he replied, "Freedom. The fact that every day I can get up and do largely what I want to do without looking over my shoulder to see if there is a government censor or secret policeman spying on me or someone who prevents me from saying what I want to say, prevents me from reading what I want to read, or prevents me from going to the church I want to attend. We're one of the freest countries on earth."

I was getting close to the end of our list of questions. I told the senator that we were almost through and asked, "You have come up against an incredible amount of obstacles and opposition in your work and your career. Is there a source from which you continually draw faith?"

Senator McGovern replied, "In my life, notwithstanding the fact that the public has sometimes disappointed me, my political faith still rests on the conviction that through reason and common sense, you can move the American public in a constructive and worthwhile way. I don't hold to the view that the American public is illiterate, or ignorant, or stupid. I have to confess, I'm disappointed with some of their political judgments. I thought they made an enormous mistake in '72"—he laughed, without a hint of self-consciousness—"when I was running against Richard Nixon. I may be the only one who thinks that, but I'll go to my grave thinking that we missed an opportunity in '72 to put this country on a much more hopeful and constructive course.

"But having said that, I'm still glad I tried. I've had times when I've been tempted to do it again. I'd also like to see if somebody else'll come along with a bold and progressive and humane message and call this country to a higher standard."

It looked like we were just about through. Senator McGovern mentioned that he had to wind it up, because he had to take the little girls to the airport. I was about to ask Kris if she had anything to add, but before I could finish my sentence, I saw my mother, out of the corner of my eye, looking like she was ready to burst. In retrospect, it had probably been virtually impossible for her to keep quiet during that whole hour. Her voice quivered as she asked the senator if he thought our problems today seem too big for leaders to put their arms around.

The senator said, "Whether it's to expand the welfare system or provide universal health care, the question now that you hear in the Congress, in the press, and throughout the government is: How can we afford it? We didn't used to raise questions like that twenty-five or thirty years ago when we were talking about the New Frontier or the Great Society or the New Deal. It was just taken for granted that if we had a major national need, we had to respond to it. And so I think we're in an unprecedented situation today. We've accumulated an enormous deficit that puts a kind of a lid on everything we want to do, as far as expanding the liberal agenda is concerned. I don't think that people are against national health care or against dealing with the welfare problems of poor dependent families. What they're worried about is the cost. Those are the things I hear being debated in the Congress these days. It's much different from when I came to the Congress way back in 1957." My mother listened intently, nodding her head, and then the interview was over.

He agreed to let us take pictures, and we took a whole round of the four of us. When we finished, Senator McGovern told us that earlier that day he had tried to take a picture of the girls with Judge Ginsburg and he hadn't been able to get the flash to go off. My mom piped up and offered to take a picture of the three of them. The consummate grandfather looked at his watch, knowing that he had little time to spare. Kris tipped the balance, saying that we would send him copies before he left for Austria. "Let me go see how my little granddaughters are doing out there and we'll see," he responded.

The senator returned with a little girl on each arm. They looked to be about nine and seven, the older one in a tie-dyed T-shirt and the younger one in stripes. McGovern made a round of introductions and the girls were very polite and not shy at all. When Kris ventured, "How about that picture?" the senator looked as though he thought she would never ask. The three of them went to the chair in the corner where we had conducted the interview. Senator McGovern sat down and the girls climbed on his lap. The older one seemed to be well on her way to a career in the performing arts, because she settled herself on her grandfather's lap and struck a dramatic pose while the younger one just smiled. He squeezed them tightly, poked his head between theirs, and then grinned so wide I thought his cheeks might split. The flash went off once and then again and the girls jumped off the chair to scramble back to their coloring books, the older girl giving us a flourish with her tiny hand as she exited and closed the door behind her. The senator watched them, beaming, and then snapped out of the doting spell when he realized he had to get them to the airport.

Senator McGovern went back to his desk and put his glasses back on. My mother had been planning on treating us to a nice dinner after the interview, and she asked the senator if he could recommend a restaurant. I think my mom just couldn't tear herself away, even though it was obvious to Kris and me that we should leave so that he could take care of the girls. But McGovern could not help himself, his generosity exhibited in his ten-minute description of three different restaurants, describing their menus, prices, and proximity. We settled on the Prime Rib, which received the senator's glowing recommendation.

It was finally time to say good-bye. There was a round of handshakes and Senator McGovern wished us well with the project and asked us to keep him up-to-date. When it was my mother's turn to say good-bye, I saw her face flush. She extended her hand and I saw her eyes get watery. The senator took her hand in his

Senator McGovern and granddaughters

and she said, "As someone who voted for you in 1972, it would be a great sadness to think that you don't believe that the thirty million you touched don't share in the same feeling of loss that you do."

The senator smiled warmly, pumping her hand, and then the handshaking stopped, but he didn't let go. "Well, I think a lot of them do. A lot of them do . . . It's just too bad we couldn't have won. I really do think that it would have changed the direction of the country." My mom withdrew her hand and I was glad that the tears had not actually spilled out but merely welled, and she said, "It was certainly an honor meeting you."

I think that day, her feelings were shared unanimously.

BACK IN NEW JERSEY   6/30

(Shainee)

Today we interviewed Senator George McGovern in his office in Washington. We had the very entertaining experience of being accompanied by my mother. Just when I was beginning to feel like a grown-up . . . She was actually a welcomed addition and was very careful not to cramp her child's style by being overtly motherly. She also gave Kris and me a new set of eyes through which we could watch our own child begin to take shape.

After the interview, we went to the Vietnam Veterans Memorial, which Kris and my mom had never seen before. In fact, during all of the Washington, D.C., sightseeing visits that my mother dragged my sister and me on, she had never taken us to the memorial. I'd only been there once and it had been an incredibly emotional experience. I warned them about going on an empty stomach, but we were already so close, and seeing it seemed fitting after spending the afternoon with the senator.

We parked the car in a lot near the end of the mall that stretches from the Capitol Building to the Washington Monument. We got out and first walked toward the tower of the monument, which was surrounded by a circle of American flags at half-mast for Justice Brennan. We were all tired and looking forward to a decent meal. My mother was busy playing cameraperson, trying to shoot the two of us as we walked with the monument in the background and giving us direction so that her footage wouldn't look "posed."

Say "Cheese" for Mom

Kris and I walked back and forth dutifully, but as much as I love my mother and her joy in taking pictures, I made a very poor shoe choice this morning and was getting cranky as a result. So my mother's directorial debut was cut short and we headed toward the memorial.

There is a long path that winds down the length of the mall to the memorial, a low, dark stone wall that seems to rise from the earth in a way that makes you believe it belongs there. It begins on one end, only a few inches off the ground, and then rises gradually, as the earth sinks, to a height of about seven feet. When it reaches its apex, it turns a ninety-degree angle and gradually descends back into the ground. The names of the dead are etched in plain block letters over every inch of the wall and can be read as you walk its length.

It wasn't crowded today, but there were enough people with flowers and messages written on paper to remind us of the difference between visiting the wall out of respect and visiting it to look for a particular name. Kris ran her fingers along the inscriptions. There were too many of them, she said, and as I watched my mother's eyes gliding over the wall, I knew we were all thinking the same thing. My mother had to say it. "How much smaller would this wall be if he had won?"

She seemed to have recovered from the emotional reaction she'd had to meeting George McGovern, and asked the question matter-of-factly. She was back to being the mother that I recognized and loved so dearly—smart, compassionate,

Vietnam Veterans Memorial

and strong, but certainly not emotional. We got to the end of the path and stood behind a guy with a big backpack who was flipping through a book enclosed by a Lucite podium. The book listed the names of the dead so that loved ones could find out quickly which panel of the memorial the name was inscribed upon. The man was flipping pages frantically. He looked to be around our age—from the size of his backpack he was obviously traveling—and his face was stony. I wonder if he was looking for his father.

We walked by, leaving him alone in his search, and a family walked past us the other way. They had a little boy, around five, who was holding his grandmother's hand as he asked, "So this is a whole wall of dead people?" His voice was so sweet, so innocent. He could very easily have stepped out of some overly sentimental public service announcement. But in real life, it was a chilling question. We all heard him and the woman seemed uncomfortable that he had spoken so audibly. She looked at my mother nervously and smiled, ushering him past us. My mother smiled back, a smile that was knowing. They had lived through it, we had not. But now we understand more.

GEORGE STEPHANOPOULOS

FORMER CHIEF AIDE TO THE PRESIDENT

THE WHITE HOUSE

(Kristin)

If our intention with *Anthem* was to perform a kind of sociocultural biopsy of America, then starting with the heart seemed the logical approach. In one way or another, all roads lead to our capital, and we were determined to get as close to the epicenter of American society—the government—as possible. We debated about who we'd most like to talk to and ultimately decided to go straight to the top.

A one-on-one with the President of the United States may not have been an entirely realistic goal, although we did request a meeting. I was a bit stunned when I called D.C. information for the White House and upon dialing was received by a human voice answering, "White House. How may I help you?" I felt a strange wave of reassurance ripple through me as I realized that our government truly was accessible, at least at this level. I stuttered, "Well, we wanted to fax a meeting request to the . . . the President." I was met by silence but was quickly transferred to another extension where I was given a fax number. One fax away from American leadership! I wondered why I hadn't thought of asking for the President's fax number years ago.

Just to cover our bases, we decided to pursue a backup, on the off chance that the President should, for some reason, prove too busy to see us. We were, after all, just two twenty-six-year-old women planning what, at this stage, could have ended up being an elaborate home movie. So, being realistic, we focused on someone who embodied the youth and vigor for which the Clinton Administration had become famous (or, in some cases, infamous). Eager, telegenic, and extraordinarily young for his position, with an apparent all-access backstage pass to the President, we decided George Stephanopoulos was our man. He worked hard, he smiled *genuinely*, and he usually spoke off-the-cuff, without the predictable self-monitoring of most politicos.

We faxed George twice and called about ten times, until one day a youthful voice on the other end of the receiver said, "George is into this. When do you want to do it?" At the time, it was only our second "yes," so we explained that we'd have to work out a few details. A few hundred details later, we set a date.

Even though Stephanopoulos wasn't our first interview, I was still feeling a bit insecure about running our equipment. The thought of getting into the White House and then forgetting to unpause the record button, or setting the wrong sound level, caused me great anxiety for the days leading up to the appointment. I was well aware that if anything went wrong at the White House, a "do-over" would not be an option.

The White House

I had the razor-sharp focus and silent sweats of an Olympic hopeful as we wove through the confounding streets of our capital city. But we had a hard time finding the White House. I think we both assumed that we would just *know* where it was—as if we'd been born with that information, a psychic sense of our society's center—so neither of us had bothered to look up the address before we got in the car. "We'll find it," Shainee said reassuringly, as she drove. "Everyone who lives here will know where it is."

So we pulled over and asked just about every individual on the streets who looked busy and governmental, not to mention a few tourists. We were greeted with myriad reactions. Some clearly assumed we were psychotic President stalkers and just shook their heads and kept walking. Others looked rather wistfully in a direction—always a different one—and tried very sincerely to explain how to locate and, in fact, penetrate the White House. Some people knew exactly where it was but not how to get inside. We were told that the main street that used to lead right to the building was closed off indefinitely, thanks to an episode in which a man in an overcoat nonchalantly leaped over the White House wall in an attempt to off the President. So much for accessibility.

After a string of wrong turns, we sensed we might be getting closer, as castle-like gates loomed over a street called Avenue F. We drove up to each of these sets of gates, but no one would acknowledge our presence. Desperation wafted through our open windows as time ticked away, and the nape of my neck heated with paranoid thoughts of missing our appointment at the inner sanctum. Shainee and I are just as capable of being as skeptical as the next big-city cynic, but there was something about visiting the White House that softened us, and made us surprisingly starry-eyed and nervous. Coming from Los Angeles, the capital of publicity and hype, we weren't easily awed. But no matter how one feels about the American government and the people who run it, the center of world power still represents hope and possibility for so many people.

With Shainee making one illegal turn after another, we frantically drove the circumference of a structure that seemed to be connected to what might be the White House. I tried to shoot everything with the video camera. Between U-turns, Shainee dubbed us "the White House impaired." A sympathetic security guard, apparently not on the White House payroll, finally pointed us in a direction that seemed trustworthy.

We pulled into yet another impressive-looking gate and were finally greeted by a guard with a clipboard. "We're here to meet with George Stephanopoulos," we said hurriedly, hoping he'd react accordingly. He methodically checked the list with the point of his pen until I reached the verge of a scream. Finally he said, "Let me see your identifications, please," and we scrambled for our driver's licenses. A few long moments later, he returned to the car and said, "Drive up and stop. The canine's going to check your car."

The "canine" was a friendly, tired-looking thing with big paws and a job to do. He purposefully encircled our car, guided by another guard who then "okayed" us to move forward to another gate. Upon reaching the next point person in the obstacle course, we were officially late for our appointment.

I began to feel gasps of relief as we finally spotted the white canopy of the West Wing in the distance. Donna Shalala cruised by us in a Mustang convertible, as if in slow motion, and I got *very* excited. I felt like a small-town celebrity spotter. We parked and entered under the white awning, which looked a lot like an uppity tennis club—perhaps a leftover touch of Nancy Reagan.

The security guard of the West Wing front door instructed us to turn off our camera and then phoned Laura to come retrieve us. Laura was a blonde young Californian who explained, as we ascended a staircase, that about 3 percent of the White House staff worked in the West Wing and that it also housed the presidential living quarters. I had turned the camera back on at this point, as Laura admitted that she was new to the White House and hadn't absorbed all the rules and regulations for media people. She said we could shoot as long as someone didn't tell us not to. That seemed fair. I wondered how many people, if any, had filmed these hallways and mysterious doorways as we walked on extra-thick carpeting toward Stephanopoulos's office.

Shainee turned a corner and loudly crashed the tripod she was carrying into an antique wooden credenza. "Watch the White House furniture," I said with nervous laughter. God knows, that credenza was probably a gift from Churchill to Roosevelt or something. The guard posted on the Stephanopoulos route shot us a disapproving glance, just before he spotted the tiny red recording light on our camera and asked, "You're not running that, are you?"

"Yes, actually. Laura knows we are," I answered diligently as I kept walking.

Laura assuaged his concern, but he squeezed in the last word as she walked away: "Well, as long as the President's not going to be involved."

Shainee and I had already escaped into Laura's office while the guard was handing down his decision. The office was connected to Stephanopoulos's via an open door, so Shainee popped her head in. Stephanopoulos unexpectedly jumped out of his chair to greet us.

He was chipper and charming in a pair of jeans and a blue silk shirt that looked as if it could have been a Christmas gift from his mother. Shainee and I had already gone through the anxiety of what to wear. Laura, over the phone, had assured us that weekends were very casual at the White House. So I wore my jeans and T-shirt while Shainee opted for the one dress that she carried at the bottom of her duffel bag.

Laura, George's assistant

After the introductions, we set up in George's office. As we worked, Shainee reiterated our goals for George's benefit: "We've been talking to people who are shaping the country, on the assumption that although we have our traditional icons—our Founding Fathers and Mothers—the country is, in a sense, still being 'founded.' " I chimed in, "We're interested in different people's perspectives on whether or not we are living up to our country's lofty ideals . . ."

Shainee finished my thought. "We're asking people how they feel about—and currently define—American heroism and the American dream."

We began by asking George about his childhood. "*This Is Your Life*," he replied with a laugh, and then described his youth in Massachusetts, New York, and Ohio. He mentioned that his father was a Greek Orthodox priest, and I instantly gained a new perspective on George. I thought about how strange it must be for him to have to call his political opponents "the religious right," having been brought up in a rightly religious humble home. I wondered if he considered himself a religious man as Shainee asked him about the chain of events that had led to his privileged position as right-hand man to the President.

George ascribed it to luck. "The smallest pieces of chance can make the biggest difference in your life," he said. "I moved to Washington in 1982 after college, and I was working for the Arms Control Association, which was a nonprofit think tank set up to fight nuclear weapons proliferation. And I had been there for six months on an internship when I went to work on Capitol Hill.

"There was a man I used to see in the park," George continued, "who was kind of crazy, but he made some sense in his craziness. He would walk around with a sign that said he would offer ten thousand dollars to anyone who could prove that nuclear weapons stopped war. I would talk to him.''

George Stephanopoulos

George smiled. ''One day toward the end of the internship, I walked back in the building after lunch, and my boss said, 'Hey, George, your friend is trying to blow up the Washington Monument.' This man had taken a van, said it was filled with explosives, and that he was going to blow up the monument to make his point about nuclear weapons. Since I had been nice to him, my boss said, 'You know who he is. You should call the police.'

''All the news stations were monitoring the police channels, so that night I was on *Nightline* as an 'arms control expert.' '' We all laughed, realizing the media's *need* for George, just for that moment, to be an expert, and he continued, ''I had just interviewed for a new job that day with a new congressman from Ohio. He had been lying home in bed with his wife watching TV, and he called me up the next morning and said, 'George, if you can get yourself on *Nightline*, you can come here and get your job.' So that was my first big break.''

I loved the absurdity of this ''big break'' and wondered if George ever thanked the guy for trying to blow up the Washington Monument.

George went on. ''I talked to Bill Clinton that September and again felt very lucky. We met and clicked early on, and I decided to get in my car and drive to Little Rock. And it turned out to be the best decision of my life. A lot of people weren't willing to move down to Little Rock at that time. And I thought, 'Oh, I have nothing to lose. I'm young. And he's a good man with good ideas.'

''I frankly didn't think he had a strong change to get elected. At that time everybody said Bush was a shoo-in. But the President—now he's the President—had seen that people were hungering for something different, even that early on. The campaign just snowballed. It was a roller coaster for the next year and a half. But it turned out, a year and a half later, we'd won. And that led to this.''

Shainee leaned over to adjust George's microphone. The silk of his shirt was too flimsy to keep the microphone clip still, so it kept flipping over and would record only mumbles and loud sounds of the mike raking across his chest hairs. As Shainee bent over, the third button of her dress popped open. Neither of us realized it until later in the interview, when I saw George's eyes uncomfortably darting beneath Shainee's steady gaze. Shainee went on, unaware of the distraction, and asked George to expand on his earlier comment of "people hungering for something different" and how it related to the recent change in the political tide toward conservatism.

"In many ways, people know what they don't want more than what they want," said George. "It's much easier to be *against* something. And sometimes there are good reasons for that. People have good reasons to be cynical over the last twenty or thirty years, whether it's Vietnam or Watergate or just the experience of hearing politicians promise things year after year and knowing that in their own lives, no matter how hard they work, and no matter how much hope they have, their actual life conditions don't change very much. So, people have a reason to be skeptical.

"And I think one of the things that we fell victim to in the '92 campaign is . . ." Suddenly I heard a familiar voice speaking to Laura outside the door, a few feet to my left. Almost subconsciously, because I was so focused on George through the camera eyepiece, I wondered how I could be hearing a familiar voice in the White House. Then I felt that same surge of adrenaline warming the nape of my neck as I had outside the grounds. I kept both eyes on George while he kept talking . . .

". . . we raised expectations, great hope. And I think we made good on a lot of those promises. But people don't necessarily *feel* that difference in their daily life. Change takes a long time to be felt."

The familiar voice was growing more distinct. It was unmistakably a soft-toned Southern sound. My heart began to pound, as in an instinctual fight-or-flight reaction to a predator or high school crush. President Clinton was apparently standing just outside the door, waiting patiently to be acknowledged. I did everything I could to keep my arms still, my legs planted, and my eye directed through the camera. George hadn't finished his entire thought, but he sat still, looking like an adolescent whose dad had just come through the front door looking for his missing car keys. He tried to continue but was unsuccessful. "The President's out there. I'd better see what he needs."

George got out of his chair and unclipped his microphone, freeing himself to go to the door, which he left ajar behind him. Shainee and I proceeded to devolve into four-year-olds. "It's Bill Clinton, it's *Bill!*" I whispered to Shainee. We'd heard he was away for the weekend.

"What happened to Camp David?" she whispered back, her voice full of shocked glee. I watched the President through the generous foot-wide crack in the door. He wore a pink-and-green plaid madras shirt, khakis, and Top-Siders. There we were, ten feet away from the first presidential candidate we had ever voted for, who won!

Shainee was immobilized on the other side of the room, glued to her chair, so I whispered a play-by-play from my vantage point. Later, of course, we would both have complicated fantasies of what we *would* have done if the scene were ever played out again. But in our shock, we spent long minutes exchanging nonsensical whispers and suggestions.

Shainee egged me on. "I dare you to go to the door."

"I dare *you!*" I challenged back. "I can't run out there with a camera."

We both realized, I think, how ridiculous we were being, but we shared an unspoken pledge that we would never judge the other for it. We lapsed into silence and listened as the President's voice emerged from behind the door like the Wizard of Oz speaking from behind the curtain. We could hear bits and pieces, but one thing was obvious from what I could see of the President's face: he was agitated. His fair skin turned pinkish as he asked George, "Is that in the record, too?!" George answered him, but we couldn't make out his reply. For some reason, the President's voice was more audible than George's. "Please spare me all the sanctimony," the President declared. Just then I saw him raise his hand like a preacher reaching up to God. "I mean," added the President, "I could wear their asses down!"

I was shocked at how serious Clinton's face was. It didn't appear that he was angry with George—it seemed to have to do with someone else. The Senate, I thought, or a journalist maybe. Just then, as I was trying to decipher the situation like a nosy neighbor with her glass to the wall, I saw his face. The President was staring right through the door, into my eyes. I watched myself, as if it were an out-of-body experience, meekly respond with the great profundity of "Hi."

The President smiled back with a nod, and asked George, "What are you doing in there?" I realized we probably looked like a potential scandal, me suddenly paralyzed—seeming quite guilty of something—and Shainee with her unbuttoned dress. At best, we were suspicious.

President Bill Clinton's hand

"These two women are interviewing me for a documentary about America," George replied in answer to the President's question.

The President, much to my surprise, probed further. "What are they asking?"

George replied, "The last question was about the changes between '92 and '94 and why the tide . . ."

All I could think was why couldn't we just bust through the door and ask the President the question ourselves? But just then George walked back into his office. Startled, I whipped the camera back to its original position toward his desk. "Sorry about that," he offered, knowing damn well the last eight minutes had been one of the highlights of our adult lives.

"I guess you could say my office is in a pretty good neighborhood," George joked.

It was true, his office was in *the* neighborhood, as in next door to where the President and First Lady snuggled up at night to watch *Nightline* and brainstorm about solutions to world crises and more job promotions for George. We all got repositioned, and I remiked George's silky shirt. He picked up—effortlessly—exactly where he had left off.

"I just told the President about the last question you had asked me—what happened between 1992 and 1994. His shorthand answer was that 'the wheel ran off,' which is just another way of saying that people had gotten all of these expectations run up, and they weren't fulfilled, and it just stopped dead in its tracks. Our job is to try and tap into that hope and sense of possibility again."

George went on to talk about the public's inclination to say "no," as opposed to supporting change. I agreed with George that, as a public body, although we cry dissatisfaction, we also secretly prefer the comfort of the status quo. George explained that compounding the apparent fear of change is a media system that offers a platform for both truths and untruths.

I knew George believed what he was saying, that the Clinton camp had been given a bit of a "bad rap" by the media. Early on, the news machine did seem to capitalize on any visible weaknesses until thin cracks in the wall became gaping holes.

I think the improbability of any human filling such large shoes explains Shainee's and my unexpected physical reaction to laying eyes on the man. The figure became larger than life, almost mythical in proportion—here was a man who had the power to affect millions of lives that he will never even know by name. I got immense satisfaction out of the fact that the President, albeit indirectly, answered one of our questions, and I proudly dictated "Mission accomplished" into my imaginary Dictaphone. I was just starting to reinhabit my body when I heard Shainee asking George for his contemporary interpretation of the idea of "government of the people, by the people, for the people." Shainee asked, "Are we living up to that mandate?"

George pointed to big money and lobbyists as the primary sources of the dysfunction in the political process. "Not on the very big issues, but in the day-to-day work of Congress, the institution is still beholden to lobbyists—to people who have the money to access the system, make the contributions. It influences the policy-makers' world view, and that skews the entire enterprise."

Then George looked down at his watch. "If you don't mind waiting, I have to go to a meeting. I'd be happy to continue later on . . ."

"That's fine. We can wait—if *you* don't mind," I said.

"Great. Make yourselves at home, play some music, whatever," he offered as he grabbed some papers and disappeared through the door to the President's office. Again the words of Rita Dove came to mind: "I think it is specifically American that we feel doors are open—or if they aren't open, that we should open them and walk through them.'' Dove had prophetically defined our White House experience and, quite possibly, the experience of our whole trip.

George's cabinet

Then Laura walked in and caught me surveying George's collection of stuffed animals, which included what appeared to be his alter ego, Curious George. ''George said we should wait for him,'' I said, turning to face her.

''Okay,'' Laura said. I stared at her and had two simultaneous thoughts. One: she seemed very nice and unpretentious about her season box seats at the White House games. And two: Was she aware of how lucky she was?

Given her intimate knowledge of the goings-on in the White House, I decided to ask her something I'd been very curious about. ''So what's the real scoop on Dr. Joycelyn Elders? Why was she fired?''

''Joycelyn Elders?'' she asked, seeming confused.

Oh, no, I thought but didn't dare say it. I knew she had just graduated from college—maybe she'd just been too busy studying to read the newspaper, I hoped. The phone rang, and Laura, saved by the bell, went to answer it.

As Laura hung up the phone, another West Wing assistant popped her head in. ''Are you going to Don's party on Friday?'' she asked.

''Who's Don?'' asked Laura, the new girl on the block.

''You know,'' explained the visitor, ''the cute guy in Education.''

Shainee and I stood side by side in George's doorway observing the interaction. It truly was the most enviable campus life in the country. ''This is Bob Dole's worst nightmare,'' Shainee said to me under her breath.

Laura walked back in to talk to us. As we never stopped thinking of our project or its needs, Shainee asked Laura if she knew any influential Republicans we could interview for *Anthem*.

''It's funny, I don't know any Republicans,'' she replied. ''The circles are very separate. At least that's my impression. All the people I meet my age are Democrats. Even the bars; there are Republican bars, and there are Democratic bars. And the two never meet.''

We were still curious about what Stephanopoulos and Clinton were meeting about. Just hearing the President say the word ''asses'' had made our trip worthwhile, but we couldn't stop wondering what had spurred his intensity. Shainee fished for what was going on. ''If you don't mind me asking . . .''

''Oh, not at all,'' Laura assured us, and went on to explain that the heated discussion was about the military bases closing. Apparently, the *Los Angeles Times* had printed inaccurate information and the President wanted to know how that happened. The pieces of the President's conversation suddenly began to make sense. In any case, it was refreshing to see the President get angry. His media image has been rather controlled and passive, and seeing the President unplugged, genuinely frustrated, and cursing made me have that much more empathy for him regarding the kind of decisions he had to make on a daily basis.

While Shainee and I were waiting, we looked around George's office. He had a few pictures of the President. One was of George standing over Clinton writing at a desk, inscribed: TO GEORGE: HERE YOU ARE, PUTTING WORDS IN MY MOUTH AGAIN. HAPPY BIRTHDAY. BILL CLINTON. I wondered why Bill had signed his last name on a friend's birthday photo—I guess presidential protocol. Also hanging on George's wall was a blown-up photograph of himself, Bono, and Michael Stipe standing next to each other at a party. The caption was from a British music rag that said: PICTURED HERE AT THE BENEFIT ARE BONO OF U2 AND MICHAEL STIPE OF R.E.M., CHATTING IT UP WITH SOME BLOKE. Shainee and I had recently sent Stipe an interview request, and we had not yet heard back. We stared up at the photograph, hoping it was some sort of six-degrees-of-separation foreshadowing.

At this point, Shainee and I began to experience competing blood sugar drops. I started to think of all the desperate things I would do for six small Nabisco peanut butter crackers. We asked Laura if there was anywhere nearby to grab some chips or something, assuming one of the early Clinton Administration mandates would have been to install a twenty-four-hour snack area. Laura walked us outside and pointed us to Donna Shalala's building, just across a walkway from the West Wing.

We walked through a number of oversized doors that magically opened as we approached them. It was White House à la Walt Disney. The halls to this attached building were entirely empty, not even a guard in sight. I had an overwhelming urge to race down the polished marble floors and slide on my knees like a rock star, just to say I did it. But we had already spent enough time in the White House to know that Big Brother was watching us somewhere, somehow. So we followed Laura's directions to the unmarked snack room, which, much to our relief, contained more vending machines than I had ever seen in one room before. We were alone in the cavernous space of sealed snacks, which we toured with coins in our sweating hands. I felt like Charlie Bucket in the chocolate factory.

When we returned, Laura informed us that the meeting was going to go on for a while longer, so she offered to give us a tour of the White House. We accepted. We were waiting in George's office when George came back from his meeting two and a half hours later. I felt bad and really just wanted to leave him alone, but he sat back down in his chair and picked up the microphone. "Sorry about that," he managed through a deep sigh.

"Oh, it's so okay," Shainee said. "We were just taking in the sights."

Shainee asked George about the changing face of heroism, a question inspired by our tour of a building decorated with memorials to past leaders. George replied a bit wearily, "I think today, leaders are torn down, almost for sport. So often when you get into public life . . . well, like what happened to Dr. Foster, who tried to become Surgeon General. Here's a man who worked for thirty-five years as a doctor, delivered thousands of babies, headed up a medical school, was a real trail-blazer in trying to fight teen pregnancy, and then he's nominated for a position in Washington, and it becomes a political football. Entire staffs of people are assigned to destroy him. And that's worked against Democrats and Republicans alike. Good people are not going to want to get involved in political life if the price is tearing down your entire being.''

This idea was on the minds of many people we met on our trip across the country. A wise man who lives on the land, Wes Jackson, would later lament the loss of thoughtful, provocative leaders of our country's past, saying, ''Why can't we have people like that in government today?''

Wes knew the answer to his rhetorical question, and Stephanopoulos knew it, too. If the individual is very human, why would he or she trade their human-ity—and that of their family's—for a job, no matter how noble? Only a few would be willing, and in those, decency and righteousness would be the exception, not the rule. On the other hand, I wondered if a lack of willingness to sacrifice a little comfort for the greater good wasn't at the root of our national shortcomings. In the history of our country, there seems to have been no shortage of men and women who were willing to expose themselves, personally, in order to do public service. Shainee and I trusted that these kinds of people were still fighting the good fight; they probably just weren't covered on the five o'clock news. Ultimately, these were the people we were in search of on our trip.

Perhaps foreshadowing his own fate, a little over a year after we had this conversation, Stephanopoulos would resign for reasons we could only imagine were the very ones we were discussing. Of course we could not have foreseen that when we asked him what allowed him to make the personal sacrifices the job demanded. ''You are constantly part of different battles and struggles that wear you down and that often cloud the broader purpose that you originally entered political life for,'' George answered quite honestly. ''But if you do keep that sense of perspective—and remember that there will be many more days away from this job than in it and that you should use every one as best you can—it does help. It doesn't mean it always helps at six in the morning when you're trying to drive into work or at eight at night and you're in a fight with a reporter or a member of Congress over some battle that may seem meaningless in the long run—but it does help in the overall approach to the job.''

I felt this was as close as George could get to just being George—the American, not the politico. We asked him a personal question, and he gave a personal answer, albeit in second person. And it was there that we officially ended the interview, recognizing George's exhaustion, and we thanked him for being so immediately receptive to meeting with us. He gave us a sincere good-bye as we left, retracing our steps down the carpeted hallway.

We passed the credenza that now bore Shainee's indelible mark, went down the stairs and toward the entrance guard. We thanked Laura for taking such good care of us and for being the one to bring *Anthem* to George's attention. She was another living testament to the fact that assistants not only run the White House, they run the world.

The last images we saw as we were leaving the West Wing were beautiful black-and-white photographs that were hung on the corridor walls, pictures of the Clintons and the Gores captured in various real-life moments: the President at work in the Oval Office; the President and Hillary huddled at a rainy funeral; the President and Vice President in discussion at a conference; the President whispering intimately into Hillary's ear. This last was my favorite—it begged the viewer to imagine just what he was confiding. The final photograph, nearest the door as we left, was one of Clinton and Gore waving good-bye. For that moment, they were waving good-bye to us.

Encountering President Clinton the way we had was more resonant for us than meeting him formally with a curtsy and a "Nice to meet you, Mr. President." We had seen genuine passion in his face. Bill Clinton *is* an American. He eats french fries, wears khakis, and has a temper. We felt privileged to know this firsthand.

Shainee and I talked as we headed for the car. We realized, although the day had far outweighed all expectations, that we were a little disappointed. Shainee looked almost gloomy. "I think the last three years have emotionally and spiritually aged George," she said sadly. "He was so fiery during the campaign and just after Clinton got elected." We saw something in George that we hadn't expected: restraint. We had all watched him enter the White House as an earnest and exuberant thirty-one-year-old. The man we left that day possessed a caution hidden behind charming eyes that have learned certain hard truths. George had apparently had his political coming-of-age, like a young father who instinctively begins to adopt, unbeknownst to him, the characteristics of his own father.

Jefferson Memorial

We drove in silence, absorbing the experience, toward the closest diner. We walked in, ordered coffee, and headed for the two pay phones against the back wall. We called our parents, boyfriends, and closest friends and retold our White House visit and presidential encounter until we were both hoarse.

Early evening had fallen by the time we left the diner. As we drove past stoic monuments, most of them at a distance, we got lost trying to leave the city, as would always be the case with us and D.C. We ended up retracing our path and passed the impenetrable gates on Avenue F that had denied us access only hours earlier. I thought of the White House, which I now knew how to find. I thought of how comforting that was. I thought of the fearlessness and openness that this country and its political body was founded on and how courageous and necessary it is for the people walking these streets, who have chosen to work *for* their fellow Americans, to reside solely in that historic frame of mind.

As Jack Healey would later say to us on the steps of the Supreme Court, ''Thomas Jefferson once said, 'Democracy is for the angels,' and I believe democracy is inherently messy . . . but you expect something from this city. This is governmental leadership and it is their job to excel at decency.''

A FRIEND'S COUCH IN CHICAGO   7/11

(Shainee)

Today was one of those days that I fantasized about when we first began thinking about our trip. There is a romanticism to being "on the road" that I very admittedly subscribe to. We are anonymous as we glide across the states, stopping to look through every open window. Because the experience of each day is new, every sense seems sharpened by unfamiliarity. It is freedom of a kind that I have never before experienced and with it comes a sense of peace.

Two days ago, we left the familiarity of the East Coast to head west, into an area of the country that neither one of us knows very well. The change is almost immediate. Seventy-five miles outside of Philadelphia, we were already in G. Gordon Liddy Land. There are very few FM stations outside of urban areas, and the AM stations seem to be crawling with talk shows. Kris doesn't really find the right-wing AM radio that entertaining, but I think I'm hooked. She gets angry and yells back at the broadcast and then pops in some of our music as a retaliatory stab. But sometimes if she falls asleep, I can listen to it for quite a while. I think of Doug talking about Rush Limbaugh being historically incorrect about almost everything he says and I try to decipher what it is about this largely hateful talk radio that mesmerizes millions of Americans. Regardless of how long I listen, I know that what I hear and what the regular listeners hear is very different. It is fascinating and dark and so very wrong. I don't get angry really, but sometimes very sad.

Fortunately, we brought a couple of books on tape with us. We started off with John Steinbeck's *Travels with Charley*, read by Gary Sinise. Steinbeck was in his late fifties when he set out, with his dog Charley, to rediscover the country that he had been profiling for so many years. The book is the story of his trip. My sweet boyfriend gave me the audio version when we first decided that we would actually leave Los Angeles and it has proven to be quite inspiring. We began listening somewhere in Pennsylvania. Since Steinbeck left from New York, his trip caught up with us right around Ohio. We had the wonderful experience of driving through the Midwestern states as we listened to John Steinbeck's words describe them. We're hoping that our journey will continue to cross paths with his.

We stayed in a motel just across the Pennsylvania/Ohio border and woke up this morning to a 400-mile drive. We are feeling pretty defenseless against the available food choices, and the concept of a good cup of coffee is not a common one in most areas. But we have found truth in one of Steinbeck's aphorisms: no matter what, we can usually count on a good breakfast at any motel coffee shop or truck stop, no matter how remote. In fact, sometimes breakfast is a wondrous meal with real blueberries in the pancakes and bacon from a local farm. Otherwise, thank God that Taco Bell serves Bean Burrito Lites, especially for our dear Kris, the near vegetarian. Life on the road is much easier for a carnivore like myself.

In addition to the lack of nutritional variety, the middle of the country gets a lot of flack for its reportedly uninspired landscape. But I find solace in the endless acres of farms. I like the order of the plow lines and patchworking of colors that separate the crops. The giant irrigation machines are my favorite, the ones that look like monster metal cockroach sprinklers.

I don't think that anyone would disagree that "American" has historically signaled "agrarian," but driving across the states of Pennsylvania, Ohio, and Indiana, it's difficult to imagine what it must have looked like two centuries ago, when the land was filled with small family farms. We see huge farms that resemble the industrial seas of Jersey City, with smokestacks and giant concrete structures punching through the flat horizon. The farm buildings look like factories just barely surrounded by stuff that is alive and grows. Once in a while we see a smaller farm, off the highway, with a family home, and we wonder how they can compete.

Today I suggested that we get off the highway so that we could shoot some older farms with afternoon light. We didn't know we'd be leaving the highway and entering seventeenth-century Germany.

We got off the mighty coast-to-coast I-80 somewhere around Elkhart, Indiana. I thought Kris was going to explode with joy. She's never seen an Amish or Mennonite community, not to mention person (not counting Kelly McGillis and Harrison Ford). I, on the other hand, like most children who grew up anywhere near Lancaster, Pennsylvania, have been to the Pennsylvania Dutch country. But I've really seen only the touristy version. And I didn't know there was such an extensive Amish community outside of Pennsylvania.

We drove around the tiny farming community and did several "copter shots" of the immaculate farmhouses and their crops. We redefined the term "copter shot"—which, in movies, is a shot taken from a helicopter—during our visit with James Redfield. It is named after our discovery that one of us can shoot great angles out of the sun roof of the car while the other one drives. We've also developed a version of "tracking shots" where one of us actually sits on the roof of the car and the other one drives, but we can only do that in very rural areas and at slow speeds. We usually bicker a little about who gets to shoot those—it's kind of like an amusement park ride.

Anyway, today we were doing copter shots and tracking shots of absolutely gorgeous, real-life "amber waves of grain" when a man in a horse-drawn black buggy drove through our frame. Kris almost knocked me over trying to get a good shot of him, and then brought her torso back into the car, gasping, "Oh my God, did you *see* him?" What followed was a couple of hours of chasing Amish photo ops. It was actually kind of embarrassing and probably a little obnoxious, but we thought it was an important snapshot of the country to add to our library of footage. The people were all surprisingly tolerant and polite about the fact that these two women in a station wagon, one hanging out of the roof, kept doing video drive-bys of their homes.

At one point, we inadvertently followed an Amish family home. We became obsessed with capturing just the right image of their blonde little baby girls, who were staring at us from under their bonnets from the back window of their buggy. They were alternately shy and giggly, making faces for us and then hiding. Ultimately, the buggy ride was too bumpy for us to grab the shot in focus. We finally passed their horse, and their father gave us a hearty wave, which is good because later today we found out that the Amish religion forbids them to allow themselves to be photographed. We hope that waving means he forgave us.

I tried to recall information from my fourth-grade field trip to Lancaster to fill Kris in on the unique Amish way of life. For one thing, they don't use electricity. Amish children go to school only until the eighth grade, where they are taught usually by an unmarried woman who has also gone to school only until the eighth grade. The Amish marry only each other. They also don't pay for—or accept—social security or welfare, because they believe in taking care of their own. The Amish maintain their own dialect of seventeenth-century German, in addition to speaking English in school and High German while worshipping. They govern themselves. Each Amish community is autonomous, settling disputes by a vote of each member in the community.

The astounding thing is that the children are encouraged to leave the shelter of their individual communities in their late teens. They call it *rumspringa*, or running around. When they return, they must take a vow of faith, and it is only then they are baptized. Apparently, most of them return and opt to live in the community until they die.

The Amish speak well of the American experiment. It's amazing that it is only in this country, the "melting pot," that the Amish communities have managed to remain as they always have been—separate. The original European communities have all been absorbed or assimilated. If it weren't for William Penn's "holy experiment" in religious tolerance, the Amish customs and practices might never have been preserved. The communities are a testament to why the Amish came here in the first place—religious freedom.

It is a simple life, in a truly self-sufficient community, based on separatism and maintaining a way of life that existed three hundred years ago. Somehow they remain unaffected in a world of technology and multiculturalism. Only in America.

W. DEEN MOHAMMED

ISLAMIC RELIGIOUS LEADER • SON OF ELIJAH MUHAMMAD

CHICAGO, ILLINOIS

(Shainee)

The bow-tie-appointed, immaculate young men who walked the strand on Venice Beach, handing out flyers and *Final Call* magazines, were a familiar sight during the four years that I lived there. They were members of the Nation of Islam, and I always marveled that they could look so neat in their heavy dark suits after spending all afternoon in the sweltering Southern California sun. They were determined and committed, speaking in strong, low voices as they extended their hands to passersby.

Venice Beach had been known for some time as a haven for drug users and sellers and, more recently, for gang activity. Surprisingly, it was the Nation of Islam—and not the LAPD—that contributed significantly to my level of comfort and feeling of safety. They were very successful in controlling the drug traffic in Venice and protecting families in the community. Quite often I would see them posted on corners, in front of suspect buildings. They were a respected army, exuding strength and pride. But their fundamental tenant of separatism didn't jibe with the liberal live-and-let-live mantra of bohemian Venice. Why did a group of empowered young people subscribe to a leader who spit out messages of intolerance?

I've never really understood Louis Farrakhan. Why exactly does he poison the good that he inspires with loathsome words? Kris and I had both been working with teenagers from different sections of Los Angeles before we left the city and had known several kids who looked up to Louis Farrakhan as their role model. We had strongly considered pursuing Farrakhan for an interview, but our research pointed us toward a less incendiary voice—that of Imam W. Deen Mohammed, whose followers are comparable, if not larger in number, to those of the Nation of Islam.

W. Deen Mohammed is the son of the late Elijah Muhammad, who started the Nation of Islam after his spiritual leader, Wali Farad, mysteriously disappeared in 1934. When Elijah took over, his family was on federal assistance and he had a following of approximately 8,000 black Americans living primarily in Chicago and Detroit. When he died in 1975, his followers numbered between 150,000 and 200,000 nationally, and he had carved a place in history for himself and his family. One of his best-known ministers was Malcolm X, who broke with the movement in 1964 and was assassinated eleven months later. After Elijah Muhammad's death, his legacy of leadership fell to his prophesied successor, W. Deen Mohammed, the seventh of his eight children. Although Imam Mohammed had been excommunicated on two occasions, largely for challenging his father and some of the tenets that he preached, Elijah had left no doubts as to whom he wanted as his heir.

Imam Mohammed initiated a radically different era of leadership among the Black Muslim population. Where his father had preached a message of separatism and warned against the "human beast" (white people), his son called for a new sense of patriotism and a classic interpretation of Islam based on the Quranic concepts of dignity and social equity. He urged black Americans to identify themselves with their land and their flag. In 1985, he dissolved his organization, the American Muslim Mission, to unite its members with the international Muslim community. His goal was not to focus on the political Black Nationalist movement that his father had generated, but instead to stress the religious and spiritual goals of Islam.

Louis Farrakhan had also been a revered leader within the Nation of Islam when Elijah Muhammad died. But by 1978, it had become quite clear that the Nation was veering from its traditional path under the Imam's new leadership, so Farrakhan decided to split off and form his own group. He retained the earlier beliefs and the Nation of Islam name. The two men have not worked together since, though they are related by marriage.

The first time we ever heard of Imam Mohammed was when we found his invocation before the United States Senate on the Web. He was the first Muslim in history to offer an invocation on the Senate floor:

> Let us pray that our great nation's two centuries of national life may inspire other nations to move toward social and economic justice for all. Grant that her big heart for charity, compassion, repentance, and mercy continue to beat strongly within all of us. Grant that Americans always have more hope than troubles and ever grow in goodness and wisdom. Bless Americans to always cherish our freedom and the noble essence of the American people.

It seemed odd that neither of us had ever heard of this man. We'd had no idea that there was another eminent Black Muslim leader nor did we know how extensive his following was.

Imam Mohammed has not been a victim of media overexposure for the simple reason that he doesn't seek out the spotlight. He preaches peace and interfaith cooperation. He has established dialogues between the leaders of Islam, Christianity, and Judaism. He was, in fact, chosen to participate in President Clinton's 1993 Inaugural Interfaith Prayer Service as the country's Muslim representative. Imam Mohammed represented Muslims at the 1988 World Parliament of Religious Leaders Meeting in Oxford; he addressed the 1990 Islamic Conference on the Persian Gulf Conflict as the American Muslim leader; and he delivered the keynote speech at the Muslim-Jewish Convocation in early 1995, which marked the first publicly recognized dialogue between top Islamic and Jewish leaders in the United States. He also has his own television and radio shows. But when we looked for a biography of the Imam in our encyclopedia, we found him mentioned only in the biographies of his father and Louis Farrakhan. We had to find out more, and fortunately, he agreed to be interviewed.

We arrived at the *Muslim Journal*, a newspaper that reports on the American Muslim community, in the afternoon and were met in the parking lot by the Imam's assistant, Rafah. Rafah was dressed tropically for the sweltering Chicago heat in a straw hat and a batiqued shirt—a far cry from the wool-suited young men on Venice Beach. He was jovial and called us both "baby sister" as he grabbed our equipment—without even asking if we needed help—and led us inside.

We entered the newspaper's office, which doubles as the Imam's headquarters, and were joined by one of the reporters, an Arab man in his thirties. The office was staffed predominantly by black women who wore the traditional Islamic dress of long caftans and headdresses. Everyone was kind and cheerful, making us feel like honored guests. Rafah led us upstairs to a room where an impressive spread of fruits was laid out with several juices. Par for the course, we hadn't eaten, but didn't dare touch the fruit, not knowing who it was for. The reporter, munching on a peach, watched us set up and finally asked if either of us liked fruit. "It's for you," he said. We blushed and split a banana while we tested sound levels.

Rafah brought the Imam in a few minutes later. He is a medium-sized man in his sixties with a slight roundness that is common for his age. He has salt and pepper hair, beautiful flawless skin, and amazingly white teeth that are impossible to miss on someone who smiles so often. He shook both of our hands heartily, greeting us with enthusiasm about our journey and making sure that we had sampled the fruit. We didn't have very much time, as the Imam had a speaking engagement later that afternoon, so we set up quickly and got started.

We talked about the beginning of the Black Muslim movement and the man who had started it all: Wali Farad. The Imam described the environment of 1930s America and explained why Farad had ascended so quickly as a leader. "This man had a strategy to bring a change to blacks or African-Americans, to those who were living in the ghetto, those who were dissatisfied with America, those who were even dissatisfied with black leadership in America. He appealed to them, and he had a plan to give them faith in their own minds and faith that their future was in their own hands. It wasn't really the religion of Islam, even though we had the name of Islam. It was really a kind of Black Power religion or Black Nationalist religion and God was, for us, a black man. At the time, the movement was heavily focused on materialism, but in spite of that, ironically, we became very spiritual people under the teachings of Farad.''

The Imam pointed out that black Americans were already living under very poor conditions, but the Depression had changed the situation from bad to worse. Of course the natural inclination was to demonize the oppressors—white people. In addition to poverty, the Jim Crow laws made it even easier for Farad to encourage blacks to move away from White America and become separate. ''As you know, the civil rights movement and Dr. King changed everything, with the help of other good people in this country, like the Jews who were willing to sacrifice their lives alongside blacks. With help from the general American population of sensitive souls, we have one law now.''

The Imam went on to explain that as the Nation of Islam gained strength and notoriety, the movement attracted attention from the international Muslim community. The media began to pay attention to the Nation of Islam's charge that white people are the cause of all of the evil in the world. Muslims from other countries began to question Elijah's teachings, saying that they didn't sound like the spiritual teachings of Islam. At a young age, the Imam began to voice opinions on Islamic interpretation that opposed his father's.

''I am a person who believes in the dignity of all human creation. I became acquainted with the dignity of the human person in the Declaration of Independence, which taught me the best ideas of this society of American people. I consider myself to be a patriotic person as well as a devoted, practicing Muslim. So during the Black Power days, in the mid-sixties, some leaned more toward Farrakhan, but the solid foundation was with me, and that's how I came into the leadership.''

We weren't sure what kind of relationship the Imam had with Minister Farrakhan, but we had to ask him his opinion of why the media focuses so much of their attention on Farrakhan, when a good portion of Black Muslim Americans are not a part of the Nation of Islam—a fact that is consistently unmentioned by the press. He didn't have negative words to say about Minister Farrakhan's media-courting ways.

''I don't feel compromised by Farrakhan and the popularity that he has in any way. He is intelligent, he is very informed, he is not naive, and I believe he is capable of changing. It is possible for Farrakhan to take on a more political image that would position him better to really do what is helpful—more social reform and dealing with economic problems. I would welcome that change. I would give him my support. I am hoping for it.''

I told the Imam that I had read a speech that Malcolm X had written when he was in Mecca, where he talked about renouncing racism. He also came to the conclusion that he actually did believe in the concept of ''life, liberty, and the pursuit of happiness,'' even after railing against America for so long. Malcolm X's revelations during his trip to Mecca sounded similar to what the Imam was hoping for from Farrakhan.

Imam Mohammed agreed, saying "A lot of nationalized American citizens from Muslim countries believe Malcolm went to Mecca to make the pilgrimage. They thought that he had come with a new mind and that he would become an Imam. Never. Malcolm was a Black Nationalistic thinker. Before he left, he said he still believed the white man was different from the black man and inherently different from other human beings. Shortly after he arrived in Mecca, though, he announced that he didn't see white people as he did before, that all races should work together. I think he believed that before. In fact, if you look through his past, you will find that he had some very close white friends. Malcolm was not foolish. Malcolm was a man who was following a plan."

The Imam went on to say that although Malcolm X was the emerging political leader of the Black Muslims, he didn't always understand all of the religious practices and teachings of traditional Islam, so he asked Imam Mohammed for tutoring. "Malcolm and I became very close friends and I was aware even back then that Malcolm bought into part of the Nation of Islam's myth but also rejected part of it. So I think, yes, there is a comparison to be made between Malcolm X's speech in Mecca and the possibility for a shift in attitude from Farrakhan. Farrakhan could easily make a statement that would not hurt his image with his following, but would clear the way for him to be identified as a social reform teacher and someone who would help the black man get up off his knees."

Imam W. Deen Mohammed

I asked him if he believed that there is an American dream that is attainable today. He responded without hesitation, "Certainly. I am a part of it. I am a dreamer now in America. I think the American dream is like the American life, always growing. The Constitution is an elastic document, the American people are an evolving people, and we are coming closer and closer to the beautiful perfect idea that we all have in our vision. We are all a part of that and I do believe in it. I believe, with the help of others, that we can play an important role in increasing the desire for an ethical society for the whole of humanity, that this whole globe will become one big living room for all people. That's my dream." The Imam paused and chuckled heartily, adding, "Not that we won't have our privacy. The living room receives the guest, right?"

Apparently, we were the guests who had stayed too long, because another man came just then to inform us that the Imam had to be whisked across town. He thanked us for including him and insisted that we rest in the air-conditioned office as long as we liked. Kris and I gladly took him up on the offer and sat around the table with Rafah and the reporter for another hour, happily feasting on fruit.

STUDS TERKEL

AUTHOR/RADIO SHOW HOST FOR WFMT

CHICAGO, ILLINOIS

(Kristin)

It was our third day in Chicago, and I was on my sixth day of an unexplainable stomachache. I kept thinking it would go away, but I was haunted by my mother's voice telling me, "Get to a doctor!" I didn't *want* to go see a strange doctor in a strange town so that he could tell me that I had been afflicted by a common road disease caused by stress, eating badly, drinking vats of diner coffee, and sleeping irregularly.

We were on our way to meet with Studs Terkel, a writer who had given a voice to so many Americans in his works of oral history—a consummate interviewer who had earned the well-deserved title "America's Chronicler." While in my early twenties, I had read two of his books, *Working*, about workers—both blue-collar and white-collar—and *Hard Times*, about the Depression. They made a huge impression on me, and I never forgot the unusual name on the covers—Studs. He was a personal inspiration to both Shainee and me. Many of the topics of our own film—such as the American dream, heroism, and inspiration—were subjects that Studs himself had spent a lifetime examining through the eyes of other people.

After weeks of trying to catch Studs at the radio station where he does his show, I finally convinced a sympathetic station intern to give me Studs's unlisted home phone number.

A gravelly voice answered the phone when I called, identifying itself as Studs. After I explained *Anthem* without taking a breath, he said simply, "I'm out of it." I blurted out a little laugh at this sweeping statement, unsure of what, exactly, he had meant. It seemed like a peculiar thing to say, particularly because I knew his latest book, *Coming of Age*, was slated to hit the bookstores soon.

"Out of *it?*" I questioned.

140

"I'm out of the *business*," he said.

"Business" clarified things only slightly for me, but I took it to mean he was taking a break from being the voice of a nation. I decided to push the issue just a little, not ready to give up so easily on a man whose perspective we both considered to be so insightful and pertinent. Plus, Studs was one of the people I was sure I had to meet before I died, and knowing he was eighty-two kept me on the phone until I convinced him to see us.

While in Chicago, we stayed with one of my boyfriend's friends, a vibrant redhead from Louisiana named Elizabeth who has a cozy one-bedroom apartment in the heart of the city. Unfortunately, the apartment was even cozier than usual, as it lacked air-conditioning and we had arrived the same week as the heat wave that made headlines nationwide. We experienced the hottest days in Chicago's history—peaking at an all-time windy-city record of 106°—having driven literally into a state of emergency.

As we headed toward Studs's home, the radio aired announcements advising people to stay in air-conditioned homes or buildings and rattled off rescue hot line numbers for all counties. One station gave surreal accounts of cows exploding on the surrounding farms. It felt eerie pulling onto Studs's abandoned street, which was perfectly lined with beautifully restored old homes.

We stepped up to the front door and read the note taped above the knocker: PLEASE RING BELL SEVERAL TIMES. We did. Moments later, a jovial man wearing a red shirt and chewing on some nuts opened the door. I had heard Studs almost always wore red shirts—and red socks, too. The man said hello, but it was difficult to hear one another over the loud Italian opera coming from a turntable in the next room.

He yelled, trying to compete with a soprano. "Come in! Come on in and meet my wife, Ida."

Ida shook our hands, directing her salutation into the camera lens as if it were a person. "Hi, I'm Ida."

Studs shook our hands, and when he did, I noticed the trademark rubber band around his right hand that I had heard of. He proceeded to spend a good deal of time trying to spell Shainee's name after she introduced herself. Early on, we saw the direction things would go that day—Studs Terkel would be doing the interviewing, not us, which was just fine as far as we were concerned.

"Where's your anchorage?" he inquired, still yelling while we all migrated into the living room, closer to the music. Studs headed for the volume control on the record turntable as we began to shout our answers back to him. I made a mental note to use the word "anchorage" more often.

Studs began analyzing our anchorage, asking questions about New Mexico and commenting on Philadelphia, as well as suggesting people we might possibly be related to. "Martin Gabel has the same last name," he pointed out. "He was an actor and a narrator of radio plays in the thirties and forties. And Hahn . . . as in *Emily* Hahn—a woman very celebrated for her adventures."

It turned out that Martin Gabel was indeed Shainee's cousin—something I didn't know until Shainee acknowledged the miraculous correlation to Studs, who had already moved on to something else. "Here, have a couple of nuts, some cashews," he encouraged, giving us each a handful. "Have you guys interviewed Ralph Nader? Because of the whole consumer thing. Who else have you done?" he probed.

We recited our list. "Rita Dove the poet?" he repeated back to us with enthusiasm. "Great! And Andrei—was he pretty good?" We were about to answer. "So it's a kind of counterattack—a lot of the people you don't see in the media. Well, that's a good group," he announced with a smile as a seal of approval.

We slowly came to realize through the course of the day that Studs has a hearing disability. Occasionally, we had to just roll with the oft-changing direction of the conversation, understanding how frustrating it must be for a professional listener to have a hearing impairment. It was the equivalent of his beloved soprano having to sing with laryngitis.

Studs Terkel

Ida had disappeared, but soon returned to offer beverages and advice on where to set up the interview. You could tell Ida ran a tight ship by the immaculate appearance of their house and by the mint-condition 1950s furniture, which looked as if it had been lifted right off the set of *I Love Lucy*.

I stood in awe of Ida as she galloped from one end of the house to the other. I knew she was eighty-three because I had already asked. I also noticed that there was hardly a gray hair on her head or a line on her impish face.

Studs took a seat in his favorite chair, where we had set up the cameras. "Oh, sit up, Louis," Ida insisted. "When you sit like that, you have ten chins," she added, I guess to give him an incentive. So Studs's given name was Louis. I wondered where the nickname had come from.

"*La madre!*" Studs cursed back to Ida with a big smile. "I speak gibberish Italian, too," he said as an aside to Shainee and me. "Why don't you direct movies?" he suggested to Ida. "Why don't you become a director?"

"I'm just trying to be helpful," Ida said, in self-defense.

"Yes, ma'am," Studs acknowledged respectfully.

We asked Studs to do a sound check for us, to test the level of his voice. "Talking. I like this level, a sort of conversational level. A nice easy way. Not so much projecting, since I'll be talking to one person, really. See, the idea, to me anyway, is you are talking to *one* person, not to hundreds of thousands. In other words, not addressing multitudes," he declared. He looked over at me fiddling with the camera. "Look at you doing that. How did you learn? You decided to go into this way back?"

Just then the phone rang with a throaty shriek reminiscent of antique wind-ups.

Studs answered—and continued to answer—as a conversation between him and his book publisher was interrupted by a series of disconnections. Studs became visibly frustrated with "modern technology," as he called it, easing his anger by cursing at the phone in Italian every time he was disconnected. "They're gonna call back again," he would continue to warn us. "I'm sorry about this—it's about my book tour. God."

"Don't worry about us. We're not in a hurry," Shainee assured him.

"Okay, I'm ready," Studs announced a few moments later, hanging up the phone and clapping his hands. He took his seat again. "Do I look distinguished enough?" he asked, smoothing his hair with his hands. No one answered him. We thought he was asking Ida, but she didn't answer. He asked again.

I took the cue. "Downright handsome," I decided, taking in his shock of white hair framing his animated face, which was backlit in an ethereal sort of way.

"He doesn't look very good," Ida chimed in, sitting on her established perch, shaking her head from side to side. "Your belt," she explained. "You've got your pants pulled up in a strange way."

Shainee and I turned our heads to Studs's waist. Ida had a keen eye. Studs had pulled up his baggy pants and cinched them like a potato sack.

"All they see is chest up," he assured her. Ida, who did not seem convinced, continued to shake her head in disapproval. "Okay!" Studs said to us with boyish excitement. "I'm ready." He then broke into song—a piece of Italian opera—before he began to talk about the chain of events that had led him to the place he was today.

"My life and what I do is really an accretion of accidents," Studs began. "My hope was to be a lawyer like Clarence Darrow. And so I went to law school. A very unhappy three years. I was thinking of the law in human terms, and in school it became property and contracts. I found it very dull. That's how it began. I didn't want to become a lawyer. My dream was to have a civil service job. Every Depression kid dreamed of having a nine-to-five job. I took the civil service examinations in 1934 to be a fingerprint classifier for the Department of Justice. And I qualified; I got recommendations from Melvin Pervis of the Chicago FBI, the man Hoover hated because he got all the credit for capturing John Dillinger.

"I was able to get my Freedom of Information files a couple of years ago and there was an exchange of letters between me and the Director, J. Edgar Hoover, and I'm writing to him in longhand, asking, 'Where's my job?' And I see another letter in the files. Someone, a teacher—I think from the law school—wrote, 'We didn't find Mr. Terkel a very good student. He did only one thing, criminal law. And further, he was not the highest type of boy.' That was the quote. I thought, 'Gee, not the highest type of boy.' And sure enough there was a memo from Hoover: 'Cancel the appointment with Terkel. We discovered he is not the highest type of boy.' So, had I been different, I might have wound up Efrem Zimbalist, Jr., or even better, Clyde Tolson.

"So that's what I almost became," Studs continued. "And then I was on a WPA job, the Work Projects Administration of the New Deal. The New Deal governmental works saved the lives and self-esteems of millions of families. But we seem to have erased that part of history. The people who condemn big government today—if I can offer my editorial right now—are the ones whose daddies' and granddaddies' asses were saved by the New Deal. That's the irony.

"See, one of the things that gripes me most today is our erasure of history. We are erasing or perverting our history. And the young, through no fault of their own, know little of yesterday. In a sense, we're suffering from what I call a National Alzheimer's Disease. Culturally, there is no yesterday, no memory of it. And thus, some of the outrageous events taking place in our society are succeeding, because we have no sense of the past."

I remembered John Waters saying that people today believe history started the day they were born. I wondered if Studs and John were right about the fact that the "disease" was striking my generation specifically. Would this National Alzheimer's Disease continue on through the next generations, slowly erasing our historical tracks like a heavy snowfall?

"After my WPA job, I joined a theater group at the time the CIO was being organized under the Wagner Act," Studs continued, becoming more visibly animated. It was obvious he was recounting a time in his life that had made him happy, even proud.

"So I joined a theater group that played before labor unions and picket lines and soup kitchens. I was in a play, *Waiting for Lefty*, that was about a strike. So I became an actor. And Chicago was the home of radio soap operas then, so I became a gangster on the radio. The only trouble with that was that I was always getting killed, and thus out of a job. So one thing led to another, and I became a disc jockey before the term 'disc jockey' was used. And then TV came, and Chicago was the home of an original kind of television—improvisation. I was a host of a show called *Studs' Place*. But 'my thing' ended suddenly because of Joe McCarthy and the Red Scare."

Studs told us that his show was canceled by NBC because he refused to say he had signed petitions "by mistake." Studs explained, "I didn't say I was duped. A number of people did, to save their jobs, and to this day people think I was a hero because I defied the system. But that's not the truth. The reason was my ego! Coming from my family, I couldn't say that I was too stupid to understand what those petitions meant. As a matter of fact, I feel pretty good about signing those things. So that was it, and I was out of a job for a long time.

"Then one day I was listening to a radio station that usually played classical music, and I heard Woody Guthrie. I had never heard anyone in Chicago play a Woody Guthrie record except me, when I had my disc jockey show. So I called up and said, 'Oh, I'd like to be with you guys.' And they knew of me and said, 'We'd love to have you, except that we're flat broke.' 'So am I, so we're even,' I said. And one thing led to another. I started to do interviews, and accidentally it began."

From Rita Dove to George Stephanopoulos—and including many others—I noticed our interviewees attributing their accomplishments to "chance, accident, or luck." Some of it, I suspect, was that we were drawn to people with a lot of humility, but I do think another quality each of these people had in common was a willingness to seize a moment of being in the right place at the right time, an ability to leap at opportunity and risk failure.

Studs went on to explain that soon after he started his radio show and began interviewing people on the air, he decided to travel around the country and talk to a cross section of Americans about different subjects like the Depression, war, and working. "So that's the story of my life," he declared. "Somewhat expurgated, but nonetheless true."

I realized that, in Studs's case, his answer would have been shorter if we'd asked him what he *hadn't* done in his lifetime.

Shainee asked what had shaped his sensibility—his perspective on the world. He talked about his family and growing up in the men's hotel that his mother ran during the twenties and thirties.

"It wasn't a flophouse," Studs explained. "It was a nice clean little place where railroad workers, toolmakers, craftsmen, firemen, and retired men would stay. And that hotel lobby was always full of guys before the Depression hit. And I'm not romanticizing the past here, but the men back then read more. So I think those guys enlightened me a bit.

"But more than anything, I think it was my mother and brothers who had the greatest influence on me. My mother was following the American dream. She reached for the brass ring but never quite caught it."

Throughout the interview, Studs spoke of his interest in and concern about the "working class"—a topic he has examined thoroughly in his writings. "It's a word that is out of context," he explained. "We don't use the word 'working class' anymore. We say 'middle class' for everything." Studs sneered, "You make $2,000 or $20,000 or $200,000, you're middle-class, because it's a state of mind, see . . . Thus, we have one class of people. We're supposed to be a classless society, which is the joke of the century when you think of the gap between the haves and the have-nots today—how so few have so much. The number of billionaires during the time of Ronald Reagan increased manyfold. How does a person get to be a billionaire, unless he gets dough from someone else? Billionaires! And more and more have-nots. It's a very class-*full* society, not classy, unfortunately.''

It was clear that Studs liked to challenge the inherent contradiction found in an equal rights, free commerce society. He, like Rita Dove, believed that by shedding light on someone else's life experience and life circumstance, it was possible to infuse readers and listeners with compassion and empathy—maybe even for people who had never before thought to care about each other.

Shainee asked Studs if there was anyone, a contemporary, whom he admired. ''I will say, just off the top, George McGovern. Now, people will laugh when they hear that. McGovern, 'that wimp,' some would say who don't know better, though he flew God knows how many missions in a bomber plane over Nazi oil fields during World War II. But that's beside the point. Here's a man who had the courage to speak out against Vietnam very early on, who recognized the impulses of women, and people of color, and others as well, no matter who they were.''

I noticed that Ida had quietly snuck away; I could hear her in the kitchen, washing dishes and doing secret Ida things. Before Shainee could ask the next ques-

tion, the doorbell rang. Several times. Ida came out of the kitchen, wiping her hands on her apron, and opened the door to a delivery person. She accepted the package, placing it on the staircase where other packages lay unopened. I caught her mumbling, ''So many books. How is one person supposed to read all of these?'' as she turned to go back to the kitchen.

I asked Studs if he received a lot of books in the mail, and he said yes, admitting that it was a bit of a burden, as he is always being sent books to review, give quotes, or personally critique. You could tell he was flattered and felt quite obligated to the pile that just continued to grow. He must have been especially curious about this latest addition, however,

Double-exposed photo of his book's arrival

because, without a word, he took off his microphone and walked to the stairway. He picked up the padded envelope, probably still warm from the heat outside, and ripped it open. ''Oh my God!'' he shouted. ''It's the book! It came!'' He rushed the bundle over to Shainee and me. ''What do you know, the book came!'' he said, cradling it proudly.

As I got closer to the thick hardcover book, I saw its handsome face: *Coming of Age* by Studs Terkel. ''Is this the first time you've seen it?'' I queried.

''Yeah! What do ya know!'' He smiled sweetly as he flipped through the pages, gently caressing each one but not stopping on any particular page. Ida came out of the kitchen to see what the racket was all about. "It came! The first copy of it, and there are the quotes," he pointed out to Ida, bringing her up to speed on our discoveries thus far. Studs turned to the back flap and held it open, and we all looked at the author's photo. "Look at that distinguished shot," he said wryly, "like a Renaissance prince or a godfather."

"Let me see," said Ida, taking the book into her own hands, figuring she'd be the judge of that. "Oh," she cooed in agreement, "this is a wonderful picture, as a matter of fact."

After we all had a chance to properly examine the new arrival, we resumed our positions and asked Studs how he feels his writing contributes to his readers. "I don't know if my writing makes a contribution," he offered. "I *hope* it does. Remember, the writing is mostly the words of other people. I write a long introduction, I talk to people, introduce them, but it's their words, except when I do a memoir."

I now understood that a significant part of Studs's excitement over the arrival of the book was not about proudly caressing the pages he had written but, rather, honoring the words of others he had managed to collect. Studs continued telling us about events that had been inspired by his books . . .

"The incidents that happen now and then make me feel good. Like when people stop me on the street here in Chicago and say, 'Ever since I read *Working*, I'll never again be rude to a waitress.' That sort of stuff—to help that person realize what it is to *be* that other person. What it is to *be* a teacher or a washroom attendant or a CEO who's just been canned. Or during *Hard Times*, what it was like for an ordinary person—whether it be a businessman or a blue-collar guy or a housewife—to live during the Depression in the thirties. So when that person said, 'I'll never again be rude to a waitress,' I felt good about that."

Studs had grown up in the age of Humphrey Bogart and John Wayne—heroes who tended to embody idealism, strength and humanity. The detective and the cowboy seemed to represent a stoicism of the common man. Shainee asked Studs how he had seen the American hero change during the course of his lifetime.

"What is a hero?" he asked us rhetorically, in return. "What is a hero in America? Now we have movies today and television shows raking in millions, multimillions, and the hero is a clod, a zombie, as portrayed by . . . Alan Schwar-zenegger or Sylvester *Sta*-llone or *Sea*-gal," he overenunciated, giving them all fresh identities.

Shainee and I managed to suppress our reaction to Studs's renaming of Arnold as "Alan."

"These are heroes who hit people," continued Studs. " 'You 'its 'em!' There was a great comic years ago named Spike Mulligan. He was a genius. He was the teacher of Peter Sellers. He did these characters, one of them did this skit: 'What do you do for a living?' someone asks him. 'I 'its people,' he says. 'I 'its little old women, too, see, I 'its her.' It's sort of a takeoff on W. C. Fields, who hits old women. You're the hero, you see? 'You 'its people.' But instead of being clown figures that you look down upon with disdain—it should be with disdain, Fields would loathe what they represent—we cheer them.

"So these heroes are the ones offered, rather than someone who's in the community, part of it, speaking for others who can't. See, there's a perversion of language as well as a perversion of ethics—a perversion of sense. What is a hero? What is a man or a woman? Tom Paine, a personal favorite, expressed these ideas—the rights of man—in his most celebrated work, *The Age of Reason*. That book was read by hundreds of thousands, by the way. They *read!* Hundreds of thousands out of a population of what, five million? It would be like a twenty million audience today for a book! Not *Die Hard*." Studs shook his head.

The idea of a hero being a part of the community—a platform for the voiceless—inspired Studs to go deeper with the question. "So what is a democracy?" he posed, linking the concept of heroism to the very foundation of our country. "A community of thoughtful, participatory people," he answered himself.

"The sixties, by the way, is a decade that's put down. But, in the sixties, there were those who went to the South to register black voters and those who protested the war. So there were causes, and they did go outside themselves. But that's put down, of course, by those—to use a quote by a woman named Joan Nesley: 'The sixties is a favorite target for those who take delight in the failure of dreams.' But 'participatory democracy' was the phrase they used. Participatory democracy should be what this country is all about, and that was the dream of those who founded it. Of course you take part. Of course you're part of the community. That's what a hero would be about."

We started to talk about the birth of the country, specifically the founding principles and our inalienable rights. " 'Life, liberty, and the pursuit of happiness . . .' " Shainee stated the familiar phrase.

"It reads well, doesn't it," said Studs. " 'We hold these truths to be self-evident.' " He continued, " 'That *all* men are created equal.' 'All' is the operative word. And now we're experiencing Supreme Court decisions that suggest we go backward. We have the Bill of Rights that goes all the way down the line—continually being attacked and misused and abused. And so the battle to achieve true freedom and equality goes on. As far as hope is concerned, without hope there's no point. Am I optimistic? Not very, no. Am I hopeful? I have no alternative, unless I put my head in the oven.

"There was a woman named Jesse de la Cruz. She was a farm worker. She became active when César Chávez formed the Farm Workers union. Jesse had a phrase for the Mexican people. I won't get it right in Spanish, but it's something like '*Esperanza muere lo último.*' It means 'Hope dies last.' So I got hope. No alternative. But am I optimistic? Boy." Studs paused. "Carl Sandburg has a poem: *The People, Yes.* I say, 'The people, maybe.' "

Prior to our trip, my assessment of the country—based mainly on information offered by the evening news—had been a daily dose of: "The people, not likely.'' At this point in the trip, we were at least in solid agreement with Studs's hopeful ''maybe.''

We were curious what Studs thought about the American dream, considering he had verbalized his concerns about the current and future state of what he too called ''the American experiment.'' ''Well, of course we have a dream,'' he said matter-of-factly. ''What was the American dream originally? It began with people from England, Ireland, Eastern Europe, the Mediterranean, Italy, Mexico, Asia . . . all following a dream. That was the dream—a new land, avoiding conscriptions of other countries, prejudices, and poverty in the hopes of making a better life for themselves and their kids. The irony is that many of the kids today are uncertain, lost, and worried, saying, 'I'm not going to be as well off as my old man.' The dream was always 'My kid will be better off than I am.' Now the dream is reversing itself.

''So maybe our culture—the worst aspects of it—is embraced all over the world. In China the slogan is 'It's glorious to be rich.' In Red China! Which, of course, means the world has been turned upside down. There was a song in the American Revolution called *The World Turned Upside Down*. We now see it enacted. And everywhere in the world, we see the worst aspects of American pop culture. But we're still losing, because when these kids say, 'I won't be as well off as my parents,' something has happened to the dream.''

Studs sat silently for a few seconds. I couldn't stop thinking about the slogan ''It's glorious to be rich.'' It reminded me of the 1930s and '40s American advertisements encouraging consumers to drink lots of coffee, ''a good and natural stimulus,'' and smoke cigarettes ''as throat protection against irritation and cough.''

I wasn't sure if Studs had finished his answer, but he suddenly broke his silence and asked, ''Could I get a copy of this interview? I could use some of it on my radio show.''

Once a working man, always a working man. ''Sure,'' we said, ''no problem.''

''Sorry,'' he apologized. ''Go ahead with what you wanted to ask me.''

We started to explain to him that the narrative structure of the film would be our road trip and that we'd be interested to hear his ideas on the mythology of the American on the road.

''The idea of the nomadic American has always been with us,'' he began. ''Whether it be Jack Kerouac's big classic, *On the Road*, or whether it be a far greater book, *The Grapes of Wrath*. Steinbeck was able to tell the story of the many by focusing on the one. That was his theme. The short chapters were many families, like the Joads, clogging the road in their jalopies, hopeful to reach the land of milk and honey, and the larger chapters were about this one family. And so the road . . . remember, the frontier has always been out there, heading out for the territory. What territory now? The Atlantic and Pacific have been spanned. What territory? There has to be a new territory *within*.''

Other people we would later meet also spoke of the notion of our modern Manifest Destiny now needing to be directed within—the idea of exploring the possibilities and potential *within* a society whose physical borders have been expanded to their limits.

"Einstein said—I love to quote Einstein," admitted Studs, "because nobody dares contradict you. Einstein said, 'When the atom was split, everything in the world changed, except one thing—the way we think, and we have to think anew.' He meant in terms of the global village," Studs explained. "And unless we do that, catastrophe awaits. That's more or less a paraphrase of what he said. And I'm not going to disagree with Einstein."

Shainee and I could both tell Studs was getting a little tired. We'd been talking intensely for quite some time. I could hear Ida filling glasses with ice. Something cold sounded good.

"We just have two more quick things we wanted to ask you," urged Shainee.

"Go ahead," Studs said, being a good sport, having been on our side of the fence many times.

"If you were traveling cross-country with us, what would you be most interested in asking people in America right now?"

"There isn't any one question," he answered, adding, "I think it has to be a combination. What they want out of life; what has influenced them. Do they question authority? And if so, what kind of authority? Whether it be the doctor or the President or the head of the Americanism Committee—whatever it might be—majority opinion. Is the majority always right? I often think about the term 'minority opinion.' Maybe it's just a minority-*expressed* opinion, and is actually a silent, or silenced, *majority*."

Shainee started to ask Studs if there was a story or an idea that he could think of that would begin or end with the phrase: "Only in America." I loved the way Studs answered questions by telling stories. Before Shainee could get the rest of the last question out, Studs had already latched onto a story that he wanted us to hear—a story he wanted to end with.

"This is a story of revelation and transcendence," he said. "It's a biblical, powerful story. It's about a guy I know, C. P. Ellis, who lives in Durham, North Carolina, and who was once the Grand Dragon of the Ku Klux Klan. He grew up poor. Terrible time. A naturally sweet gentle guy, he heard all his life that being poor was 'That goddamn nigger—he's responsible.' His father was a Klansman. That's what he learned, and all of his life he believed that, and then he joined the Klan. What a powerful feeling it was to have that sheet on him, that hood on him. Suddenly four hundred people were looking at him, marching toward that illuminated cross. He wanted to be somebody.

"So," Studs continued, "there he is and he's fighting and challenging civil rights people in the beginning when they were picketing department stores to have black clerks there. And he and this woman, Anne Atwater—a black woman—were devout enemies. And one day they were tossed together—some funds came in for schools during the Carter Administration and everybody was invited to this gathering. The Ku Klux Klan, the Southern Christian Leadership Movement, the White Citizens Council. He shows up, and people say to him, 'Are you *crazy*, being with them?' And he says, 'Well, my kid's involved here, and I don't want them to get all the money.' One thing leads to another, and he and Anne Atwater end up on the same committee together, and slowly they get to know one another. And one day she comes in crying. He says, 'What are you crying about?' She tells him the black kids are attacking her because she's been seen in these meetings with a Klansman. He says back to her, 'My boy came home crying because the white kids were teasing him that his father was going around with the black agitator.' And the two of them start crying, feeling the pressure. And then they hold on to one another, realizing they're the same people.

"Time passes," Studs continues with the story, "and C.P. begins to notice things. He's walking down the street looking at a black man, thinking, 'Is he the guy who's keeping me poor? He's as bad off as I am. He's worse!' He said he would get calls when he would break up those civil rights meetings, big shots saying, 'You're doing great, Clayburn, you're doing great, C.P. Keep it up!' And the next day he'd walk down the street and those same men would cross the street not to be seen with him. He thought, 'Am I being used by them against the black man?' And then he took a job as a janitor at Duke University. And the next thing you know, he's organizing the union. The union is eighty percent black women, and he wants to run for paid full-time office. He figured he didn't have a chance, running against a black man. So he faced the union, saying, 'You know me. You know who I am.' 'Yes, we know you,' they said back to him. And the next thing you know, he had won. They voted for him four-to-one because of the work he was doing there and then.

"And so today he is able to say, 'This is me now, the same person who had cried with joy when Martin Luther King was killed, and now I read everything King wrote; I have every record of his speeches . . . This is C. P. Ellis today.'

"To me, this is a great story . . . of possibility . . . of transcendence, of unstacking the deck of a deck that was stacked all of his life. That, to me, is a hopeful story. I'll use that as my parable," Studs said, nodding his head.

It was comforting to know, given how much Studs had seen in his extensive lifetime—how many lives with which he had intimate contact—that he still believed in the innate goodness of people. I regarded Studs as an expert on people—their behavior and natural inclinations. He had spent most of his life observing people, talking to them, and documenting them like the Jane Goodall of an asphalt jungle. So the fact that I now knew that Studs's hope for us—the people—would survive at least as long as he did gave me lasting peace of mind.

Just as we had finished, Ida came through the swinging kitchen door with a tray. "Do you like apple juice?" she asked. "It's organic."

As we drank the juice, I asked Ida how long she and Studs had been married. She calculated for a moment. "We just celebrated an anniversary—fifty-six years," she said, choking slightly on her juice.

"I have to see this ear doctor," I heard Studs, behind me, explaining to Shainee. "I got this hearing aid and the doctor's gotta clean my ears out for the rest of my life. Would you mind dropping me on your way? I have an appointment at three-thirty."

"We can take you wherever you want," Shainee assured Studs, audible in my periphery.

"What's it like being married to Studs? Or Louis, I should say. Where did the nickname 'Studs' come from?" I asked Ida, wondering two things at once.

"Yes, it's Louis," Ida confirmed. "Studs is a nickname. It came from the James Farrell novel *Studs Lonigan*—a Depression-era book about an Irish kid." She had answered the easy question and just looked at me, apparently hoping I might ask something else and forget about the "being married" question. I just looked back at her, and she started to laugh. "In most ways, it's been a lot of fun," she chuckled.

Studs lifted his glass of organic juice high into the air. "Here's to you," he offered as our four glasses met in the middle.

"Cheers," we said back. "To your book, and to your fifty-six years together."

"We'll rest a minute, and then we'll scram," Studs said, informing Ida of his newfound ride to the doctor's office. A minute later, Studs was on his feet, walking in and out of rooms, whistling an intricate tune. I wondered if it was the house favorite—some kind of work-ethic tango. My grandpa had always said to me that if you were born in the Depression, a big part of you never grows out of it. To Studs, there was no sense in wasting time or potential, he always found something to keep him focused and busy.

After we packed up, I walked over to Ida. "Thank you for letting us come into your home. It's been a real honor for us to spend time with you both," I said as we shook hands.

"Well, he gets a kick out of this kind of stuff," Ida confided.

"He's been a big inspiration for us," I admitted, hoping she'd repeat it to him over dinner. "Traveling around the country, talking to people, and trying to understand why they do the things they do—what it feels like to be them. When we read his books, it touched a nerve in us."

"Is that right?" she asked earnestly. I thought maybe it made her happy to hear that Studs's work had penetrated the generational barrier. Studs walked back through the room, leaving us in the wake of whistle.

We bid good-bye again to Ida, who held the front door open, waves of visible heat sneaking in as we made our way out. "Oh, it is hot! Oh my God," exclaimed Studs. "This is our record, you know! It's hot as hell!"

We quickly piled into the car, Studs riding shotgun, all of us saying grace for the invention of the air conditioner. As we drove away, Studs explained that he had never in his life been behind the wheel of a car. Surprising, considering Studs's well-known traveling adventures. As it turns out, he always managed to convince a friend with a driver's license to join him. "Now, both you guys know how to drive a car, huh?" Studs inquired, seeming impressed.

"Yeah," we said, being reminded that not everyone takes the skill for granted.

"I'm talking like I'm from another planet." He laughed. "I take the bus. If I weren't going with you, I'd be taking the bus. I have a nice seat against the window. Is this the first time in Chicago for both of you?"

Yes, it was. Before we left Los Angeles, Shainee and I had determined that we'd surprisingly only been to about eighteen states between us. Illinois was not one of them. "Chicago is quite a remarkable town," Studs said proudly. Shainee asked him what he loved about his city. "It's my roots, it's everything," he said simply. "You'll see the lake more when we go around," he added, pointing his finger east.

As we drove, we passed by a number of unleashed fire hydrants, erupting like cold lava volcanoes while barefooted children danced underneath them, screaming and laughing with relief. Studs tried to convince us to drop him off a few blocks away from his doctor's office, trying not to put us out. He explained that he was used to walking a few blocks from the bus stop. We tried to talk him out of it as we sat behind a string of cars stranded in front of the State Street bridge. Sirens screamed while fire trucks wet down the bridge, which was expanding from the heat.

By the time we neared his doctor's office, we had convinced Studs that walking would not be wise. I was watching the few people on the street from the comfort of our car—tightly sealed like a Ziplock—and they didn't look so good.

"This is fantastic," Studs said, as we rounded the corner to his doctor's office. "Well, listen, kids, the best to you," he said, sticking his hand out to both of us for a farewell shake. "You two are very good. I like you," he said, as if someone else besides us was in the car listening. And with that, he opened his door, and holding it almost to brace himself from the heat, he gave us detailed directions back to Elizabeth's like a true automobile driver—not forgetting one turn or helpful landmark.

Studs's serenade

He closed the car door, and I rolled down the back window to wave good-bye. Studs, with both arms outstretched, his *Examining Your Doctor* book clenched in one hand, began to serenade us, curbside, with an Italian operetta.

To his wife, he is Louis. To the rest of us, he will always be Studs—the man who gave a voice to the working class, the disenfranchised, the disillusioned, the dreamers, the debutantes, the waitresses, and the wise elders of our vast country. J. Edgar Hoover may not have believed him to be the highest type of boy, but the grown Studs Terkel has proven himself to be the highest type of man. It seems this kid from the Great Depression found himself a pretty steady nine-to-five gig— humanizing the human race.

REMEMBERING CORNFIELDS IN AMES, IOWA   7/18

(Shainee)

Iowa is surprising. It's pretty and we hadn't heard. Lush and green, with sprawling white farmhouses and small quaint towns. We arrived this afternoon, come to visit Kris's boyfriend, who's working here for the summer on a movie about tornadoes. We thought it would be fun to take a short break and see him. We found him on the set and were a little bit taken aback by the glaring differences between our film and theirs—just when we were beginning to believe that we are actually making a *movie*. They have a crew of over 200, a chef, and a *rain machine*. But we held our heads high as we were introduced, and the well-meant question "Oh, you're making a film, too?" followed us from the drivers to the production assistants.

We nodded our heads faithfully, Kris clutching one of the cameras as proof.

Ames, Iowa, is not the most likely place to find a massive Hollywood film crew. There is a tangible nostalgia here for a version of America that I have seen only in Norman Rockwell paintings. I have always felt that I was missing out on some quintessentially American experience, because I never lived on a farm. This place evokes a sense of longing that I have not felt since I was a kid.

I grew up in a "development," a group of single-family homes all modeled on the same five prototypes, laid out on symmetrical lots of land on streets with thematic names (e.g., trees or presidents). The "development" grew to be very popu-

Kris, the crew, and the rain machine

lar in the Northeast during the postwar fifties and went on to become a major contributor to the metamorphosis of small-town America into suburban America. A childhood in the suburban Northeast is determinedly filled, brimming with housing, schooling, car-pooling, and so on. It was a contained and measured lifestyle with few surprises, so, being a kid, I quite naturally acquired a longing for what I did not have—open spaces, the undiscovered, and mobility. Luckily, our particular backyard bordered on a farm . . .

It was a small South Jersey farm that harvested a few acres of corn or peas every year and also ran an undoubtedly more profitable horseback riding school. That farm provided some of my most cherished fantasies when I was growing up.

I spent a lot of time daydreaming about riding horses, coming of age in a haystack, feeding pigs something mysteriously called "slop," climbing silos with endless numbers of siblings . . . And whenever I wanted to live it, all I had to do was go and sit between the cornstalks with a book or stroll the path around the fields with the obligatory prop, a walking stick.

The farm was surrounded by neighborhoods on two sides, an apple orchard on the other, and a hospital across the street. My grandparents had told me fairy tales about the fledgling suburb, where they had come to live twenty years prior. They said that the land used to be covered with farms and orchards as far as you could see, from all sides of that first tract of housing. We had three apple trees in our very own backyard to prove it, and every fall we would try to eat a bite or two of the wormy fruit.

I loved that we had dysfunctional fruit-bearers in our backyard: their fruit was flawed and it didn't bother me a bit, our trees were relics of the great orchard that once flourished on the other side of our backyard farm.

My sister and I would tell any visitor who would listen about the endless orchards of the past, pointing at our three measly trees. Our lot of land had been blessed and we would boast to all of the other kids in the neighborhood about what grew on our "property," as the under-twelve crowd had termed it. The word "property" became common usage with the young locals, particularly useful when Kid 1 got mad at Kid 2. If Kid 1 said, "Get off my property," Kid 2 would have to oblige, but the rules of our vernacular also stated that Kid 2 could stand at the property line, refusing to leave the scene, and retort, "It's a free country."

Wishful thinking

Growing up, I resented the boundaries—represented by fences and landscaping—and fell even more in love with the boundless farmland and orchards. I didn't register the fact that a farm was someone's property, too. The farm instead symbolized the untouched and unknown. The farm was something we had all missed out on. In my mind, behind our house there was something precious and pristine: wilderness and forest. And it was while I was mistaking a farm for wilderness and an orchard for the forest that I began to form early ideas about how land becomes property in a free country.

When my sister turned eight, I shared the secrets of the farm with her and gained a companion trailblazer. We were very fortunate to have one of those moms who caught on quickly, so when we would tell her that we were going out to "count our acres" or were "heading into town for supplies," she would tie a kerchief under our chin and call it a "bonnet." Years passed without my mother ever questioning how the spirit of an eighteenth-century pioneer had entered the body of her child.

It wasn't until after I hit puberty—and became distracted with less wholesome fantasies—that I abandoned the imaginary world of the farm. Eventually, one afternoon, my mother did ask me where the infatuation with wormy apples and life on the farm had come from. The only answer I could come up with was: "It makes me feel like an American."

When I was a kid, my idea of America and "the American" did indeed resemble a Norman Rockwell painting. I felt deprived in some way because Norman was nowhere to be found in the suburbs. None of his impressions were a part of my family's past, which had been located in Europe in the nineteenth century before they settled in New York and Philadelphia. There wasn't a farmer among us. I felt cheated and questioned why this mythology couldn't be found anywhere in my own experience. I felt as if I had inherited a genetic memory of a fading version of the American dream. Tract housing and strip malls grew where apple trees once stood. Frontier was turned into farmland, farmland into cities. We certainly have a dream with an identity problem.

DOROTHY BETTS

WAITRESS

AMES, IOWA

(Kristin)

As we headed through Iowa into Kansas, making our way toward Wes Jackson, we passed by the kind of prairie landscape that had become most familiar and comforting to us: silos, open fields, cows, farmhouses, and lonely windmills. You could say we were silo-obsessed, particularly with the indigo blue ones. Silo spotting had become one of our favorite road games.

Although there were thunderclouds looming in the distance, the summer sun beat mercilessly down on us through the windshield. "I need food," Shainee chirped, as she invariably did about every two hours. Traveling with Shainee was like traveling with a baby bird who needs constant feedings and lots of protein. I, on the other side of the food chain, have a metabolism akin to the mammalian ocean order and cannot ritually devour cheeseburgers, fries, and milkshakes like the bird people.

We pulled off the highway into a relatively unpopulated area on the outskirts of Ames, Iowa, picking the one restaurant we could find—Perkins. Our waitress was a salt-and-pepper-haired woman named Dorothy who was probably in her sixties. She was spry and attractively stocky, her butt swinging a bit with her stride. We ordered, then talked with her for a few quick minutes, but she wouldn't let herself get too wrapped up in conversation, always keeping one eye on each of the other tables in her station. But she did explain, when we pressed, that she was the oldest waitress in the place "by far" and leaned in to whisper, "I run circles around the twenty-year-olds—if I can say so myself."

We were both dying to know Dorothy's story, so when she came back with my sandwich and Shainee's burger, we asked her if she would be willing to do an interview. She thought about our proposal for a minute and then agreed. She explained that we wouldn't, however, be able to shoot it in Perkins because "they are a chain and have strict codes." She phoned her friend who worked in a smaller "more relaxed joint," and we all agreed to meet there after Dorothy's shift.

Dorothy was there when we arrived, having already picked out a booth in the back. We sat down across from her and started right in, as we felt immediately comfortable with her. She didn't seem nervous, which was unusual for someone who'd never been interviewd before, particularly on-camera.

Dorothy in action

She explained that she'd been working at Perkins for fifteen years. We asked her if she liked it there. "Very much," she replied. "Otherwise, I wouldn't stay." Dorothy realized she still had her Perkins pen tucked behind her ear. "Oh, let me put this away," she said, as she slipped it into her purse by her feet. "It's a good company to work for," she continued. "I like the customers, the local people."

We talked about the "local people," those who had been raised on farms like Dorothy. Dorothy then revealed the unexpected—that she too had the movement gene. "I spent ten years traveling around the country. I saw a lot of the country." She smiled. "Enjoyed what I saw, but I just kind of like Iowa."

We suddenly understood why we had been drawn to Dorothy. She too had seen for herself the beauty of the country, and that made the staying that much more fulfilling for her. Dorothy already knew what we were just discovering: that rootedness was savored when preceded by exploration.

We asked Dorothy about her travels and what she did to support herself. "Waited on tables. Just moved around. Different jobs, wherever the mood struck and wherever I decided to go."

She smiled, knowing she probably didn't have to qualify this for two fellow Gypsies. She glanced up at the ceiling, then looked back at us and said with a hint of pride, "I probably saw just about every state, except Alaska and Hawaii. I came back to Ames because I had two sons at Iowa State. I decided to spend some time with them and I just"—Dorothy paused—"stayed."

We probed a little more about why. "Well, I think part of it is that it's home. And the seasons—I'm used to the changes. I'm a farm girl. I feel at home with the people around here because fifty percent or more of my customers are farmers or people who lived on the land at one time. And I just like the country here—it's beautiful, and I enjoy my drive back and forth to work because I can keep an eye on the crops and what's going on. That's what I'm used to. It's just a good place to be."

I wondered if simply observing the daily rituals of farming from the vantage point of her car was enough for Dorothy or if she missed living on the land. She

assured us that she had had enough of farm life and just watching was indeed enough.

We asked Dorothy if she had seen farm life in Iowa change since she was a little girl. "Yes, to a point," she began, "because—and this is dating me—but I grew up on a little farm during the Depression. My dad used to tell me that if it wasn't for the fact that he had bought the farm from his father, he would have lost it. In other words, sometimes you can let payments slide. I come from a large family; there were eleven of us. Prosperity was just not a word any of us knew back then. At the time I was growing up, Dad owned the first tractor he ever had, which was a little tractor with metal wheels, and there is just no comparison to the machines they have today. So there's been a lot of changes in the mechanics of farming, but the basic idea is still the same. If you go to your average Iowa farmer, it's a matter of living on the land. Their concern is getting the crops out, getting the crops in, raising their animals. But they're right there to help their neighbors when they need help. They're concerned about the others, not just themselves. So the way of living is basically still the same."

It was interesting to me that Dorothy thought that the technological changes were less notable than the unchanging approach to the way of life—the community ethic of farming. That's what connected her to her home.

During our conversation, Dorothy explained that she had once been married. "We reached the point where he stayed where he was, and I stayed around here— and everywhere," she explained.

Dorothy seemed to me to be one of those people who had grown comfortable with herself, anchored by years of life experience. It was apparent she liked her job and appreciated the simple fact of being alive. Shainee asked Dorothy if she believed in the notion of an American dream.

"Oh, very definitely!" she enthused. "Very definitely. And I look back on my entire family, who came over here from Germany with nothing. I get a little provoked when I hear people complain, because I look back at my own family—I come strictly from the Iowa farm on both sides—and Mom and Dad did not have a lot. But they raised a family and they were able to support themselves until the day they died. We never had to take care of them. I look at all their children now, and they have families that are doing the same. I look at mine. My four boys have all graduated from college, working themselves through. And now they're supporting their families. They're not millionaires, but they've done it on their own. They've done it strictly through hard work and a wish to achieve what I guess you might call the American dream. I think that the American dream exists for anybody who wants to work for it."

Dorothy's eye twitched slightly, making her look like she knew a secret.

"It's out there. It exists, and I think it will continue to exist. And I look at other kinds of things that we have—the freedom to do as we want. I look at my oldest son, he decided to go to Australia. He's still an American. If he ever decides to come back—and he may—he has the freedom to return. You can just kind of strike out on your own here. I look at myself. I'm not rich, but I'm happy, I'm content. I don't have to ask anybody for anything. I work for what I have."

She leaned her elbows on the table, coming closer to us. "I grew up before World War II and isolation, when we seemed to want to stay to ourselves. We didn't want to reach out. I think we have to realize that the world has gotten so small that we can have an American dream, but it's got to be shared. Because we can't live by ourselves.

"I talked to my son in Australia on the day he got married. I sat looking out my west window and watched the sun go down while he watched the sun come up over in Australia. And it really made us both realize just how small this world is—when you can sit and do that from opposite ends of the earth. There is no way, anymore, that we can keep our American dream to ourselves." Dorothy had her own real-life analogy to the global village that many had cited.

We asked Dorothy if any particular person had influenced or shaped her way of thinking and her life—whether they are well known or not.

"If I were to name a well-known figure, I would say Abraham Lincoln—the things he believed in, how he treated people, and his ideas. But if I wanted to pick somebody that was not well known, I would pick my father. In some ways, I guess he reminds me of Lincoln." I remembered Rita Dove saying that it was good to have heroes, as long as some of them are close to home. Dorothy said that her father just believed in people. "And he instilled that same spirit in me."

Shainee asked Dorothy what she appreciated most about living in America.

"The beauty of the country," Dorothy declared. "You've heard of the red clays of Georgia? Well, I found out they really are red! I saw them! And I used to ride through the Rocky Mountains; I just love those mountains in the fall. I would see picture postcards of the area that looked like somebody just took a paintbrush and dabbed all these colors all over. But it's not coloring. It's not fake—it's real. I would ride through the mountains and wonder what the pioneers must have thought of seeing them for the first time in their little wagons. On wagons and horseback, they must have seemed even *more* tremendous."

Dorothy looked through the lens of the camera right at me. I suddenly became more aware that we were *interviewing* her. I was so used to my micro viewfinder perspective that I had actually forgotten about the camera. In a moment of pause,

I caught Dorothy's eyes closely examining the camera and my hands on it. Her eyes moved over to Shainee, who was looking down at our list of questions. I could tell Dorothy was thinking, with some detectable envy, about how we were spending our summer.

"We've been lucky to be able to just travel around, stepping into people's lives for a moment, asking all kinds of personal questions," I offered, as a response to her silent question.

"Yeah! I think what you're doing would be interesting—meet the people, see what's going on," she said, slowly nodding her head. After answering Dorothy's questions about why we had ventured out together, I was curious if she had journeyed with someone or flown solo. "So did you travel by yourself?" I asked, wondering if I would ever be able to survive years on the road *alone*.

"For a lot of it, yeah," she said with a little pride. But her fair cheeks turned pinkish, and we could tell there was more to the story. "I also did some of my traveling by semi." I loved the image of Dorothy riding shotgun, pulling the horn whistle, and managing the CB radio and the tape collection.

I couldn't help but ask how it was that she came to travel by semi, even though I knew the answer was probably a whole other interview.

"Oh, let's just say I had a very good friend," she quipped with a wink, "who took me around, and that was part of the reason why I did so much moving around. And then, as friendships sometimes will, I went my way and he went his.

But I've never regretted the time, because I learned so much, and I saw so much of the country that I wouldn't have otherwise."

Dorothy seemed so sincere when she spoke of the land and her urge to see more of it. "I think my dream would be to have my little old car and a sleeping bag and just enough money so I didn't have to work. And I'd just start driving. I think that would be . . ." Dorothy didn't add the word, seemingly unable to find one that would do her feelings justice.

"That would be your American dream?" I asked.

"That would be my American dream." She smiled. "Maybe someday I'll make it."

"I have a feeling you'll be passing us on the road!" I said.

"Oh, maybe I'll *follow* you," she said laughing. "I won't be in a big hurry at all."

WES JACKSON

FOUNDER OF THE LAND INSTITUTE

SALINA, KANSAS

(Shainee)

We first heard the name Wes Jackson while we were staying with Elizabeth in Chicago. For three nights, Kris and I shared the pull-out futon in Elizabeth's un-air-conditioned living room during the worst heat wave in Chicago's history. It was taxing enough that we had to share motel rooms, but the same bed, in 106-degree heat, was enough to put me over the edge.

We were all up one night—too hot to sleep. Elizabeth thought Kris and I were being babies. "It's not *that* hot" slid off her native Louisiana tongue with sugary ease. We rolled our eyes and I told Kris she was touching me again, her leg on my side of the futon. Elizabeth was checking out our itinerary, asking about various people, and throwing out suggestions.

It was a familiar scene. Every time we would stop to stay with someone or ask somebody for help in getting in touch with someone (like their second cousin's ex-boyfriend's stepmother who was currently dating the man who ran the publicity firm of whoever we were tracking), we would get suggestions. I'd say a good 30 to 40 percent of our final list of participants came that way.

Elizabeth was no different. She couldn't help herself. She asked where we were headed next and we told her we'd be stopping to see Kris's boyfriend in Iowa before heading down to Tennessee. Elizabeth urged us to detour through Kansas to see Wes Jackson, who had started the Land Institute, where he was studying and experimenting with an innovative philosophy of farming. Wes had called Elizabeth's family years before to see if he could use some of the land on their plantation for one of his research projects. (Yes, Elizabeth actually grew up on a plantation in Louisiana and it *is* still operating.) Elizabeth gushed about how impressed she was with Wes and his work, saying that we absolutely needed to speak with him.

We called the Land Institute the next day and they faxed us some information. The institute was started in 1976 in Salina, Kansas. Wes was working to steer American farming back toward sustainable agriculture—a philosophy of farming that does not destroy the land. The goal is to try to mimic natural ecosystems, specifically by looking at the polycultural makeup of the native prairie and how it sustained itself before white men started farming it. In a nutshell, the idea is to move away from growing annual crops, which require pesticides and fertilizers and drain the soil of its nutrients, and restore the land to growing several different perennial plants at once. This method fights insects and weeds organically—and could produce food that is more nutritionally complete.

The technical descriptions sounded a little bit like an advanced botany course, but a quote from one of Wes's essays leaped out at us: "Will our grandchildren be able to eat in the year 2080?" For the answer to be yes, according to Wes, farming as we know it would have to be drastically transformed. Most of the institute's ideas date back to biblical times, such as using more animal power so farmers have the ability to breed their own plowing replacements, rather than having to scrap equipment and buy new machinery on a regular basis. It all sounds so retro, but it's surprisingly regarded as revolutionary and progressive.

After reading the institute's press kit, we knew we had to meet Dr. Jackson, whom *Life* magazine had named one of the most important people of the century. Good enough for us. Wes was obviously a busy man who traveled considerably on speaking tours, so I wasn't optimistic when I called him at the Land Institute. But before I could identify the Muzak song while on hold, Wes barked, "*Yallo?* Tell me your story."

Our request sounded ridiculous—even to me. "Hi. We'll be driving through your town in four days. Wanna meet with us?" My query was met with apprehension. "I spend my afternoon with you and I never hear from you again and you don't use anything I say, right?" Wes replied. There was a hint of a Kansas twang in his voice and he was a little on the gruff side. I quickly assured him that we would be using as much of the footage as we possibly could and that we thought his voice would be a valuable addition. "Fine, I'll see you at one o'clock on Friday afternoon, in my office," and he hung up. I had only one more question: Where was his office in relationship to Iowa?

The answer was about 400 miles southwest. We left Dorothy on Thursday afternoon and drove south on I-35 to stay with a friend's family in Kansas City. Kris and I had met the Rudds in Los Angeles when they had come to visit their son, our dear friend Paul. They are sweet, loving people and we were looking forward to spending a night or two in a home with a resident mom. We were not disappointed to find a full spread of tea, lox, and bagels waiting for us when we arrived after midnight.

We ate and talked and drank in the attention and affection. We were both a little weary at that point, having been on the road for almost two months. Then came the real treat: we got our own rooms! Kris slept in Paul's old bedroom on a pristine water bed. I got the guest room. It was heavenly.

Mrs. Rudd got up and made us breakfast before she went to work the next morning. We'd be making the 350-mile round trip from Kansas City to Salina, returning that night, and then leaving the next morning for Memphis via St. Louis.

It wasn't an incredibly stimulating ride, visually. Kansas is brown. In fact, the overall theme of the state seems to be wheat—everywhere. It is the color, the commerce, and the pride of the region. Kansas is also perfectly flat. The horizon does not fluctuate; the black of the road stretches to infinity. Driving across the state is a bit hypnotic, but fortunately someone was reading *Charlotte's Web* on the local public radio station, so we were set. It was one of my favorite chapters, when Wilbur is at the state fair competing against all of the other fattened pigs.

Salina wasn't what we expected. According to our map, it is smack in the middle of the country, so we assumed we'd find consummately charming Middle America, U.S.A. It was Middle America, all right, but not especially charming. There were several choices of fast food, the requisite Super Wal-Mart, and a few automotive stores. It was a little depressing and disappointing—when we were expecting just a hint of the Kansas that *The Wizard of Oz* nostalgia could conjure—but by this point, we were used to having our romantic notions deflated.

To me, Salina looked like the valleys of Southern California: flat, prefab, and uninspired. Undaunted, we found the correct dirt road leading to the Land Institute, only after following the wrong dirt road to a lone farmhouse where lines and lines of large wet bras dried in the dusty wind. To say it was hot out was an understatement. We stripped down to the minimal requirement of clothing and went in search of Dr. Wes Jackson.

We walked into the office, a small converted ranch-style home, and were greeted by a pleasant woman named Alice who said Wes was expecting us. While she called him, we looked around. One of the men who was working at "the Land," which is the institute's nickname among its residents, introduced himself. His name was Ken Warren and he said he'd heard we had made a trek to speak with their guru. "Is that what we should call him, too?" Kris kidded him.

" 'Resident philosopher' is the term we use," he answered half-seriously. "You're so fortunate he was able to be here," Ken said with a big smile. From the looks of things, "the Land" was an enormous endeavor, and from the posted list of books and articles published by Dr. Wes Jackson, the term "guru" actually seemed to be a consensus. Kris asked Ken how long he had been living there.

"About three months," he replied. "Brand-new. I've been a friend of 'the Land' for a good long time, hard not to be when you understand the logic of it. I finally just abandoned the other things that I was frivolously doing and came out here and decided to get into real work."

"What were you 'frivolously doing'?" Kris pressed.

"Oh, I was pretty much into the brokerage and banking business for the last twenty years. It's a big change, but it feels pretty good. Wes is kind of a loner right now. He wants to be on his own. So he has moved out of his office, which I'm now in, and moved over to a shed in the woods, Walden-like."

Kris commented that he must be going through his Thoreau stage. Ken laughed and asked if we'd ever met Wes before. We said no. "Oh, you're in for a treat," Ken went on. "He's done everything, a real Renaissance-type guy. I think you'll enjoy him."

Just then Alice got hold of Wes, who wanted us to meet him down at his house. Ken wished us luck and we went back to the car to get the equipment. An unsuspecting intern in his twenties walked by and Alice snagged him to take us over to Wes's house. His name was David, he had ragged strawberry-blonde hair with a full beard, and he walked like he was on a perpetual pogo stick. David sounded like he was from my recently abandoned Venice Beach. "I'm an intern here at 'the Land,' " he said. "It's pretty sweet."

After we loaded David down with our tripod and an extra bag, we followed his bobbing body down a path, through tall dry grasses and unidentifiable croakings from polycultural flying things. He asked us how we heard about Wes and whether we had read any of Wes's books. Since we had known of Wes for only a couple of days, we had to fudge. We didn't want to let on how little we actually knew about their guru.

"We're walking through the herbery right now," he pointed out. "A collection of native prairie plants that Marty, one of the ecologists, went around Kansas and collected. And this is our garden. Those really big plants are sunflowers getting ready to blossom—they're just great."

David was right, they were great, willowy and inviting. They were the only actual sunflowers we had seen in the Sunflower State.

"All of it's organic," he continued. "Even the seeds are native organic seeds. This is gama grass here, one of our candidate species for the perennial. That's a classroom and an intern garden next to it. And if you guys want to go for fresh vegetables, it's all for you. We have so much food in there, we can't eat it. It's all free picking.''

David made a sweeping gesture with his free hand and I saw Kris's eyes go wide. The garden was gorgeous, replete with huge tomatoes, their vines climbing five-foot stakes. Kris whispered that we should pick some vegetables to bring home to the Rudds. We arrived at Wes's little cabin on the prairie and said our good-byes.

Wes opened the squeaky screen door into his office and offered us metal chairs. He was a hearty-looking man with gray-ing hair, ruddy cheeks burned by wind and sun, well-worn farmer jeans, and a button-down shirt. His massive weath-ered hands suggested a lifetime of hard work. He was wearing more clothes than anyone should have been that day, but he showed no signs of discomfort. We, on the other hand, were looking a little frazzled, I'm sure. Kris rested the camera on Wes's desk, commenting that it was a nice hot Kansas day. Wes settled back into his swiv-eling desk chair, his large hands clasped casually behind his head, and answered, ''Just right. Keeps the riffraff out.'' He was grinning like the Cheshire cat. ''So you're the camera person?'' he asked Kris in a deep, rich Kansas growl.

''We're the *everything* people,'' she clarified. ''It's a two-woman show.''

''Well, I can see you must be entrepreneurial types. I mean, you're busting out on your own to do this. Your parents must think, 'Well, you know, they had to do it.' '' We all laughed. What followed was a good-natured inquisition about our quest, which I think we passed. We rattled off the list of the other interviewees and Wes asked us about Studs in particular. ''I bet he's a hoot.''

Kris confirmed his suspicion. ''A *very* big hoot.'' Wes went on to say that Studs's books had had a lasting impact on him, especially *Working*. We agreed.

We went outside to get Wes set up. It took us a long time to figure out the best option for power in the middle of the Kansas prairie, and we apologized for the delay. But Wes waited patiently, kidding us while we scrambled. ''It's okay. I always like to help the young complete their assignments, even when they are self-imposed.'' We found an extension cord and I began by asking Wes to explain his work in layman's terms.

"Well, our work is different than the usual brand of sustainable agriculture, in the sense that we look at the way natural ecosystems have worked, and we pay attention to data coming from tropical rain forests, alpine meadows, coral reefs, and our friends working with the traditional crops. If you look at the way the native prairie works, it runs on sunlight and features material recycling. And contrast that, say with a wheat field, which is dependent upon the extractive economy—the use of fossil fuels, the use of chemicals that are harmful to humans and livestock.

Wes Jackson

"So we're saying that a future agriculture ought to be based on the principles of natural ecosystems, based on the way the world has worked for millions of years. We've only had agriculture eight to ten thousand years, and during that period of time, agriculture has undercut the very basis of its own existence through soil erosion. So we say we're working on the problem *of* agriculture, rather than working on the problems *in* agriculture."

We knew from what we had read that Wes's railing against annual crops had occasionally made him unpopular with the mainstream farming community. According to Wes, King Wheat, the local cash cow, was one of the biggest offenders—a statement that did not improve Wes's popularity with fellow farmers.

Wes went on to discuss the mission statement of the Land Institute.

"When we began, it was: 'Devoted to a search for sustainable alternatives for agriculture, energy, shelter, and waste management.' Now we have a mission statement that says something to the effect of when people, land, and community are as one, all three benefit. But when they become competing interests, all three are exploited.

"The ecosystem is used as a conceptual tool and is applied to people, land, and community becoming one thing. We understand wholeness when we talk about the liver; one liver cell does not a liver make. We understand wholeness when we talk about all the organs put together to make up a body. But when we talk about wholeness that has to do with trees, and people, and soil, and microbes, and so on, the concept eludes us.

"But we think natural ecosystems are the organizing principle. See, if you just think about community in that equation—if people can get consoled by going to one another instead of going to a shopping mall, think about what that means as far as how much less money they need to live. I was just among the Amish last week in northeastern Ohio, and the only food on their table that didn't come from their own farms was the peaches.''

I'm not sure if many people would necessarily cite the centuries-old agricultural philosophy of the Amish as an example of progressive farming. But the recurring theme of community had already been established in our journey by many people—whether it was Studs's definition of participatory democracy, Dorothy's suggestion that we must learn to share the American dream with the rest of the world, or Ben and Jerry's beliefs in social responsibility. Kris and I were learning to expect that almost everyone we would meet prescribed community as a panacea. Wes's solution was a community of *all* of the elements that make up life, not just people.

The heat was so incredible that I worried about Kris standing so long with the camera. She was looking a little flushed, but Wes seemed immune, happy to bake. Just the same, Kris asked Wes if he wanted her to get him a drink. "Where is it?" he asked.

"I don't know—in your house?"

Wes laughed, saying, "That's what I thought." Kris laughed right back, saying he didn't really think we carried a cooler around, did he? I interrupted their banter by asking Wes to describe another of the Land's projects, the reestablishment of the small town.

"Yeah," he said, "I can talk about the demise of small towns in rural communities. I think Wendell Berry said it well in *The Unsettling of America*, his very great book: 'We came with vision, but not with sight.' We came with visions of former places, but not the sight to see where we are. He also said that as we came across the continent, cutting the forests and plowing the prairies, we didn't know what we were doing, because we didn't know what we were *un*doing. Wendell went on to say in that book, with the title's double meaning, that first came the conqueror, then came the settler, and the settler effectively turned the native into a surplus people.

"We never really atoned for that sin. And the consequence is that we're now all candidates for surplus people. Dan Luten wrote a paper in which he said that we came as a poor people to a seemingly empty land that was rich. And that we've built our institutions based on that perception of reality. Poor people. Empty land. Rich. And now we've become rich people in an increasingly poor land that's filling up. So, the consequence of the industrialization of agriculture, and greater agricultural efficiency, is that these people who are now on the land will be the new surplus people. And so they've effectively, because of the nature of the economic system, been driven into the cities."

Wes's notion of surplus people was telling in its simplicity. We took the land from Native Americans and decimated it, ignoring their practices of keeping it fertile; consequentially, they became "surplus" or excess people. They no longer fit into the economic culture and were therefore destroyed culturally, relegated to exist traditionally only on the fringe. Now, we were doing the same thing to our family farmers through the industrialization of farming and management of land. They become excess, rendered purposeless; therefore unnecessary and have no choice but to move to the cities. This migration kills the small towns, which in turn kills the agricultural community. It is a circle of demolition that we began hundreds of years ago and are racing to close. Wes explained the consequences further.

"The consequence, of course, is devastating, as Wendell Berry has pointed out," he said. "Now we're losing our *cultural* seed stock—the people with the know-how. Because agriculture is a product of culture. And losing this cultural seed stock to the likes of Silicon Valley, where kids grow up in shopping malls and Little League, and worse. Now the cultural information that was hard-won over the last eight to ten thousand years, the discipline and so on, is lost by treating crops and livestock only as accoutrements of civilization.

"We think that the place to begin to reverse this is at the community level, because when we were creatures in the Upper Paleolithic, we were tribal. And community is civilization's upscaling of the tribe. And community works the same way the liver works—without thought and on demand. Community we can do well, and it seems to me that the possibility of a different economic order that's not dependent on an extractive economy is inherent in that."

The elements of an ecosystem work together to sustain one another. Why shouldn't groups of people? Wes's argument was that culture and nature have common ground that needs to be reclaimed. It was a convincing argument, one that gave testament to our own experience of uncovering innumerable connections between ostensibly dissimilar strangers.

Wes also explained that Wendell Berry is a good friend of his. We talked about Wendell's discussion of the husbandry of the land. Wes had some ideas on the topic.

"The dominant ideology now is economics," he declared. "There was a time when the church controlled our thinking, and we built cathedrals to the glory of the church. And after the Enlightenment, the nation-state dominated our thinking, although people still went to church. I'm speaking about Western civilization. That peaked out with Hitler and World War II. Then it's economics that dominates our thinking. So as the church built the cathedrals, the nation-state built the capitals, and economics built the shopping malls. We're saying that ecology ought to be the next round, and this time it would be wilderness that dominates—that not made by human hands, unlike the cathedral, or the capital, or the shopping mall. This is a practical necessity we're talking about. This is something that our future suste-nance and health are going to be dependent on."

We talked a little bit about the roots of the American dream that stemmed from a land-gobbling Manifest Destiny.

"The American dream," Wes explained, "has been based on the idea of either infinite resources or infinite substitutability—if we give any thought to it at all. We've lived with this great illusion of abundance. Where there isn't abundance, we'll just be smarter. And then comes the substitutability.

"Manifest Destiny, always looking westward . . . Right out here on the north end of Salina is old Highway 40, and the street is called Pacific Street because it was called the Pacific Highway. I think of that every time I cross Pacific. This country was always looking to where more land was, no matter that that land was dry.''

Wes was revising our romantic notions about farm life in the middle of the country. He spoke in terms of land rape and a dangerous lack of concern. We hadn't been unaware of the price the land has paid in the name of opportunity, but it was wholly different sitting on a prairie with the dry smell of grass in the air, the soil under your feet, and the buzzing of insects in your ears. Wes's words struck deep.

Later, Wes's fears would be echoed by Willie Nelson, who would tell us that every civilization in the past has collapsed because of soil erosion and the inability to feed its people. It seemed that the Highway Commission of Kansas was definitely not taking that long view, because it had proudly posted signs that read 1 KANSAS FARMER FEEDS 101 PEOPLE PLUS YOU at intervals along the road. I had read that Wes objected to this slogan, so I asked him about it.

''It's an outright falsehood. You have to be very careful that you don't use the word 'lie,' because I don't think people meant to lie when they made the signs. What they mean is that one farmer who relies on the extractive economy of fossil fuels, chemicals, and machinery, plus all the people and energy that go into manufacturing those pieces, feeds a bunch of people.''

Wes continued, ''See, the problem with the industrial mind is that it's predicated on the assumption that knowledge is adequate. And we all know that we are billions of times more ignorant than knowledgeable. I mean, the hole in the ozone layer comes out of a knowledge-based worldview; global warming comes out of a knowledge-based worldview; acid rain comes out of a knowledge-based worldview. Well, if we start with the recognition that we're fundamentally ignorant and always will be, then an ignorance-based worldview—which is our long suit—would force us to remember things, hope for second chances, keep the scale small, and be far more tentative than we are right now.''

I had promised Wes on the phone that we would occupy only thirty minutes of his time. We had already gone way over, but Wes didn't seem in a rush, and Kris and I loved listening to the way huge ideas poured out of Wes's mouth as naturally as most people recite the alphabet or the Pledge of Allegiance. He was a disarming combination of Mr. Green Jeans, some of my more interesting college professors, and a proselytizing evangelical.

"What is it about the land that makes you so passionate?" I asked.

Wes paused. He rubbed his hand across his face and then answered matter-of-factly, "Well, I have children. I've got a grandchild. About to have another. What could I do that's better? What else is there to do? I mean, in a way what I'm trying to sell is a kind of insurance. It seems to me ordinary prudence would say, 'Let's hedge our bets. Wouldn't the culture want to have an ace in the hole?' "

He changed gears and continued, "The agriculture we're talking about, even the sustainable agriculture, was validated by the National Academy of Sciences in a major report way back about 1990. This is not some agriculture for a bunch of hippie farmers anymore—the most prestigious scientific body in the world is validating this work. So if our side just keeps trying to make sense, keeps pushing it, maybe this whole culture will come to its senses, particularly the politicians.

"Right now, I think the politicians are mostly chasing their tails on nonissues. The health issue is important. The abortion issue is important. But why isn't soil erosion an important issue? Why isn't chemical contamination of the countryside an important issue? And why isn't fossil fuel dependency an important issue? When the fossil fuel is gone, if we haven't figured some things out, we're going to be going to nukes. And if we go to nukes, we've got to repeal Murphy's Law. So there's a whole bunch of stuff that just seems to me is not in the national discussion at anything close to the level it ought to be."

I asked Wes why he thought people were so resistant to embrace the facts and the institute's practices.

"Well," he replied, "let's put ourselves at Kitty Hawk that day, December 17, 1903. I think there were only six bystanders there, and I don't think they knew the significance of what was going on. But if we had been standing there, wouldn't we say, 'You'll never get that thing to carry as many people as a train'? We'd probably all say that. The Wright Brothers could not have imagined the 747, the Piper Cub, the SST, the Learjet—any of those things. Well, I think people probably look at our work—and even though we've shown perennialism can provide high seed yield, that a polyculture can outyield a monoculture, and that there's no trade-off cost—that may be a Kitty Hawk, but it's not acres and acres of corn. It's not the train carrying a lot of people. To go from the principle to the expanded possibility is a difficult jump.

"You see, that would be a paradigm shift. I think that's the right word to use there: 'paradigm.' Taking the earth out of the center and putting the sun at the center. In a sense, what did that matter?" He laughed before continuing, "But it does matter how you treat that top two or three inches of soil that stand between us and starvation."

Kris brought the camera down and sighed deeply from physical and mental exhaustion. The heat was taking its toll on us both, but I was more worried about Kris, because she had been standing so long with the camera. I knew it was time to start wrapping things up. I asked Wes what he thought the future of the land and farming would be if we failed to embrace the ideas he was suggesting.

"Well, I don't know what's going to happen to land and to farming, any more than I can predict the arrangement of the cars of two wrecked freights that have hit one another head-on. All you can say is there's gonna be an unpleasant mess.

"We have a local auctioneer here that's been auctioneering for thirty years and sold a lot of farms at farm sales. He was able to tell us about the blood and guts that goes along with the change in farming from family to corporate. He says it used to be, at the farm sales, there'd be the dad and the son. Now the sons aren't there. Farmers are getting older. There's gonna be more and more corporate-held farms. Wendell likened it to everybody in a room fighting with one another, and everybody fights until there's only one man standing, then he goes around and picks everybody else's pockets. What we really need is a whole bunch of people standing.

"So I do think that there is a danger to a sustainable food supply. Now, that's hard to imagine. But if you jump off the Empire State Building and get all the way to the tenth floor, you may say, 'Well, everything's going all right so far.' It's a matter of a perspective. It might not be that quick sudden stop that we're looking at, but there could be a pretty serious splatter."

Wes finished his assessment of the future of farming: "If you're living beyond your means in your household, you want to know about it. We're clearly living beyond our means as a nation. We can understand this at the household level, but when we expand it to the national level, we just deny it. Freud said no person believes in his own death. So the gift of denial is part of our problem.

"Aldo Leopold said that there are two spiritual dangers which come from not owning a farm: the belief that heat comes from a stove and that food comes from a grocery store." Wes snickered. "Dan Luten was telling me that there was someone who said, 'Why do we need farms so long as we have supermarkets?'" he finished incredulously, shaking his head.

We asked Wes one last question. If he were traveling with us, what would he ask the people we met?

"I'm always interested in whether somebody's joined the fight or not. I mean, that's how we picked our students here. We want them to be smart and to have joined the fight. And there are ways you can find out whether they've joined the fight. Like, what are their passions?"

Wes had summed up a good portion of the purpose for our journey. We wanted to find out who had "joined the fight," what their fights were, and why they were fighting. We were finding that the people we had wanted to meet were—more often than not—warriors.

Wes had earned his doctorate in genetics, coupled it with his own version of responsibility, and joined the fight against what he called the "violence to creation." He came back to his roots to challenge what he saw as the destructive, golden monocultural annual crops of Kansas wheat to build an experiment that is

Walden for him and Mecca for his students. One of the Internet articles we read described Wes as "part bison and part Isaiah the prophet," in reference to his call for a new vision of global agriculture that even he thinks will not work for another hundred years. Yet he is unwavering in his appeal to farmers to stop relying so heavily on human cleverness and instead to rely on nature's wisdom.

We walked back to Wes's office with him. He decided he didn't have time to show us around, so he picked up his pink phone and arranged for us to take the self-guided tour. Then Wes said he was on to us. He said that obviously we knew if we promised only a twenty- or thirty-minute interview and got someone going who "loved to hear themselves talk," that they would "carry on with senile rapture." He called us tricksters and we admitted he'd figured us out. He walked us to the door and said, "All right, ladies. A blessing on you. I'm with your spirit. Good luck with your project." And the squeaky screen door closed behind us.

Kris and I walked away from Wes's little cabin near the Smoky Hill River and went to pick some tomatoes. As we were leaving, we heard Wes talking on the phone from the garden, joking and laughing. Kris still had the camera on as we passed the blackboard that Wes used during outdoor classes. There was an eraser's swish through the middle of the sentence, but we could still make it out, and Kris muttered that she hoped the camera could read it. It said: I SUSPECT THAT AMERICANS ASK, "WHAT IS SACRED?"

(Kristin)

I remember the first time I was bitten by the open road bug. I was eight and my grandpa initiated our fishing trip ritual one day after he reached his threshold with my eccentric grandmother. My mother and I lived a mile away from my grandparents in Albuquerque at the time, and I came home from school one Friday to find Gramps on our couch eating cookies and milk, apparently waiting for me. "There are too many chiefs in this outfit," he said. "How's about you and I go fishin'?"

And so we did. From then on, I always kept a secret fishing bag packed for emergencies. Escaping with Gramps was the kind of fun I imagined Pippi Long-stocking had on a *regular* basis. We focused only on our own unearthly sagas. Grandpa was a cowboy at heart and the first person I met who passionately loved to drive. With that vital ranch and road combination, he always insisted on hitting the road no later than 5 A.M.—cowboy hours, I guess. In the quiet early morning dark, we would pack the car with the usual cream cheese and olive sandwiches, vanilla wafers, ginger ale, Velveeta, pickles, crackers, fishing poles, tackle box, our fishing licenses, and Hank Williams tapes. And we would begin our race against the sunrise. The ritual of our fishing trips was the one thing Gramps and I could always count on.

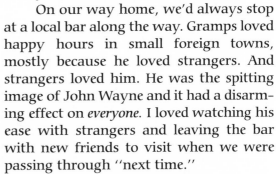

On our way home, we'd always stop at a local bar along the way. Gramps loved happy hours in small foreign towns, mostly because he loved strangers. And strangers loved him. He was the spitting image of John Wayne and it had a disarming effect on *everyone.* I loved watching his ease with strangers and leaving the bar with new friends to visit when we were passing through "next time."

Grandpa was a retired Air Force colonel and had a dignity about his mysterious ice-blue eyes. He loved America, and as we drove on roads big and small, he instilled in me a respect for the liberties we easily enjoy on our "free soil." Living in New Mexico, I found it was impossible to ignore the details of Native American history missing from our schoolbooks. Gramps would explain—as best he could, having his own strain of prejudice—the plight of the Indian and the loss their people endured in order for us to live on this great land "settled" by our ancestors. He would talk about the Founding Fathers and what they intended this country to be like and then joke about the Founding Mothers, who were *really* the ones in charge. And on those roads, when the sun was lighting our path, he would let me drive, as long as I promised to never tell my mother.

From the perspective of those tall, swiveling bar stools and driving those Southwestern roads with a pretense of "catching fish," I developed a curiosity that would never go away. Although we truly did cast many lines, to this day, he and I have never caught one fish. Gramps and I haven't been able to take many road trips together in the last few years. But at twenty-six, it was my longing for the familiar feel of the untraveled road that steered me to *Anthem*.

WARREN LEWIS

MAYOR OF WARREN'S TOWN • OWNER OF WARREN'S PLACE

NORTH MEMPHIS, TENNESSEE

(Shainee)

After we left Kansas, we went to St. Louis, where we stayed with the Clarkes, the parents of another friend of ours. This time we were spoiled Southern-style, with cheese grits awaiting our signature midnight arrival. We spent the next day with Carolyn Clarke driving around the city in the rain trying to find a riverboat pilot to interview on the great Mississippi. We didn't have any luck, so we hit the road late that afternoon.

Kris and I headed southeast on I-55 toward Tennessee. Our destination was Memphis, to meet with a man named Warren Lewis. I learned of him because he was the subject of a great short film by a friend of mine called *Burn Heads*. Warren had gained more than fifteen minutes of fame for his hairdressing technique of burning hair, rather than simply cutting or shaving it. He had appeared on talk shows and in newspapers for burning famous heads and had leveraged this small good fortune to his advantage, claiming a position of leadership in his community. Warren's Place grew from a barber shop to a barber shop/T-shirt store/soon-to-open deli/beeper dealer/community center. Warren employed as many as he could and was always ready to expand. Eventually, the city of Memphis designated about ten acres of North Memphis as Warren's Town, appointing Warren the mayor. Warren had turned his little shop into a city hall.

We arrived in Memphis way after midnight on a Sunday. We had planned to spend an hour or so at Warren's the next morning and then devote our afternoon to enjoying the city of Memphis *without* our cameras. We thought we'd have an easygoing, informative day like regular tourists, with a stop at the Lorraine Motel, the site of Martin Luther King, Jr.'s, assassination and now the National Civil Rights Museum, and a perfunctory stop at Memphis's most famous attraction: Graceland. Par for the *Anthem* course, we had no idea what we were in for.

It was over 100 Southern degrees outside when we pulled up in front of WAR-
REN'S PLACE—HOME OF ORIGINAL HAIRSTYLES. North Memphis was an uninspired section

of town that felt thick with humidity.
There were several housing projects, some
fast-food restaurants, and not enough
businesses. We parked in back of the shop,
but when I got out, a man who seemed to
be guarding the front door said I needed to
move the car to where he could keep an
eye on it. Warren had warned me about
the area on the phone, but like most risky
neighborhoods, North Memphis looked
more forgotten during daylight hours
than dangerous.

A couple of guys had gathered at the
front door of the shop by the time I had
reparked the car. They made up a good
part of the staff: tailor, shoe shine man,
several barbers, T-shirt man, and beeper
man. We were led inside the building, through a small video arcade, and found
Warren Lewis holding court with a few locals at his barber chair. *We Are the World*
was playing and under the fluorescent lights stood a not quite tall, thin black
man with a white beard and very thick glasses. He waved his elegant long fingers,
motioning us to come closer. "Well, we finally meet. What I'd like for you-all to
do, if you would, is to look at the whole place. Look at it and then we can do what
you need to do."

Warren's voice is somewhat surprising when you meet him in person. He
speaks with authority, but his register is usually high-pitched and he has a bit of
a lisp. Nonetheless, he was the mayor/boss/grandfather/barber of the close to fifty
people in his shop and he had an indisputable presence. Kris and I followed Warren's direction and walked around the shop for a while, each with our own camera,
speaking with the various merchants of Warren's Place. I realized that the shop
could have doubled as a successful strip mall if the rooms were actually storefronts
rather than part of an ever-expanding house. Warren still lives on the top floor. I
stopped to talk to the very amiable Mr. T, who was manning the T-shirt counter.
When we discovered that we were both Rutgers alumni, he *really* wanted to chat
and told me several "History of Warren's" stories. My favorite was about how
Warren began the craze of burning football numbers, names of teams, and so on
into the heads of local boys. I guess to Warren's other titles we would have to add
trendsetter. I let the camera glide by all of the faces in the shop, from the mothers
waiting for appointments, to the boys who had recently been added to the barber
staff, to all of the children who were milling around and playing video games. It
seemed that several of the employees brought their children to work with them,

so "daycare center" must also go on the list of services provided by Warren Lewis. The kids, fascinated by the camera, followed us around, asking, "Are we in it?"

Warren's name was being called from all over the building. He was obviously in demand, but he caught up with us in the newest addition to his place: the deli. "Everything you see here is going to be expanded in a big way. This is going to be the deli, sitting room, and all that. Mm-hmm. I want you to see upstairs. We're just getting it all together. You met Mr. T?"

Warren was brimming with enthusiasm and chatted all the way up the stairs. We arrived on the second floor and entered into a shrine of sorts. There were several awards and newspaper clippings hung on sky-blue walls, along with framed photos of Warren burning celebrity heads like Jay Leno and Jesse Jackson. Warren led us from wall to wall, explaining that he had appeared on the *Late Show with David Letterman* and *The Gong Show*, too. Apparently, Warren had been as far as Japan to display his pyro-talents. One wall was devoted entirely to the blueprints for the future of Warren's Town. It was impressive and we both oohed and aahed.

We decided to do the interview in the back of the shop, which was deserted and, for the moment, relatively quiet. We sat Warren in a barber chair and he yelled to a young stylist in the next room to turn down the soap opera she and her client were watching. Warren began by giving us a thumbnail sketch of his background.

"Originally, I was born in Philadelphia, Mississippi, sixty-two years ago. We moved from Philadelphia down to Mole Head and I left there and came to Memphis in '51. I walked into a shop and asked if the man had an extra barber chair. He said, 'Yeah, I have a chair.' Asked if I could have it, he said, 'Sure.' That's where it all got started, and I've always had a lot of customers ever since. Only fifty cents in Memphis for a haircut back then—I got to keep half. I made eighteen dollars, went back to Mississippi, brought my wife-to-be back here, and got married. So I've been here forty-two years now—be forty-three in December."

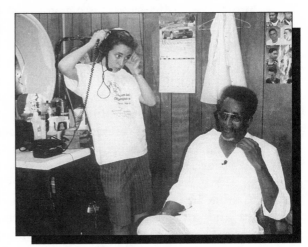

The mayor of Warren's Town

"So all the things you see me doing is original, like the burning heads and stuff. I didn't go to barber school, but I've taught a lot of people how to do hair. I'm from a family of seventeen and my mother used to kill a lot of chickens. Sunday mornings, we would take a piece of paper or shuck or something to burn the feathers off. That's how I got the idea of burning hair."

Warren went on to explain why he moved to Memphis and why he stayed.

"Oh, I like Memphis. Wherever you are, you have to adjust and adapt to the environment. I had never been to a city before I came to Memphis. I couldn't explore my ideas in Mississippi, so I came on up here. This is a town where there's opportunity for people that's wanting to get up and do something. You know what I'm saying?"

Warren was a very effective advertisement for Memphis. He was obviously very proud of his community. Warren told us how he got started working in—and for—the community, beginning with a youth service and a food bank. "About fifteen years ago, I was working as a special deputy sheriff, and they asked me what I want to be doing here in North Memphis. I got the idea of Warren's Town, so I could help many people with food and clothing. Isaac Hayes was working with me at the time. He would fund me and I would help people. We was talking to the city and to the county, and they passed a resolution to name this whole area after me. We went to them, and they named it Warren's Town. What I plan to do is clean it up. Make it livable and presentable to people who come through. If I make the first step, then people will come in and help. But if you not doing nothing, people not gonna help you do nothing. That's the way I feel about it. Mm-hmm."

Warren said that Warren's Town was made up of about ten acres. There were plans for a wedding chapel, assembly hall, and several stores. "I got so many people attached to me, and I can't let the whole neighborhood down. This is crucial. We need jobs for kids out here twelve to seventeen. If you give them a job, they'll work. We used to have two streetcars sitting in front of the shop that would take kids from one project to another to clean up around. The projects would pay me, and I would divide the money equally among the kids. That's how Youth Services got started. Now, Youth Services is doing a big job around here in Memphis. The people down at City Hall said, 'Look, we want to help you,' and took over the program.

"The trick is not to give up. Sears give me two truckloads of toys and put it in my warehouse one evening. The next morning there wasn't a toy in there. Somebody stole it all. But I don't let it get to me. Next time we'll get them to the children. So that's where we are at this point. Now, the next step, if you give me about six months more, then some of these projects I was telling you about will be in progress."

Warren finished his discussion of the North Memphis community by telling us that Elvis used to live three blocks away and had a delivery route, so Warren occasionally saw him around. He said the neighborhood had great potential to be more than what it is, given its proximity to downtown Memphis.

I asked Warren where he drew his faith and how he thought he kept hope alive. "I don't know. It's strange how things happen, but it's all comin' together, as you can see. 'So a man thinks, so is he.' You can tell how I think by what I'm trying to do. You got to plant some seeds in order to reap the harvest, no doubt about it. If a man don't work, a man don't eat. Mm-hmm."

Warren went on to say that it was still possible for young people to be successful. He explained that the work ethic and attitude of people hadn't really changed. "You've got to be able to hang in there. And have to have stickability to do things, you can't be no fly-by-night."

Warren pointed to a teenage girl walking across the next room. "There's my granddaughter. My granddaughter's fifteen, she got two jobs, she drives, she's smart in school. Only fifteen years old. But like I'm saying, she could be lazy like a lot of young ladies. The poor box's gonna be with us always, but they don't have to be *that* poor. You have a choice in this country to be anything you wanted. I want to be a role model for some of the kids out here. If I can just help one or two of the kids, then I think my living won't be in vain."

It was obvious that Warren was keeping a lot of people busy, because it was getting louder as we went on. There were the sounds of electric razors, laughing and gossiping and children playing tag. Warren seemed mostly oblivious, maintaining a cool camera composure. Once in a while he would finish a thought and snap his head toward the next room, yelling, "Keep it down in there! We got equipment going in here!" There would be a titter of young women's giggles and then a hush that would gradually give way to the same decibel level of activity. Then Warren would yell out again. It didn't seem to bother him, so it certainly didn't bother us. I asked Warren what he had found influential in his youth.

"When I was growing up, I wasn't really around very many people. We was farming and all. One of the reasons I left farming was we would make about fifty or sixty bales of cotton a year. And at the end of each year, my daddy would get what you call a settlement out of the crop, and the man would tell my dad, 'If ya'll work a little harder, you get out of debt next year.' And I still don't understand why: all that work and no money."

Warren paused to think about what he was trying to convey to us and leaned into the camera, speaking more softly. "One of the things I'd like to say on the record is that one day my throat was swollen, my ears were swollen, I had three abscess on one of my jaw tooth back here. We were living in the country, picking the cotton. I asked my boss lady for two dollars to get my tooth pulled, and she said, 'Can't you pull it yourself?'" Warren paused. "But what hurts people helps them. If she had given me the two dollars, I probably would still be there, picking her cotton.

"Sometimes I wonder why I'm the only one in business out of all my brothers and sisters. It's not easy, but no one told me it would be easy. Ya know, who would have thought, come from fifty-cent haircut to fifty-dollar haircut? I've almost touched all across the world since I've been doing hair. I've burned my way from Mississippi to New York to Hollywood to Japan. I was even supposed to go to London. But the bigger you get, the smaller you feel. You've got to humble yourself to a certain point."

"Do you believe that there is an American dream?" Kris chimed in.

Warren looked back at her matter-of-factly and said, "Mm-hmm, that's what I'm doing." He chuckled. "Yeah, I believe in the American dream. But see what happened, a lot of people in doubt about the American dream. But they don't know they got to do something first. 'Ask not what your country can do for you, ask what you can do for your country,' so to speak. That's the way the American dream is gonna have to function."

Warren continued with a smirk, "Oh, I would like to *not* work. Like a lot of people. But I can sleep at night now by me working like I do. I ain't got no problem with that. So the American dream is based on you. It's open. It's wide open for anybody. It's up for grabs for a person like me in North Memphis."

We talked about the problem of people who do work hard but still can't get ahead.

"If I'm making thirty-four dollars a week, thirty-two dollars I carry home to two kids. It's very difficult getting ahead making minimum wage. But at the same time, how do a person with four or five kids making minimum wage make it, while a person making fifteen dollars an hour can't make it? You have to balance the budget, balance your money. There's no way around it. You can't have all the luxury cars, the jewelry. Look how much I got on, all these diamonds." Warren laughed as he wiggled his bare spidery fingers at us.

We told Warren that we sometimes asked people what they would do as President of the United States. He was very excited by the prospect. His face lit up as he almost jumped out of his chair. The idea was evidently not a new one to Warren.

"If I was the President, I could make a *good* one! This is what I believe—I'd stop everything, smooth everything, balance everything out, and start over. That's the only way! I'd try to get everybody working. Back when I was a little boy, they had a thing called the WPA. People cleaned up the countrysides and all. Everybody made some money. There's no reason for a well, healthy person in this country that shouldn't have no job. It's no reason, and that's the way I feel about it. This is for the record. Why can't that be here? I might need the presidency to do it. Now Jay Leno says I need to burn the President's hair." Warren laughed and continued. "But if I could just be the President for a while, I believe I can make things better. It would be no worse."

Warren stopped for a second to gather his thoughts and then finished with a fireworks finale of aphorisms and biblical references. "It really tears my heart up to see some of the things that goes on. The houses in this neighborhood haven't been painted in forty years. Forty years. So every time I get ten dollars, I invest eight. Every time you want a Coke, you can't drink a Coke, you gotta drink some water. Water's better for ya anyway. So what I'm saying is: every penny you get you can't waste it. The Bible speaks of waste. You know, when He fed all those people fish and philo and bread, and He had them pick up all the fragments. They had to pick up all the fragments and carry it with them. They didn't leave no scrap food. I just wish things were different. Since they not, if things ain't right, you have to make them right. Somebody throw you a lemon, make some lemonade out of it, right? If they throw sand on ya, get some more and make some concrete.''

When Warren broke into a wide grin, we realized he was done. Kris let the camera rest on her hip and expelled a big sigh, telling Warren that he should have his own show. Warren couldn't think of a better compliment and answered proudly, ''You can see I'm not very camera-shy.'' We all chuckled and broke down the equipment.

When we asked Warren if he would show us how he burns heads, he readily agreed and told us purposefully, ''Follow me.'' We followed Warren into the shop where he informed an unsuspecting young boy that he needed a haircut. The boy looked at the camera and sheepishly climbed onto the chair, trying not to crack a proud smile. Warren showed us a box of the long white cathedral candles that he uses as fire wands. He lit two and explained how he can use them separately or together. The boy didn't flinch as Warren expertly combed his hair with flames, his head beginning to smoke. It was odd and fascinating.

''Does anyone ever get burned?'' I asked.

''I burned a man once,'' Warren responded vaguely without removing his attention from the boy's head. ''But now, this boy has real thick hair. Everybody don't burn the same.'' Kris watched, intrigued, and asked if burning was easier than cutting. Warren said it was for him, then said to me, ''Like for your hair, I burn the split ends, it stays even longer.''

Warren and Kenny

Kris chortled, coaxing me, ''Shainee, I think you need a haircut.'' I decided to take a rain check. It was time to leave and we asked around for directions to the Lorraine Motel. Mr. T, who was lingering at the door, responded, ''It's not called the Lorraine Motel anymore. It's called the National Civil Rights Museum. Yeah, it's on . . . Hold on. Kenny! Do you know how to get to the Civil Rights Museum?''

By this time, Warren's chair was occupied by a man in a glittery blouse circa 1976 who was getting his hair relaxed: Kenny. ''Second Street to Vance, make a right on Vance, and a left on Mulberry. Is Mulberry a one-way street, Mr. Lewis?'' The men bickered back and forth about the best route to take to the infamous street that is home to the Lorraine Motel. We eventually left the salon with Warren calling after us, ''Ya'll stay in touch now.'' We promised we would.

Our hour with Warren had turned into the entire afternoon. Kris and I finally made it into the car. As we discusssed our impressions of the obviously well-loved man with a youthful exuberance, we tried to follow the conflicting directions to the infamous Lorraine Motel. Kris and I were both starving at this point, and wrestled with the idea of stopping for food, but we were worried the museum might close before we got there. So we decided to go without and drove in a low-blood-sugar stupor to Mulberry Street.

MARVIN BOOKER

MINISTER • VOLUNTEER NATIONAL CIVIL RIGHTS MUSEUM

MEMPHIS, TENNESSEE

(Shainee)

The area surrounding the Lorraine Motel was not what we expected. There were hardly any signs of life or commerce and the once-beautiful brick homes and businesses have been replaced by a ghost town. It was an ominous feeling to know that this part of the city had once been bustling and thriving, the place where Dr. Martin Luther King, Jr., always chose to stay when visiting. I wondered if his assassination had marked the beginning of the demise of the area.

As we approached the Lorraine Motel, we saw a proud polished testament to modern architecture attached to a fifties-style motor lodge. The museum had been built as an addition to the motel and featured a futuristic-looking powder-blue finish that shone blindingly in the sunlight.

As soon as we got out of the car, my eyes focused on a flowered wreath mounted on the second-floor balcony of the motel. It was impossible to miss as you approached the museum's entrance, a large white circle of flowers marking the place where Dr. Martin Luther King, Jr., was struck by a fatal bullet on April 4, 1968. I felt a blanket of sadness wrap around me as we approached the spot. The impact was absolutely unexpected and I will swear that even today, the horror and loss of that terrible moment in America's history lives at that motel. It grips you and overwhelms you the moment you step foot on the grounds.

When we went inside the museum, a sweet young girl informed us that there was no admission fee that day due to a special event. We were relieved, considering the fact that we had three dollars between us. She had a Pepsi in her hand when she informed us that, no, the museum had no vending machines or snack bar. Now we were in big trouble. I had begun to see black spots from faintness and the girl must have sensed our desperation. I handed her a dollar and pleaded for two more Pepsis from wherever hers had come from. She half-tried to explain that the machine was for employees only, before she disappeared and returned with the cans. We thanked her as if she were Ed McMahon at our door and sat down—at 5 P.M.—to savor our first meal of the day. After a few satisfying sips, I almost forgot the heat, the humidity, the sadness, and the empty belly. People eyed our sodas longingly as they passed by and we smiled like teacher's pets. One man came over, wiping his brow, and asked where we had gotten the drinks. We told him of our reconnaissance work and when Kris offered him a sip, he accepted and sat down.

Reverend Marvin Lewis Booker was dressed in a three-piece, light-wool, double-breasted blue suit on this uncomfortably warm day. He spoke with an unusual cadence and asked us what we were doing. We explained that we were in the middle of making a film, traveling around the country, and had stopped to take in the museum. We asked him about the tables we'd seen set up in front of the museum.

Reverend Booker explained that various groups were handing out leaflets, protesting the fact that the government poured millions of dollars into the museum and left the surrounding neighborhood to rot. He then identified himself as a volunteer at the National Civil Rights Museum, whose job it was to deliver the Reverend Martin Luther King, Jr.'s, speeches to visitors. Kris and I looked at each other wearily. Reverend Booker accepting a sip of Kris's Pepsi was what James Redfield would call "no coincidence." So much for being tourists. It was time to retrieve "the twins" from their brief nap.

We followed Reverend Booker outside and he stood in front of the plaque that commemorates Dr. King's speeches. The second-story balcony where Dr. King was shot hung over Marvin's head. We asked him to explain what he does. "Well, I'm unemployed right now but I am a minister of the Gospel and before becoming a preacher in 1979, God gave me the ability to do Dr. King's speeches and the heart to deliver them as if Dr. King himself were delivering them again. So this is what I do. I see to it that the words of Dr. Martin Luther King are kept alive.

"Ralph Abernathy placed here at this motel, about twenty-five years ago, this plaque, and it says, 'They said, one to another, behold, here cometh the dreamer. Let us slay him and we shall see what will become of his dreams.' " Marvin pointed to the plaque next to him. It was apparent that he was about to give us an example of his talents. As he prepared to orate, his entire body tensed and he seemed to grow three inches taller. What followed was a very moving experience.

" 'I say to you today, my friends, even though we face the difficulties of today and tomorrow, I still have a dream . . . It is a dream deeply rooted in the American dream. . . .' " The familiar first words of Dr. King's famous speech rolled out into the hot Memphis afternoon. The entire speech followed, and even though I'd heard the words countless times I was rapt. Marvin emulated Dr. King's inflection precisely. By the time he finished, the ghost of Dr. King truly walked among us. Marvin ended with Dr. King's words, lifted from a spiritual, " 'Free at last! Free at last! Thank God Almighty, we are free at last!' "

Marvin returned to his body and was met by transfixed stares. A group of people had gathered around him and some children were peering out at him from inside the museum, from inside Dr. King's motel room. There was audible sniffling. Marvin paused, then addressed the small crowd.

"The spirit of Dr. King is still very much alive today. The movement and the struggle are ours to overcome. It is now our cross that we must pick up and carry on, the unfinished business of Martin Luther King, Jr. To make the American dream a reality where all men and women, where all little boys and all little girls can live in a nation that is free from corruption, free from diseases, free from poverty, free from violence, free from fear. Where they can grow up and become model citizens and give to this nation and to our world a new sense of morality, a new world order of justice and brotherhood, whether their minds are completely and totally educated to the truth of the fact that out of one blood God made all men to dwell upon the face of the earth. We are all brothers. This was the message, and this is the living legacy of Martin Luther King, Jr. They slew the dreamer to slay the dream, but the dream lives on." The reverend paused, and looked at Kris and me. "Thank you."

We thanked him in return, both a little taken aback by the impact that he had on us and the people who had gathered around. Fascinated with Marvin's passion and sense of duty, we were curious about his background. Apparently, he had been living in the motel when they closed it down for renovations.

"I lived there from May of 1983 to January of 1988. And on January 4, 1988, when they closed it down and the state took over for renovation, I had to leave. I'm happy that I was forced out because this place is remarkable. It does tell the story, and Dr. King would have wanted this. Dr. King was a lover of history. He was a history student. And Dr. King respected history. And Dr. King would have wanted this history of the civil rights movement to be known. He said it in 1956"—Marvin began to channel again—" 'I want young men and young women who aren't alive today, who are going to come into this world with *new* privileges and *new* opportunities . . . I want them to know that these new opportunities and privileges did not come without somebody suffering and sacrificing for them.' "

We thanked Marvin again and told him we'd keep in touch. His ability to conjure ghosts was eerie and draining and cathartic. We left him with an elderly woman who had heard Dr. King speak several times. She was overcome with emotion and clinging to Marvin's arm.

Kris and I separated for a rare private moment, to experience the museum. Inside, a visitor could start at the beginning of the civil rights movement and physically move through the entire chronological experience, with an interactive timeline that included diagrams, recordings, paintings, photographs, printed biographies, and film footage. The last exhibit was Dr. King and Mrs. King's actual motel room, pristinely preserved with his big Cadillac still parked under their window. In an hour, the museum gave me more insight into the civil rights movement than all of my years of schooling.

By this time, we had only about forty-five minutes left before the museum closed. It wasn't crowded—most of the few visitors were black families. I set a pace for myself and seemed to end up at each display with one family in particular, a young couple and their three-year-old daughter. We listened together to an actual recorded conversation between President John F. Kennedy and Governor Orval Faubus about the National Guard's presence at a forced desegregation. We watched footage of the first Atlanta sit-in together, and we arrived at a replica of Rosa Parks's bus together. At first, I felt as though I was becoming an intruder in a very private family experience. But by the time we reached the bus replica, although we had yet to speak to one another except for an occasional "Excuse me," I felt that the shared experience had linked us.

There were statues of people inside the bus, marking exactly how it looked when Mrs. Parks had boarded. We stepped inside and began to read descriptions of the event that were printed over the windows where advertisements would normally be. As the woman and I were reading, her daughter came bounding onto the bus and sat down in a seat toward the front. As part of the exhibit, a man's voice came over the speaker, saying, "Please move to the back of the bus." The little girl promptly got up, her mother still engrossed, and moved to sit in the last seat. When her mother had finished reading, she looked around for her child and called out, "Pumpkin, why are you sitting all the way back there?" The child responded matter-of-factly, "Because 'the man' told me to."

Tears welled in the woman's eyes as she turned to me and said, "Let's hope she never understands what she just said." I nodded, my stomach dropping as she gathered her giggly little girl and stepped off the bus.

Kris and I made it into the Kings' motel room at the same time. We were the only ones there. We walked slowly, reading every minute of how he had spent his last day, how he had stepped outside his room to speak with Jesse Jackson and been shot, and how Reverend Jackson had to call Mrs. King to tell her.

You have no choice but to come face-to-face with the spirits that still reside at the Lorraine. The emotional presence in that room was incapacitating. I felt limp and angry and so very, very, sad. Kris and I didn't speak and we respectfully avoided looking at each other's wet faces. Eventually, the security man came in to tell us that the museum had closed and that we would have to leave. I wiped my face on my T-shirt and stood outside of the room so Kris could finish. We didn't speak until we got into the car. Kris picked up the map and said, "Let's skip Graceland."

FIG TREE DINER, SALLISAW, OKLAHOMA   7/26, 10:50 A.M.

(Kristin)

We crossed the Oklahoma border at sunset last night—the trees along the highway were silhouetted by the parting sun, which looked like a melting Bombpop laying on the horizon. We were grateful for the sight of the Sallisaw Motel. We ate a Pizza Hut pizza in our room while we performed our nightly *Anthem* rituals and then tried to sleep through a heavy storm, an all-night tornado watch. This morning Shainee was so excited that the rain had broken the pattern of hot sunny days that she went running through the parking lot puddles in her bare feet.

We are now sitting in the comfort of a red vinyl booth, eating grits at the truck stop diner near the motel. Shainee's reading across from me and we just realized that the Joads from *The Grapes of Wrath* hail from Sallisaw. We seem to be following in some of the footsteps of John Steinbeck's Americans.

Good news. I just called Dr. Maya Angelou's office (for the ninety-third time) to see if her staff had an answer as to whether or not Dr. Angelou would do an interview for *Anthem*. I asked for her scheduler, as I had so many times before, and engaged in our overly familiar dialogue. "Hi, this is Kristin from *Anthem*. I'm just calling to see if you had heard anything from Dr. Angelou about the possibility of her participating in an interview. We could be in North Carolina in about . . ." Her scheduler did not immediately respond, "No, I'm so sorry, Dr. Angelou has still not had an opportunity to review your request . . ." Instead, she said, "Yes, Dr. Angelou would like to participate in an interview for *Anthem*." I was struck speechless but managed to get out a thank-you and a promise to call back in a few days to confirm a date.

Shainee didn't believe me when I came back to the red booth and told her Dr. Angelou had said yes. It would be too weird not to have to call the North Carolina office every other day, just to ask the same question. Next to Hunter Thompson, Dr. Angelou has been our longest and most tenacious pursuit. She has been a part of our routine, a part of our daily inner and outer dialogue. Getting a yes is the equivalent of the dog catching the car.

AMARILLO, TEXAS   7/26, Midnight

(Shainee)

I couldn't tell you what motel we're in. Today was a blur of heat, miles, and disbelief. We woke up in a tiny town over the Arkansas/Oklahoma border called Sallisaw. There was a tornado watch and I never saw a sky that color of slate before. The slate tried to become blue as we got back on I-40 headed west toward New Mexico. After our first twenty miles, the summer sun took her rightful place in the sky and the day became unbearably hot—the radio told us it was over 100 degrees.

Yesterday, we heard an odd noise emanating from our dashboard but didn't think much of it until today, when we lost the vital capacity for air-conditioning. Air-conditioning has been one of our few steadfast amenities during this trip and, as with most valued friends, we didn't really know how much we would miss it until it was gone. The air immediately turned dry and dusty. I was very aware of exactly where my legs were in contact with the leather seats and open windows blowing hot wind in our faces provided no relief. We drove more than 100 miles, not speaking: dripping, praying for an unlikely Arctic front, and dreading the 400 miles left between us and Albuquerque. There was no sign of civilization visible anywhere from the highway, only endless cattle ranches. A roadside mechanic did not seem likely to appear. Finally we saw a sign that said, OKLAHOMA CITY—32 MILES.

Last night when I was charting our route on the computer, I pointed out to Kris that we would be traveling past Oklahoma City. If we wanted to make it to New Mexico on time, we wouldn't necessarily be stopping. But one of our goals *is* to create a time capsule of this moment in America's history and Oklahoma City, in the three months since the bombing of the Federal Building, has been at the forefront of the nation's consciousness. We debated about stopping but both decided that we were still feeling overwhelmed by the idea of all the misery caused by the blast—and the relentless media coverage—the wound it left, still fresh. It is one American site that we did not want to see for ourselves.

But that was last night. Today, the agony of the heat—and our need for a mechanic—ultimately won out, and I pulled off of the Interstate at an exit that said DOWNTOWN OK CITY.

We found a mechanic in the Yellow Pages at the first pay phone we saw. We followed his directions and, in spite of all of our trepidation, found ourselves driving past the very images of destruction that we had been trying to avoid. It was a weekday afternoon in downtown Oklahoma City—and the place was deserted. There was no one on lunch break. There was no one running errands. Not one single person was walking the streets.

And there was also no glass—anywhere. Every window of every building was boarded up with wood—where there were buildings left, that is. The Federal Building has been razed. There are chain-link fences surrounding the heart of the blast area, festooned with huge banners and signs that read GOD BLESS OKLAHOMA CITY and STRENGTH, COMPASSION, AND COURAGE. The fence was covered with notes, handkerchiefs, pacifiers, and other memorials. There was devastation everywhere. Piles of rubble lined the streets, and everything from the post office to the phone company was shut down. We looked on in silence, wondering where everyone was.

When we dropped the car off, Mike, the mechanic, said it would take a while before he could tell us anything. He suggested we get something to eat, thought for a moment about our dining options, then told us to try a diner called Sweeney's. He couldn't think of anywhere else that was open. We walked over to the restaurant, reluctantly lugging the cameras, famished and hot. The epicenter of the blast was to our right and we couldn't help but be transfixed.

Inside Sweeney's, we got a table. The restaurant was fairly empty, considering it was the only one open. A few people looked at our cameras, but they were obviously immune to them by this point. We asked the owner, David, if we could interview him and he agreed. He promised us a couple of his secret recipe jalapeño cheeseburgers and said he'd be right over. Kris didn't have the heart to tell him that she

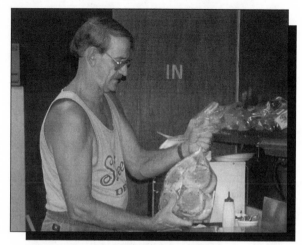

David Hoke, owner of Sweeney's

didn't eat red meat; he seemed so excited to cook for us. A few minutes later, he came over with plates piled high with Oklahoma beef. They smelled amazing and he grinned with pride, watching our faces as we took in the aroma. Kris even broke her own rule and dug in. David sat down with us and began to talk.

He told us that the bomb had taken away most of his clientele. "A lot of them died and the others are still too traumatized to go to work. Besides, the only people making any money right now are the glass-makers. We got our windows replaced the first week so we could stay open, but most businesses are still shut down." His tone was stoic as he continued, saying that he had been to over fifteen funerals and was still trying to help out a lot of friends and family who had been directly affected by the tragedy.

I thought about my father's stories of air raid drills held in grade school during the height of the Cold War. The drills had instilled terror in millions of children, who fully expected the Communists to attack at any moment. Of course they never did and I thought about how shocking it must have been for people of his generation when the attack finally came at the hands of fellow Americans. This was *never* supposed to happen in America.

Kris and I felt self-conscious and thought it was odd for him to pour all of this out as if he knew us. But apparently, streams of people—and sometimes entire families—had already made the pilgrimage to Oklahoma City during their summer vacations. And *Sweeney's* had evidently become for others what it became for us today: the symbolic gathering place at which to pay your respects. We were only two in a long line of mourners who had come through this restaurant. Three months, fifteen funerals, and six new panes of glass later, this man was still making his jalapeño burgers. It's hard to accept, but life somehow manages to go on in Oklahoma City.

When the time came to check back with Mike, we thanked our host for lunch and walked back to the garage. Mike said there was nothing he could do about our air conditioner unless we wanted to wait for two days until he could get a part in. We said we couldn't, with dread in our voices, and he was nice enough to call ahead so the part would be waiting for us in Albuquerque. It seems we have no choice but to cross the state of Texas without the luxury of cool air. Sometimes our journey dictates itself.

JUST OVER THE NEW MEXICO BORDER   7/27

(Kristin)

"It's 105 degrees," the radio informed, as we approached a new state. WELCOME TO TEXAS—DRIVE FRIENDLY, the sign urged, boasting the Lone Star flag. My leg hung out the open window—it was open because our air-conditioning is still on the blink. Shainee and I were both in a desert mirage daydream state when I caught a glimpse of the sirens in my sideview mirror—objects suddenly becoming much closer than they appear. *Another* speeding ticket for my riding partner, Ms. Andretti. At least we're moving around all the time, and maybe the cops won't realize this is the same "Shainee Gabel" who's been stopped in every other state.

I've grown accustomed to riding shotgun, having mastered the responsibility of changing tapes and dispensing snack rations, as well as operating the camera to capture images along the way. We usually only tag-team when Shainee is tired. One more ticket and I would become designated driver, and Shainee would be relegated to permanent passenger. Unless, of course, we took Doug's advice and changed her name and identity.

We quieted the radio as a wide-brimmed Texas Ranger sauntered over to Shainee's window and took off his *CHiPs*-inspired sunglasses to get a better look inside. I couldn't control the urge to capture the happening on camera, so I kept it rolling while he leaned in, like a cop out of a movie, twisting a toothpick in his mouth, silently assessing the situation: the mound of everything we owned hiding from the pounding heat under a blanket in the backseat. He squinted one eye and shifted his weight to one foot. "So are you two related or are you *friends?*" he asked cocking his eyebrow with his last word.

Shainee, the suspect

Shainee and I exchanged a look of "Is he really asking that?" and then responded in unison, "We're . . . *friends.*"

The ranger proceeded to ask Shainee to get out of the car and follow him back to his. I swallowed heavily, my confidence going down with dry air. I couldn't figure out what he was up to. We were in one of the smallest towns in Texas, and as it was my first time in the hefty state, I very much wanted to love it. I didn't *want* to have some stereotypical encounter with a narrow-minded Lone Star ranger to retell, particularly when we were almost safely over the border.

My imagination raced while I watched every move the ranger made through the sideview mirror, the rearview mirror, and the camera eyepiece, which I kept pointed at his car throughout the ordeal. More than ten minutes later, Shainee came back to the car and slammed the door, ticket in hand. "What did he ask you?" I pressed her.

"He asked why the car had Florida plates, and I admitted it was stolen," Shainee quipped. "And then he wanted to know what was under the blanket, and I told him, 'Drugs to pay for our movie.' He asked how we knew each other, and I assured him we were lovers." Shainee then started the car and added, "But he obviously didn't believe any of it because he gave me a ticket anyway and let me go."

I watched the ranger in my sideview mirror writing up his report in his patrol car engulfed in the cloud of dust we'd left behind, and we continued *slowly* on to New Mexico.

JIMMY SANTIAGO BACA

POET • WRITER

ALBUQUERQUE, NEW MEXICO

(Kristin)

After our interlude with the Texas Ranger, we continued on to Albuquerque, where an interview and an air conditioner part awaited us. I moved away from New Mexico when I was seventeen, and going back is always emotionally stirring for me. My body feels internally altered once I am inside the state border. I find myself wanting to dig into its desert like a dog that eats dirt to quench a deep mineral desire. The surroundings conjure memories of growing up as a single child in a single-parent home, rain dances at my grandparents' ranch, weekend explorations in the Sandia mountains, and a general sense of wonderment. The muted colors, the goodness and accessibility of the people, the Native American presence and storytelling, and the whispering desert wind set this place apart from other places for me. As Studs had said, "It's my home. It's everything."

Several people we had encountered in our travels had suggested that we interview a New Mexican poet, Jimmy Santiago Baca. Shainee and I occasionally stopped in bookstores to do research for upcoming interviews, and on one particular occasion I was drawn to a collection of poetry by Southwest writers. As I flipped through, I happened upon a poem about New Mexico. I wasn't too surprised to find the familiar name of Jimmy Santiago Baca on the page, as synchronicity had defined much of our journey up to that point.

Shainee and I decided it was time to try and track down Mr. Baca. After we called all ten "J. Baca's" listed with the Albuquerque operator, we got a lead. It wasn't Jimmy but someone who knew Jimmy—the poet, the local hero. I dialed number after forwarding number, and was told over and over that "Jimmy doesn't live here anymore." I was beginning to get the impression that the man we were looking for didn't want to be found. Finally, I reached a voice mail box with an innocuous but promising outgoing message: "Hi, this is Jimmy. Leave a message." I did. And several more after that. In the meantime, I contacted Baca's publisher, who confirmed Jimmy's evasiveness but said that he would try to help find him.

About a week later, Shainee and I were making our usual to-do lists in a forgettable Arkansas motel when the phone rang. It was Jimmy Baca, but he didn't seem particularly happy about returning our call.

After I described our project, he suggested we interview a friend of his in Arizona. I explained that we'd love to hear more about his friend, but we really wanted to interview *him*. We talked some more and he reluctantly agreed to give us his home phone number and said to call when we got closer to New Mexico. I took down the number, and we left it at that.

Weeks later, we called Jimmy from a pay phone outside a double-wide trailer post office in Cuervo, New Mexico. Surprisingly, he agreed to meet us and gave us his address. I admit, we wondered if Jimmy would still be living there when we arrived.

Shainee and I drove the dirt roads of the Black Mesa Valley, on the west side

of Albuquerque, until we came to the house. Two guard dogs came to greet us at the fence surrounding the property, and Jimmy followed. "I don't know why I agreed to do this," he declared as he reached for the padlock. "I hate interviews." From what we had read about Jimmy, I wasn't entirely surprised by his inhospitable welcome. But he did swing the gate open and actually told his dogs *not* to bite us.

Jimmy introduced us to his sons, Gabriel and Antonio; Beatrice, the mother of his children; and a few of his friends who were visiting for morning coffee. We sat on the porch, under an old elm tree, and had coffee with them. Jimmy asked us where we grew up, what we were all about, and, in a roundabout way, why we were trying to ruin his day with this interview. At least he had a sense of humor.

We handed Jimmy a gift we'd brought with us—a bag of bananas, tobacco, and corn—a traditional Native American goodwill offering. Then I answered his first question, "I grew up here until I was seventeen. This is still my home in a lot of ways." He didn't reply but arched his thick eyebrows, suggesting that he *might* let us stay.

After we'd been there for a while answering *his* questions, Jimmy seemed to relax a little, so I decided to ask him if he would elaborate on the author bio on his book flaps.

After a pregnant pause, he began to speak. "I was born in Santa Fe and grew up in southeastern New Mexico, in the plains over the mountains on a sheep farm—a sheep ranch in a little village. Then I went to an orphanage. Then I lived on the streets. Then I went to a detention home. Then I went to the county jail. Then I went to prison." Jimmy laughed nervously, took a breath, then a gulp of coffee. "And then I fell into paradise," he said, "I guess I had paid enough penance . . . so here I am in paradise."

Jimmy made a sweeping gesture with his arm, referring to the breathtaking mesa that surrounded his home. The vista provided a sense of boundless physical freedom and a majestic setting to inspire artistic expression within the warmth of his family's home.

I had read that by the time Jimmy was five, his mother had been murdered by her second husband and his father had died of alcoholism. I also knew that Jimmy was in prison by the time he was twenty and had spent four years in isolation before he was eventually released for good behavior. I asked Jimmy how he had become a poet while serving a prison sentence.

"I was giving out coffee one day in the pen," he said, "and this one guy threw a cup of coffee at me because he wanted me to give him five cups, and that was enough of a provocation where I had to decide, then and there, what I was going to do with this guy. And I decided I was really tired of fighting. And the guard opened the cell and left me alone with this guy. I looked at him and I thought, 'There's gotta be something more to life than just fighting like this. There's gotta be a better way to communicate.' And I walked away. I was humiliated because I had always prided myself on being a really good fighter. It was the hardest thing in the world to do. I felt like the greatest coward . . . There was no place for a young Chicano to turn other than to fulfill the stereotypical image of a Chicano being a fighter.

"I had to talk to somebody or else I would have gone crazy, so I decided to try and talk to a piece of paper. The idea of consciousness being born—that's what that act was for me. I also began to write letters expressing my concerns about the society I lived in—the judicial system, racism, and my emotional immaturity. I had never learned how to read and write, so I was just starting to understand the world. That's why I started writing—from a deep sadness."

I asked Jimmy how he had taught himself to read and write, and he described a ritual of hiding under his blanket with books and a flashlight every night. Ultimately, he said, it was gaining command of language that saved his life. As fate would have it, the books were poetry, and in those late-night, dimly lit reading marathons, Jimmy deciphered John Keats's poems of love—a word he says he had no context for until later in his life.

We began to talk about Jimmy's prison sentence, and he explained the details surrounding his "beef," as he called it. It was the first time he had been arrested as an adult, on a drug-related charge. He also said that he happened to have been innocent of the crime on this particular occasion.

Regardless, the judge found him guilty, and Jimmy strongly believes that the decision was racially motivated.

Jimmy sat silently, reliving that fateful day. With visible effort, he pulled himself back to the present.

"My act of forgiveness for society was that I picked up the pencil. And that was a sense of 'I forgive you, society. I'm gonna try one more time to do it your way, and we're gonna see how this goes.' "

Jimmy began to write. He found that putting words together was cathartic, a way for him to express his anger and sense of loss. Eventually, someone at the prison suggested that Jimmy submit his writing to *Mother Jones* magazine. And so he did. Much to his surprise, his writing was accepted, and within a few years, he had four published books and had won the American Book Award for *Martin and Meditations on the South Valley.*

Jimmy explained what motivated him during those early years. "What was happening behind bars and what was happening on the streets was horrible," he said. "The story of poverty and discrimination in this country doesn't seem to ever change. I fell into despair and lost faith on several occasions; I would lose faith in myself. But through it, I kept writing; I kept talking about what was happening."

Jimmy's large gray eyes weren't just looking at us; they seemed to be magnifying everything around us. My chair somehow felt a little larger than it actually was—my coffee cup, awkwardly oversized, caught in his stare. I wasn't intimidated but was conscious of being closely observed. Jimmy was like an enormous fishing net catching everything as he quietly culled the area. He stared directly at me and asked, "Do you not think that poverty is a crime?"

He didn't wait for my answer, opting to answer his own question. "I do. I think it's a crime that we should have poor people living a life of oppression, having to struggle to pay medical bills and reaching a point of despair watching their kids suffer."

Jimmy spoke from a lifetime of experience. I was curious about what sustained him now.

"Do you know what losing faith is?" he asked back pointedly. Jimmy answered our questions by asking his own.

"What keeps me going," he continued, "unequivocally, is my beautiful girlfriend, Beatrice, my children, and my friends. The give-and-take of the respect we have for each other. You'd be amazed how far respect goes, if you have nothing else. Like bringing fruit to a new friend." He paused and offered a little smile. There he was, I thought, the person I'd glimpsed when I first picked up a book of his poetry.

Oppression

Is a question of strength
of unshed tears,
of being trampled under

and always, always,
remembering you are human.

Look deep to find the grains
of hope and strength,
and sing, my brothers and sisters,

and sing. The sun will share
your birthdays with you behind bars,
the new spring grass

like fiery spears will count your years,
as you start into the next year;
endure my brothers, endure my sisters.

We wondered what gave Jimmy the energy to endure. "I always felt that I could deal with these things that go on in a person's life—living in poverty, worrying over bills, how you're gonna raise your children, the school situation, whether your children are going to be a victim of a drive-by shooting, the corruption of politics, and when you go to the hospital, you know you may die if you don't have a buck in your pocket. You fight to deal with all of that, and then there comes a point in time when you realize that you can't, that you need help.

"Ultimately, there comes a place in your heart where you open the last door, and you see the horror of horrors, and that is that you can't do it. What I was never able to do was ask for help, and what I found myself doing was praying to God, saying, 'You gotta help me with this, man, 'cause I just can't do it anymore, I'm really sorry.' And then, in that act of surrender, you begin to become vulnerable again and are being reborn through the act of asking for help."

Jimmy clearly didn't express himself in a linear way. Some might say his style of communication is disjointed, but having spent time around Native American cultures in the Southwest, I had learned about a cultural emphasis on oral tradition and oral history—wisdom and teachings often being passed down through stories that were nonlinear and sometimes took days to tell. I always loved the thought of someone beginning to tell a story, going to sleep, and then waking up to pick up where they had left off. The Hopi Indians believe that to truly answer a question, one must talk around it and work toward the center, entering the fiery heart of truth as if through the rays of a sun. Jimmy continued with his point, headed for the center . . .

"I believe that my source of faith comes from my community," he said. "It comes from people helping people. That's just how it is. It has to be that way. Otherwise, I don't see any other way out. If we don't have a community, we have nothing."

Once again, Shainee and I were reminded that for most of our interviewees feeling a sense of community—and being supported in times of crisis *and* celebration—was of paramount importance. "That was the dream of those who founded [the country]," Studs Terkel had said. "Of course you take part. Of course you are part of the community." Many others would express a fear that we were losing our sense of community, and that as those relationships fell away, so did the foundation of our civilization.

"How do you define inspiration?" I asked Jimmy.

"It's like those little flecks of gold you find in the gravel when you're panning some old river." Jimmy sat, quietly thinking, then went on.

"One day I was watching this carpenter build some steps and he was quite good. He mitered the side, like this." Jimmy made a smooth hand gesture, whistling to emphasize the imaginary board's perfection. "And he fit in all his boards and then, on top of that, he had precise ridges running so he could put little borders so it would never come apart. I've tried to live my life like that. I try to shape my life so that it's the kind of stairway that people can come and go on, and it can hold their weight and the kids can play on it. Inspiration to me is as simple as when I'm mean, and Beatrice is nice, and I look at her and think, 'I want to be that way. I want to be nice like her.' Inspiration, to me, is a process that is ironed out over a long period of time."

There was usually one particular and identifying moment in each interview when I felt—by way of my sternum—that something had been uttered which I absolutely *needed* to hear. They were like one of those flecks of gold Jimmy had mentioned, a moment of clarity finding its way to our pan.

Jimmy looked at us looking at him. "I had some misgivings when you guys showed up here," he reiterated, as if his initial greeting was no longer fresh in our minds. "I thought, 'Oh, I shouldn't have said yes.' I'm so used to people coming into my community and just taking and taking. But what you're doing is solid." Jimmy paused, then decided, "I'm glad I did this."

We talked about preconceived notions and first impressions and then he laughed out loud. "Walt Whitman said something about the contradictions of life," Jimmy recalled, "that he was perforated with them. I think I am as well." I heard the echo of Doug Brinkley's voice, paraphrasing that same Whitman passage: "I contradict myself. I am large, I contain multitudes."

We sat in silence a lot with Jimmy, more so than in most interviews. We didn't feel the need to rush, and I also didn't feel the need to respond to everything he was saying with overt gestures.

"So can we stop for a few minutes?" Jimmy asked, breaking the silence.

While Jimmy took a break, we talked to Beatrice, who had been sitting with us, sharing in our silence, smoking cigarettes, and drinking coffee. As we talked, Gabriel rode his dirt bike in slow circles around us. At that moment, I remembered reading in one of Jimmy's books that he had met a woman, later in his life, who was the first person who was ever kind to him—actually, *the* woman who had given him the context for love. He had written about the transforming effect of that love on both his life and his writing. He had written with wonderment about the sons they had birthed together. As we sat, I realized Beatrice was that woman.

When Jimmy came back, I was rather surprised by his return. I figured once he was freed from the chair, he would have come to his senses and suggest we were finished. Beatrice looked at Jimmy while she put out her cigarette, "Doesn't he have a beautiful face?" she said to no one in particular. "A beautiful head?" He did—Jimmy's crew cut crowned a perfectly shaped head and striking features. He was a sturdy and handsome man, with a severe indentation between his thick eyebrows that gave him a permanent look of concern. He also sported a thin mustache anchored directly over his upper lip, which reminded me of John Waters's—only slightly more butch.

Jimmy Santiago Baca

I wanted to ask Jimmy the question we asked everyone: "What does the American dream mean to you?" But I was afraid that just the utterance of the phrase would be offensive, as Jimmy had made it clear that many of his people had been faced with something more akin to an American nightmare. Jimmy, however, seemed to be one of the great dreamers, so I decided to go ahead and ask.

"Good God," he exclaimed as I blinked, waiting for him to tell us to get the hell out. But he continued. "The American dream has had no validity for my people whatsoever. In order for a Chicano to be even partially accepted in this society, you have to call yourself Spanish and you have to pronounce your name 'Baker.' It seems the American dream is to have a new house, a new car, a nice fat bank account, to have the law working for you, not against you. We haven't had that. What we've had is old cars, no education, and no medication for the sick. When you try to get medical attention, they ask you, 'What's your insurance company?' What is the American dream for us?" Jimmy repeated our question, taking a breath. "The American dream for many of us is living without a dream. And that's just . . . existing."

Jimmy looked out at the desert and continued. "All my life I've had to cover who I am." He said this matter-of-factly, without a trace of the anger that he had said once defined him. "And that's not a complaint, it's just a fact. It's a fact I would rather not have had to live with. I didn't particularly *want* to be oppressed; I didn't want to be different; I didn't want to be chosen as the oddball out. I wanted to be part of American society; I wanted to play in the games, see the movies. I wanted to do the things that other kids did, but I wasn't given that opportunity.

They just said, 'No, you can't.' 'Why?' 'Because you're brown.' 'Okay, I won't.' It's a tremendous effort to try and see the goodness in America every day when it's got its foot on your throat.''

Jimmy patted his own arm like an old friend, then chuckled to himself. ''The American dream has been a lot of cholesterol and fat when they told us it was good for you. We all died really early of heart attacks, man! I tell you! 'Here, eat this dude!' '' Jimmy laughed loudly as he motioned a plate being shoved under his nose. He then dramatized a heart attack at the table for us à la Redd Foxx. He continued to laugh, and although Jimmy's laughter was the contagious kind, it felt, at that moment, strange to join in.

It was getting hotter outside as the sun passed directly over us. I gathered my hair into a ponytail and pinned it to my head, then asked Jimmy about his thoughts on the future for both himself and his community. Jimmy, never missing a beat, looked at me. ''You got a clean homesteader's face,'' he declared. I wasn't sure whether it was a compliment or whether the road had worn me beyond my years. While Jimmy pondered my previous question, an image of me and Willa Cather on a flat, lonely plain, delivering a calf, lingered in my mind's eye. Jimmy pierced the vision with his words.

''My people have practically no culture left,'' he said. ''So, therefore, we must start again by reaching into the subconscious mind and reclaiming the archetypical images and the metaphors that will help our people heal themselves.''

Jimmy smiled. ''I just love the way you turned the word 'anthem' into what it really means. Just beautiful. What is America's *real* song, if it's not all these wonderful people who are struggling to make sense of their lives in America—and who are doing a pretty good job of it? That's the real anthem. Before every baseball game, we oughta have somebody stand up—some old white woman from Appalachia—and talk about how she fed thirteen kids for thirty years. That'd be the anthem! Then start the baseball game!''

Shainee and I were both stunned that someone had articulated our goal, the gathering of voices in a way that we had only secretly imagined it. Jimmy knew what ''anthem'' meant to us: ''a song of praise; a sacred choral composition.''

We stopped talking again, and I looked out over the mesa, which was illuminated in golden light as the sun fell closer to the ground. I asked Jimmy about the land he and I grew up on—what it represented for him and why he had chosen to continue to call the Land of Enchantment ''home.''

Jimmy explained that since he was a boy he looked to the earth as his mother and the sun as his father. ''The land is sacred to me. Black Mesa is sacred to me,'' he said. ''You forget how good it feels to look up through tree branches at the sky and just let the breeze walk over your face. Or running out after the rain onto the prairie; you stand out there and you just know that you're loved. And when we take that away, then we take who we are as human beings away.

''Earth has always been an unending marvel to me. When you see a beautiful valley or mountain, somehow there is an instinct that tells us part of its innate integrity is part of us. And you feel a little bit more proud to be a human being, a little more worthy, a little more meaningful, after having touched the mountain. And sadly enough, even my people need to remember how to respect Mother Earth again. We have to be reminded that this earth is ours; it's our mother from generation to generation.''

For Jimmy, the land seemed to hold an even deeper meaning and purpose in his life than most, and it was reflected in his spoken word and his writing. He admittedly seems to search for himself—his identity—there in the land, his surrogate parent.

Jimmy's son Gabriel leaned over with a cupped hand and whispered into Jimmy's ear. ''Gabriel wanted me to tell you,'' Jimmy translated, ''that he found dinosaur bones up on the mesa. He can take you up there to look at it later if you'd like him to.'' We asked Jimmy to tell Gabriel that we'd take him up on his offer.

Meanwhile, somewhere in him, Jimmy had been processing an answer to one of our first questions about what inspired him to write. Although hours had passed since I had asked, it wasn't surprising that he had finally come to the heart of the answer. ''There are endless reasons for continuing to get up every day and write, but at the base of it, I write out of love,'' he said. ''You know how an addict takes opium? It's an act of love. It brings that feeling of love; it's a desire for love. And how the little infant screams for milk at night? That scream is an act of love: 'I want love!' Or a young woman who tells her parents, 'I'm not living with you anymore. I'm going to be with so-and-so.' Even though it's the worst decision she could ever make, it's an act of love, for her—love. Writing encapsulates all of those things for me. It's the first act of love I ever knew. And it will probably be the last, because when I die, I'll be laying down, probably thinking of some Rilke poem, and I'll float away in that poem and never come back to my body.''

Jimmy's head went back and his eyes closed. I remember thinking, he is both the mother and the infant in his metaphor—the desire to love, and be loved, equally strong. He seemed desperate to make up for lost years. But as much as Jimmy is now capable of loving people, a piece of him seems to still trust his love of language—of the words that saved him—a little more.

After the interview, Gabriel led Shainee and me across the mesa toward the mountain in the distance. Shainee hadn't run camera for an interview in a while, and she was physically exhausted from the day. So she explored the base of the mountain while Gabriel led me up to the secret spot he had discovered one day after school. With each crunching step over mesa gravel, I felt childhood memories, long buried, creep back—my youthful excavations, settling secret desert caves, and finding mysterious bones and buried pieces of Indian pottery. I had known never to take any home, as I was taught an ancient wrath would most certainly descend upon any pillagers. But, as with Gabriel, the fun for me was always in the search.

We came back to the house for some water, and Jimmy and Beatrice invited us to stay and have dinner with them and a few of their friends. Much to our surprise, Bill Moyers's PBS series on poets, featuring Jimmy, was airing that night.

We had known about the series and had actually heard Moyers talking about it on NPR, mentioning Jimmy's piece as one not to be missed.

Gabriel leads the way

Once again, Shainee and I acknowledged that we were by chance in exactly the right place at the right time. For dinner, we ate a traditional New Mexican meal of tortillas, "hatch" green chili, refried beans—all homemade, and all tastes that I had long missed. I had eaten this food all through childhood; it was grounding and comforting to be tasting it again. We all sat together enjoying a dessert of sopapillas and honey, watching Jimmy being televised into his own living room.

Saying good-bye that night was awkward, having shared such an intimate day and knowing how much it took for Jimmy to open his door to us to begin with. For days after we left, I felt the urge to call Jimmy and Beatrice just to say hello. But I never did. I guess like Jimmy, I trusted they knew, without us expressing it, how much the time together had meant to us.

ON THE WAY TO COLORADO   8/1

(Kristin)

Being in the desert with Jimmy reminded me of a trip I took to Arizona when I was younger. I camped out with a friend of mine who was staying on the Hopi Indian reservation north of Flagstaff. He was assisting Titus, a 104-year-old Hopi corn farmer and spiritual leader, with his daily chores.

My friend took me to look at some petroglyphs near the reservation. There was one called *The Hopi Life Plan*. Also known as Prophecy Rock, it stood tall and alone. My friend explained that the petroglyph that illustrates a Hopi prophecy dates back several thousand years. The prophecy tells of a new world in which "an inventive light-skinned people would come—lost in a world of their own invention." That's how my friend, translating for Titus, explained it to me, while we circled around an evening fire.

Titus went on to say that originally, the Hopis had not feared the coming of the "light-skinned" people, as it was foretold that they would bring a great gift of inventiveness that could potentially be applied toward compassionate ends. They hoped it would be so.

The full prophecy takes many days to tell, but the rock illustrates the crux of the Hopi vision: a crossroads. Which leads me back to our current trip, on which so many people we have met have expressed a belief that America is presently standing at a crossroads. Not all of our interviewees are optimistic, but the majority seem to be struggling to stay hopeful. No one, so far, has been willing to predict which road we will ultimately take.

I remember standing in front of that lone, inscribed rock and seeing a timeline that went from left to right as the future gradually became the present. The image began with a line that emerged out of the earth and evolved into a diamond shape that symbolized a collective rooting into the land—everyone on the continent settling together. The line continued and then split off into two roads: one high, one low. On the lower road, a stick figure walked alone carrying a planting stick. He was slouched slightly to show that he had "lived a long and happy life," Titus later explained, looking himself like the drawn figure. Above the aged stick figure, on the upper path, were four beings with straight backs drawn almost three times larger than the lower being, illustrating their power.

Unlike the man below them, the four beings' heads were floating above their bodies. This, I was told, shows a disconnection between their power and their wisdom and intellect. The upper path of "the inventive people" begins to zigzag as the four large beings attempt to dodge disasters created by their own inventions. On this path, there is a dependence on the creation of even greater inventions to reverse the destruction of the previous ones. The Hopis had predicted that while these two paths were separated, all beings on both paths would experience losses, such as family breakdown, ravaging of nature, incurable diseases caused by the inventions, changing weather patterns, an increase in mental disorders, destructive gossip, and ever-increasing violence in the "large villages."

As my eye continued to follow the paths, there was a point at which they seemed to come back together. My friend explained that the intersection only symbolized the *possibility* of coming back together. "A window of time to reassess," he had said, "an opportunity to reconsider our choices, which is marked by three world shake-ups." World War I and World War II are described by the prophecy in vivid detail. "The third has not yet occurred," he said, staring at the rock, all of which left me with an emptiness in my gut.

My eye continued to follow the paths, the upper carrying with it the beings—heads still disembodied—toward "a stairway to riches that leads to nowhere," Titus later clarified. The drawn stairway had ended suddenly in midair. The Hopis believe that as a nation on the timeline, we are quickly approaching the last connecting point—the third shake-up—where the long-term future will be determined. The interesting thing about the prophecy is that it outlines more than one possible outcome; the Hopis believe humans to be co-creators of their own destiny. One prophesied precipitate is a great war that ends all creation as we know it; the second is that the north and south poles will flip and water will wash over the land; and the third is a global change of heart, where people will correct themselves, changing their behavior patterns, and begin to share the same language, metaphorically speaking.

I had asked my friend what the circles around the chest of the stick figures symbolized, as the upper and lower beings' circles differed. He explained that it was the heart and that because the being on the lower path had surrendered to the creator—his ego staying out of the way—he had the clarity of *one* heart. The upper path beings, who had two circles, were endowed with a duality of heart, symbolizing a positive innate quality to care for others and to authentically love others, while also having the capability of turning away from others' suffering and pain. They lived with a split heart.

Jimmy had argued that it should be a crime for people in America to be suffering from poverty and political injustices. He had wondered why we don't take responsibility for each other, how we are able to abandon our own. I can't help but wonder if Jimmy's concerns are in any way connected to the split heart of that high road.

I have remembered and thought about these pieces of the *Prophecy Rock* story many times, but now that I've seen more of our country and talked to a number of strangers about the past, present, and future, that solitary rock suddenly seems to hold a greater significance. I now wonder if that rock doesn't have something to do with the crossroads that people are identifying in *Anthem*. My friend had explained that in the mid-1940s, after the explosion of the atom bomb on Hiroshima and Nagasaki—a historical event that is predicted by the same Hopi prophecy—the tribe leaders decided to make their prophecy public. They hoped to shed some light on the changes that were taking place in our time. Although most people have ignored their teachings, considering the Hopi prophecy to be just a story, the Hopis hold the belief that many people are already sensing the approaching intersection—the impending future—and their prophecy will offer confirmation for those people. The Hopis also acknowledge the complexities of freewill; people may not see—or perhaps *choose* to not see—the crossroads, and the path they travel.

Hanging with Jimmy also made me think about the paradox of the low road being the *better* choice, since, in common American parlance, the phrase "the high road" signifies the path of most value.

SNOWMASS, COLORADO   8/5, 3 A.M.

(Shainee)

As a child, I always dreaded the first of August. It meant the beginning of the end of summer; June was the "Friday" of summer, August the dreaded "Sunday." This year I have mixed feelings. June was, in fact, a difficult month of acclimation and technical boot camp, but now the dust seems to have settled. We're halfway through shooting and we've become comfortable with our rhythm, drifting out of one meaningful encounter into another memorable experience. Meanwhile, we've stopped trying to write everything down, knowing that each day is too rich to recount on a regular basis. Hopefully, when the time comes, the rule of our muse, John Steinbeck, will prove true: that which is most important and worth retelling will remain indelible.

The West is magnificent, the section of our trip that I have anticipated the most. The land is shockingly beautiful as we move from state to state, and I have become addicted to perpetual motion. I have also come to love every mundane

ritual of our travels, from late-night fuelings in remote truck stops to the terrible free coffee offered in every nameless motel we wake up in. I have begun to dread returning to a life that is stationary and routine. Solitude and anonymity have the strange effect of providing solace to the soul; it's ironic, considering we have come in search of the connections that bind us all.

We drove through the Rockies today. They are truly awesome. I-70 winds westward out of Denver and, within fifty miles of the city, becomes a magnificent scenic route. Our eyes have become saturated with beauty after two months on the road, but the Rockies are indeed magical, rising like enormous green monoliths with white summer snowcaps as we drove through a series of sun showers. The sun dipped in and out of dark clouds and rain splashed on our windshield so erratically that we gave up on trying to turn the wipers on and off. We opted instead to watch the play of light from the sun and clouds on the lush green mountains. Just when we became accustomed to the startling contrast between green and white, the giants turned adobe red as we wound past historic mining sites, through the Eisenhower Memorial Tunnel, toward Glenwood Springs.

I drove the distance, Kris shot. The road was frightening, built into the sides of the giants, barely wide enough for cars, and with no real safety guard separating road from sky. The frequent signs alerting us to RUNAWAY TRUCK RAMPS did not make me any calmer. It's hairy in the summer; I can't imagine what it's like with snow cover. Our destination today was a tiny dot on the map called Woody Creek, nestled in a valley. We have come in search of a legend: Dr. Hunter S. Thompson.

We've been calling Hunter since Doug gave us his number in New Orleans. He never picks up his phone. He never calls us back. We keep calling. At first it was kind of a game for us, then it became another of our rituals. We pull into our motel for the night, clean the cameras, label tapes, and then one of us calls Hunter and has a delightful conversation with his answering machine. Doug told us that Hunter is up all night, so we call at all hours. I actually feel as if we already know him, though we've never spoken to him.

In the meantime, we've tried to brush up on his background. In college, I read *Fear and Loathing in Las Vegas*, the story of a search for proof of the existence of the American dream. Hunter's conclusion was that the dream is dead. Now, our crash course revealed more. Besides revolutionizing journalism by stressing the experience of the journalist and the behind-the-scenes story (lovingly termed "Gonzo journalism"), Hunter drank beers with Jimmy Carter, rode with the Hell's Angels, was a correspondent for *The National Observer* (among other magazines), turned a town upside down by running for sheriff, and has led two generations of readers into

One of many futile calls

an America that he depicts as dangerously close to the edge of demise. His wild exploits are the stuff of myths.

Doug has assured us that Hunter is in town and knows we're here, but it could be an ordeal trying to get Hunter to actually do an interview. He is notoriously unfond of having cameras pointed at him, and we gave up on trying to secure anything concrete with him a long time ago.

So we decided to take a break here, at our halfway mark, relax a little, and hang out in one of the loveliest areas of the country while we try to tempt Dr. Hunter S. Thompson into seeing us. The worst thing that can happen is that we spend a week outside of Aspen catching up on phone calls and faxes and getting a little R&R. I vote for horseback riding. Kris wants to raft.

Besides, friends of friends have lent us the use of their condo for the week, and it kicks ass! We have our own rooms, bathrooms, living room, dining room, and a patio with a magnificent view—where I sit now in an iron chair. We've stepped into our own version of *The Prince and the Pauper* and have changed places with our royal twins for the week. After we had spent the last three nights sleeping on the floor, opening the door on our very own palace was exhilarating. We high-fived and scurried to run steaming baths.

We've decided to wait until tomorrow to call Hunter. We're going to talk to Doug one more time before we actually begin our quest. So for tonight, it was a quiet dinner in the town of Aspen, which I can only describe as "posh quaint." I'm looking forward to seeing the village by day, but the influence of the rich and famous is apparent even in the dark. The nineteenth-century façades of a once-bustling silver mining town hint at the Wild West of a hundred years ago. But the storefronts house names that I recognize from Rodeo Drive. It is a strangely invented community, situated here amid natural wonders. I can only wonder how someone like Hunter Thompson has managed to survive here for so many years.

SNOWMASS, COLORADO—MISSION ACCOMPLISHED 8/6

(Shainee)

Well, we finally met the man. We were ready to spend days calling and cajoling, but it all happened so quickly.

We spoke to Doug soon after waking and he told us that we should call Hunter and tell him that we would wait for him at the Woody Creek Tavern every day this week. Doug said he wasn't sure if Hunter would show, but we should just hang out and cross our fingers. He also gave us a twenty-minute lecture on the perils of Hunter Thompson and again absolved himself of any further responsibility. We promised him we were prepared.

Woody Creek
ROD & GUN CLUB

HUNTER STOCKTON THOMPSON, EXECUTIVE DIRECTOR

Apparently, Hunter's not too keen on picking up messages, because when I tried to call, the tape said, "Box full, thank you for your call," and hung up on us. Eventually, I got through. "Hi, Hunter. It's Shainee and Kristin calling, friends of Doug Brinkley, and . . ." In the middle of the usual recitation, the phone clicked and a ragged voice barked through a speaker-phone, "Yello. Yello?" I was stunned. "Hunter?" I ventured.

It was him, and I dutifully suggested that we meet at the tavern. He said that maybe we should just come up to the house instead. I paused, a little startled, and rushed, "Sure. When?"

"Well, this afternoon might be nice."

This afternoon. Could it be that simple? Hunter gave us directions and we said we'd meet at five. I hung up and Kris pelted me with questions. When she had figured out that Hunter had answered, she had scrambled for the DAT machine to record the conversation, as we did with most calls, and we were now both wrapped in the microphone's cord.

While Kris unwound us, I told her how surprisingly pleasant and welcoming Hunter had been. The eternal optimist, she harrumphed triumphantly, saying Hunter couldn't possibly be as difficult as everyone says he is and that Doug was probably overreacting. Well, tonight we spent a good ten hours with Hunter, and I can't say that Doug was overreacting entirely.

We arrived at Hunter's this afternoon. His home is called the Owl Farm and is settled on several acres of opulent green valley floor. He lives in an abandoned wooden schoolhouse and has two peacocks that strut his property freely. We pulled up on a gravel driveway in front of the main house; a guest house stood about thirty-five yards to our left. A sprinkler system was watering the several acres of lawn. There was no one in sight.

But we were soon met by Deborah, Hunter's assistant or, more accurately, guardian angel. Deborah lives in the guest house and has been Hunter's personal assistant for about fifteen years. She is a thin, leggy woman in her fifties; tall, with clear blue eyes and a no-nonsense attitude. We found her crouching over one of the sprinkler heads in running shorts and a T-shirt. She was rather wet.

She got up and introduced herself, wiping her hands on her thighs and grumbling that one of the timers was off. Doug had told her all about our project and she thought it sounded really interesting, adding, "I hope Hunter won't be too much of an effort for you," with a raised skeptical eyebrow. As she led us inside the wooden home past a bison's head, a rifle rack, and a few smaller stuffed animals, an ear-rattling siren rang out and Deborah cursed to herself as she went to turn it off. It was dark; the blinds were closed and the walls were knotty pine. The television blared CNN. Deborah said Hunter was getting dressed and offered us drinks and a plate of cheese and crackers that had already been set out and covered with plastic wrap. We chatted a little about Doug, then Deborah left to go next door and change out of her wet clothes.

There was no sign of Hunter. Not a peep. Kris and I looked at each other, whispering, "Now what?" Everything seemed normal enough. We ate cheese and looked around at the house. One entire wall is covered with notes and chapter headings, topped by a sign that reads POLO IS MY LIFE in big letters. There are pictures, letters, and notes taped up over every remaining inch of wall space: everything from a photo of the Kennedys to a bumper sticker that says IMPEACH REAGAN.

Finally Deborah came back. She hit the play button on the answering machine, and the voices of everyone from Roxanne Pulitzer to Lyle Lovett to the Woody Creek postmaster poured out. Every call was voice-stamped after 2 A.M. She scribbled down the messages and when she realized that Hunter had not yet emerged, she yelled toward the back of the house, "Hunter! These girls are waiting out here for you! Come on now!" When her bellow was met with silence, she proceeded to give us a course on our duties as Hunter's escorts for the evening. Apparently, we would all be going out.

Deborah grabbed a duffel bag full of stuff and began to pack it with more stuff, explaining as she went. "His cigarettes will be in his pocket, lighter goes over here, cellular phone underneath the goggles, an extra flashlight, there are also three in the car, and this pocket holds all of his filters." She packed the bag like a pro, shooting out the instructions like a drill sergeant. She yelled again, not looking up from the bag, "Hunter!"

Finally he appeared, shuffling into the room in a large white terry cloth robe, slippers, and a baseball hat, his FDR cigarette filter dangling from his mouth. He seemed a little groggy but affable. We made our introductions and he sat down in a chair behind the kitchen counter that doubles as his desk. Hunter is a tall, lanky man with an unusual way of moving: his legs seem to want to move faster than the rest of him, dragging his torso reluctantly behind. He's also a little difficult to understand. At first he sounds as though he's mumbling until you realize that he simply doesn't employ the use of inflection that often. Once we adjusted, we could understand him perfectly.

Hunter settled in with a vodka and orange juice and told us he had just gotten off the phone with Doug, who had been filling him in on some of our escapades. I can just see Hunter in his room, calling Doug to ask him one last time why he should hang out with these two girls who were in his den. Doug must have really talked us up, because Hunter asked us to tell him the story of President Clinton's surprise intrusion on our interview with George Stephanopoulos. We recounted it, a little self-consciously, but he did chuckle at the telling. He said we'd have to learn to tell it in more detail if we wanted the whole thing to sound even better than it had actually been.

Just then a fax came through. Deborah grabbed it off of the machine and told Hunter it was from Ed Turner, the head of CNN. Apparently, Hunter and Ed have been faxing each other back and forth about the current state of American media for quite some time, needling each other mercilessly. Hunter asked us to do a live reading of the faxes, with Kris playing Ed and me playing Hunter. We happened to have our DAT recorder on which captured them word for word.

We began with a Fourth of July fax from Hunter to Ed, offering an idea. Hunter proposed a Television Journalists Hall of Fame, saying that maybe Jimmy Carter would let Ted Turner (who, incidentally, is no relation to Ed), Ed, and Jane Fonda build it on his land in Georgia, and the Rolling Stones could play the opening. Hunter thought President Carter would be honored and offered to propose the idea to him himself. He signed it: IT'S YOUR CHANCE AT IMMORTALITY. YOU'RE WELCOME, DOC. Hunter interrupted every so often as I read, to make sure that I said every syllable correctly. He knew the fax by heart.

Kris then read Ed's reply:

Dear Doc:
     Two hundred and nineteen years ago, some very brave men assembled to risk all for an idea. The idea of freedom. That regardless of one's own circumstances, an opportunity to succeed by one's ability should be a guarantee of government. And so I am, of course, struck dumb by the silliness of your idea to create a Television Journalists Hall of Fame. Doc, we don't need more nitwit awards in this Dodge. What we need is quality reporting and writing and honest intent. And a commitment to do the right thing by our forefathers, and for that reason I am becoming a Rwandan terrorist.

Have a good and safe Fourth and remember that those warnings printed on fireworks larger than two feet in length are written by dweebs trying to rob you of your fun.

Seize the moment, E.T.''

It was a little surprising that the man who oversees CNN's programming has time to read a fax from Hunter and whip one back within the half hour, day or night. The play continued; it was now my turn again.

Dear Ed:

It's about time you took yourself off the O.J. story. You are a victim of the Peter Principle because of the guilt you feel, because of the millions of goddamn hours you've squandered and wasted for a whole generation of doomed children all over the world who will grow up stupid and stunted because you relentlessly deprived them, during the most impressionable years of their lives, of all news about anything except the vulgar O.J. trial. The Lindbergh baby and Dr. Sam's bushy-haired stranger were nothing compared to the damage you've done. Think about it, Ed. That slime you have on your hand is a lot worse than blood.

Kristin read Ed's response:

This endless seminar on television journalism continues, although even the most brainless sprayhead would have picked up more quickly, and it makes me worry that this silly thin air you've been breathing is dimming the brain's electrical circuits or you have acquired the very real disease sweeping Washington which permits you to speak clearly and forthrightly out of both sides of your mouth. I think we should draft a proposal to the EPA to thicken the Colorado air, perhaps by piping in some New York City air or the backup from a good brimming Paris sewer. Television news *is* O.J. O.J. *is* television news. Everything about the one is related to the other.

Seize anything, Ed.

The final fax from Ed—the one that had just arrived—wrapped up every recent news story with one giant fictionalized conspiracy theory. It was a little too warped to repeat, but I'll just say that he somehow linked David Koresh to Susan Smith and concluded that one day there will be an all-pervasive media force that will communicate solely through cartoons. It ended:

The real enemy will be an electronic one . . . And finally the echo of human kind will be a chattering, ''Th-th-that's all, folks!''

Seize your neighbor's wife, E.T.

With this, Hunter finally got dressed. He made us borrow jackets and told us we would be riding in his convertible. We were about to meet the Great Red Shark of *Fear and Loathing* fame, an impressive car—long, sleek, and fire engine red. She slept in the garage hooked to a battery charger. Hunter said we should all sit in front as he removed the cables and slammed the hood shut.

Kris and I got in gingerly, pretending that Hunter Thompson taking us for a spin in his infamous car was no big deal. We were absolutely calm and poised until Hunter backed out of the driveway with a roar and leaped onto the narrow road that winds through the foothills of the valley. We both yelped—loudly.

Hunter drives very, very fast. Some people might have been scared, but Hunter's been driving these roads like this for over twenty years. If he hasn't crashed yet, why would he crash today? We were calm believing that Hunter only seems like a reckless driver. In reality, he and the Shark are one with the road, and he expertly predicts every twist and turn.

Hunter seems to open up with the car's engine, relaxing and leaning into the ride. Kris asked him if he drives with the top down in the winter, too. *He absolutely does.* I asked him if he's ever hit anybody. *He absolutely has not.* Kris chuckled, explaining that I tend to drive fast, too, and relayed the number of speeding tickets I've received thus far on our trip. Hunter responded with a nod at me. ''Well, you must appreciate this then.'' I certainly did. We flew over the back roads, the sun settling over the mountain tops, the wind screaming in our ears and Hunter's tape deck chugging out Little Village's *Why Get Up?* I recalled Doug's initial call to Hunter, remembering the words ''high fun factor.'' I took a chance and said, ''Maybe you'll let me drive sometime.'' Hunter thought that *was* pretty funny.

No one drives the Shark but Hunter. *Everyone* knows the rule.

Kris asked Hunter if we could shoot some of the drive, and he said we could shoot whatever we wanted, as long as he knew the camera was on and we would light him a cigarette. We lit cigarettes for all of us, Hunter passing around filters, and relaxed as the Great Red Shark transported us to a restaurant called Sheffy's in a neighboring town.

The Great Red Shark

When we walked in, it was obvious that everyone knew Hunter, and greetings were called out from the bar and neighboring tables. The maitre d' sat us outside on the patio, and Hunter ordered three margaritas, three glasses of champagne, and three banana daiquiris. Kris and I tried to protest, but before we could get any words out, Hunter had already ordered two dozen oysters, three salads, two pastas, four crab cakes, and three pieces of chocolate cake—all ''to go.'' The flurry of drinks came quickly and the food followed shortly thereafter. None of it was wrapped to go—except for one plate of pasta for Hunter to bring home to Deborah—but Hunter didn't seem to notice.

We ate and talked over a long dinner. Hunter asked us a lot of questions about ourselves and the project, nodding and puffing on his cigarette as he listened intently to our answers. He liked to talk politics and sports, and had an encyclopaedic knowledge of both. He was genuinely concerned that we always have at least one fresh drink before us, and I grew a bit worried about the pile-up of untouched beverages and entrees. It would have been humanly impossible for us to keep up. Hunter ignored our failure and paid the check when we weren't looking.

We didn't get back to Hunter's until after 2 A.M. We hung out till three, with no one making any mention of an interview. We're expected back at the Owl Farm in ten hours. Tune in tomorrow.

The OWL FARM   8/7, 5:32 A.M.

(Shainee)

We are not well. I think I might die here.

STILL IN SNOWMASS, TRYING TO RECOVER 8/9

(Shainee)

I feel like we've spent the last few days on another planet: Hunter's World. The elusive answering machine voice that plagued us for so many nights has morphed into a living, breathing man who represents a full-time job. We are with Hunter every minute of every day that we are awake, which seems to be always. He is a man who really should be dead, given his inimitable way of life. When I asked him why he isn't, he replied simply, "It is my karmic punishment that I am still alive." I cannot recount *all* of the madness that we have witnessed and partaken in. Besides, I don't think it's necessary; anyone who has read any of Hunter's work has heard it all already, and it is all quite true.

But I will try my best to recount some of the highlights of the last few days. The other night I went over to Hunter's house alone, because Kris's boyfriend flew in to spend some time with her. I wasn't completely comfortable with Hunter yet; Kris and I were still in the beginning of our full immersion course on the Hunter lifestyle. He's overdue on a story he is writing for *Rolling Stone*. It's called *Polo Is My Life* and it's about Hunter's journey into the decadent polo world of Florida. The pretense for us spending so much time with Hunter is that we are supposed to be helping him with this article. Many have gone before us and failed.

I went in with a positive attitude, thinking, How hard could it be? It was hard. When I arrived, Hunter was already awake and had a terrible headache, the pain was radiating down his neck. There was also the distinct smell of skunk in the front of the house and Hunter cursed "the wretched beast." Needless to say, he was cranky, and his morning "orange juice" and vitamins didn't seem to be doing the trick. One of Hunter's neighbors was visiting and called his tenant, a masseuse, to come over and work on Hunter's neck.

I wasn't sure what to do with myself, so I went outside on the porch to sort out *Polo Is My Life*. It is intended to be an article first, then a book, so I tried to organize the chapters by page number as best I could. The peacocks were poking around on the front lawn, the sun was setting peacefully behind Hunter's parking lot of old cars, and there were the sounds of night birds beginning to sing.

Then the bellows of Dr. Hunter S. Thompson getting a massage rang out in the warm evening air. I worked quietly, flinching whenever Hunter screamed. At one point, I heard him fly off the table, accusing the young woman of trying to kill him. Fortunately, she didn't take him seriously and continued to work. Eventually, the screams gave way to deep moans of relief and Hunter, back to his old self, yelled out to me to keep a shotgun handy in case I spotted the skunk. He seemed to think that the animal was after the peacocks' food. I assured him I'd keep watch.

The hours went by. I went into Hunter's office to look through files that had been left by the last person who'd tried to organize his book. A Macintosh graced his office, yet the manuscript was typewritten. I asked Hunter if anyone had ever put any of the book into the computer, and he said he thought there might be something there but didn't know how the machine worked.

I found an outline of the book on the computer and printed it out. Hunter was astonished that I had located it. I put it down in front of him and showed him how I had compared what he had finished writing to the requirements of the out-line and that there were a few chapters that were half-finished. I suggested we work on those first. I put everything in a pile and circled the page numbers of the relevant chapters. Hunter just stared at me.

"What?" I asked.

"Fascinating. You have one of those linear minds. Your thoughts form a nice little row, don't they?"

I couldn't tell if he was mocking me or being sincere, so I just smiled. From what I now know of him, it was probably a little bit of both.

I was trying to move Hunter logically through a plan for tackling the rest of his story, but he's a master of diversion. I tried patience, earnestness, indifference, and firmness. Every approach was futile. The man just did not want to write that night—he would do anything but. We talked, we watched television, we smoked, we received guests. At some point in the evening, I ceased to be a writing assistant and became simply a spectator. In fact, Hunter caught me watching him accus-ingly during the third unexpected visit from a random friend and said menacingly, "Just remember. I'm watching you as closely as you're watching me." I laughed at my own transparency.

Around midnight we went out for a while—got some food at Sheffy's and then had a drink at the tavern—before returning to his house. We talked a lot and then were silent. I enjoy Hunter's company immensely—he is incredibly intelli-gent, he makes me laugh, and he's one of those people that seem to know some-thing about everything.

At about 5 A.M., however, I told Hunter I had to go home. He asked if I was sure I didn't want to try to find the skunk—he would teach me how to hunt. I lied, saying that I thought the skunk was long gone. I had actually spotted the creature invading the peacock cage at around 3 A.M., but I had opened the door wide so he would be sure to get out. Now I lied again and said the smell wasn't that bad anyway.

Then Hunter said he wanted to give me some gas money for the drive home, although we are staying exactly three miles from his house and he knew it. He opened a drawer. It was stuffed with cash and he took a fistful of twenties and handed them to me. I said it wasn't necessary. Hunter got very serious, saying that I had put in a full night's work organizing his book, and he wanted to pay me for it and for a tank of gas. He said he knew that documentary filmmakers never had any money—it was a rule—and he wanted me to have it. He pushed the money into my jeans pocket and was very firm that he wasn't going to take it back. I said, "Fine," and counted the wad when I got in the car. He had given me $120. I put it back in his drawer the next day before he woke up.

Our next adventure with Hunter took place at a conference given by the National Association for Criminal Defense Lawyers, cohosted by Hunter's attorney and friend Gerry. Hunter is the poet laureate of the association and spoke at the meeting about his Fourth Amendment Foundation and privacy rights.

He read a speech that he had jotted—during Gerry's introduction—on the

Poet laureate

back of a bumper sticker that said KEVORKIAN FOR SURGEON GENERAL. He was charming in his straw hat and brightly printed shirt, peering out at the audience from behind thick yellow glasses. Everyone was thoroughly entertained, and Hunter invited the audience back to Gerry's house for a party.

Before we went to the party, we had to go back to Hunter's so he could change. While Kris and I waited, a blonde woman in her forties appeared at the door and walked right in. It's surprising how many visitors Hunter gets—for a recluse. And no one ever seems to knock. The woman at the door turned out to be the Woody Creek postmaster.

She sat down at the counter with us, poured herself a drink, and told us that Hunter's fans call or show up at the post office at least once a week, looking for Hunter. "They have been for thirty years." She said that his post office box is always full of letters from fans and readers. I felt a little sorry for Hunter, listening to her. But the postmaster said that the whole town protects Hunter and always has.

Then her vodka and diet Sprite kicked in a little, and she told us stories about Hunter's secret good deeds. The postmaster who had preceded her was an older lady who had spent her whole life at the job. She was very dedicated and always discreet—even in the midst of the mania surrounding Hunter in the seventies. Every year Hunter would slip her some money to take her one annual vacation, to visit her sister. The secret contribution continued for almost twenty years.

Our suspicions were confirmed. Hunter's wild, obnoxious side has been well publicized, but few people know he can be sweet. Of course we needled Hunter when he emerged. "It's no secret what a nice guy I am," he joked.

We had a hard time getting Hunter to actually leave for the party to which he had invited 200 attorneys. We had to pack the duffel with the requisite flashlights and other paraphernalia, and then he insisted we give him a haircut. This definitely went above and beyond the normal requirements for coaxing someone into an interview—in fact, Hunter still hadn't officially agreed to be interviewed. However, Kris and I must be among a very few people who have said, "Stay still" to Hunter Thompson and lived to tell the tale.

We went to the party, Hunter dapper in his new 'do. We drove up in the Great Red Shark and people immediately swarmed around him. A woman from Texas, with large blond hair, leaned into the car and asked me if she could take Hunter's picture. "I guess so," I answered, "but you should probably check with him." She snapped away on her yellow disposable camera and Hunter was magnanimous, to say the least.

Very few people spoke to Kris and me, and we didn't really understand why until we talked to one woman who was there with her husband. She asked us what we did, and we explained that we were making a film and trying to get an interview with Hunter. She punched her husband in the arm and said, "See! I told you. You're always so judgmental." Kris and I just looked at each other. We had been sitting with Hunter most of the night and were waiting on him because of his bad neck. Documentary filmmakers, concubines—whatever.

THE OWL FARM   8/10, 4:31 A.M.

(Shainee)

I am sitting in a room that only a taxidermist could love—and does. Sinéad O'Connor's *Emperor's New Clothes* is on replay and I think this is possibly the eighth time we've heard it. CNN is competing with Sinéad's voice, and the sound of a typewriter—being used by someone who can't type—is audible over the din. Dr. Hunter S. Thompson is writing. The legendary Jerry Garcia died two days ago, and *Rolling Stone* called Hunter for a piece, even though he's two months overdue on the last one he owes them.

   He's finally working, after hours of typical Owl Farm chaos. Kris is attempting to help extract pages. I'm about to pass out on Hunter's couch; but before I do, I have to get this down. Tonight, when we arrived, I was in a very melancholy mood for reasons I will not bore anyone with. Hunter took one look at me and said, "You're sad." I nodded my head yes, choosing not to explain, and he didn't

Writing break

press. About an hour later, Hunter had finished the morning ritual that began when he woke up at 4 P.M. We were scheduled to go on one of his so-called "sunset rides," and for the first time since we arrived, I didn't perpetuate the running joke of asking to drive his beloved 1973 red Chevy Caprice, with 254 horsepower and racing suspension.

   We went on the ride, Hunter driving on the wrong side of the road, music blaring, the whole bit; stopped for dinner, where he had to order his signature six of everything; then he got in the car again to head to another party in Aspen. We were driving along a winding dark back road when, without warning, Hunter slammed on the brakes and got out of the car. Kris and I were a little unnerved. Although our experience has been entirely the opposite, we've heard enough wacky stories about him to make us wonder. Kris leaned over to me and said, "This is it. He's gonna kill us." But he didn't. Instead, he came over to my side of the car, opened my door like the perfect gentlemen he can be, and said, "Your turn to drive."

   I knew that this was Hunter's gift to me—his way of cheering me up. It worked. I was so touched by the gesture that I forgot all about my bad day. Hunter's friends were astonished when we pulled up with me at the wheel. He ignored all questions as to why he had broken his thirty-year rule.

It was a blast driving the Shark, although Hunter didn't let me drive in quite the same way that he does. I had to stay under the speed limit, and I felt like I was driving with my grandfather every time I heard Hunter's foot hit the floor as he roared, ''The brakes! Put on the brakes, you crazy child!''

I got to drive home, too. We got back here to the Owl Farm about 3 A.M. and Hunter passed out filters for our cigarettes as we settled in to assist him with the pell-mell of his daily wee-hour writing ceremony. These, I think, must be the good old days.

THE OWL FARM   8/11, 6:45 A.M.

(Kristin)

Even though my body is wracked with exhaustion, I can't fall asleep. Today was an especially enlightening and taxing twenty-four hours at the Owl Farm.

Shainee, Hunter, and I took a long "sunset drive," as we have the days before, and stopped at a local haunt for the usual overordering. Hunter has insisted on buying dinner every night so far, which is a little uncomfortable for us, although I understand he believes it's the gentlemanly thing to do. But tonight he asked me to sign his credit card bill while he started the car—chocolate silk pies "to go" in hand. I got into an argument with the hostess, who had helpfully added a 50 percent tip to the bill. "He always tips that much," she insisted indignantly.

"Not when I'm signing the bill, he doesn't," I explained. "Why don't we agree on a generous, reasonable percentage, like the one the rest of your customers give," I suggested, changing the tip to 25 percent. Apparently, Hunter's generosity is legendary in Woody Creek.

After more driving, we headed back to the Owl Farm for some late-night writing. Deborah asked us to encourage Hunter to get some pages done. A few days ago, I had asked Hunter over gazpacho what inspired him to write. "Fun," he had said simply. "I need to have a lot of fun, then I can write." Well, we'd managed to squeeze in a few hours of fun, and I, for one, was ready to burn the midnight oil for another chapter of *Polo Is My Life*. Shainee seems to have made some progress in organizing the existing chapters.

Hunter procrastinated for a good hour, threatening to "flog" Shainee with an oversized egg beater he found in his kitchen. We've learned to ignore Hunter's threats, staring back at him with stone faces, not speaking. I think it amuses him.

I put paper in the typewriter, which Hunter interpreted as an overt act of aggression. He suddenly decided we should call Studs Terkel and say hi, explaining that he and Studs go way back, which was news to us. "Oh, yeah, I did his radio show for *Fear and Loathing*," he said, adding that Studs had been—without really trying—instrumental in a moment that helped keep Hunter's career on track. Hunter explained that he had wanted to abandon the book tour he was on at the time. "The publicity people were swines," he grunted. But he had been scheduled to go on Terkel's show and had decided to do this last interview before going into hiding. He ended up having such a great time with Studs that he decided to stay with the tour. It proved to be a very wise decision.

Hunter demanded Studs's phone number, which I reluctantly gave him while glancing at the clock. It was only 8 P.M. Chicago time, but I still felt it might not be respectful to call at this hour. Hunter dialed before anyone could dissuade him, and greeted Studs on the other end of the line. "Studs! This is Hunter. Hunter!

Hunter Thompson!'' Hunter and Studs proceeded to have a reunion conversation, catching up on lost time.

Hunter always uses a speakerphone, so we could hear the whole thing. Studs seemed excited and surprised to hear from Hunter and doubly surprised that Shainee and I were still on the road and at Hunter's. Studs yelled encouraging words to us over the speaker. After giving our best to Ida, we hung up, taken aback, momentarily, by the connections between the people we were meeting on the road. There is nothing better than a Studs Terkel or a George McGovern story told by Hunter Thompson, and vice versa.

After a couple of hours, Shainee sagged, her big eyes at half mast. She fell asleep on the couch to the sounds of CNN broadcasting the day's news yet one more time. I sat at the typewriter as Hunter paced back and forth in the kitchen, dragging on his filtered cigarette. He dictated, I typed. We got down about five good pages, in which Hunter described a summer afternoon visit to Jimmy Buffett's Southern mansion. Buffett is a personal friend of Hunter's, and a big fan of polo, which is how he fits into the book.

Hunter struggled a bit for the right words to end the story. ''Damn!'' he yelled in frustration. ''I've written some good shit in my life.''

''I know you're brilliant, Hunter,'' I told him. ''So it's too late to convince me otherwise. Plus, I've read a lot of your good shit.''

I'm not a fan, per se, of Hunter's works. Although I appreciate his singular voice, I guess they're not manifestations of my personal fantasies, in the way they are for many of my male friends. But, after talking to Hunter, and reading some of the personal letters he's shared with Shainee and me, I have gained a better understanding of and admiration for his wit and intellect. Shainee and I do not idolize Hunter; we respect him. I think he senses the difference and maintains a safe distance between himself and the idol chasers, which he can smell from a mile away.

''I need to take a swim,'' Hunter declared abuptly, explaining that it helped him relax before bed. I looked at the clock above the stove: 5:10 A.M. I was bleary-eyed, but, as always, Hunter was persuasive. He can make taking the garbage out sound like an event not to be missed. I got my suit and woke Shainee to ask her if she wanted to go. She looked at me like I was the lead character in her nightmare and stumbled toward Deborah's house, looking for a bed.

Hunter and I wove through the deserted backroads. We had left the top down, but Hunter blasted the heater when he noticed that I was shivering from the mountain air whipping in and out of the exposed Shark. I love driving with him; it inspires a heightened sense of both peace and suspense.

''I'm going to take a hard, sharp turn to the right,'' Hunter warned as we screeched around a corner into a long driveway. He cut the motor and the lights as we rolled closer to a large, quiet house hidden in the middle of the woods. Near the house was a cabin containing an Olympic-size indoor pool. Hunter explained that he has an agreement with the people who own the house—something to do with a lawsuit—access to their pool being part of the settlement.

Hunter grabbed a flashlight and pointed one toward the door of the cabin. He had a key with which he unlocked the door to the giant, humid room. The fragmented lights from the bottom of the pool illuminated our way like a disco ball, and Hunter parted the water within seconds. I watched him proceed through a silent ritual of movements and strokes, looking like an underwater yoga master. I slipped into the other end of the misty pool and challenged myself to an underwater somersault match, occasionally coming up for air and visions of pristine stars shining through the glass ceiling.

When we got out, I too felt relaxed, but energized. We both ran outside to the car as though someone was coming after us with a shotgun. We laughed, dripping wet, and jumped into the Shark. Hunter swung the car around, peeling out of the dark driveway.

The sky was growing a shade lighter. Hunter took an unfamiliar turn, heading up a mountain. Blazing a trail through the brush, he stopped the car suddenly, put it in park, and stared straight ahead over the plateau in silence. For a few moments we were quiet. I think it's actually in those moments of silence that we understand each other best.

Soon we witnessed the orange and yellow debut of a Colorado morning, and I wondered if this too wasn't part of the daily Hunter ritual. He seemed to have timed our arrival by the minute. We watched the sun come up until there was no doubt it was staying. "Once you get used to space, it's hard to go back to civilization," Hunter said as he put the Shark in gear and began to follow our trail back to the main road.

One thing Shainee and I have appreciated about Hunter is that he has gone out of his way to show us the beauty of this part of the country. Hunter loves this land and often talks about it "and its imminent destruction by the groping hands of nearby Aspen land rapers." In frustration, he has also talked about leaving— moving before the developers move in on him. But I bet that Hunter lives here until he dies. As much as it changes, it's still his home.

We pulled back into the Owl Farm, the sun beaming and me ready for bed. Before I could say good night, Hunter was pulling food out of the refrigerator, insisting that he make us a meal so we wouldn't go to bed hungry. I agreed, even though I was more tired than hungry.

He whipped up a pesto pasta dish, avocado salad, and unwrapped his favorite chocolate silk pie. "Do you want to watch *Being There*?" he asked while whirling

Kris and Hunter

around the kitchen. I suggested we eat outside in the quiet of the porch; my sensory system was short-circuiting. I was so tired that I didn't attempt to help. I went to sit outside, the peacocks keeping me company.

Hunter emerged, carrying trays to the deck, where we sat in the stillness of early morning, eating, talking and laughing, keeping one eye out for skunks. I liked many things about this man, but most of all, I would say, I liked his sense of humor. The muscles in my cheeks ached from exercise—days of nonstop amusement.

The meal was delicious—yet another surprise from our constantly surprising host.

"Good night," I eventually said to Hunter, squeezing his shoulder and thanking him for our breakfast-hour dinner.

"Good morning," he said, only just beginning to look tired.

HUNTER S. THOMPSON

JOURNALIST • NOVELIST

WOODY CREEK, COLORADO

(Shainee)

On what was supposed to be our last night in Aspen, Hunter finally agreed to do the interview. He could procrastinate no longer. To this day, I think he would have preferred it if we had just come to visit, with no purpose other than to play. But he claimed that he truly wanted to participate in our documentary.

The three of us went out to dinner that night, having finally convinced Hunter to let us treat. He took us to the Snowmass Country Club, but it didn't go very well. He was obviously unnerved at the prospect of being interviewed and thus a little cranky. When the waitress told him that he couldn't smoke at the table, things got weird. Hunter told the restaurant staff, quite audibly, that they had degraded themselves to the quality of an IHOP—an IHOP with a bar. We canceled our order and got Hunter out of there. Kris paid the bartender, telling him that I was sick and that we had to go immediately. We took Hunter home.

Gerry came over, which only added to the brouhaha. Hunter fidgeted with his cigarette holder as he barked at us about the lighting for the interview. He didn't like being lit from above. "I just think it's a very bad way to photograph. This is the kind of light you get in the police station." Kris tried to assure him that the light was not unflattering. Hunter prepped himself for the interview with the right hat, a plastic hand that he attached to his shirt's placket, and then turned the TV to CNN. He kept flipping through the channels, trying to find anything to do besides begin. Gerry got him a drink. Finally Kris ventured, "Are you ready?"

"Yeah. What kind of time frame are we looking at?" Hunter glanced around nervously from the camera on the tripod to the Steadycam in Kris's hand. He asked if both cameras would be running the whole time. We said yes, it would make the film easier to edit, and just when we thought he was ready to start, he asked us to turn the cameras off. He had already set up a flashlight to shine directly into the lens of the stationary camera, rendering it useless. We breathed deeply and turned everything off.

Finally he seemed set. I was hoping that at best, we would get a few solid answers from him before the agitation took over. Since our window of opportunity would be short, I figured it would be better to dive right in while I had his attention. I asked him if he could discuss the changing face of the American dream. It seemed a safe question, given that he'd written much on the subject. In retrospect, it was a poor choice.

"*Talk* about it? I thought we were going to ask questions. You want me to make a speech about the American dream?"

"Sure. We'd love that," I responded.

"I'm sure you would, but I don't have it in me right now. Ask Bill Clinton for that shit. No, I'm not going to make a speech about the American dream." Hunter huffed and turned from the camera, grumbling, "Man, out of cigarettes, too. What else?"

Hunter did not do well in the hot seat. He was articulate, funny, and charming—except when he saw the red record light. I was a little panicked at the thought of not getting any usable footage. The phone kept ringing every two minutes. Hunter kept fidgeting. I stayed silent, thinking it would pressure him into saying something. He finally spoke.

"Well, we all know that there is a mythology about the American dream. I went to look for the American dream one time in Las Vegas. I finally found the American dream. It was the old Psychiatrists Club up on Fremont Boulevard or something. And it had burnt down several years earlier. It's documented. So how's that?"

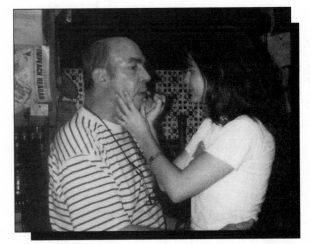

Hunter primps

It was a beginning—a story Doug Brinkley had already quoted to us. Then Hunter decided that he could not go any further without applying an unsettling shade of red lipstick to his lips. "I want the lipstick! I insist upon it!" Kris had to put some on, too. I was far enough away to escape this fate, and asked Hunter who he had found influential.

"A hell of a lot of people. J. Edgar Hoover, Roy Cohn. They were in charge of law enforcement for fifty years of this century, and are you aware that J. Edgar Hoover was a monstrous bullfruit? I mean, a flaming fruit? The kind of queen who didn't really shave. Ms. Mary, they called her. Head of the FBI, through seven or eight presidents. Every American's view of law enforcement has been influenced by J. Edgar Hoover. Mostly because of his outrageous public relations. But more because of the files he kept on everybody. For fifty years, this guy controlled the political throat of the President. And you wonder why the American dream got into some kind of trouble? Welcome to J. Edgar Hoover Country. Not much different now.''

Kris asked, ''What about the Founding Fathers?''

''They were a huge influence on me. I think they were an amazing bunch of people. Thomas Jefferson was hopelessly insane, you know that? He was insane. And Ben Franklin was a convicted felon in England. He was a member of the Hell Fire Club. These were degenerates. One of my ancestors signed the Declaration of Independence. Richard Stockton, a lawyer they said was from New Jersey but who actually came from Virginia. I was shocked when he was identified as a lawyer from New Jersey.''

Hunter was losing steam fast, so I tried to push on, asking if there was anyone living today who had influenced him.

''George McGovern is one of them. Despite appearances and all rumors you may have heard, I have been working in politics for a long time, about thirty years. George is the best person I've met. Bobby Kennedy once called him the most decent man in the Senate. That was in 1966. George is not President. Neither am I. Michael Jackson might be soon. I think he will be the third-party nomination after Perot.''

We knew that Hunter's friendship with McGovern dated back to his coverage of the 1972 election. I asked him if he thought things would be different now if McGovern had won.

He laughed. ''Yeah, he'd be in jail.'' Then seriously, ''No, there would have been an interlude of decency.''

Gerry leaned in and handed Hunter a refreshed Scotch and water—just in time—as I asked Hunter if it bothers him that he has a bunch of freaky people trying to hunt him down all of the time, calling him an icon. Hunter smiled. ''Who do you have in mind?''

Kris replied, deadpan, ''Us.''

Hunter puffed on his cigarette for a second and said simply, ''At times. It depends. It's an hour-by-hour thing. It's been quite a trial.'' Just then a moth flew in front of Hunter's face, distracting him. Hunter swatted at it like King Kong swatted the helicopter and finally crushed it, throwing it to the ground for a final stomping.

''Did I get that bastard?'' he asked sincerely, and Kris just laughed. ''Was there something funny there?''

''Just enjoying your charm,'' she offered.

He seemed satisfied with that and complained, ''I can't believe I'm being forced to carry the intellectual weight here,'' taking a long pull from his drink. Gerry and Hunter then launched into a very long conversation about nothing in particular, eventually leading us back to the subject of politics.

"The good people are always the failed ones," he stated. "You see, politics is basically the art of controlling your environment, and there are a lot of ways of doing that. Environment is more than beer cans on the side of the road and people spraying too much weed killer. Environment is Newt Gingrich, for instance. He is part of our environment, mine anyway. Yours, I dare say.

"And to choose *not* to help control your environment is like going into battle and choosing the low ground. 'We'll defend the swamp. That way they can't get behind us.' Politics really is, in theory, the only way in a democracy that we can play on a level court—which is insane, of course. It's not level, and it's not fair. But we can play on it. I speak in a broad sense, of course.

"There were some very good people in politics, unsung heroes: George McGovern, Jimmy Carter, and others. The real problem with this country is the Democratic Party has become obsolete, useless for about thirty or forty years—ever since Roosevelt and Truman. Truman was the last really Democratic President. Truman beat Dewey and that's when politics was fun. Since then, it's been a parade of whores, with good people—the exceptions—always remaining as the failed ones."

Wow. Somehow, when Hunter wasn't looking, we had gotten an opinion out of him. After some anecdotes about terrorizing his neighbor Jack Nicholson and another about being bitten by neighbor Ed Bradley's (of *60 Minutes*) dog, I asked if he had any hope for the country's future.

Hunter looked me right in the eye and said, "I knew you were going to say this. What does it all mean, Alfie?"

"I love that song. '*What's it all about, Alfie?*', you mean," Kris chimed in.

Hunter stood corrected. But he was right. We'd promised not to ask him anything too philosophical, and "What's it all about, Alfie?" was his way of telling me that I'd strayed into forbidden territory. I reminded Hunter that the night before—when we were prepping him with our list of questions for the seventeenth time—he had told us that we didn't know anything about America. He had said that our generation was still too young, that we had missed most of the important stuff.

We had made Hunter promise to fill us in *while* the cameras were running, but the argument had obviously not been effective. He had been reluctant, saying, "Naturally, I get a little kicky when I see a red light go on."

We never really understood Hunter's uneasiness in front of the camera. He certainly loved using them. He had three video cameras of his own and a closet full of still cameras and Polaroids. You could not stop the man from snapping away maniacally once he got going. But when the camera was turned on him, all hell broke loose. I can only posit—as Hunter's colleague Tom Robbins would later lament—that those who choose to communicate through the written word are often not as comfortable with the broadcast word.

We tried to hold Hunter to his promise to tell us what we did not know about America. He offered, "The American century is going to end here. This is a doomed structure. If people would accept their diminishing expectations and diminishing hopes, then maybe we could survive. But that will never happen. A lot of people thought that's what Jerry Garcia stood for. The Hell's Angels certainly did.''

I saw Kris glance at a bumper sticker that read HUNTER S. THOMPSON FOR PRESIDENT. She tried to resurrect the situation by coaxing Hunter into talking about his experience running for the office of sheriff of Aspen. He would have no part of it, so we asked him the ''What if you were President?'' question instead.

''I'd be in jail, probably'' was his firm response.

''All right, even if you were in jail being President, what would be your focus?''

''I'd have a good deal, I suppose, if I were a President in jail,'' Hunter quipped. ''They were going to lock up Nixon in a closet underneath the Capitol stairs, you know. That was the only place they had for arresting the President. It was about the size of a bathroom.

''Oh, you poor girls. It's a miracle you've gotten this far. How many people have you interviewed? Now you're going into Crow country, evil country, Wyoming; Montana; Cour d'Alaine; Idaho. Mark Furhman just recently purchased a home in the Cour d'Alaine area. That's probably a good place to go. We probably should do some shooting tonight so we can get you prepared. I'll give you a cheap shotgun—that you can keep.''

We were off on a tangent again. Hunter told us he'd teach us to shoot after the interview—that skunk was still lurking around somewhere. We gave it one last shot and asked Hunter about the root of the demise of the American hero.

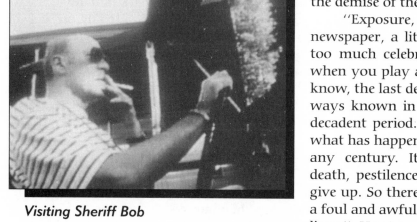

Visiting Sheriff Bob

''Exposure, I think. A little too much newspaper, a little too much TV, a little too much celebrity. You got to lay low when you play around on that level. You know, the last decade of any century is always known in English literature as the decadent period. You have to understand what has happened in the last ten years of any century. It's always plague, fear, death, pestilence, and failure. People just give up. So there's no surprise that this is a foul and awful period in a lot of people's lives.'' Hunter reached behind him and pulled out a reference book that he said chronicled the timetables of history. He was looking for proof of his conviction but never found it. After a few minutes, he closed the book.

''Well, I'm not going to sit here and do research. Let me just assure you: either I'm right or I'm wrong. But I will tell you that any research at all on this, done by a person of your gender and eminently destructible tender age, will prove that there is a threat of darkness. The last ten years of a century, people generally tend to give up. So it's no surprise at all that this is not going to be a constructive period in human history as we know it. It could be, but history is deeply against it. And if I were twenty-six at this time, I'd be pissed off myself. It's the end of the American century, period. From now on, you're all gonna know what it was like to live like a Venezuelan in 1975."

Hunter then told me to stop staring at him with "doe eyes," because it wouldn't work, and that about wrapped it up. We hoped we had gotten enough footage to piece together and we put the cameras away. As we packed up, I got the feeling that Hunter thought he'd let us down. He puffed on his cigarette, the blue light of the television shining in the lenses of his glasses, and said, "Well, you definitely got something, but the real interview came through osmosis." Hunter was right—our week with him had been marked by a series of lessons and insights. Most important, we felt we had made an unlikely friend.

We were scheduled to leave the next day. We went over to Hunter's house in the afternoon to say good-bye. He persuaded us to go for one last "sunset drive" in the Shark, and we drove around, dropping in on Hunter's friend Sheriff Bob, and then over to Sheffy's for one last dinner. We stopped for gas and I went into the adjoining 7-Eleven with Hunter—while Kris guarded the Shark—to buy him yet another flashlight and some batteries. He brought one of his Polaroid cameras

with us and took pictures of the teenager behind the counter and the only other customers in the store—a couple of guys in flannel, with short hair on the front of their heads and long hair down the back.

Then he asked the kid behind the counter to take a picture of him and me and the flannel guys. Hunter handed it to me and said, "Here, take this home. It's your father's worst nightmare."

We bought twelve lotto tickets and went back to the car to scratch them off with Kris. We sat in the convertible, the cool Colorado breeze ruffling our hair, puffing on Hunter's filtered Dunhill Reds, and played lotto. We won four dollars and Hunter went back in and bought more batteries with the winnings.

For Shainee's dad

We ended up back at Hunter's at midnight. We had planned on leaving in the afternoon, since we had to be in Pinedale, Wyoming, the next day at one o'clock. It was a good seven-hour drive, but Hunter didn't seem to want us to leave. He would never have admitted it, but I think he was a little sad to see us go. We were certainly sad to leave. When we finally said we had to hit the road, Hunter followed us out to the car with sodas and some sandwiches that Deborah had made. He checked our gas gauge, wiped our headlights clean, and asked if we had enough duct tape.

"Duct tape?" we asked in stereo.

"You must have duct tape . . . and flashlights," he said, pulling two rolls of duct tape out of his jacket pocket, the flashlight and batteries we had just bought out of another pocket. Then he retrieved a bright yellow flashlight from the Shark—one we had admired the first night we met him. Kris told him that he had a very gallant side and that we had laughed more with him than on the rest of our trip combined. Hunter hugged us and said simply, "I pay attention, and history will absolve me."

And with that, we waved good-bye to the Owl Farm and the legend who lives there.

(Kristin)

There is no interstate from Aspen to Pinedale, so we are relegated to small highways and back roads. Shainee is progressing at her typical breakneck pace, determined to get us to Pinedale in half the time and buy us a few hours of much-needed sleep. I'm not sure I'll ever be able to decipher this writing, but our new flashlight is already coming in handy. However, the possible purpose of the duct tape remains a curiosity.

I got the camera out before we passed the Colorado town of Baggs to shoot the signs at the state border: LEAVING COLORFUL COLORADO and ENTERING WYOMING—A GREAT LAND OUTDOORS. As the signs passed me through the viewfinder, I got a chill up my spine. It may have been a melancholy brought on by lack of sleep, but I had a sudden moment of heightened awareness of what an ephemeral experience this trip has represented. I feel like I'm at a parade, perched on my dad's shoulders, and once the spectacle has inched past where we stand, beyond our view, we will never see or know that piece of it again.

I know Shainee and I will never again take a trip like this—neither together nor alone. We will, instead, talk about this trip, the one we took when we were twenty-six, for the rest of our adult lives. "Remember when Ken Kesey called Hunter's house after Jerry Garcia died?" "Remember when we thought Hunter was going to kill us and instead he let you drive?" Thinking about how Hunter—now only moments behind us—is already a memory leaves me with a sweet sadness of things to come, and things passing as quickly into "remember when. . . ."

I can't believe we're finally on Wyoming soil. I just remembered a recurring dream I had before I left Los Angeles. It always took place in Wyoming in the summer months, at a quiet ranch where I contentedly worked under an endless, surreal-blue sky. The dream was particularly haunting because I had never been to Wyoming or anywhere near there, and I had always wondered what my subconscious was trying to tell me.

As our trip's days turn into weeks and weeks into months, I feel myself becoming a less career-driven, results-oriented girl and more a woman who seeks happiness and wholeness through a *process*. A few states back, I started defining "success" as finding the best glass of Southern lemonade I could get my hands on. Being a passenger on a summertime drive, with my feet hanging out the window, I've discovered a finer appreciation for the cast-away slivers of life, the shavings that can pile up on the workshop floor and be ignored, stepped all over.

This has not been an easy transition for me. Paradigm-hopping is painful, actually, as one can hold tightly to things that define them, even if they're detrimental. Growing up in the seventies and eighties, I had been reminded again and again that it was most important to shape one's life and identity around a career, whether it be social work or running a Fortune 500 company. Although family had been an implicit part of the equation, *balance* was rarely discussed. I am beginning to realize that the element of balance—something a lot of people we've met have addressed—can make excelling at one's work that much easier.

I just realized that I haven't had that dream about Wyoming since Shainee and I left Los Angeles.

JOHN PERRY BARLOW

CO-FOUNDER OF THE ELECTRONIC FRONTIER FOUNDATION • GRATEFUL DEAD LYRICIST •

CONTRIBUTING WRITER FOR *WIRED* • RETIRED CATTLE RANCHER

PINEDALE, WYOMING

(Kristin)

I was so curious about this man we were about to meet, with whom we had been communicating for many months via E-mail, a relatively new tool for me. Shainee, my personal cyber-guru, had brought Barlow to my attention after reading some of his articles in *Wired* magazine.

As a third-generation cattle kid, John was a man of the old frontier, yet also a pioneer of the new frontier of cyberspace. Years ago, John had stumbled onto the then-uncharted cyber-territory while writing songs for the Grateful Dead. The Dead and their followers were one of the first ''communities'' to set up a cyber-camp in order to communicate—it was an especially useful tool, given their nomadic nature.

John had initially purchased a computer to try and save the family ranch he had been running for seventeen years. Since then, John has focused most of his energies on taming this new frontier. He helped usher the term ''cyberspace'' into public discourse and, with Mitchell Kapor, cofounded EFF, the Electronic Frontier Foundation, which is dedicated to maintaining constitutional rights—particularly the First and Fourth Amendments—in cyberspace.

We were to meet John in a park overlooking a wide, running stream across the street from his house. We were on time, surprisingly, but we didn't see a man—young or old—anywhere in the park. We had no idea what John looked like, but we did know, from his last E-mail, that he would be driving directly from the airport to meet us. He would be returning from Jerry Garcia's funeral that day. I wasn't sure how I felt about doing an interview with someone right on the heels of a good friend's funeral.

Knowing how unpredictable travel can be, I napped in the park while Shainee opted for ice cream from a shop around the corner. I awoke to the sounds of a car pulling into the gravel driveway across the street. A man in a cowboy hat got out of the car and walked over to the passenger's side to assist a white-haired elderly woman. I spotted Shainee sitting on a huge rock near the house as I stood up and grabbed the camera, with a hunch that this was probably the cowboy we had been waiting for. I moved toward the house, pulled the lens cap off the camera, and asked, "Is that you?"

"It's me," he answered knowingly. "Sorry I'm so late." We assured him it was fine. "Nice hat," he added, looking at my head.

I had forgotten that I was wearing Hunter's "Gonzo hat" given to me as a parting gift. "Thanks," I said. "The man himself handed it over."

"How is the man himself?" he asked.

"He's fine, actually," I said. "*We're* almost dead, but he's fine."

"I'm sure you are!" John said, laughing heartily. "His nervous system has been case-hardened. But Hunter's a good one," he added with reverence.

John and Hunter actually had a lot in common including a generation, friends, and a personal mission. We had spent much of our time with Hunter talking about the First and Fourth Amendments, a subject about which he's passionate. And John works tirelessly to uphold the same amendments for people maneuvering through the so-called information superhighway.

"It seems you've had a long, hard week," I said to John.

"Yeah," he replied, explaining that he had gone to Australia and Minneapolis on business before taking a flight to San Francisco for Jerry's funeral. There was more space between his words when he spoke of Jerry. "I can't seem to get my mind wrapped around it. I couldn't cry about it until yesterday and then, only briefly. He was a very close friend. It's just, it's just too . . . the ways in which it affects the world, at least my particular slice of it, are so thorough and fine-grained that it's just too much to try and take on at once."

John came back from his reverie and changed the subject. "So who else have you talked to on this odyssey of yours?" We listed the ever-growing group of names, tracing our steps backwards, stopping with Andrei Codrescu's name. "He is terrific," John interjected. "I love that guy; he is a very soulful dude.

"You guys have really set out on a terrific thing for yourselves here," John decided, squinting in the long rays of the afternoon sun. " 'Let's go out and meet every famous, interesting person in America!' What an excellent scam!" he declared with his robust laugh.

"You have to be naive enough to think that you can do it," Shainee admitted, giving away our secret.

"That's kind of the message of a lot of what I do," John explained. "If I came out of the cattle business a middle-aged, broken-down rancher to become some kind of computer guru in six years, then this stuff can't be all that hard."

"It's only been six years since you first used a computer?" Shainee repeated in shock.

John nodded his head. "Six or seven."

We asked John why he had gotten out of the cattle business. "Well, I've often said, 'There's more money in bullshit than bulls.' But I was gonna lose the ranch if I didn't sell it," he explained. "I figured it was better to sell it on my own terms than to watch somebody do it on the courthouse steps." He explained that he didn't really have a permanent residence anymore, but that he still visits the ranch, and sometimes takes his three little girls there to play. It was apparent the ranch remained close to his heart, even though his name was no longer on the deed. He promised to take us there before we left.

John's personality had a disarming effect. I got the feeling he was so unguarded, in part, due to his friend's sudden death. John probably didn't have the energy to keep up a front for visitors right now—judging from the underlying vulnerability to his stocky frame and bearded face.

As we headed toward John's house, I noticed that the sun was trying to set. We had only about an hour of usable daylight left in which to do our interview. We realized that would be cutting it close, so John generously invited us to spend the night in the little gray house across from the park and tape the majority of the interview the following day at the ranch. Avoiding another bad motel sounded like a great idea to us, and since we knew John came from the Grateful Dead tradition, in which it was cool to crash on a new friend's floor, we accepted without hesitation.

John explained that he was divorced and that his mother, the white-haired woman I had seen, lives in the house part-time so he and his daughters can spend time with her. We walked into the house to meet the cast of Barlow characters: Miriam—John's feisty ninety-one-year-old mother—and two of his three daughters, Anna and Leah, ten and twelve years old, respectively. Amilia, his third and youngest daughter, was away camping with a family friend in a teepee in Colorado.

While we sat in the kitchen talking to Miriam, Anna, and Leah, John talked to someone on the phone about an Internet chat he was scheduled to do with New York Mayor Giuliani the following night. It was then that we discovered that Miriam had been a lifelong registered Republican—probably the most unorthodox, radical Republican the state of Wyoming has ever known.

"What do you think about the Grateful Dead and their music?" I asked, a subject that seemed to have been on everyone's minds the last couple days.

"Well, I love them to pieces!" she declared with joy. "I've known Bobby Weir since he and Johnny went to school together. See, I knew them a long time before they were the Grateful Dead." She told us how much she loved their shows, especially watching from backstage. She was always impressed, she said, by their "improvisational techniques."

Shainee and I sat with Miriam, transfixed, until the spell was broken when John walked back into the kitchen, suggesting we start the interview. We followed him out of the house with our equipment, heading toward the bridge across from the park. The girls ran up behind us, not wanting to miss any fun.

We reiterated, for John's benefit, what our interview would be about and asked him to give us a context for his present endeavors by sharing some of what had led him to this place in time.

Miriam

"Well, I was born right near here. I actually went to a one-room schoolhouse and rode through three miles of snow to get there; it was a pretty nineteenth-century existence. At a certain point, I got into a lot of trouble and got sent away to school, where I became close friends with the guitar player who would eventually become the rhythm guitarist for the Grateful Dead. When I look at all the odd forks along my path, I sometimes feel like a thinking man's Forrest Gump. You know, I just stumble into things that actually amount to something.

"When I went away to college," John continued, "that was a real eye-opening experience, because I found out that most people these days come from . . . 'Generica.' So the motivating factor in my life ever since has been finding new ways to actually create place and community." The notion of community was being addressed in *every* context on our trip, it seemed, even cyberspace with web sites and chat rooms—the newest adaptation of community.

"That is the underlying subtext of a lot of the things I've done that otherwise seem completely disconnected," John explained. "That was why I did the Grateful Dead. When Weir wanted me to try writing songs with him, the thing that motivated me was that I could see that the Deadheads had a community of sorts, even though they didn't have a place. And the thing that motivated me to go to cyberspace was following them there, but for the purpose of creating a community." John was full of surprises. I was certain that he was the only former Republican county chairman in America who had been writing songs with the Grateful Dead since 1971.

"So, anyway, I went East to college," John said, backtracking to his school days, "and spent a good deal of time at Millbrook with Tim Leary. I was a full-raised hippie and I still am, without any hesitation. I went to India, actually sat on a mountaintop with a holy man, completely, once again, by accident." John laughed. "The holy man mostly wanted to know about automobile mechanics. I think he learned more than I did. But when I came back, I stopped at the ranch and things were in kind of a dreadful state. I was on my way to California to work for Warner Brothers Records, but I decided I'd run the ranch for six months and then go about my business, because I never really wanted to be a rancher anyway—what a terrible coil that is.

"But I ended up doing that for seventeen years. There've been a few other major odd forks that aren't in my bio, 'cause you can only say so many contradictory things about yourself before it starts to fade into some kind of a blur and people can't get any kind of a handle on it. But I like having those contradictory things in my life, because another one of my missions in the world is to get people to accept paradox. I think one of the reasons we have so much inner and social conflict is because we don't think something is true until we've resolved all of its contradictions. Which means amputating half of any reality and turning it into something that we made up."

Shainee asked him what had inspired the inception of the Electronic Frontier Foundation. John replied, "The EFF is something that got started because I had an experience with the FBI that made me realize that the Feds were about to come to this place, cyberspace, that I had only just identified as being a *place*. They certainly didn't recognize it as a place, but it felt like one to me from the first time I got there. And I could see that the Feds were about to come there to subdue the natives. So we founded EFF to try to educate authority on digital issues."

John talked about EFF's particular defense of the Fourth Amendment as it applies to search and seizure in cyberspace. "EFF was created in order to help preserve the Bill of Rights in cyberspace. We were focused on how one would go about conveying rights in such a dimension. We knew it was going to require a complete rethinking of human relationships and how they could be regulated. So we began by tackling a specific problem, and then realized we had grabbed hold of a very large problem—since the notion of 'rights' in this new realm was a brand-new can of worms. The government didn't understand what they were dealing with well enough to know how to do a responsible search. I mean, if they were doing tax fraud, for example, in a conventional office situation, they would go in and get the files that mattered and business could proceed. But in this case, they were taking . . . they were going in and grabbing every single magnetic medium and everything that could relate to it. In one case, they even confiscated a clock radio!" John laughed at the absurdity.

Shainee drew John back to his ideas about Generica—as he called it—and how the idea of community relates to cyberspace. "Well," he began, "in order for a community to exist, it has to be able to form its own culture and ethics and social contract. And for the federal government to try to impose their completely inapplicable will on the place: A, it won't work, but B, it will screw things up . . . It would be a tragedy to have the greatest free place that human beings have ever created polluted by fear at the get-go. Because really, as much as anything, it just has to be the kind of place where you can go and say anything you want and publish that to the rest of the human race without constraint.

"We are now in a collective hallucination in this country that is distorting all of our political processes completely, because people are making their map of the world based on information rather than experience. The net, in my view, has the capacity to become much more like experience than information. In cyberspace, you can at least ask questions in real time about the phenomena that you're sensing. You can't do that with Morley Safer. As much as he may seem like a personable guy, he doesn't know who you are, and he never will.''

John looked down to Anna and Leah, who were wading through the water in their shorts. The temperature was dropping fast and I knew the water had to be freezing cold. I was reminded of how much you can learn about a person by watching their kids.

''Anna Bear!'' John yelled. ''You monster! You girls are going to fall into the crick.''

''So!'' she squealed back. ''Can I just dive in?'' she asked, then dove, without waiting for an answer.

''I wouldn't stop ya,'' John said, more to us than Anna.

Leah followed her sister's lead, falling into the water, giggling.

''They're definitely not 'girlie' *girls*,'' Shainee declared.

''Oh, yeah, they are!'' John disagreed. ''All three of them have a very strong girlishness, in spite of their general resilience. There is nothing intrinsically girlish about being weak or whiny, you know. I think the model of the future is women that are really feminine is some respects but also really . . .''

''Warrior?'' I suggested.

''Yeah,'' John said. ''Sort of like Tank Girl.''

Just then Anna and Leah ran up the bridge toward us, dripping wet.

''I'm going to take a shower,'' Anna informed us as she passed us. Leah followed, her attempting to clean her glasses with her wet shirt.

''Throw your clothes in the dryer before you take a shower,'' John insisted, watching them go. ''These girls are gonna be a force loose in the world,'' he said, his eyes staying on them. ''And I'm just delighted by that. Another one of my missions in life is to end the dominance of my half of the species. And I don't mind being a traitor, either. I feel very strongly about this. We've done a shitty job for twenty-five hundred years. I think it's time to let you take it.''

''We're ready!'' Shainee said without hesitation.

''I know you are,'' he agreed, looking not to us, but downstream. The sun had finally set, leaving us shrouded in deep blues. We headed back to the house, all complaining of hunger. None of us had really eaten that day, so we went out to dinner and got to know each other a little more over fried chicken, biscuits, and homemade pie. Our dinner conversation revolved mostly around Grandma Barlow's haircare tips. She attempted to convince all younger, less experienced people at the table of the benefits of once-a-month hair washings. ''You're all *ruining* your hair overwashing it,'' she insisted. ''I have gone seventy years washing my hair once a month. And I have had beautiful hair *forever*.''

"I don't think Vidal Sassoon would want this information to get out," I ventured, buttering a hot biscuit. "His stock would crash."

After dinner and more family discussions, Shainee and I lay in the attic in darkness on sheets covered in cartoon prints. I fantasized about staying in Wyoming. Forever. I had felt so immediately at home here, it was overpowering. I lay there imagining explaining to Shainee, the next morning over coffee, why I knew that I must stay in Pinedale, maybe even with John and Miriam. I would tell her that my plan was to get a job on a ranch where I would work with my hands and fall into bed at the end of each day exhausted by pure physical labor. After all, this had literally been my *dream*, the recurring dream that had first compelled me to talk to Shainee about leaving our city and exploring the country. Here I was, in the very place I had dreamed about. I had arrived. I convinced myself that Shainee would understand why I needed to stay; she was wise, and I trusted she know that some choices in life had to be made impulsively.

I stared at the moonlit ceiling with the terrible and guilty feeling of not wanting to go on with our trip. I did not want to cross the next state line. The things I had come to desire for my life were here.

I drifted to sleep.

The next morning I awoke, but not early. It was almost 11 A.M., I saw, as I looked at my watch in disbelief. Neither Shainee nor I had slept so late since we started our trip. I felt the repercussions of having given over our internal clocks to Hunter, and a tinge of anxiety crept into my body. Then I remembered the decision I had made before I fell asleep, and I knew that the decision was the source of anxiety. Shainee was still asleep, so I creaked down the pull-down ladder and listened for signs of life. There were none. From where I stood, I could see John's mother asleep in her bed, her long silky hair on her pillow, princess-like, and John's door still closed. I was surprised that two people who had grown up on a ranch could sleep in so late. But then I remembered what John had been through in the last week.

The night before, John had shared some stories from the funeral, including one about driving off the road into an embankment before the service. John and his passengers had had to get out and collectively heave the car back onto the road. Everyone except for Bob Dylan, that is. Dylan stood back silently, surveying the effort. John said it had been the only time he'd seen Dylan smile that day.

I sat on the living room couch in my pajamas, staring at a grocery bag brimming with mail. It had obviously accumulated in John's absence. Just then John's door cracked open, and he emerged. I was sort of embarrassed (despite the fact that I had decided this was going to be my new home) to be found sitting in my pj's on this man's couch, when I had met him only the day before. Looking at each other with sleep in our eyes, we said, "Good morning," and he acknowledged the grocery bag with a pointed finger as something that needed to be attended to.

John planted himself cross-legged on the floor and began to sort the mail by type and priority, weeding out junk mail, not saying very much. I thought about revealing my new identity and address (his) to him, but I decided I shouldn't ven-

Cyber cowboy

ture into the explanation until I had a cup of coffee in my hand. If he was a real cowboy, he'd have a pot of coffee ready in no time. After sorting most of the correspondence, he stood and went to the kitchen. I sat still and listened for the sound of a spoon scooping grounds, and was relieved to hear it just on cue. That's a sign, I thought, I really *can* live here. Soon after, Shainee and Miriam arose.

John delved into his phone messages while Shainee and I dove into a bowl of cereal. I decided to wait until the end of the day to tell Shainee I was pretty sure I should stay. Here.

While waiting for John, we talked to Miriam some more, who was never shy about offering an opinion or her unique brand of commentary. "My father was a civil engineer; he surveyed a lot of this country," Miriam explained, as a response to our prodding her about her family history. "My parents were poor as church mice when they moved onto the ranch. Essentially, the ranch was my home for about seventy years, I suppose."

Grandma Barlow was from the stock of women who had shaped America with their bare hands (before living on the land went mechanical). I asked her what she appreciated most about this part of the country. "Oh, it's my home. There's room to breathe. People are nice. It's not a complicated life, like it is some places. We used to have a good legislature; now it comes and goes. People who are in local government are generally like the people in the federal government—they go there for the money or the power. When the Russians had the chance, if they had dropped the bomb on the Pentagon and the Capitol, we could have started all over again, and we might have managed. But we have such an entrenched bunch of graft . . . I mean, it's just feeding on itself!" Miriam paused. "I think often the people who should be running the government are generally too busy running their own lives and businesses."

We asked her if she thought the American dream, which she had defined as "owning a home, sending children to school, and happiness," was still alive and well. She answered by telling us a story that illustrated the changes she had seen. "Norm and I would drive in a snowstorm, after Christmas, all the way from Salt Lake City to Jackson, Wyoming, to celebrate New Year's Eve with our friends. We would always have a wild time, you know, a big deal. And now Jackson is inundated with the rich, the art galleries on every corner. The economy is gone. The ranches are gone. Jackson is a horrible example of what we hope doesn't happen to Pinedale, but it's already happening. It's happening to Colorado, Utah, Wyoming. California is moving in on us. They've ruined their state, now I presume they want to try and ruin ours. It's bringing in dangerous inflation. In Salt Lake City, you can buy a real good $10,000 house for about $200,000." Miriam chuckled with detectable disdain and sipped her tea.

Shainee asked Miriam if she thought role models in America, particularly for young people, had changed. "Oh, yes, or why would Jerry Garcia be a role model?" Miriam left it at that and then warned us, "I will talk you to death, and I will digress."

John, sitting at his desk in another room, must have heard her, because he responded, "Yeah, we need to go soon!"

"Whatever you say, dear," she yelled back to him. "But don't say it and then sit there for another half an hour!" John did not respond. Miriam winked at us with another sip.

A few minutes later, John walked into the kitchen. "We better get going if you guys are gonna make it to Montana," he urged.

"Montana!?" I screamed in silence.

We swung by John's ex-wife's house down the road, picked up his daughters, and then headed out to the ranch in the red family Suburban. Grandma Barlow rode in the front seat wearing dark, wide sunglasses that looked like welder's gear. The rest of us rode in the back with Willie, their large dog. I was bubbling with secret excitement at the thought of getting to the ranch, all 7,000 acres of it.

We drove past the BOX R ranch sign onto the property, crossed a number of cattle guards, and stopped in front of a quintessential ranch house. Everyone in the car was silent, except for Willie, who was panting with anticipation. Everyone just stared at the still house—nothing in it or around it stirred, not even another dog. Anna broke the silence. "Did they paint the roof? That's not the right color." Tipping his Stetson up for a better look, John stared at the roof that he had probably repaired many times, and, without answering, slowly moved his boot from the brake to the accelerator. We drove a couple of miles up the single-lane dirt road and parked. Grandma Barlow opted to stay in the shade of the truck as Willie led us up a hill to a plateau overlooking the acreage.

"Down there's where I went to school," John said, pointing. "I'll take you down there next."

"In that teeny house?" I asked. "How many kids?"

"Oh, the most we ever had was seven," John said, still looking in its direction. "And then I lived there the first seven years I was back on the ranch." I wondered what greater significance the number seven had in John's life.

I have never seen a structure before or since that reminded me more of Thoreau's Massachusetts cabin. The fact that John lived there for seven years, through

Wyoming winters, shed even more light on the man standing before me. Let's just say he wasn't wearing that cowboy hat as a fashion statement. I followed John as he deliberately walked toward a clearing.

"This is where I always used to come to think about things," he said, his eyes on the ground.

"I can see why," I said, my eyes on the horizon.

"This is also where I got married," he said. I suddenly realized why he was looking down. His eyes were tracing a rock pattern—one that he had laid out many years earlier. "See that line of rocks?" he asked, pointing to a line extending from the circle. "I came out here at dawn and put that line of rocks toward where the sun rose. We got married right around sunset and put that other line of rocks toward where the sun set."

My eyes shifted downward; I didn't know what to say. The circle had been formed on land that was no longer his, in honor of a marriage that had ended.

"What does it do to your mind to grow up here?" I wondered out loud.

"It makes you want to have it expanded," John said without hesitation.

"Apparently," I said as Shainee and the girls walked up, followed by a buoyant Willie.

"We can talk about the frontier here if you want," he suggested. It seemed like a good idea, as we had a 360-degree view of the unblemished frontier as a backdrop. I held the camera, framing John in a wheat-colored landscape that went on forever.

Shainee asked him to explain how he had made the transition from this frontier to the new frontier and particularly how our heritage of Manifest Destiny had affected the shift.

"All the time I was growing up here," John began, smacking his lips like he had just taken a swig of whiskey, "I had a real vivid sense of having been the first generation to run out of a frontier to go to, because just about everybody back to the genealogical horizon had been right on the leading edge, and they'd come into this general area in the 1870s. My great-uncle was the first white man to ever spend a winter in this part of the world. This is like the last place in the lower forty-eight that was settled because it's very cold. But there was no place to go beyond this, so in spite of all this space, I always felt like we'd reached the end of the line, and I felt kind of cheated. It was no longer a matter of building something, it was suddenly a matter of *maintaining* what was here.

"So I stayed here for seventeen years thinking about the frontier and the end of it. And being a rancher instead of a settler. But at the point that I discovered cyberspace, I realized that there was a whole new area of frontier that was being developed that would always be frontier, would never *not* be frontier—there was an unlimited potential for it to go on being so. There would always be new areas to settle and work out. And so I felt a natural tendency to go there and be part of that process. There's just an itch in our genes—*g-e-n-e-s*—that's always existed in this family," he said, taking a beat. "But I miss all of this space," John looked around him. "Real space, not virtual space—this is . . . *space.*"

John's eyes stayed on the boundless landscape for a moment, and then he turned to lead us back down the hill toward the car.

We drove to the schoolhouse, which was surrounded by tall wildflowers—a burst of color that hadn't been stepped on or over since they'd bloomed, it seemed. John walked over to the schoolhouse and sat down on the lip of the doorway. He told us that his teacher of many years was the first black schoolteacher in Wyoming.

John's schoolhouse

"A brave soul," he added. "She was also the only black person in Sublette County at that time."

Shainee continued the interview by asking John how he believed cyberspace would influence the future of human relations and communications.

"Well, what we're doing at the moment is creating an environment whereby anybody with an opinion can share that opinion with the rest of the human race, without restraint. Now, it may be that it's an opinion that the rest of the human race is not interested in, either because it's ridiculous or because it's obvious or artlessly stated. But if you've got something truly fresh to say, you're not going to be prohibited from saying it because it's so fresh that the publishing apparatus or broadcasting apparatus that used to sit in the middle between you and any sizable audience doesn't like you to say it.

"I would say that that is an enormous empowerment to the individual— genuine freedom of expression. There has always been the myth of freedom of expression. But the fact is, I think it was A. J. Liebling who said, 'Freedom of the press is guaranteed only to those who own one.' Well, now everybody can conceivably own one with a truly global reach."

Then Shainee asked, "You've spoken about some of the hysteria and paranoia that surround this developing environment. Why do you think the Internet is so threatening to government structures?"

"Well," John began, "the idea that anybody should be able to say whatever they think, whether it fits the dominant paradigm or not, is incredibly threatening to everybody whose power depends on widespread belief in the dominant paradigm. There used to be bumper stickers around that said: 'Question Authority.' Lately, I see them supplanted by bumper stickers that say: 'Question Reality.' Which is much more effective and insidious, because the way in which authority gets itself established is by getting everybody to assume that there is a reality, that reality is a fact and not an opinion . . . I honestly think that there is really no stable power relationship in the world right now that isn't going to be either eliminated or completely reconfigured by digital media. It makes everybody who's got power uncomfortable. And well it might.''

We wondered which historical figures had inspired John's passions. ''Well,'' he began, ''given what it is that I'm trying to do and the other people I'm trying to do it with, I'm obviously really inspired by Jefferson, Paine, and Madison. Because what those guys were doing was trying to take a look at the political process with completely new eyes. They felt like they had come to a new land, that the human race had come to a new place in its history, that reason and a generally educated populace had endowed humanity with a whole new set of possibilities, and they wanted to create forms of government that would be appropriate to those greatly enhanced conditions. Which is how they designed the government of this country, and I think it's still as enlightened a shot as anybody's ever taken. So, I think about trying to obtain the social contract of cyberspace, and trying to come up with methods of ensuring some level of order and civility in that environment with the same kind of complete openness of opportunity that they had.

''I wouldn't want to compare myself to them in any other respect. Those guys were not of the sort that you get on a regular basis anywhere in the world; they were sort of Leonardo da Vinci–class human oddities. These were extraordinary people who had a profound understanding of the essential qualities of humanity and how those were likely to relate to one another, and what was in the nature of government to try to accede, and what was in the nature of individual human beings to abuse. I wouldn't say that I have those kinds of insights. But I certainly feel a sense of kindred spirit with them.''

Aware that we were in a state that prides itself on having preserved much of its landscape—A GREAT LAND OUTDOORS—we asked John what he appreciated most about Wyoming.

''I love Wyoming for its reality,'' John answered. ''This is a pretty nonvirtual place. This is a place where things are right there in front of you, where the reality that you experience at any given moment is of a nature to reach out and kill you. Which is great. It gives everybody an edge. You are expected to say what you mean here and live by it. You are expected to behave according to a set of ethics. You are expected to be interdependent with your neighbors. Generally, people figure that lawyers are for people who are too gutless to shoot, which is sort of a good thing and a bad thing. I don't know, Wyoming is still a lot like what the rest of the country used to be, prior to television and suburbia.''

As a final question, we asked John what he valued most about being an American, regardless of which state he called ''home.'' ''Well, I'm so dismayed with the general condition of America—philosophically, psychologically, and spiritually—that it's hard to say what I value most about being an American,'' he said, stopping for a moment. "This is a country that consists largely of people who didn't fit, or who were dissatisfied, or burned with a kind of ambition. Our genetic pool here is all the soup of the dissatisfied. And that gives us a lot of virtues and liabilities that I think you lack everyplace else. It gives us an exploratory impulse that is a good thing to build a future on. It also gives us a rootlessness and restlessness that is highly alienating, especially now when we're not going to new places where we need one another. Now when we move to new places, we're going to some new place in the suburbs where we *don't* need one another, where things are sort of set up for that purpose.

"But," he added, finally acknowledging what he did appreciate about his country, "I guess the thing I like most about being an American is the passion of it, the willingness to embrace the future, the gullibility of it, the lack of skepticism. Those are all deep American tendencies that I enjoy having inside myself." John paused, taking in the summer splendor around us and listening to his girls giggle, out of our sight in a nearby field.

"I think this is changing," he continued. "I don't know that this is any longer a national trait, but it has been the case that Americans really loved liberty. I think there's plenty of evidence that the majority of us do not, at this point." He looked either disappointed or distressed by what he saw as the erosion of liberties. "But to the extent that it was ever part of this country's philosophical heritage—I love to be free. I love it when other people are free. I understand that freedom is the ability of that person that I find intolerable to be free; that's where liberty resides, it's in the rights of the most odious person you can think of. And I love to be in a context where they have as many liberties as I've got.

"I guess the other thing about being an American . . . is a belief that human beings are basically good. And I think that's changed; that's been severely damaged by the media, and I'm not sure that that's a dominant belief here any longer. But I think it's certainly a much more positive way of proceeding through the world. And it's my way. I really am of the opinion that a stranger is a friend I haven't met yet. I'm not one of these parents who teaches his children to fear all strangers because they're threats; I look at them as opportunities, for my beautiful daughters as well as myself. And the last thing I would want these girls to believe is that they couldn't turn to a stranger. Who else are you gonna turn to in certain circumstances?"

A stranger is a friend I haven't met yet. I'd heard it before—first from my grandpa who I think was quoting Will Rogers; it was a great motto for the road.

On that note, we packed up the equipment and all piled back into the Suburban, followed by a panting, smiling Willie.

"Tell the dog to get in the back!" ordered Grandma Barlow. "He doesn't believe he should sit in the back. Thank God I don't have a sense of smell anymore. I don't have to smell him stinking up the car."

"How do you know he smells at all then?" asked John.

"Well, he's a *dog*," she asserted.

Back on the dirt road, John stopped the car and squeezed his body into the center console, his hat flattened by the roof.

"What are we doing?" asked Leah, not understanding the new seating arrangement.

"Anna wants to try driving," John said, struggling to get comfortable.

"This is crazy, if you should ask me," Grandma Barlow said, then realized no one was taking her up on her offer.

"Okay, how do I do it?" Anna asked, holding the wheel, ready to go.

"Are we really down to the 'How do I do it?' level?" John asked.

"These girls have to get to Missoula, dear," Grandma Barlow reminded. "How many delay tactics are you going to pull on them?"

I was hoping for at least a few more. "We're fine," we assured the carload.

On our drive back to the little gray house, I sat by the open window. Like Willie, I had grown to love that spot. I shot scenery going by, mostly more of the unadorned Wyoming landscape. I thought about many things at once: about going places where we no longer needed one another; about John letting Anna drive, even though her tiny feet could hardly reach the pedals; about all the ways I had seen

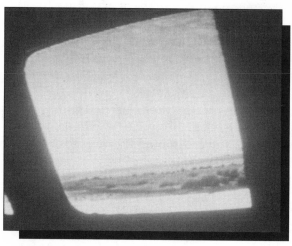

The favorite spot

John empower these girls, who would indeed be—thanks to their parents—a force to be reckoned with. I also thought about the old Barlow ranch, and I hoped the new landowners cared for it like it was a consecrated, living body, the way John and his family had.

If owning land and a home that you take pride in is the most widely accepted definition of the American dream, then I wondered if John felt denied of his. Perhaps, instead, he felt an even greater freedom having no permanent address for now, his only home being the new and spacious frontier he shared with millions of others—millions of friends who were yet to be met. Maybe walls weren't comforting to him anymore, like they are to most people. Maybe cyberspace felt like a more dependable place to hang a hat.

In thinking of "home," my mind wandered to *Anthem* and how our project was alive in me. I thought of how all those who had invited us into their home and had made themselves vulnerable to perfect strangers gave me a kind of pride and sense of responsibility in seeing that their voices be heard.

And I re-embraced my part in this mission like one does a relationship that's been momentarily taken for granted. Suddenly I was so relieved that I hadn't yet had coffee when Shainee came down the attic stairs that morning. I might have opted to tell her my plans. I might have momentarily forgotten about these gifts I had been given—the road, this challenge, my thirst, a mission, and one other person to share every step and every memory, including ones that can't be written.

We got back to the house and said good-bye to Grandma Barlow, who quickly disappeared into her room for a nap. We gathered our belongings and sat with John on a bench, watching him map out a sensible route for us to Montana. He's the guy you hope to catch when stopping to ask for directions.

"I think you're off on a great adventure," John declared. "Take care of your-selves."

I thanked John for his time, and energy, and . . .

"Hospitality," Shainee added, completing the thought. I wasn't sure if John was sad to see us go, but as we reached that awkward moment of saying good-bye to someone who is no longer a stranger but not yet a friend, he reached out and hugged Shainee and me. And not a pat on the back like a distant cousin at a family reunion, but the good squeezing kind.

Anna had gone off to play. I hugged Leah good-bye.

"Tell your sister good-bye for us," I said while John moved toward the house, almost out of sight. "And take care of your dad."

When we pulled onto the 191 interstate toward Montana, it was still a bright day, everything reflecting silver and white. As we drove toward Yellowstone, the sky seeming to stretch wider and wider, I said to Shainee, "*Anthem is* my Wyoming dream." *Anthem* was the wide-open, indomitable West that appeared in my sleep-ing vision, my hands working it, my heart a part of it.

The dream. There I was, my nose out the window, living it.

THE ONLY MOTEL ROOM IN MISSOULA, MONTANA   8/15, 4 A.M.

(Shainee)

Today we left the Barlows. Every few days we begin a new abridged love affair. We never stay long enough to really get to know each person or place. So we never have to fall out of love; we move on when the feeling is fresh and with it comes a small pang of loss.

We headed north on 191 toward Jackson and soon caught up with the Snake

River, which meanders along the valley floor. We drove through the relic Western town which, as Mrs. Barlow said, seems to have gone the route of most great tourist attractions, becoming quasi-tacky. Nonetheless, the Grand Tetons will not be compromised. They are the aristocrats of mountains and jag into the air wildly, their crests still white at a mile and a half high.

We made our way toward Yellowstone, planning to drive through the park to cross over into Montana. Unfortunately, the park's entrance fee is ten dollars, and the speed limit is forty-five miles per hour. So it was an expensive and slow forty miles that wound through the very first national park in the country and the very first national park on our trip. We felt okay about making a contribution to the National Park Service, but we were pretty bummed about getting yet another ticket! This time it was Kris, at least. She was not happy when we were stopped by a pubescent ranger. He clocked us at sixty-five.

In 1872, the United States set aside over 3,400 square miles as "pleasuring ground for the benefit and enjoyment of the people"—Yellowstone. We haven't really had enough time to visit any national parks yet on our trip. Today being no different, we missed the waterfalls and herds of antelope, bison, moose, and elk that still run free, but the drive was enough to offer us some of the most magnificent sights that we have encountered thus far.

Yellowstone, in some areas, is downright strange-looking, full of gurgling, bubbling geysers and "mudpots" that pop up out of the earth, reminiscent of a fantasy Star Wars terrain. We also saw a large forest that had fallen victim to a recent forest fire. The naked trunks stuck out like needles on a porcupine's back, adding to the eerie, barren feel of the land. It is exquisite country, and I hung out the window shooting as much as I could before the sun set.

We have found one thing that we have in common with the rest of the tourists—we all have cameras. No one just sits and watches Old Faithful erupt; you have to take a picture of it, record it. In fact, even before everyone had cameras Americans had a tradition of sending home sketches and observations of the West. On the Internet, I found the journal of a young woman who had visited Yellowstone with her family in 1896. She wrote very descriptive accounts of exactly what we saw today. I can only hope that someone will find our impressions of this wondrous place still accurate in another hundred years.

Kris and the Grand Tetons

It is disturbing to note, however, what people will do to get the right picture. When we were in Pinedale, waiting for John Perry to arrive, I went to an ice cream parlor. Two teenage girls behind the counter were talking about the third Yellowstone tourist that year to be hurt by an animal. Evidently, a couple visiting from Japan had taken their baby to the park and had come upon a baby bear. The man tried to pose his child on the bear's back for a photograph and was of course attacked by the bear's mother. The baby was fine, but the man was injured badly. One teenage girl told the story to the other as she was dipping my scoop of mint chocolate chip. The second girl just shook her head, saying, "They really should translate the animal warnings into Japanese, but you'd think they'd know better. That'll be a dollar twenty-five, please!" she said to me cheerily.

Old Faithful

I paid for my cone, thinking that Kris and I had taken some serious chances in the name of the right picture, but even we have our limits when it comes to wild creatures. Although some might say that Hunter came pretty damn close.

DANIEL KEMMIS

MAYOR OF MISSOULA

MISSOULA, MONTANA

(Kristin)

We pulled into Missoula, Montana, around 3 A.M., but without our customary econo-motel reservation. We tried almost every hotel and motel in the city, only to be turned down by a string of sympathetic desk clerks: "Sorry, we're full . . . summer vacationers." We couldn't believe it. We'd never been shut out of a town, and the next "hotel town," we were told, was more than an hour away. We were ready to sleep in the car when a policewoman pulled up beside us. We explained our dilemma, and she suggested a shelter.

We decided to try one last corner of town and spied a hotel that we hadn't yet tried. A clerk—who looked like a young Ozzy Osbourne—said they had no clean rooms, but two people had just checked out. "If you give me a minute to clean, you can have it." We were too tired to even care about what sorts of things were probably happening until 3 A.M. in this now available room. We accepted.

We followed the clerk into the room with our baggage and insisted on helping him, which entailed changing the sheets. I could tell by the way he handed me the sheet that he had never before folded hospital corners with a guest. Pushing his long hair away from his eyes, he said good night. After two hot showers, Shainee and I were fast asleep.

We arrived at City Hall the next morning still exhausted, our slightly jittery hands carrying Circle K coffee cups. A graceful-looking fellow of about fifty emerged from an office and introduced himself as Mayor Kemmis.

Kemmis is the first publicly elected communitarian official in the nation. Communitarian thought—a relatively new but quickly spreading political and social philosophy—argues that one's individual liberties have a direct relationship to one's involvement in the foundations of society: family, school, and neighborhoods. In essence, communitarians believe that with rights comes responsibility. It was an idea that certainly dovetailed neatly with much of what had been on our previous interviewees' minds.

Mayor Kemmis invited us into his office and affably informed us that he had cleared his schedule for the rest of the day, with the exception of one unavoidable city zoning meeting. He offered to first take us to lunch at the weekly food festival in the town square, near the carousel.

It was a low-clouds, rainy day in Missoula—the only bright color being the giant swatches of saturated green on the surrounding mountains. We walked through town, Mayor Kemmis leading, me lugging our equipment. Kemmis greeted the citizens we passed on our way to the town square, with ''Hello's'' and ''How are you?'' until we came to a large tent packed with people and a selection of international food. We found a bench by the river and sat down with some lo mein.

I had an urge to call Andrei Codrescu and tell him that Missoula had a Pakistani restaurant.

During lunch, the mayor explained how much he liked going out to public gatherings, like the Wednesday food court and the farmers' vegetable market. ''You get to talk to people about things that they wouldn't necessarily call the mayor's office about,'' he explained.

Citizen outreach

After lunch, we walked over to the nearby carousel, with its elegant bobbing horses and organ music. The handmade Missoula carousel was not your average merry-go-round; it had an old-world charm and an unusual story. The mayor told us that a man had come into his office one day with a painted wooden horse to say that, although it would take him more than ten years, he'd like to build a hand-carved carousel for Missoula. The man wanted to know whether the city would accept the carousel as a gift. Mayor Kemmis sent him through the proper channels, the park board and the redevelopment agency. Word got out about his mission, and before he knew it, the man had dozens of volunteers at his door wanting to carve and paint horses with him. The work of hundreds of Missoulans produced a carousel with thirty-eight horses, two (wheel-chair-accessible) chariots, and a band organ in less than half the time expected. "It's the first carousel hand-carved anywhere in the world in sixty years," the mayor said, admiring it. "Now it really does belong to the whole community."

Kemmis asked us if we wanted to go for a ride. "Of course," we said, and he walked up to the old-fashioned carnival ticket window and purchased ten tickets.

"Why did you get ten?" I asked him, thinking he must have wanted to do the whole interview on the carousel.

"Oh, I just like to carry them around with me," he responded, slipping the extras into his pocket. An image flashed in my mind of the mayor telling his secretary that he had to close his door for an "important call" and then climbing out his second-story window to sneak a few laps on his favorite stallion.

Just then I looked over to the whirling horses and saw something that made me blink twice. Two men—apparently the sheriff and the chief of police—were mounted on two very unofficial-looking, albeit blue, horses. The pair smiled serenely as they rolled past us, tipping their hats. It was a charming, if somewhat absurd, moment.

Shainee asked the mayor if the chief of police and the sheriff came down to ride often. "I think just on Wednesdays," he answered. This is another one of those small-town big towns, I thought to myself, where the mayor knows the carousel schedule of other local officials. No one could accuse him of not being an active mayor.

When the carousel stopped, the chief of police and the sheriff dismounted their blue horses and moseyed over to the ice cream parlor. Against her better judgment, the carousel manager agreed to let us ride with our conspicuous camera, and we were off! The mayor and Shainee were neck and neck happily chasing me. After the ride ended, we decided it was time to get serious, so we walked through drizzling Missoula to a nearby café to warm our bones with coffee, and start the interview.

Shainee and I were intrigued by communitarian thought because it challenges the idea that American freedoms and rights are handed over to you at birth, like a passport that never expires. We wondered if something in Kemmis's childhood might have been the seed that inspired his belief that individuals live and die by the support and success of their community.

Shainee asked him about his background, and he spoke of a childhood on a small family farm in eastern Montana. The farm had been located in one of the harshest climates in the country, which required community cooperation. "Unfortunately, in the long run, the farm ended up being a little too small to support our family," Kemmis concluded.

He explained he'd been intrigued by politics ever since he was a boy. He spent the first ten years of his political career in the Montana State Legislature, including one term as minority leader and one as speaker of the house. He then came to

Missoula, convinced that he could make a more tangible difference in regional politics. "Essentially, I wanted to find a way to make people a part of the political process at the community level. That's why I ran for mayor, and this is my second term," he said.

We asked Mayor Kemmis what he hoped his work would contribute at the community level. "I see a city like Missoula as a living thing. During the heyday of the Greek city-state there was a really strong sense that communities were alive, and that's where the language of the 'body politic' came from. People saw it as a *living* body." Kemmis said he tries to recapture that image to instill a sense of the community as organic and interdependent in

Shainee and the mayor

its constituents. He went on to give examples of how citizen participation has turned Missoula around, citing the cleanup of the river, which had previously been a dumping ground; the once-unkept surrounding parks and undeveloped natural areas, which have been restored and linked by hiking trails; the carousel; and the town trolley. Kemmis feels that people are inspired by their previous accomplishments to do more. He continued, "That to me is what democracy has come to mean—a growing sense that people can have by feeling their own community become stronger and better, knowing it's because of their work. Missoula is a very capable town, which means that it's a democratic town."

Months before we met with Daniel Kemmis, Shainee and I had stopped by George Washington University to talk with Dr. Amitai Etzioni, the co-founder of the communitarian school of thought. Our encounter with Dr. Etzioni had been brief, but we did walk away with a basic understanding of his theories and some strong arguments for the importance of mandatory citizen participation. Our discussion with him had inspired us to find and interview Mayor Kemmis.

One thing that Etzioni had said, with regard to the relationship between self and community, was: "The original document of the country was created in an era in which America was a set of very small, very tightly knit, very religious communities. The total population was less than three million. And so, in those days, to argue only *for* rights was wonderful, was hopeful, because to communities then, freedom and rights were like air and water—they were like sunshine. Now it's two hundred and some years later, and we find ourselves in almost the opposite situation. What we took for granted two hundred years ago—the *inherent* interest in citizen involvement, having not had it prior—is now what needs building up. We now need a bill of *responsibilities.*"

Montana Elevator Company

Dr. Etzioni illustrated his point by telling us about a study. It showed that young Americans feel very strongly that if they are charged with a crime, they are entitled to a trial before a jury of their peers. "Which they *ought* to feel entitled to," Etzioni added. But when the youths were asked to serve on a jury, they mostly said, "Find someone else."

"It's indecent!" Etzioni declared. "It's indecent to take and not to give."

Now, sitting with an elected public official who subscribes to Etzioni's philosophies, we wondered what it was about Missoula that had drawn Daniel Kemmis to apply this philosophy here. "I don't know if you could ever fully articulate in short terms why you love a place, any more than the subtleties of why you love a person. In this case, it's an identity that comes so strongly from bringing together people and landscape. Over time and generations, people are selected by the place, they find a niche in the place . . . Physically challenging places, like Missoula, encourage a kind of entrepreneurship . . . and entrepreneurship has got almost an ecological side to it. The way that people fit their lives together creates a richer and richer texture in a place like this."

We had gotten caught up in discussion and had lost track of time. Mayor Kemmis looked down at his watch and realized he had to go to his zoning meeting. He asked us if we wanted to go back to his office, take a nap on his couch, and finish the interview afterward. I guess it was obvious we hadn't slept much. The idea of taking a catnap was tempting, but we opted to borrow his office to make some phone calls.

The mayor left and we got out our interviewee follow-up list. We called the usual suspects, including Robert Redford's office, Walter Cronkite's office, the Chicago Bulls's publicist, and Willie Nelson's lawyer. The calls all went as scripted: "I don't have an answer for you. Call back next week . . ." Except when we called Willie's lawyer, who told us that Willie had decided to meet with us.

Elated, we dueted the chorus from every Willie Nelson song available to our collective memory. Luckily, the mayor's door was closed.

The mayor returned from his meeting just as cheerful as he had been before he left. I could tell he was the kind of person who was always pretty chipper. And why shouldn't he be? He loves his life, and he loves being mayor of this city that feels more like an idyllic town. He suggested we go back to his house to finish our discussion. We agreed and followed him past rows of modest homes that were built rather close together—a curious American tendency, even in spacious states, that John Waters had pointed out months earlier.

Mayor Kemmis's wife opened the door to greet us, while their teenage son hovered around one corner of the living room. We walked out to the backyard and set up on their wooden deck.

We imagined both Kemmis and Etzioni probably felt that heroes in a communitarian society would be those who took the most responsibility in their community. We asked Mayor Kemmis who had influenced him most. "The people who influence me are those who are really attentive to their personal mission, because I believe we all have one. And out of that attentiveness comes a kind of authenticity that has a tremendous power to it. That's what I see in somebody like the writer Wendel Berry."

There was that familiar word again: "mission." Shainee asked Kemmis about his personal feelings on America's future as we approach the new millennium.

"I feel optimistic about humankind," he said, explaining that he doesn't like to think in nationalistic terms. "I feel optimistic about life on the earth, even though in so many ways you can find decay and things getting worse. What I see and what I seem to be drawn to are those places where healing is taking place, where strong nodes of wholeness are emerging . . . Missoula is an example of that kind of community to me."

"Where do you draw the energy to do this every day?" Shainee asked.

"Well, I do get tired *sometimes*," he said, laughing. "Winston Churchill once said, 'History is just one damn thing after another.' And I often feel that way sitting in my little office. But the more time I spend in the work that I do, the more I come to feel a *part* of something that's moving—something that's growing. When talking to young people who are trying to figure out where to position themselves, I find myself saying to them, 'Just do good work.'

"There's one other dimension that I might talk a little bit about," Kemmis added—he seemed to be asking for our permission to add a final thought—before continuing. "There's something about the kind of anxiety that we often bring to our work that seems to not be quite right or productive. Let's just say, if this city is, within itself, trying to achieve a greater wholeness, then it's not up to me and it's not even up to all sixty thousand Missoulans to make it happen. If we worked with what was there, and added our energy to it, almost as a gift, rather than feeling this tremendous burden of responsibility—which I think does make us anxious—then I believe we could actually move things further along. What it finally comes down to, I think, is a question of grace—of being able to move gracefully through the world and through our work, rather than cutting across the grain.

"So, a lot of times now, I look for the path of greatest *grace*. And by that I don't mean ease, because there's always work involved. But maybe sometimes we need to do—and force—less, and in that way contribute more." Kemmis's last comment burrowed under my skin as we thanked him and said our good-byes.

I can honestly say that Kemmis's theory on work and grace was one of those indelible ideas that has since had a profound and lasting effect on my life. The idea

was so appealing: to not try so hard and, in the act of relaxing, allow things to find a more natural way of bringing themselves together. It was like the Missoula carousel principle: built by many hands, it took two years to create, rather than ten. The carousel was a community effort, and a perfect example of Daniel Kemmis's entire philosophy about government and the American people: "Everyone builds it, everyone rides on it."

I have seen that, for me, doing "good work" sometimes becomes more about my ego saying "I can do this, I'm going to make this happen, find a way, and push as hard as necessary until it shifts the way *I* think it should." I can chase something down just for the sake of the chase, getting lost in the effort. But there's always another way. "Work and grace, not work and muscle" echoed in my head. We are so acculturated in America to believe, even as young women, that "might makes right." I was amused by the irony of being reminded of the feminine yin approach by this tall and manly Jimmy Stewart character.

Partly because we were both experiencing another blood sugar drop and partly because we were thinking about all that Mayor Kemmis had said, we set out in silence toward our next destination: Glacier National Park. Somehow, though, we took a wrong turn on our way out of Missoula and found ourselves in a dead-end alleyway. Obstructing our path was a wall with a sloppily painted message in large letters: NOBODY FOR PRESIDENT.

MEDORA, NORTH DAKOTA, AFTER OUR LONGEST DRIVE   8/20

(Shainee)

Montana was dreamy and extreme. It is aptly named "Big Sky Country," with big everything—mountains, plains, animals—and, of course, that endless blue sky.

After our afternoon with Mayor Kemmis, we realized that we had to rest or we would never make it back across the country in time for our next appointment. We picked a good place to do it: Whitefish, Montana. Whitefish is situated right outside Glacier National Park, which actually became Waterton-Glacier International Peace Park in the eighties, when the Canadian and American sides of the park officially merged. The union is intended to symbolize the bonds of peace and friendship between the two countries.

I visited the area once before as a teenager and was overwhelmed by its loveliness. Kris has never been to Montana, so I insisted that she had to see Glacier before we left the state. We took a break from the sterile life of the motor lodge and opted for a very charming little bed-and-breakfast for about the same price. We spent a day exploring the neighboring towns, but the jewel of this region is the park and the lake that it surrounds. Entering the park, I realized that even my fondest memory did not do it justice. Kris and I were both awestruck by its beauty.

One billion years of glacier movement have produced breathtaking sedimentary sculptures in the northern Rockies. The ancient ice has carved dramatic layered mountainsides flanking impossibly deep canyons with white waterfalls springing from every corner. The lake is a mile deep and the water shines like rare aquamarines. Kris and I took a hike up through very dense forest. The trees are ancient and massive, with moss running over every inch. We each picked up walking sticks and climbed to the top, over rocks embedded in a cragged mountainside stream. At the top of the crude trail we reached a clearing with a large pool of bright kelly-green water, which ran off in three pristinely white waterfalls from the surrounding cliffs. It was absolutely astounding. God did a good job on Montana.

At the end of the day, we stopped and had hot tea at one of the nineteenth-century resorts that still dot the park. We sat in big old wooden Adirondack rocking chairs on a shale patio overlooking the lake. The air turned chilly as the sun went down, and we had to put on every layer that we have with us. Intrapark transportation is still provided by a fleet of apple red 1920s cabs. With their rumble in the background, a huge fire in the enormous lobby hearth, and waiters dressed in whites, it was easy to imagine ourselves stepping off the steam train from Great Falls seventy-five years ago. But after a couple of days, we had to snap out of our dream world and get back on the road.

We left the park this afternoon and headed east on U.S. 2. Montana quickly becomes a vast plains state as you move away from its western borders and the Rockies. We had over 500 miles to drive—endless stretches of road and wilderness without any hint of civilization. We sped through Great Falls and landed on State Highway 200, which would take us all the way to the North Dakota border along the Lewis and Clark Trail.

We stopped in Lewistown for gas and food and found ourselves in the middle of a Cowboy Poetry Gathering sponsored by the state. I pictured the poetry "slams" I had witnessed in Los Angeles cafés and tried to substitute men in Stetsons and plaid shirts for the angry young artists with bleached blond hair. But there was no time to check it out for ourselves. We pushed on, the front of our car becoming an icky collage of very large dead Montana bugs.

Around midnight we crossed the state line into Medora, yet another "authentic" Western town with one too many T-shirt shops. Medora was founded by a French marquis who came to the Badlands in the 1880s. He built a huge chateau and named the area after his wife. Medora's other famous resident was Teddy Roosevelt, before he became president. The town is a strange contradiction, offering tours of the French château followed by refreshments at the Rough Riders Hotel. But the oddities of American tourism can no longer faze us.

Tomorrow we get to drive yet another enormous state in one day. We must be in Minnesota in twenty-four hours.

ROGER ZINS

HAY-GRINDER

NEW SALEM, NORTH DAKOTA

(Shainee)

We barreled across the barren plains of North Dakota for what seemed like days, getting hungry in the early afternoon. There was no relief in sight. Gone were the McDonald's and the Shoneys that we had scoffed at for months. The tables were turned and we were desperate for the option of fries. After about 100 miles of growling stomachs, a sign that said SUNSET INN CAFÉ sprung up out of the flat horizon, trumpeting an oasis.

The Sunset Inn is the quintessential truck stop diner. It has a chrome counter that runs the length of the restaurant, with brown vinyl booths lined up under the windows and walls painted institutional green. Two waitresses in ruffled polyester aprons leaned familiarly on the tables, yakking with customers, a pot of coffee in hand. There was a card game going on in the corner between four white-haired men in flannel and there were women having a kaffee klatsch in the other corner of the restaurant. They obviously all knew each other. The chattering hushed when we walked in. We took a seat and ordered a couple of grilled cheese sandwiches, knowing it wouldn't be long before someone would ask, "Where you gals from?"

The inquiry came from the end of the counter, where a middle-aged man in a blue baseball cap sat drinking a soda and smoking a cigarette. There was an enormous truck parked in front of the café that had a contraption on the back. It reminded me of a cement mixer, and Kris and I were speculating about its purpose when the man interrupted to tell us the truck was his.

He introduced himself as Roger Zins and explained that he was in the hay-grinding business. He was a friendly, open man who spoke methodically in the region's very distinctive accent. His *o*'s were long and round and the *a*'s came from the back of the throat, harsh and short. He was pretty chatty, so we asked if we could do a little interview after our meal. Roger was excited by the idea; he had never been interviewed before. We briefly explained the interview format while we waited for our order to arrive. When the

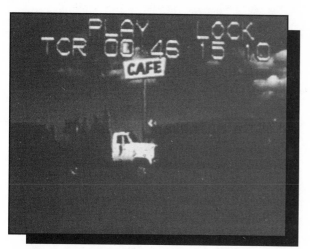

Roger's rig

waitress brought our sandwiches, Kris and I wolfed them down. Then we set up our stuff. I asked Roger to tell us about himself. He jumped right in. "As the present time, I'm living on a farm site in a community called Raleigh, North Dakota. I've been doing custom hay-grinding since 1972. When you talk hay, so many people will relate to these big round bales you see along the road. Well, my machine grinds them. The cattle will utilize the feed a lot more if it is ground. It minimizes waste."

We had seen the huge golden rolls of hay dotting the Great Plains from Texas up through North Dakota; we hadn't realized that it was someone's job to grind them. I asked Robert if he enjoyed the work.

"I enjoy it. The busiest time of my year is usually the wintertime and I don't really enjoy it so much when you're standing out there in forty-, fifty-, sixty-below wind chills. But I've always been an outside man, so I guess this is the kind of work an outside man would stick to for a long time. It also gives a person a chance to kind of move around. You aren't sitting in one place all the time doing the same thing. I reach out approximately 120 to 130 miles from home."

We told Roger that we were asking people their opinions about America, the land, its heroes, and the American dream. I asked him how he felt about the future, from what he's seen in his part of the country. Roger answered, "Well I'm a person who listens to people who've been in different parts of the world. I've never been to any other country and a person kind of hates to say it, but I personally feel that it's only getting worse here. As times change and the country progresses, things should always be getting better. But just looking at the chaos and the way things are going economically . . . I just have a gut feeling that eventually something is going to bust loose in this country. I hope I'm wrong."

Given Roger's pessimism, I asked him if there was anything that he would like to ask the American people himself.

"I'd need time to think about that. If this whole thing was aired, maybe there's things I wouldn't want aired. Sometimes you say the wrong thing, ya know, and you wish you wouldn't have said it. This part can be cut out, right?"

Even in the sparsely populated Great Plains, the promise of the media was both enticing and frightening. We assured Roger that he was doing great and asked him if he had any heroes. "John Kennedy," he responded. "I don't know, it just seems like back in the day of John Kennedy—I was about ten or eleven years old when he left us—the country, in general, seemed very comfortable and satisfied with the work he was doing and the way he was ruling the country. He was working for the people. Since then, it seems like the country is no longer for its people anymore."

Roger had a son who was around ten or eleven. I asked Roger if he thought his son had anyone to look up to in that same way that he had admired President Kennedy.

"Well, he seems to be all wired up about the Dallas Cowboys. That's all I hear about from him when I'm home. I would say he honors them probably as much as I did our President back then."

Roger fiddled with his lighter for a second, thinking, and then answered our earlier question of what he'd like to ask people himself. "Well, this is a good question: Would people sooner live in today's society or have the type of living and governing we had, say, thirty, forty years ago? I think that would be of real interest. I know for me—I wouldn't mind driving the vehicles we have, the machinery we got—but I would sooner go back to that way of living. Times have changed so considerably just in the last, say, twenty years—far too rapidly, I feel. Faster than what the average person can handle. It's not a gradual change, it's too much of a rapid change."

We listened, nodding, although you wouldn't know that anything had changed at the Sunset Inn since the day John Kennedy was killed. If we subtracted our video cameras from the scene, it *was* 1963. Roger continued, "Maybe here in North Dakota, we are comparable to the way people in California and Florida may have been, say, twenty or thirty years ago. From what I understand, change starts from the south and works its way north. And that is one reason they have always called North Dakota 'backwards' and 'isolated,' because we are always the last to know."

"So, if you're feeling the change, you know it's *really* happening," Kris responded.

"It's happening," Roger said definitively. "What you people are coping and living with in California? I maybe wouldn't even be able to make it one day out there. I've never been in California, so I don't know what you people have there, but I've heard a lot about it."

Roger spoke of California like one of the foreign countries he had heard people talk about. We moved on to our final question, whether Roger felt the American dream is still a reality. He thought for a second and responded, "Oh, I don't know. To some people, probably. Most people will stick with something they're comfortable with, especially if it makes 'em a halfway decent living. I really never did have a dream. The hay-grinding just happened. Everybody's got to go out and get a job when you strike out from home. Eventually, I made a business out of it. And here I am today."

Thirty or forty years ago, many would have said Roger's life *was* the exact definition of the American dream. Certainly, Warren Lewis thought building his

Roger Zins

own barber shop was the American dream. Perhaps it is the images of how others are living, which have penetrated even the remotest regions of our country, that have given Roger the idea that owning your own business and doing work that you enjoy does not represent the dream. How often does Robin Leach make it to North Dakota?

It was time to get back on the road. We asked Roger to state his name and tele-phone number on camera and he did, joking, "When I see the movie, I'll have a chance to see how your trip went, but sometimes it may take a few years before a film is put to work. Ya know?" Roger knew the drill. He waved good-bye, smiling under the baseball cap that proudly boasted ZINS CUSTOM GRINDING, and went back to his cigarette and Mountain Dew. The waitresses and the old men playing cards in the far booth waved, too. The kaffee klatsch in the corner resumed its normal level of buzzing. The door closed behind us, with the tinkle of wind chimes as we walked out past the hay-grinder's truck.

WINONA LADUKE

CO-CHAIR OF THE INDIGENOUS WOMEN'S NETWORK • FOUNDER AND DIRECTOR OF
THE WHITE EARTH LAND RECOVERY PROJECT • ENVIRONMENTAL ACTIVIST

WHITE EARTH, MINNESOTA

(Kristin)

We should remember to get shots of the lake on our way
back," Shainee and I said in unison, driving toward Winona
Laduke's home. We just looked at each other. Speaking verbatim in
stereo was starting to occur on an almost-hourly basis. But it was during our drive from Montana toward northern Minnesota that we finally
acknowledged this previously unmentioned phenomenon between us:
our own form of ESP. I imagine this is common among people who co-
exist twenty-four hours a day for an extended period of time. I wondered
if the paired explorers of the past had also written about this or if they
just kept it to themselves, not wanting to deal with the hassle of explaining or proving it. But quite often, Shainee or I would manage to verbalize
whatever the other was thinking during our silent moments in the car,
no matter how abstract. Or Shainee would answer a question I had been
silently asking myself. We fell into communicating through subtle gestures and eyebrow raisings, turning blinking into a new alphabet, our
own Morse code.

The 1,000-mile drive from Montana to Winona Laduke's house
wound down as we breezed through Fargo, North Dakota, and headed
over the Minnesota border. I guess the directions I had been given over
the phone were what one might expect for a modest home in the middle
of an 837,000-acre reservation: "Take a left at the 'Raspberries U-Pick'
sign, make your third right onto the unmarked dirt road, follow that
down about a mile, and you'll see it set back into the woods on your
left . . ." It was one of the few times Shainee and I were on equal navigational footing. A map was useless.

We had first read about Winona in the *Utne Reader*'s list of 100
Visionaries and had heard about her from a number of people we respect,
among them a few of *Anthem*'s interviewees. We contacted her through

the Land Recovery Project in northern Minnesota, where she lived. Getting her on the phone was no small task; we were clearly dealing with a woman on the go.

Since our interview, in addition to her existing responsibilities, Winona ran as the vice-presidential candidate with Ralph Nader on the Green Party ticket. Their platform advocated stronger environmental protection, greater opportunities for the disenfranchised, and a reduction in the power of multinational corporations in American politics.

We knocked on the door of what seemed to be the right log cabin. We found Winona busy in the kitchen, preparing enchiladas on the stove.

"Hello!" she welcomed us, her hands covered in chili sauce. "Did you have trouble finding me? I just have to finish making lunch for these guys who are horse-logging up the road."

Directions to Winona's

We shook our heads, not really knowing what "horse-logging" meant, but she was so focused on cooking, we decided not to bother her for an explanation. I shot some footage of Winona preparing the large meal. She had light eyes, shiny chocolate-brown hair, flawless caramel skin, and strong bone structure. She looked like an elegant tomboy.

As soon as the enchiladas were in the oven, Winona offered us coffee. A *good* cup of coffee was hard to come by on the road, so we gladly accepted the dark roast, heading with mugs in hand out back to her wooden deck. The deck was built to blend into the surrounding pine forest overlooking Round Lake, one of five hundred bodies of water on the White Earth reservation.

White Earth Reservation

We had read that although she had grown up mostly in cities with her mother and Anishinabeg Indian chief father, after graduating from Harvard, Winona had chosen to return to her roots, to her ancestors' rural reservation. We asked her if she could give us a context for her work today. "Well, I'm from this reservation, which is called White Earth, and I'm Mississippi band Anishinabeg and Bear Clan," she explained. "And I work on issues in my community—both nationally and internationally—for the restoration of our economic, cultural, and environmental foundations. I'm campaign director for the Land Recovery Project, which is seeking to get back our land base, since most of our land is held by non-Indians inside our reservation. Most reservations were created by federal law or by treaty. We have an 837,000-acre reservation, which was reserved for us under a treaty in 1867, when we said we would keep this land in return for larger areas of northern Minnesota.

Winona Laduke

"Over time, the U.S. government attempted to assimilate Indians, and part of that practice was to try and teach Indians the concept of private property, which is not a concept in the language of native people. We have a concept of collective land ownership and individual- or family-use *rights*. And so they took our reservation, divided it into 80-acre parcels of land, gave each individual a parcel, and then taxed it. We lost about 250,000 acres from taxes, because we didn't have a context for the concept of individual ownership. It happened because we have really good land here—which is why my people chose this reservation—but it's also why we don't control most of it today, because it was so desirable.

"Our story is a microcosm of the rest of Indian country. The native people on Cape Cod are another example. Or the Hawaiians. Under the Statehood Act, Hawaiians are supposed to control fifty percent of all public lands in Hawaii. They have almost nothing. So the situation that we're in is pretty common, though we're one of the worst cases of it."

Shainee asked Winona if there had been a family philosophy that had influenced her work or way of life. "I was raised in a family that believed in standing up against injustice," she began. "Ever since I was a small child, I was taken to demonstrations, whether it was for Indian people, or farm workers, or antiwar activities. I was raised with an understanding of the civil rights movement, where it was right to say something was unjust, and to bear witness against it. And on both sides of my family, I have a long history of people standing ostensibly against injustice. My politicization came through that process and being raised watching Walter Cronkite and seeing body counts on TV every night on the six o'clock news. So between my family's history and a broader sense, my view was that there was something wrong out there.

"Then one really concrete thing happened when I was about ten years old. I received a check from the federal government for $94.60, and it was a Treasury check, but it wasn't demarcated as to what it was. It was a land check. The government was paying each individual Indian who was a member of the Mississippi band, like I am, $94.60 in return for terminating our title to lands outside the reservation. Essentially, what it meant was about eleven cents an acre, and the government recognized what it had done, that it had violated the treaty and it was holding the land illegally. But instead of returning the land, the government was saying, 'We're just going to pay you for it. We're going to pay you $94.60, and that'll fix it.' That's essentially how the United States was purchased—for about $800 million. It wasn't taken by 'conquest', it was taken by treaty.''

We were particularly curious about what Winona thought of the notion of the American dream, considering she had been acculturated in American cities, while also staying rooted in the Native American way of life.

''I think the dream that is represented in America is unsustainable,'' she said simply, repeating Wes Jackson and others. ''Because the dream is born of a *concept* that is unsustainable. Right now, there's a lot of discussion about issues like sustainable development and environmentalism, and rights of peoples. But those are long-term struggles that have been going on for hundreds of years. Not just here in the Western Hemisphere, but elsewhere in the world. And to me the centerpiece of this, and I believe to a lot of indigenous people, boils down to two different worldviews.''

Winona went on to explain those differing views: land-based thinking versus industrial thinking. Winona characterized the indigenous view of land-based thinking as one belonging to people who live on the land; people who make their living from the land; and people who have ceremony and prayer which reaffirms their relationship to the land. A centerpiece, she added, is an acknowledgment that natural law is preeminent. ''The idea that natural law is the *highest* law,'' she continued, ''higher than the law made by nation-states or municipalities.

''A second cornerstone concept to indigenous thinking is that all that is around us is animate, is alive. So in our language, many nouns are animate, whether it is *mandaamin*, the word for 'corn,' or *manoomin*, the word for 'wild rice,' or *mitig*, the word for 'tree,' or *asin*, the word for 'stone'—all of them are animate in our language, which means that they have spirit. They have standing on their own. As such, when one reckons with them, it is with the knowledge that they are alive. And in response to that, we have practices where when you're harvesting, you're very respectful. Because it's our view that, for example, a deer gives itself to you. It's not because you're skillful.

''But,'' Winona went on, ''in American society, we are taught of man's dominion over nature. The idea of man's God-given right to all that is around him—that all that is around him is inferior to man and that the laws of Congress are superior to the laws of nature. Our native culture is based on the most basic notion that you never take more than you need. Inherently, capitalism is very much about always taking more than you need . . . And from that vantage point, I would argue that capitalism is intrinsically disrespectful. And being that that motive is the core of the American economic system, it's very much a problem when you look at the American dream and the price we've paid for it. I question the validity of that dream.

Man's dominion

"It was sold to us as a bill of goods that doesn't give us quality of life," she continued. "It gives us a level of consumption. Americans today, who make up just five percent of the world's population, consume one-third of the world's resources. Americans consume seven times more wood products than any other industrial country. We are the number-two consumers of energy per capita in the world, and the vast majority of that energy comes from native lands—uranium, coal, oil, natural gas, hydroelectric power.

"The chance that the rest of the world could live like we do is zero," she added. "And the thought that they should is totally based on a misrepresentation of reality. And the chance that *we* can continue living like this for another fifty years is zero; we're going to run out of resources before then. So I think we have to decouple our view of how we define our quality of life from our level of consumption. That, to me, is one of the most prominent challenges this generation faces."

We asked Winona to expound upon the idea she had raised earlier of inanimate versus animate, wondering if the difference in semantics between these worldviews wasn't one of the ways in which our industrialism is justified.

"Well"—she paused—"a lot of authors and native peoples refer to this as the 'commodification of the sacred.' The industrialized English language has been transformed, so the animate quality has been removed. So, for instance, corn is now referred to as an agricultural 'product,' and it becomes an inanimate noun; we now have dairy 'products'; and a natural resource like water is viewed in terms of water 'rights,' or acre-feet of water; and coal is referred to as a natural 'resource.'

"The Hopi people, however, will tell you that the black heap of coalfield is the liver of Mother Earth. Peabody Coal or Arizona Public Service will tell you that it's worth twenty dollars a ton delivered. It's a totally different worldview, and it permeates this culture. I spend a lot of time working on forest issues on my reservation, tryin' to keep trees standing instead of cut. And I am in constant meetings with the Department of Natural Resources and they are referring to trees as 'timber resources,' and I keep trying to assert that they are *forests*. They are *trees*. 'No,' they insist, 'they are timber resources in this number of acreage.'

"You know," Winona said, taking a breath and looking over the surrounding pines, "as Indians, we are, in the view of most of America, seen as people who are not quite in keeping with this century, who need to be moving along, who need to get caught up. It's a paradigm that I reject. Time after time, I'm talking about trying to get back our land and people say, 'What are you going to do with it?' The inference is that we have to log it, or that we have to grow agricultural products on it. I usually say, 'Don't worry, we've got plenty to do with our land.' But, sometimes I want to say to those guys, 'I just want to *look* at it.'"

Winona went on to talk about another concept that is central to her community: "a cyclical concept of life." "We don't really have a concept of Armageddon," she explained. "What we have, for instance, is *minobimaatisiiwin*, a word in our language that means 'the good life.' The ultimate translation is 'continuous rebirth.' I believe that the earth is now in a time of change, a time of cleansing. It doesn't mean an end; it means a death of one way and a rebirth to another."

Winona stopped talking and looked around her with apparent appreciation for the trees that protected her house, the water kneeling at the edge of her land, and the wind that kicked up to cool us all. Suddenly, the faint sound of a hawk's call drifted down from high above the trees. Winona squinted upward to find him.

"Oh, do you see that hawk?" she asked.

It took us a second, but we spotted it—wings spread wide against the blue sky. He soared above us, releasing three loud calls before taking refuge in one of those trees that Winona had talked about protecting. I later found out that Winona's Ojibway name is *Benaysayequay*, meaning "thunderbird woman."

Winona retraced to her pre-hawk thought. "I think that one of the wrongful assumptions," she argued, "is that there's a technological fix that's going to make everything okay. I don't believe that; I think that has to do with that linear way of thinking and with denial."

Her words reminded me of the Hopi Prophecy Rock in Arizona. Before I could ask Winona if she knew of it, she continued: "I think part of the problem in not knowing one's history is that we think the level of consumption that we've now grown accustomed to is reflective of how people in our country have always lived . . . The framers of the Constitution did not foresee the despoiling of oceans; they couldn't imagine rivers so polluted they catch on fire. But they did write about prosperity, 'life, liberty, and the pursuit of happiness.' I think environmental protection is implied in the Constitution and now needs to be made explicit. The violence of this society has outstripped the law."

Shainee asked Winona which American perspective she felt would need to shift first in order for us to collectively move toward "the balance" she was hoping for. "We are taught that we should go to school to get an education," Winona said, "to become a white-collar worker, a silk-collar worker. What's wrong with being a farmer? What's wrong with working on the land?

"There's a social pecking order here. What garners the most status is to be a movie star, or a musician, or a stockbroker. I think we need to realign ourselves to figure out what really defines quality of life. If you can't breathe the air, and you can't drink the water, and all your food has a stamp on it, I think you've lost your quality of life. I think quality of life should be based on our relationships to each other; whether we are living in places where we know someone, and whether we trust our communities. America today is about society, not community."

We asked Winona if she knew of Wes Jackson. "Yeah, I know Wes. I love Wes Jackson; he's really inspirational. If I could get him to talk to all the farmers here, I'd be set. Actually, I should bring him here for a little tour. He said he'd come up here sometime." Winona thought for a second. "There's a lot of really remarkable people out there that are doing long-term work. We all have our little piece."

Shainee asked Winona if there was a particular place from which she drew her faith and passion. "For me, my community and the land that I live from is my spiritual wellspring, and that is how I sustain myself," she said, with both strength and softness. "I live in a place where thousands of years before me, people of my blood lived and had the same prayers that I have. And I am surrounded by people who are working on these same struggles and trying to make a better life for their descendants. There are a lot of people I know who are in much more difficult situations than I am, and that in itself can give one some kind of courage.

"You look out and there are these women facing down bulldozers—or the Dan sisters, these elderly women who are protesting and getting hauled off by cops. Or these eighty-five-year-old women standing on runways in northern Labrador trying to stop fifty-ton fighter jets. There are a lot of people out there who are engaged in struggles that have a lot of integrity. And the only reason that those of us who are alive today have any rights whatsoever is because someone struggled for us—that is whether we are people of color, whether we are women, or whether we are working-class people.

"And it is really important to reaffirm and to always rearticulate that somebody dreamed something . . . somebody *dreamed* that they had the right to live with clean water, with clean air, and to raise their children in some safety of not feeling like a predator . . . is going to come and take their joy from them. That's the American dream. And that, I believe, needs to be the wellspring—aside from a spiritual one—that is the foundation of all work."

Winona was one of the few people we had met who was able to articulate the American dream in such infinite and universal terms. She was able to bring individuals, communities, and countries together under one very human definition of *the* dream.

After the interview, Winona invited us to join her in delivering lunch to the loggers she had been talking about. Shainee and I followed her van down dry, dusty roads and parked across from a steepled Catholic church. We walked away from the church into the woods, where I heard the sounds of chains knocking and heavy animal breathing. Pushing through brush, we came face-to-face with four pairs of flaring nostrils that seemed the size of teacup saucers. I have never seen horses that large before or since. They looked as if they more appropriately belonged in a Roald Dahl novel than here on earth and in Minnesota. Standing next to these enormous creatures, tending to their bridles, was a boy of about ten. The horses looked like eight-cylinder pickup trucks next to his tiny frame, and it was an awesome sight, this boy and these giants, who were indeed friends.

Horse-logging

We talked with the boy for a minute while he worked, then he directed us to where his father and a friend were busy preparing logs. We were told the logs were being gathered to build a new home for the boy's family. The trees they were loading onto a wooden sleigh had fallen during a recent windstorm that had cut a thirty-foot canal down a few miles of the reservation. So the logs were considered a gift from Mother Earth. The men loaded the gifted trees onto the handmade sleigh, secured them with chains, and "heeya'd" the horses about 100 feet forward to the road. We all moved quickly out of the path of the horses as they lunged in great tugging strides past us. So *this* is horse-logging.

Winona asked if she could try "driving" the horses. The boy's father gave her a few syllables' worth of instructions (Winona later explained verbal communication is not his strength) and handed over the thick leather reins. Winona "heeya'd" and held tight. The horses, like a train on oiled tracks, took Winona for a lightning-fast ride. When the horses came to a halt of their own free will—Winona still hanging on—she released the reins and staggered around toward their heads. She nestled her face against one of theirs, her arm around his neck, laughing like they had all just told her a great joke. Then she walked through the trees, out of our sight, but I could still hear her chuckling to herself.

Shainee and I needed to get on the road, so we bid a reluctant good-bye to Winona, her friends, and the horses, as they continued making progress in our rearview mirror.

MICAH WAGNER AND RYAN PARR

STUDENTS • GAS STATION ATTENDANTS

BLOOMSBURG, PENNSYLVANIA

(Shainee)

When we left Minnesota, we drove straight back to Chicago and Elizabeth's apartment, where we had planned to meet with Bill, our cinematographer, for the first time. He would be crossing our path and heading west as we made our way east. We hadn't seen him since the day we did camera tests in Los Angeles before we left. None of us had ever really stopped to think about how odd our arrangement was, so the fact that no one had seen one frame of Bill's footage yet did not seem odd, either. Blind faith all around.

We had finally scraped together enough cash to get some footage transferred to videotape. We wanted to make sure that we hadn't completely overestimated Bill's ability to shoot "postcards" of America that would match our experiences, without him experiencing our experiences. Kris and I had tried to be diligent in describing the regions and people we'd encountered—and the images we thought would best illustrate them—to Bill via voice mail. And we had managed to catch up and speak in person about once every other state.

Our plan was to meet in Chicago for one night to watch the inaugural footage. The lab had checked the film for exposure, so we knew that Bill's wind-up Bolex camera was capturing something, we just didn't know what. Elizabeth was in the middle of moving—straddling two apartments for the weekend—so we got the old apartment to ourselves for a slumber party with Bill.

He pulled up in his big blue pickup, which was all tricked out for life on the road. Bill and his truck are not a likely couple on first glance. Bill is a wiry guy who wears glasses, army pants cut off at the knees, and a variety of threadbare T-shirts. He is soft-spoken and shy with people he does not know. His truck, on the other hand, could easily be souped up to monster truck competition standards. It is absolutely enor-

275

mous and loud, and Bill maintains it fastidiously. We could barely make out Bill's face, which was dwarfed behind the truck's huge steering wheel, when he pulled up beeping and waving. He parallel-parked the blue giant carefully—a difficult task on the crowded streets of Chicago—and we all started talking at once.

Bill's test run

We went out for dinner and drank a bottle of wine to prepare ourselves for the news, good or bad. Then we returned to Elizabeth's, and it was time for the screening. We had only had enough money to transfer the first few rolls of film to video—about twenty minutes of footage—but it would be enough on which to base a thumbs-up or -down. We hooked up the VCR, Bill did an impromptu drumroll on the hardwood floor, and the very first shot came up on the screen—a gorgeous image of an endless sunflower field. Kris nearly fell out of her chair. While we'd been in Kansas—the Sunflower State—I had driven her crazy trying to find a field of sunflowers to shoot. We had even asked at the Land Institute why we couldn't find one. Turns out they weren't in season yet and weren't that common in that part of the state. I had been so disappointed—I love the flowers and had been longing for the sight of a whole field full.

Kris jumped up and hugged Bill, who had no idea why his sunflower shot had elicited such a visceral reaction. We took it as a symbol of the true bond between the three of us—a good omen that we indeed had a symbiotic vision for the project.

As it turns out, the shot was actually from a test run at a local field in Texas, a few miles from Bill's home. We watched the rest of the footage, and even Bill—his own worst critic—was pleased with what he had wrought. The images were beautiful and evocative, and we thought they'd mix well with our own footage. We sat up most of the night exchanging stories of our respective adventures. Around 4 A.M., Bill announced that he wanted to become a professional hobo. Kris and I supported him in his decision, agreeing that it was a life we could all get used to, and we finally went to sleep.

After a couple of days in Chicago, it was time get back in the car. We bid farewell to Bill—his monster truck pointed west, our car pointed east—and promised to meet again soon. I was expected at an engagement party in New Jersey a mere thirty-six hours later, so, as usual, we had to drive fast. About 150 miles northeast of Philadelphia, we pulled off the highway at a massive truck stop in a town called Bloomsburg to refuel the car and ourselves. Kris pumped; I went to pay and peruse snack options.

There were two teenage boys behind the counter, and I watched them as I handed over my money. One had longish blond hair and seemed to be instructing the other on procedure. The second boy, who was taller and darker–complected, listened intently as he punched our bill into the computer. Their vernacular was Beavis and Butt-Head, but there was something about them that piqued my interest. Kris joined me at the Frito-Lay display, and I asked her if she was up for an interview. She eyed the boys and wearily agreed.

First we asked if they were uncomfortable with us pointing cameras at them. They laughed, telling us, teasingly, that it was an everyday occurrence—that girls with cameras were always running after them. The blond boy said that the week before, a bunch of girls had stopped to get their car looked at and had taken three rolls of pictures of him at the gas pumps. Kris asked why they had wanted pictures. He looked sheepish and said, ''Well, they were Asian tourists.'' He seemed almost embarrassed and perceptibly P.C. hypersensitive.

The blond boy was named Micah Wagner, and his friend and gas-attendant-in-training was Ryan Parr. We began by asking who had influenced them. Ryan said he was influenced by the people that he meets every day and went on to say, ''Publicity today is so corrupt. You can't trust anything you see. If someone's made out to be a good influence to the public, they're generally not. Personally, I have role models in my everyday life that I look up to . . . my parents, my future in-laws.''

I asked if Ryan was engaged, and Micah broke in and said very seriously, ''See, we're both nineteen, but we've both been seeing our girlfriends for several years now. I've been with my girlfriend . . . Well, in December it was five years.''

''I've only got two years and five months.'' Ryan shrugged.

Micah went on. ''We're both very serious, not only about education and life as a whole, but everything.''

The semis began to pile up outside, each one setting off a bell in the store. The boys pretended not to hear and somehow managed to keep the financial transactions flowing while we asked what kind of future they predicted for themselves. Ryan said he had everything he needed except money, and he didn't know how much of that he actually needed. ''I've got the other half of the American dream working on my side,'' he added. ''I like the area I live in and I just want to keep on living here as comfortably as possible, and that's about the extent of my life. There's not a whole lot to worry about in this area, but it's changing all the time. Before you know it, we'll have as much pollution and smog as the rest of the world and just as much crime; we already do in town. But I live out in Sticksville, in the middle of nowhere. I like it out there: the grass is green, big bushy trees, running water that's still clear.'' He stopped to think, then continued. ''I'd like to be able to have my children enjoy that, too, and I think one day they actually might.''

He suddenly seemed self-conscious, speaking so openly in front of his buddy. But Micah was nodding his head vigorously in agreement backing Ryan up. We moved on to the question of equality.

"I think as it goes now, women are becoming more superior than men in today's society," Micah postulated, and it was Ryan's turn to nod his head in concurrence. "Because women over the years have used their smarts. They've used their brains to get ahead and I think they'll stay ahead and take over." Ryan looked at us and smirked, listening to his friend, knowing he was waxing a little too much for the older women with cameras. It was okay though; we were still sufficiently impressed by a younger man echoing what John Perry Barlow was so sure of as an older man.

The conversation turned to contemporary media, and Ryan observed that the only way in which the media provides role models is by focusing the spotlight on people who provide examples of how *not* to live. Micah piped back in, "What am I supposed to believe when I open the newspaper and read that a guy who just got out of jail is supposed to be the greatest heavyweight fighter that ever lived? The media's making it sound like a great thing when the man just got out of jail for *rape*. How good is that? I'm a fan of boxing, but how can I, as a fan, feel proud of a man who's going to stand in a ring and make millions of dollars when he has done something so terrible to someone else? He does not deserve that opportunity, he does not. It's not right."

Ryan shook his head, grumbling, "Only in America."

Shortly thereafter, a trucker with a big orange hunting hat walked in and looked at the boys with raised eyebrows. Micah smiled at him, handed him some change, and gave him a look that asked

Micah gets miced

him not to interrupt. The trucker put his hand up as if to say, "It's cool. No sweat," and walked out straightening his hat. Unfortunately, the manager saw the exchange and interrupted our interview. He said he didn't mind us doing our "school project," but Ryan was in training and at least one of the boys had to man the cash register. He elected Ryan to stay, and Micah followed us outside, where we conducted the balance of the interview in front of a silver gas pump marked with big red letters spelling out ULTRA CLEAR DIESEL. The sun was setting behind him, and we had to work around the trucks pulling all around us—but there was no time to be choosy.

Micah was a sport and sat down on a patch of curb between two oil spills as he began to describe his life. "I'm just an everyday person. Right at this point, I work in a mill, and I work here at a gas station. I don't want to be stuck in the mill for the rest of my life. I want and need a college education, just a life in general, even if it's a struggle. Just life. I don't want to sit stagnant."

Micah had mentioned that he worked a forty-hour week at the station, so I was a little surprised to hear that he had another job. I asked him to tell us a little about his work.

"I work at a carpet company as a utility weaver, which is someone who helps the weavers keep their looms running properly," he explained. "I basically just tie knots. There's a guy who's been there for about twenty-five years and he can do about thirty thousand ends a day—manually. The most I can do is about ten thousand, but manually, only a thousand. And here at the station, I deal with all the truckers. A good majority of them are nice, and I like this place a lot. Even though I deal with a driver once in a while that I wouldn't mind clobbering, I still like it."

Micah was very forthcoming, and I was glad that we were finally getting the chance to hear a young outspoken voice. I asked if he was planning to go to college.

"Well, I started already at Bloomsburg University, but I took a year off because of my financial situation. I'd like to get a bachelor's in biology, though, and possibly, in the future, be a veterinarian. Right now, I dabble a little, with reptiles mostly. No great contribution there, just a learning experience. But I could go to college and not be able to do it at all, you know. So I just want to do whatever I'm best at. That's what I want—what I'm best at."

In addition to Micah's two jobs and his interest in animals, he was also a writer and told us he had won a couple of local poetry and short story contests. Kris asked Micah if he was planning on staying in Bloomsburg—like Ryan—or move away for school or work.

"I don't want to live in the city because there's too much violence and I don't want to compete for a spot on a sidewalk," he answered. "This area is gorgeous. I would like to stay here or move out farther into the country. It's beautiful. It's majestic. It's peaceful. And at nighttime you don't hear a car, you hear the animals. You don't hear animals in the city; you hear a drunk guy stumbling on your sidewalk or puking in the alley. I'm just lookin' to fill my spot in this place, really."

Then Micah explained that he hadn't spoken to either of his parents in over a year and that he was living with his girlfriend's family, trying to support himself and get through school. He said money was an obstacle and that he and his girlfriend, both attending classes at the university, were barely getting by. I asked if he felt as though doors were open to him.

"No," Micah answered without hesitation. "Unless you have parents that are rich. Unless you're kissing somebody's ass. Or unless you're a welfare bum, you don't get opportunities today. You don't. If you're a normal, everyday middle-class person who barely gets by and who has just enough money to live, you don't get an opportunity anymore, because they think you can still do it. And we struggle now just to have the little we have. We always have money in our pocket, but we just never seem to be able to get ahead. Because it always takes more than what you have in your pocket.''

I asked if he thought things would stay that way after he finished college.

"Yeah," he declared. "But I don't want the things that an everyday college graduate would want—you know, a big fancy house and a nice car. That's materialistic bullshit. You don't need those things. I mean, they're nice. But what purpose do they serve? If I'm working a sixty-hour-a-week job, what purpose is a nice car gonna serve me when I only spend an hour in it?

"What I want is for my kids—when I have kids—to have the opportunities I didn't have. I want to put my money away for intelligent things. If I don't buy a $200,000 or $300,000 home, get a reasonable home instead, and save money, I can put that money away for a college education for my children."

We revisited the question of influence and I asked Micah if there was anyone that he admired. He mused, "I don't think there's any one particular person—every single person to me has a flaw that is very unadmirable. But a lot of things

people have said have influenced my life. Things a lot of great artists have said. Things Kurt Cobain has said. A lot of things the Dead have said and done.''

I asked Micah why he mentioned Kurt Cobain and the Grateful Dead specifically. He answered, "Well, Cobain was a heroin addict, and he had a very dysfunctional life. He stressed it in his music. He was very open and honest about it. And I get so tired of watching people hide who they are. Even me, who used to hide who I was to everyone—I'm very ashamed of who I used to be. And he was open and honest, even though he was still the same person when he died. For me, knowing who you are is the most important thing in life, not where you go. Just knowing who you are.''

Micah leaned into his hand, pausing as the semi behind him revved its engine. He continued matter-of-factly, " 'Cause I can sit here and tell you a thousand things I've did and a thousand things other people have did, but I can't honestly tell you who I am as a person. I don't know many people who can."

We asked him if he believed there was an American dream.

His answer was definitive: "An American dream. No. Because the American dream was lost in the dollar, it was lost in the economy, it was lost in drugs, and alcohol, and sex, and violence. I think that whole thing was lost twenty-five years ago when our parents got lost in what they think was an era. No one knows what the American dream is anymore. If there is an American dream, I'd be damned if I could tell you because I don't see one for any reason or purpose except to make a dollar. Where can there be an American dream when seventy percent of the people I know are either getting high, busting their asses to get high, or they're trying to get somewhere with nothin'?'' Micah stopped looking at the ground, and then finished, ''I don't know, cause that is confusing.''

Strangely enough, Micah was echoing the words of Roger Zins, who had argued that the American dream was valid a generation or two ago but not anymore. Micah did, however, reach for a silver lining, saying, ''You know, I guess I can contradict myself in one way, though. For the American dream, I would say it might be to live a better life than your parents lived. I would say that is everyone's dream: to have it better than their parents did when they were kids.''

''And do you think that's still valid?'' I asked.

''Yeah,'' he said. ''For everyone. Because if it wasn't, why would anybody want an education? Why would anyone want a good job?''

Micah's gaze shifted past us and we looked to see a middle-aged woman pulling up. Micah excused himself and ran over to her. She handed him a bag from McDonald's, he hugged her, and she drove away. When Micah came back, he told us the woman was his girlfriend's mother, dropping some dinner off for him. He was working a double shift. ''She's really great to me. The whole family is,'' he said graciously, stuffing his mouth full of fries. He dug into the bag and asked, ''Isn't this trip really hard on you two, as a social kind of thing?''

''No, we have a social life—we're hanging out with so many great people,'' Kris answered.

''That would be the best part, even though you're only there temporarily. But you honestly get to know the most intimate sides of the people because of the questions you ask,'' Micah said, chewing. He said he had trouble understanding, however, how we could be away from our loved ones for so long. ''Every person craves an intimate part of life, no matter how much a person wants to travel. I'm the kind of person who always needs someone there for me. I can't see two people just kind of out there, just leaving things behind. For me, the hardest thing in life, no matter how much I might want to, would be just pack up and leave. I need something intimate, I need something physical, and I need something emotional. I need something very fulfilling. I have to speak to my girlfriend every day. I have to hold her every day or else something just feels like it's not there.'' Micah just kept on eating as he spilled his guts to us.

He continued with his mouth full. ''It takes a rude awakening, like for me, who woke up in the hospital and was told, 'Oh, we thought you were dead.' It takes things like that, serious things. Three years ago, I was a regular everyday user. I did everything. You name it, I did it. I don't touch it at all now, not even dibble-dabble. I didn't go through no program. I did it on my own. I said, 'This is bullshit.' I quit smoking, I rarely ever swear. And I work where every single person swears, and I work where every single person smokes. Ninety percent of my friends still use on a daily basis, and they use right in front of me. But my life is mine, and goddamn it if I'm going to let somebody else screw it up for me. I always had an excuse. 'Dad did this.' 'Mom did that.' 'It's my life.' Mom and Dad can do what they do, but it's still your goddamn life. Don't let anybody else screw it up.''

Micah was adding an entirely new perspective to our already diverse group of opinions. He spoke of hopelessness and disenfranchisement, young people without direction. I had known them myself when I was his age and we talked a little bit about what happens when you can't drag yourself out of the pattern. Micah said that he had been forced to separate himself from some of his friends.

''I've had so many friends die. I had a friend die in front of me from a heart attack, using heroin. I sat right there and watched it. I had a friend hit and killed by a train on New Year's Eve. I've had friends killed in drunk driving accidents. They're just not there anymore. Even a lot of the kids that I used to hang out with, until I really started getting serious with my girlfriend, they're just so lost and so burnt-out, wasted; they're not even people anymore. As a matter of fact, one of my closest friends at the time was at the top of his class in computer program-ming. And he didn't even recognize me the other day from doing drugs. We hung out every day. I lived with him for eight months. That's bad.''

Micah shook his head and fiddled with his microphone cord. He informed us that Bloomsburg University is ''one of the top ten party schools in the country. We've had a lot of problems. For a while there, we had problems with gangs, even. It's a pretty rural area and it's starting to feel like the problems of the city.''

''You have *gangs* in the middle of Pennsylvania?'' I squawked. Micah was completely unfazed by my response. He said that he himself had been mixed up in the gangs at one point. I asked why.

''I missed the union, that family-type feel, where you always have someone there for you. I missed it. I haven't even been involved with it for a year or two now. It's hard to explain. When you feel lonely, you feel worthless. You feel trapped. You feel like there's nothing there. Give yourself one friend, and that can make all the difference in the world. But when you're in a whole room full of friends, and they're all willing to stand behind you, no matter what, regardless of what they're doing, you feel drawn toward it and it can really suck you in. Quicker than you can flush a toilet.''

Micah continued without any prompting, saying that there had been a bad Skinhead problem in the area, as well, that had recently been eradicated. He said that at one point he was even mixed up with some of them. ''I was a follower, and because of it, I had gotten involved with them, too, and I got marked, ya know. You probably don't even know what that is.''

We didn't.

''Tattooed.'' Micah paused for what felt like a whole minute. He seemed to be getting a little bit uncomfortable. He continued, though, swallowing hard. ''It's humiliating, because I never believed in anything they believed in the first place. I was always very against what they thought. I was involved with them for about a month, and it was because there was someone that I didn't like, that I really wanted to get even with. I didn't have any friends to back me up. So I got involved with this group of wanna-bes, hoping they would do my dirty work for me. And really the biggest reason was because of the partying, because I used to party a lot. I was too screwed up to care that they stood for everything I hate.''

Kris asked, ''Having said all that, do you feel optimistic at all about your future?''

''Optimistic, no. Hope, yes,'' was Micah's definitive answer. ''Why not?'' he asked. ''When you lose hope, there's nothing there. Why give up when tomorrow can be better?'' Micah had finished his soda and had nothing left to fiddle with. The sun was going down behind the rows of silver pumps and Kris and I still had to get to New Jersey. It was time for us to leave. We told Micah how glad we were that he had given us so much of his time and shared so much of his life with us. He smiled, saying that he was a little surprised himself at how much he had shared. We asked one last question. What made him keep going, through all of his ordeals?

He rested his elbow on one of the pumps and thought for a second before responding. ''What makes me get up in the morning is I had a niece who was six months old and had a bad liver. The last time I saw her was in a hospital in Danville. And she was really sick, really bloated. They didn't think she was going to live much longer. I was leaving, and I put my hand on her bloated stomach—she was only twelve pounds at six months old—and her stomach was as big as a basketball. She smiled and giggled, and cooed and kicked her feet. And even the nurses were surprised that she kicked her feet, because she was in a great deal of pain. That child was six months old when she died because her brain hemorrhaged from so much stress on the body.

''I can't just lay in bed and let a day go by knowing that there's something I can do—when I know that there's so many people who never have a chance to enjoy what they really do deserve. I'm nineteen years old, and there's so much beauty in people and life. I just can't let that go past me without knowing what there is. And if you sleep one day, who knows what you're gonna miss. You never know.''

At that moment, Ryan leaned out of the store and yelled to Micah to come back in. Micah straightened up, dropped his trash in the barrel next to him, and gave us a wide smile with a shrug of his shoulders. ''Back to my real life.''

We got back in the car—it was after nine at that point—and we still had a solid three hours to go. Kris fell asleep about twenty minutes outside of Bloomsburg. I put in a Nirvana tape and sang the whole way to New Jersey.

MICHAEL STIPE

SONGWRITER • LEAD SINGER OF R.E.M.

NEW YORK CITY

(Shainee)

During the summers in Philadelphia when I was in high school in the mid-eighties, they used to hold what they called "jams" at the then-crumbling JFK Stadium. They would headline three or four bands, and 60,000 people would come from all over the tri-state area to partake in an all-day, general-admission, beer-swilling, babe-ogling, amp-blasting, classic-rock heat rash. When I was fifteen, I spent a summer away from home, woeful about the fact that I was missing "everything," including that summer's biggest concert. I talked to my friend Rachel on the phone the night of the event and asked her how the show was. "Awesome," was the reply.

Apparently, I had missed out on the Police, Loverboy, Wham!, and Joan Jett and the Blackhearts. Rachel went on and on about Sting and George Michael and the glory of boys and beer. I was trying desperately to hide my misery, but Rachel saw right through it. Just before we hung up, she tried to make me feel better. She said that some new band had opened up the jam, and everyone had hated them—I was *so* lucky I had missed them. She said that no one understood their music, and some people even threw food from coolers at the stage. She couldn't remember the band's name, but she said it had something to do with seeing. That day I had missed my first R.E.M. concert. Today Rachel gladly eats her words.

The first time I met Michael Stipe, the lead singer of R.E.M., was at the Los Angeles premiere of Nancy Savoca's film *Household Saints*. The premiere was a benefit for a mentoring program for young women in film that I was running. On the day of the event, we heard that Michael Stipe might be attending. My insides froze. Here I was, living in a town where the novelty of stargazing wears off the first time you see Larry Hagman at the dry cleaner's, and I was positively clammy about the prospect of meeting Michael Stipe. At that point, R.E.M. had already released ten albums, and had been a prevailing rock band for an entire decade, always evolving.

A couple of years, a zillion phone calls, and a few skipped heartbeats later, I was about to meet him again, and yes, I was still a little clammy. We had been pestering Michael for months about participating in the project, and after much vacillation, Michael agreed to do the interview. We settled on a date when the band would be in New York for the *MTV Music Video Awards*. A couple of days before the interview, Meredith, Michael's assistant, called to tell us that Michael had had an emergency hernia surgery, but he was insisting on performing at the awards show and we would do the interview as planned.

Michael had asked us to call him at his hotel, the Four Seasons, the day before, to give him a little background on the interview topics.

OPERATOR: Four Seasons, good afternoon.

SG: Hi. It's Shainee and Kristin calling for Michael Stipe.

OPERATOR: One moment to connect you.
(Long silent pause, us breathing)

KH: Should one of us tell a joke right now?

SG: Oh, I do have the funniest joke to tell you . . .
(More silence, more breathing)

SG: This is definitely a little nerve-racking.

KH: I know. I feel like we're calling the President.

MARK: Thank you for holding. This is Mark.

SG: Hi, Mark. It's Shainee and Kristin calling.

MARK: Yes, can I place you on hold one moment, so I can get him for you?

SG: Sure.
(More silence)

KH: One of us needs to do most of the talking, so we don't talk over each other. I'm gonna let you do it.

MARK: I'm going to transfer you into him now.

SG: Okay. Thanks.

MAN: Hello?

SG: Michael?

MAN: May I ask who's calling?

SG: It's Shainee calling.

MAN: Hi, Shainee. Hold one second. Let me put you through.

SG: Okay. Thanks.

MS: Hello?

SG: Michael?

MS: Yeah. Is this Shainee?

SG: Yeah, hi.

MS: Hi, how are you?

SG: Good. How are you feeling?

MS: I'm feeling better. It's something I've never experienced before, so that's probably good.

KH: A new experience. A hernia isn't very much fun, though.

MS: Yeah, well, I didn't know how traumatic invasive surgery is. . . . It's pretty intense. I've never been encumbered by anything—touch wood—and it's been a wild couple of weeks. But I wanted to talk to you guys, just to kind of go over some stuff. It's been a while since I saw the first fax that you sent along and then the six or seven hundred after that.

We proceeded to give Michael the rundown, rattling off our list of questions, telling him we were planning to focus his interview on his thoughts on the evolution of the American hero.

MS: Okay, cool. Well, we can talk about this more when we sit down face-to-face. But I get asked a lot of stock questions, so I've got stock answers, dial-a-quotes . . . I tend to become kind of like, you know, that's card number 369—my comments on *Media and Sexism*—blah, blah, blah. I'll stay away from that, but when we sit down, if you guys are getting those kind of answers, just let me know.

Later we talked to Meredith, to schedule the exact time of the interview, in spite of the fact that Michael claimed to be a ''space cookie'' from the painkillers he was on. Meredith also gave us instructions on how to get up to his room. He was staying under a false name and to get access to him, we would have to utter a secret password, click our ruby-red shoes, and spin on our heads—or something to that effect. It was all very intriguing in a *Mission: Impossible* kind of way.

When we arrived at the Four Seasons the next day, we went to the concierge, who asked in a stylish British accent, ''You're here to see . . . ?'' He then made a strange swirling with his eyelid and eyebrow that managed to communicate that he wanted me to give him the password, so I did. The man looked me square in the eye and said, ''Right!'' so emphatically that I thought maybe it had been a trick question. He called up to the room and handed the phone to me to talk to one of Michael's staff, Don.

When we got upstairs, Michael wasn't in his room, but Don let us in. We set up our equipment around Michael's breakfast remains, which were still on the table, his magazine collection, which was scattered around, and an open box of Converse tennis shoes on the couch. Michael walked in a few minutes later in a blue T-shirt, Adidas sweatpants, narrow sunglasses, and a beautiful shaved head. He's a delicate-looking man with elegant hands and a velvety speaking voice. We all said our hellos and Michael asked if anyone was hungry. Kris said no, I said yes. He seemed like the kind of person that you could be honest with.

Michael got on the phone and ordered some food from room service. We asked how he was feeling and he said he was getting better, then he pulled up his shirt and pulled down his pants so that we could see the pink sliver of a scar on his abdomen. It was an intimate gesture—I mean, we had met him five minutes ago and here was his pelvis. But it was also endearing. The immediate dispensing with formalities could also have had something to do with the fact that upon our arrival, we realized that we had a mutual friend who happened to be visiting Michael that day. His name is Jeremy, and he played the role of fly on the wall for the afternoon.

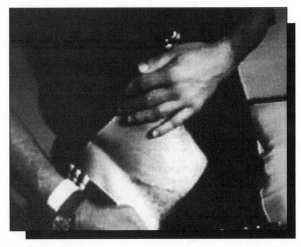

The scar

Michael sat down on the couch so we could get started and asked if either of us wore a ten-and-a-half shoe, picking up the sneakers. We both said no. Then Michael lit a Drum cigarette, and we began with our usual opening question about his background.

Michael replied, "My father was in the military, so I moved around a whole lot. Growing up, I lived mostly in the South—Georgia, Texas, Illinois, Alabama—and Frankfurt, Germany. So I've been traveling all my life. My father retired when I was seventeen or eighteen, and we moved back to Georgia, which is where our entire family is from originally. They moved to Athens because it was a big college town, and they wanted us to have the opportunity to go to college if we wanted to. I was living with a punk rock band outside of East St. Louis. I ran out of money and moved back to Athens. I started going to school there, working a job. And I've stayed in Athens because my family is there, and we're very close. I've traveled the world and the United States, but there's a part of Georgia in me, and I always feel good when I go back there," Michael said, smiling wide.

He had one of those smiles that changes a person's entire face, in Michael's case, lending an almost gawky boyishness to his persona. I asked Michael to talk a little bit more about his family and how they had influenced his life.

"My grandfather on my father's side was a Methodist preacher. My mother and father are both Christian—both raised Methodist. I was raised Methodist. I'm not Christian. But I think a lot of the better parts of Christianity—and some of the ethics that are taught through that religion—came through my parents and my grandparents to me and to my sisters.

"It's really hard to define just how close my family is: the kind of love that we have for one another is unconditional. Particularly at the end of the twentieth century, when most of my friends come from divorced or broken families."

Michael stubbed out his cigarette and I asked him if there was a particular moment when he knew that he wanted to make music his life.

"My parents were not big music fans, and so the music that I listened to growing up was mostly radio. I was living in Texas for five years when I was quite young, so it was country radio and bubblegum pop, late sixties, early seventies.

Sound check

That kind of influenced me a little bit. But when I was fifteen, I came upon the punk rock scene in New York through various magazines and newspapers and kind of found Patti Smith. I was trying really hard to like all the bands that everyone in my high school liked. I wanted to fit in and all that stuff. I never really got Ted Nugent.'' Michael chuckled. ''I never really got Styx. I never really got REO Speedwagon. When I heard Patti Smith for the first time, I knew that this was something that was so different from anything I had ever heard before—and so powerful.

''You know, I tend to take things very, very literally . . . When *The Last Picture Show* came out, the movie? I was eleven or twelve years old. I thought it was the last film that would ever be made. The punk rock ethic in those days was: 'Anybody can do this. Anybody can be in a band. Anybody can play guitar.' It was D.I.Y., and I took that very literally. And at the age of fifteen, I said, 'I want to be a singer.' Four years later, we started R.E.M. And it's gone on from there.'' Michael paused for a ringing doorbell.

Jeremy uncurled himself off of the couch to get the door. I asked Michael to name anyone, historically speaking, who might have influenced him.

''Well, the Velvet Underground are history for me. But also Arthur Rimbaud, the French poet. I read his entire works at the age of sixteen—before I knew his name was not pronounced 'Rimbod.' And you know, that's pretty powerful stuff. At one point, I was infatuated with Leonardo da Vinci, because he was left-handed. I'm left-handed, and he wrote backwards, and I wrote backwards until I was in sixth grade. He liked to draw. I tried to draw. I wasn't very good.''

I laughed, asking Michael if he too had invented things. He thought for a second. ''No. My own persona, according to some people,'' he smirked and then completed his answers on influence and history. I asked him if there was any American movement or idea that had captured him.

''Punk rock gave me something that made me feel empowered, made me feel important. I didn't feel like such a freak when I listened to it. Prior to that, the American education system in the 1960s and 1970s, when I was going to school, was already disintegrating. History as a subject was so obviously revisionist. I never believed that the Indians and the Pilgrims sat down at a table; that just didn't really fly with me. Why were all the Indians dead if they sat down at a table and they were all friends, and they swapped secrets about how to grow corn by putting fish in the ground? It didn't make sense to me.

"My sister and her husband are teachers now. I see the struggle that they have every single day, trying to rise above the kind of stuff that's handed them. I mean, to be a teacher in the mid-1990s in the U.S., I think is more like being a baby-sitter really."

Michael spoke of his sister and brother-in-law and their dedication to teaching with such admiration. I asked him if he thought that America has any real heroes today.

"I have a really strong opinion about the idea of heroes at the end of the twentieth century in the U.S. At one point, it seemed like the people we looked up to were kind of abstracted, because they were religious figures. Religion has kind of gone the way of all good things . . .

"At one point, they were politicians. When JFK was shot, that dissipated. When Nixon was caught in the scandal of Watergate, it dissipated even more. Politicians are no longer people that we look up to. I think what's left are sports figures, movie stars, and music figures." Michael paused, still thinking. "And maybe anchor people," he finished, smiling. "And that's kind of a weird place to be."

"Is it a weird place for you to be?" I asked.

"It is. I mean, it's a strange position to be in. There was a point in the late eighties, in the midst of the Reagan/Bush Dark Ages, when I felt compelled, as a person in a band, to comment on the situation that our country had found itself in. We were in really bad shape in 1979, 1980, by no one's real fault. What happened in the twelve years following that, with Reagan's first term in office, his reelection, which was astonishing to the world, I think, and then the election of, you know, 'Oh, the puppet is a little too old. Let's get the puppeteer,' and by the late 1980s, this country was so dissipated, I think.

"The ideology that was popular was one that was very elite, and a lot of people were marginalized by it and became angry . . . People were not taking care of the people around them. And so I got really political in some of our music. I don't think that it worked very well. There are a lot of musicians who are political and do a really good job. I don't think I was one of them. That having been said, I was offered the title as 'Spokesperson for a Generation.' I was like, 'I do not want that. How could I possibly fill that role?' I was really uncomfortable with it, and I stepped back . . . It's a ludicrous concept, that one person could speak for an entire generation.''

Michael's hands fluttered about as he expressed his disdain at the idea. Many people, by this point in our trip, had described media figures as a poor substitute for heroes in contemporary America. It was the first time that we had actually sat down and talked with one, though. Michael had referred to the years between 1980 and 1992 as the ''Dark Ages,'' and I asked him if he thought we were doing any better.

''I think the ripple effect from the Reagan/Bush years is going to be with this country for the rest of my life . . . The kind of ideology that Reagan and Bush put forth and the people who jumped on that bandwagon easily and readily were very very greedy. That's not something that disappears in a four-year term with the next President. There's just no way that anybody could step into office and try to undo some of the things that were done in that time period.

Michael said that he respected anyone who would have the strength and ambition to try to overcome the current gloomy situation. He continued, ''I'm very idealistic. I'm also incredibly cynical, and there's a balancing act between that idealism and that cynicism that I think really defines a lot of people my age and younger in this country right now. That being said, I can't approach anything without thinking that somewhere, somehow there's going to be a good end to it, or a good side to it. I'm an eternal optimist. That's what I've been called. I don't know if that's good or not.'' Michael shrugged.

I told him what John Waters had said about always hoping for the best and expecting the worst. ''Yeah, that's good,'' Michael agreed. Just then the food arrived—thankfully—because my stomach was beginning to make noises that I was positive everyone could hear. But my hopes were dashed when Michael said to just leave the covers on the plates and we could keep talking.

Michael continued, ''I think it's really unfair that media figures are called on—and again, I've been caught in this myself—called on to comment on just about anything in the world. I'm a singer, for Christ's sake, in a rock 'n' roll band. I don't know how a nuclear power plant is put together. When I was twenty-seven years old, I was asked that, with cameras on me, people with microphones. I don't know that stuff.

''I do know that there are bad things in the world, and people are affected by them and they become victimized by something that's much bigger than them, whether it's corporate or otherwise, and that's not good . . . But it's kind of a weird place to put a sports figure or a musician or an actor on a pedestal so high up that they are expected to know everything about everything or anything about everything, and to be able to comment on it, and truncate it, and give it a nice pull quote that will look good on the cover of a magazine.''

I asked Michael what impact he felt R.E.M.'s music has had. He answered, ''It's really hard for me to comment on how my band impacts the people who listen to our music . . . I know when people come up to me on the street or in a club and they say, 'This song really meant a lot to me,' that makes me really proud.

"Because, you know, at the end of the day, being in a rock band and being an entertainer, which is basically what I am, is not a real high calling. It doesn't take a genius to do this. I don't think I'm stupid, by any stretch. I also don't think I'm Noam Chomsky. But I mean what I'm saying, and I think what I'm saying is something that a lot of people respond to."

I asked Michael if he believed there is an American dream.

"I'm not sure that I ever quite figured out what the American dream was supposed to be. I think it's like canned peas and corn, and everything's perfect, and Formica counters, and Mom dresses like Mom, and Dad dresses like Dad and smokes a pipe, and everybody has opportunity. Is that right? Is that pretty good?

"Then again, I didn't go through two world wars and try to raise a family and go through a Depression. And finally, when it seemed the Golden Age had come, and everything was okay, and you could eat your food out of a can, you didn't have to go out in the garden and pick it, and you could eat as much meat as you wanted to, you didn't have to ration it—you know, I can't say that was invalid. Maybe those people really felt like they had deserved that, that they had been through a lot of hardship.

"My grandmother once said to me—she died this year, she was eighty-four—she said to me, 'When I was your age . . .'—I was probably twenty-four at the time—and she said, 'We had a war that would never end, we had politicians who were corrupt, we had a disease that was going to kill half the people in the world. We had children starving on the street. We had men and women who didn't have homes.' It just keeps going.

"I think what she was saying to me . . ." Michael paused and a mischievous smirk took over his mouth. "Well, going from my dear grandmother to this is maybe a little bit of a stretch, but there's the idea that every generation thinks they invented oral sex, you know? I think that's a very funny thing." Michael laughed at his metaphor of every generation thinking they invented hard times, continuing:"The world and the way that it is—the level of corruption, the level of good, the level of beauty—I think it's always been like that and there've always been periods of upheaval and violence and darkness, and then periods where things are a little better and people seem a little more tolerant and more peaceful. I think right now that we're in a period of immense upheaval and violence and corruption and ugliness."

At this point we took a little break to again address the fact that Michael still had not eaten and didn't hernia surgery recovery require that he should rest and eat? He said we should keep going, that he was running on caffeine and adrenaline. Michael wanted to know if his definition of the American dream was what we were looking for. We explained that we were approaching the subject objectively and that the film was truly based on the idea that *it depends who you ask*. We said that we had found that the definition of the American dream seemed to have evolved. Michael had an opinion on this:

"I realized at some point that I felt a nostalgia for an America that never existed. Partly it was what was taught to me in history class, and I realized then that that was not real. So I have this pride and this nostalgia for something that really is very abstracted and very fantastic and not really what happened. It's hard to realize that everything that you think and everything that you feel about your country . . . that it's kind of this invented thing."

"What do you value most about living in America?" I asked.

"What do I value most about living in America?" The big boyish grin returned as Michael proclaimed, "My freedom. Once again it ties exactly into that: What is freedom . . . ? You could talk to one person in the U.S. and they could say we live in a police state. You could talk to another person and they could say they've never had any problem at all with the law or the way the country is run."

Michael went on to talk more about freedom and, by a circuitous route, reached his conclusion, saying that the American dream certainly wasn't represented by Oliver North.

I mentioned to Michael that we were on our way to the Christian Coalition's Road to Victory convention in Washington, where Oliver North would be speaking, along with Newt Gingrich, Phil Gramm, Bob Dole, Ralph Reed, and Pat Buchanan, among others. We explained that we didn't have any conservative voices in the film and that we thought the Road to Victory would provide us with what we had affectionately dubbed "one-stop shopping." Michael laughed and said he didn't think we'd have to look hard for the blue-plate special.

Michael advised us not to bait any of the attendees at the Road to Victory. He talked about how easy it is to spawn enmity between factions. We explained that we were hoping to reflect an objective view, rather than trying to pit anyone against each other. Michael went on to say, "Clearly, to a lot of people in this country, I'm a real freak, and for whatever reason, whether they're looking at me for my job, the way I look, my sexuality and my stand on that. For me to say that my parents are Christians and that I have absolute respect for them . . . that's probably something that they haven't heard before."

Michael was right. When we did arrive at the Road to Victory conference, we thought back to his wish that the audience could hear from someone like him, someone who might be able to evince respect for difference and tolerance in this country. We told Michael that we had mixed feelings ourselves about our upcoming trip to Washington but that our trip, so far, had never let us down. "Yeah, it's had to have been a blast," he said.

"We've been lucky," Kris acknowledged.

Michael laughed out loud, saying, "Good. How often do I say that myself? I do feel sometimes like I am charmed, that somebody's looking over me. If I were to—and I don't want to die tomorrow—but if I were to die tomorrow, I would have lived the most intense, unbelievable, life-loving, thirty-five years of anybody

I know. And what more can you ask for? Not a lot. I wanna live to be eighty-four, though. I think I'm gonna be around."

"Like your grandma?" I asked. Michael nodded, smiling. "So you've got fifty years left on the planet? That's a lot."

"Forty-nine, but who's counting?" he kidded.

After the interview, we sat around the table eating "family style" as Michael called it, which meant we all picked at his food. We continued our earlier conversation about our upcoming trip to Washington, and he asked us if we could confirm that Jim Carrey was a wild right-wing conservative, something a friend of his had told him. We could not confirm that, but it was an amusing image: the putty-faced Joker from *Batman Forever* and the slippery Superdude from *The Mask* donating some of those outrageous millions to the aging Bob Dole or rambunctious Phil Gramm. "But maybe it's just a rumor," Michael concluded, scooping up the last bit of pasta from the serving platter.

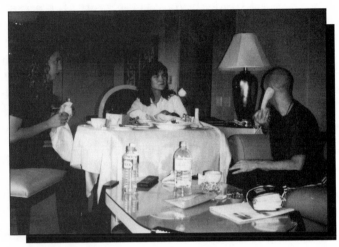

Family style

After we finished picking at Michael's food, we got into a discussion of names while we were sitting around. Michael asked me where my folks came up with the name Shainee. I explained that my grandfather made it up. He pushed, asking if it meant something in particular, one of my least-favorite questions. I told him it was an embarrassing definition, stemming from the word *shanah*, which means "pretty."

"That's not embarrassing," he said sincerely. "My name means 'he who is like God.'" We all thought that was pretty hilarious. "Now, *that's* embarrassing. Up until last year, I thought that Michael was the archangel who fell from grace and sat at the side of Satan or something."

At this point, Jeremy, who'd been nearly silent all afternoon, piped up. "Jeremy means 'goose,'" he stated tonelessly, and the quiet guy won the biggest laugh.

We offered to get out of Michael's way so that he could prepare for the MTV rehearsal later that afternoon. He said we were welcome to hang out until he left, so we did.

When we finally made our way toward the back entrance of the hotel to wait for our car to be retrieved by the parking attendant, we noticed two parked limousines with signs in the window that said R.E.M. We also noticed a guy lurking with a guitar in one hand and a pen in the other, pacing back and forth in front of the door. His eyes were darting all around, and his body language was clearly predatory. Just then a security guy came over to us and asked us if we could stand fifteen feet from the door. We tried to explain that we were waiting for our car, then remembered the cameras in our hands. He obviously thought we were press or fans and wanted us to go away.

I suddenly felt very grateful for my anonymity and for the brief two hours that we had spent with a man who was constantly being watched and watched out for. Then a flurry of people burst out through the spinning glass doors and Michael, the rock star—head down, hat and sunglasses on—was being ushered out. The predator started to wave his guitar and yell in Michael's direction. Michael waved good-bye to us as his staff shepherded him past all of us into the limo. We watched the limo drive away with Michael and the rest of the band, knowing our car would finally be pulled around now. The crazy guitar-waving man stood next to us, perplexed and deflated, holding his pen and his unsigned guitar.

A LUMPY COUCH IN WASHINGTON, D.C.   9/10, 1:15 A.M.

(Kristin)

The last few days have been a whirlwind, starting with Saturday's 7 A.M. search for the Hilton Hotel, where the Christian Coalition's Road to Victory conference was being held. It's a building the size of two football fields, with a prominent sign, but we passed right by it three times. I think it might be a phenomenon similar to Wonder Woman's invisible plane. You have to *be* a conservative Christian to spot the Mother Ship.

We have been corresponding with the Christian Coalition for months about the possibility of interviewing their young leader, Dr. Ralph Reed. Shainee and I

feel strongly that even though we do not subscribe to the Coalition's ideology, the organization's membership is large and growing, and we feel it is important to include Dr. Reed's perspective on the current state of America. Since Dr. Reed assumed the responsibilities as executive director of the Coalition in 1989, membership has grown from 200,000 to over 1,700,000.

Dr. Reed's office had agreed to a sit-down interview during the convention, but when we finally arrived, we were informed by his assistant that he would not have time to meet with us after all. Shainee and I were both struck speechless by this last-minute rejection. We had re-faxed Dr. Reed's office our materials the

day before, as requested, and I wondered if a second glance at our list of interviewees—which included names like Hunter S. Thompson and John Waters—had caused them to change their minds.

After considering our options, Shainee and I decided to attend the conference anyway and spend the weekend educating ourselves, with the hope that we could eventually convince Dr. Reed's office to reconsider. We were curious to hear what some of the scheduled speakers had to say. All we knew of most of them were the sound bites we had heard on television and the quotes we had read in newspapers. As getting beyond sensational headlines and second-hand information is one of our goals, we seized the opportunity.

We checked into the press room, got our passes, and headed for the main hall. We passed by rows of booths with displays and spokespersons from various conservative organizations, such as the Heritage Foundation, the NRA, and Operation Rescue. But the largest table belonged to the Christian Coalition, replete with Coalition T-shirts, books—including *Politically Incorrect* by Dr. Reed—and stuffed

powder-pink-and-blue Coalition bunnies for prepubescent attendees.

Early on, it was apparent that the Road to Victory was going to be a well-organized event. The purpose of the conference, as stated by its sponsor, the Christian Coalition, was to create a forum to discuss the Coalition's interest in political and social change in America and to platform the Republican presidential hopefuls. They had speakers scheduled back-to-back for two days, including Dr. Reed, William Bennett, Senators Robert Dole and Phil Gramm, Pat Buchanan, Speaker of the House Newt Gingrich, and a host of senators, governors, and mayors who endorsed the Coalition's ideology.

Check-in

We set up a camera at the back of the hall, and I walked to the front of the stage with our hand-held camera to get some close-up footage. As the 4,000 attendees shuffled in, *Take Me Out to the Ball Game* came over the loudspeaker, presumably to summon up images of heartland and family values. At eight in the morning, the thought of hot dogs and Cracker Jacks made me nauseous.

Dr. Reed was the first to take the stage. He welcomed everyone as they stood and cheered loudly. "Good morning!" he began. "My friends, ladies, and gentlemen, this is the largest gathering of grassroots pro-family activists in America this year. And we are here to send a message—to this city, to the political establishment, and to the media. And it is this: We will ride in the back of the bus no longer!" The crowd mustered quite a roar of applause for such an early hour. I was curious which metaphorical bus he was referring to. The one that oppresses middle- to upper-class white males between the ages of thirty and sixty, or the one Rosa Parks was forced to ride? I was already confused and slightly agitated, and the day had just begun.

Dr. Reed commanded the stage with a boyish charm, stating that the Christian Coalition was not favoring any one party or candidate. He explained that the Coalition merely wanted their chosen issues and concerns to be given fair and equal attention by political leaders, the public, and the "God-hating media."

William Bennett took the stage, and I felt a propensity to like him. Maybe it was because he reminded me of Norm from *Cheers*—just a guy you'd like to have a beer with. But unlike Norm, Bennett is an intellectual and political force in America, former Secretary of Education, and author of the major bestseller *The*

Book of Virtues. As the second speaker, he began with an analogy for the weekend gathering. He likened the audience to the wind, saying we were, after all, in control of the direction of the country. "The wind is the culture, the wind is the people," he said. "This [D.C.] may be where it all comes out in the end, but the culture and the American people, and changing the culture and changing the hearts of the American people, are more important than changing the government. If I had to, I would give my adversaries the government, if I could give my friends the culture."

William Bennett

He went on to talk about taking personal responsibility for the current state of affairs and not falling into the trap of placing blame on others. " 'It's them over there,' " he mimicked. " 'Nobody here is responsible.' Well, a lot of what has happened to us has not been done to us by someone else, it has been done by ourselves. And if we don't look inside, if we're only pointing outside, I think we're missing the point."

Bennett's sentiments were similar to those expressed by Amitai Etzioni and Daniel Kemmis, who also called for citizen responsibility. "Solving the problems of the federal government is not solving the problems of America," Bennett declared. "Some liberals think government is the solution to the problems of America; they're wrong. Some conservatives think no government is the solution to the problems of America; they're wrong, too. The greatest strengths in this country are in those institutions of family, church, school, and neighborhood. And that requires a great deal of *us.*

"Be mindful," Bennett warned, "of our greatest Republican, Abraham Lincoln, who got it right then and is still right today. He said, 'As a nation of free-men we must live through all time, or die by suicide. In the end, it is us.' So don't forget, when you're looking at government, to look inside, and never forget to look up."

Dr. Reed took the stage again and boasted of the gains conservative politicians had made in the 1994 elections, as well as some recent appointments. "A year ago," he began, his hands seizing the sides of the podium, "our opponents had names for candidates who were guilty of unpardonable crimes like going to church and synagogue, reading the Bible, and praying daily. They had names for people who dared to bring their faith into the public square and their issues of conscience into the political process. They called them: 'extremist,' 'radical,' 'right-wing Christian Coalition types.' We had our own names for them, but we now call them: 'senator,' 'congressman,' 'governor,' 'mayor,' 'city councilman,' 'state legislator . . .' "

Dr. Reed suddenly became inaudible as the audience's laughter and applause shook the hall. Dr. Reed smiled broadly and continued. "We gather here one year later, grateful, humble, and honored to have played a part in such a historic sea change. We have gained what we have always sought: a place at the table, a sense of legitimacy. We are an authentic voice of faith in the conversation that we call democracy. But our work, my friends, is not done. The threat that we face today is not on a foreign battlefield or from a foe's army. It is a threat within. It is a threat of our national character. It is divorce, abortion on demand, illiteracy, out-of-wedlock births, crime, drugs, family breakup, violence. It is the lives that it consumes, the hopelessness that it breeds, and the dreams that it destroys."

The room fell unusually quiet, and Reed capitalized on its silence. "You know, novelist John Updike recently wrote: 'The fact that compared to Eastern Europe and Russia, that we live well, that we live in wealth and splendor, cannot ease the pain of the feeling that we no longer live nobly.' If we balance the budget tomorrow, eliminate the deficit, and reform Medicare, but if we also lose our children, then we lose our culture. And if that happens, we will lose our nation, and then we will have failed ourselves, and failed our God, and, my friends, we cannot fail."

In closing, Dr. Reed left the audience with a prayer: "My prayer today is as the world looks at you, and looks at us as a movement, they do not see Republicans, or Democrats, or conservatives, or liberals, but they see followers of a humble carpenter from Galilee. Let us never forget that we do not bear the name of Ronald Reagan, or Bob Dole, or Newt Gingrich; we bear the name which is above every name." And he left it at that.

Dr. Ralph Reed

He retreated from the stage with a raised arm of appreciation for the extended applause, and the next thing I knew, he was striding toward us at the back of the hall. Dr. Reed stopped in his tracks about six feet from us and sat down in a seat as bright white camera lights flashed on while he placed an earpiece in his left ear. I could faintly hear a voice that sounded like Sam Donaldson coming through the tiny speaker tucked inside Dr. Reed's ear. He proceeded to carry on a conversation with an interviewer sitting in a newsroom somewhere else in America.

Dr. Reed was indeed right about one thing he had said: the Coalition has become a legitimate voice in the conversation of democracy. I could grasp only pieces of Reed's dialogue as the conference continued without him. "Ours is a pro-family, Judeo-Christian agenda," Dr. Reed explained to the camera. He then added, "It's not so much about being called the 'victor' but being called 'faithful.' '' The statement contradicted Reed's speech, in which he had made it quite clear that he and his constituency considered themselves to be essentially engaged in a cultural and political *war* that they couldn't afford to lose.

I admit, I found Dr. Reed to be more inciting than insightful. I had hoped he would do what few figures thrusting themselves into the political limelight have done: rise above the fray of petty rivalry between religious and political groups to present viable solutions to our problems.

Another speaker was introduced, but the room was so noisy, I couldn't hear the name. I watched the stage, and a familiar face framed by a helmet of white hair emerged in the wake of cheer. ''The Founding Fathers had a strong sense that everybody was equal,'' Newt Gingrich began. '' 'We hold these truths to be self-evident.' But why are they equal? Because they are endowed by their *creator*,'' he answered for himself.

''Power in America goes from God,'' Gingrich continued, pointing upward. ''Yes, I'm going to use that word . . .'' he joked to another crescendo of applause. ''Do you see now why I seem to be too radical for *The New York Times*?'' he asked with a roguish smile. He then continued on with his point: ''Power goes from God to you, and you loan it to the government. Which is why the Constitution of the United States does not begin 'We, the lawyers,' or 'We, the politicians,' or 'We, the

Newt Gingrich

editorial writers,' but 'We, the people.' The left is so profoundly and fundamentally wrong about the nature of American civilization that we have to take this on as an intellectual debate and win it on every level.

''My point being: Before you leave town, you need to visit the Jefferson Memorial. Your liberal friends will say to you, 'Well, Jefferson didn't *mean* creator when he said ''creator.' '' But go to the memorial and look at this magnificent statue, and look up and around the top, which says the following: 'I have sworn upon the altar of God Almighty. Eternal hostility against all forms of tyranny over the minds of men.' Now, why do we think he said 'sworn upon God Almighty?' He could have said, 'I've sworn upon the Constitution . . . this week's *Washington Post*.' I believe this is a clear sign that he believed it was God Almighty.''

Gingrich's point made no sense to me. Being one of those ''liberal friends'' he had referred to, I would never claim that Jefferson did not mean creator when he chose the word ''creator.'' Contrary to Gingrich's claim, I'm acquainted with a number of liberals who are devoted to their belief in God and/or a creator, and I think that faith was indeed shared by many of our founding parents. But I also learned at an early age that Jefferson—the very man who added the word "creator" to founding documents—made it clear in his extensive writings on religious freedom that one of the fundamental tenets of our new government was to keep church separate from state and end religious tyranny. And while the Christian Coalition clearly felt *they* were the ones being oppressed, their desire to impose their beliefs on the whole of America could be read as tyrannical.

The crowd was responding to someone else making his way to the podium accompanied by *The Battle Hymn of the Republic* playing over the extra-loud loudspeakers. Bob Dole was the next candidate to court the Coalition. He was not the favorite of most of the twenty or so people I asked—he seemed to fall a little too far on the liberal side for most members' liking. Senator Dole was interrupted by people in the audience shouting, "Sign the pledge! Sign the pledge!" Apparently, Senator Dole had not yet signed the Coalition's platform, pledging to be an anti-abortion president, if elected. The senator, ignoring the hollers, forged ahead to announce, "It's been a rather difficult two days in the Senate. In fact, about twenty minutes ago, I read two letters on the Senate floor. One from me to Senator Packwood suggesting that we get this behind us. And he has, as of today, relinquished his chairmanship of the Finance Committee and will leave the Senate on October 1." The crowd applauded enthusiastically—for justice served, I guess. For better or worse, Bob Packwood had become a part of our time capsule.

Then someone from the audience yelled, "Who's next?" suggesting Dole leave the podium and the next speaker be introduced. I began to sympathize with Dole, standing up there trying to rally support from an organization that had a kind of monopoly on the Republican candidacy—and his future—by virtue of sheer voting members.

A few audience members "shushed" the others to be polite while Dole went on to state his commitment to protect freedom of religious expression and, if elected, instate the conservative political framework outlined by the Contract with America. Dole declared that "liberals" and "Democrats" resent the conservatives because "the liberals don't have any convictions, they don't stand for anything . . . and they have no real hope or personal responsibility."

Senator Dole ended his remarks by hoping God would bless America, and then *The Battle Hymn*'s refrain—*Glory, Glory, Hallelujah*—struck up again. Just then a number of people moved to the podium, and an unidentified man announced that the Christian Coalition was "presenting Senator Robert Dole with the Friend of Family Values award." Elizabeth Dole proudly clapped for her husband from the sidelines.

By Saturday afternoon, we were weary from the sheer act of holding a camera for long hours of speech-making. We gave up on the main hall and its mainstream speakers and headed for the cafeteria downstairs. All the tables were full, so Shainee and I scanned the sea of strangers for someone packing up to leave. A curly-haired older woman sitting alone must have noticed us, because she waved us over to a couple of empty seats at her table. She was warm and kind and proud to be the Coalition representative for her Wisconsin chapter.

After sitting with her for a while, we found ourselves sharing similar feelings and concerns for what was happening in America. Our proposed solutions differed somewhat, but we did have a similar experience of our country, despite our cultural and spiritual and age differences. We all wanted the media to become more sensitive; we wanted our country's elders to have sufficient health care and respect; we wanted the standards for education to improve; and we all deeply appreciated the right to pursue our own interests in pursuit of happiness. It all seemed so natural, chatting openly with this woman. In fact, we got along so well that she assumed we were young Republicans and asked if we would be in San Diego later this year to help organize the Republican youth. In her opinion, our generation was the weakest link in the Republican constituency. We told her we probably wouldn't be seeing her in San Diego, because we were both registered Democrats. Surprisingly, she didn't flinch when we informed her of our political leaning.

Leaving the table, shaking this woman's hand, Shainee and I both felt our first moment of optimism during the weekend. It was reassuring that we could both agree and disagree with this stranger—expressing our opinions freely. We walked away from her, having shared some soup and common ground, and no longer quite so weary.

Newly energized, we went back to the main hall to hear Phil Gramm speak before packing up to leave. In his speech, Gramm admitted to failing the third, seventh, and ninth grades and declared with pride, "You can count on me to never be an education president. I want to finish the Reagan revolution," he declared with team spirit. I was so confused, trying to put Gramm into context with the others that we had heard. I thought we *all* agreed on higher standards for education. Did someone forget to tell Gramm's speechwriter? Incidentally, this particular Hilton is the D.C. hotel where Ronald Reagan was shot in 1984.

Pat Buchanan's nth run at the nomination

We were practically dizzy as we headed for the exit. We decided that we will *not*, after all, call Dr. Reed's office to try and reschedule the interview, but instead, begin to pursue a local Christian Coalition chapter president, like the Wisconsin woman we met. We felt and learned more from our brief encounter with her than listening to the majority of the more "polished" speakers during the last two days.

We are leaving D.C., focused on our new search for this unknown individual.

JACK HEALEY

FOUNDER AND DIRECTOR OF THE HUMAN RIGHTS ACTION CENTER •

FORMER EXECUTIVE DIRECTOR OF AMNESTY INTERNATIONAL U.S.A. •

FORMER FRANCISCAN PRIEST

WASHINGTON, D.C.

(Kristin)

When I was in my early and mid-twenties, my awareness of human rights—and violations thereof—was expanded by a man I had never met: Jack Healey, the executive director of Amnesty International U.S.A. One of the ways Amnesty had achieved its goals of raising awareness of human rights and protecting the rights of political prisoners was with huge rock concerts—devised by Jack to raise money and consciousness—and I had been one of the estimated 1 billion people mesmerized by the five-hour *Conspiracy of Hope* and *Human Rights Now!* shows. Through the universal language of music, Amnesty, with Healey's guidance, wove an international net that caught the attention and imagination of my entire generation—and countless others around the world.

Shainee was also aware of, and involved with, Amnesty, having interned with the organization during her college years. So when drawing up our *Anthem* wish list, we were determined to track down Jack Healey at his home in D.C.

It had taken us quite a few attempts to reach Jack, but when we did, he instantly accepted our invitation. He explained over the phone that after twelve years at the helm of Amnesty, he had struck out on his own and formed the Human Rights Action Center, a grassroots effort to get the Universal Declaration of Human Rights—instigated by Eleanor Roosevelt almost fifty years ago—translated into all languages and into the hands of everyone, everywhere. To me, this sounded like a daunting task, but listening to Jack, I knew he believed it was more than possible. While we were on the phone, he went on to explain the kind of empowerment he'd witnessed around the world when people learned—firsthand and in their own language—their rights, such as the right to shelter or the right not to be tortured.

We pulled up to Healey's brownstone on the southeast side of town. We knocked and were greeted by a swiftly opened door and a man whose flurry of untamed white hair, pronounced jowls, and thick glasses reminded me of an over-worked Einstein, although Jack's Human Rights Now! T-shirt planted him firmly in this decade.

We made our introductions. "You've been *driving*!" Jack declared comment-ing on the itinerary we had faxed him.

"Yeah," Shainee admitted, "we haven't really been going in a logical order because of people's schedules."

"Every time we think we're done with an area, we have to go back," I added—D.C. being the most recent example.

We decided to eat before the interview and walked over to the corner pub for a long talk and some french onion soup. Jack told us about his ambitious plans and why he and Amnesty had parted ways after twelve years. He explained, "There were certain things that couldn't be done within an international infrastructure, with a staff of a hundred." He said that he had accomplished a lot of what he had hoped to at Amnesty, and now wanted to approach human rights from a more grassroots perspective, with a people's campaign. Shainee and I were intrigued.

After lunch, he led us down the Capitol streets as we tried to decide where to do the interview. "We've got the Supreme Court here," he said, pointing to his left.

Unfortunately, it's Saturday

"Now, the Library's a little older. And there's the Capitol . . ."

Shainee and I decided the Supreme Court would be an appropriate backdrop, and we started up the white polished steps, Jack lugging some of our equip-ment. "Oh, Kris," Shainee said, stopping. "Look what it says." She pointed to the top of the building, which was adorned with a cement ribbon that read: EQUAL JUS-TICE UNDER LAW.

"That's a pretty good backdrop for you, Jack," I said as we moved closer to a Romanesque fountain on the far side of the building. "Yeah, we're still hunting for that," he said, more to himself than us.

A guard approached us from the bot-tom of the steps and asked if we had per-mission to shoot up there. "Permission?" I questioned. "We're just doing a little documentary project."

"Yeah, see, you have to get permission from the Public Information Office, which is open Monday through Friday, before you can do any kind of filming up here," he explained.

"Monday's too late," Shainee pleaded. "What about on the steps?"

"No, that's not allowed, either," he said. The guard spoke into his walkie-talkie, then started to walk away.

"This is sad. Don't we own this, as citizens?" I asked the guard, who was quickly moving out of earshot. "Oh, God!" I said in exasperation, looking to Jack.

"It's an analogy for what's going on," Jack said, turning to walk back down the stairs, away from the Jeffersonian building. " 'Public Information Office,' " Jack repeated, his head bowed. "You can only be helped Monday through Friday from nine to five."

Ultimately, we decided to set up on the sidewalk at the foot of the stairs leading up to the building. We started the interview by asking Jack to tell us a little about his childhood and life in the priesthood.

"I was born in Pittsburgh, Pennsylvania," he began. "My parents were economic refugees from Ireland, and I was the youngest of eleven children. My family worked in the coal mines. My father was killed when I was two, so we went from poverty to riches to poverty; I was raised in poverty. Then I went into the seminary, became a Franciscan priest, and then left the priesthood when I was about thirty."

Jack had a shy, unassuming quality to him. I wondered if it came from living in isolation as a monk in the socially formative years of his twenties. Shainee went on to ask him why he had left the priesthood.

"I enjoyed the seminary; it was a good way to grow up. It instilled a lot of values in me. But I came out," he explained, "because I wanted to get more deeply involved in what was going on—and going wrong—in the world. I realized I was more social-minded and political-minded than I was religious-minded, though I was religious."

Jack explained that his first job outside of the priesthood was raising money for world hunger in the late 1960s, early 1970s. Jack isn't the kind of person to assume credit for successes, but in my research on him, I found out that he essentially pioneered the now-popular fundraising technique of walkathons. Jack seemed to have strong instincts about what masses of people would respond to. "We raised about $14 million for world hunger, between 1969 and 1974, from young people walking," he said, pushing back his thick glasses. "That's when I discovered that kids were being wrongly accused of apathy." I thought of Studs Terkel's assertion that "the kids of the sixties *did* reach outside of themselves, only to be put down."

Jack went on to talk about working with human rights activist Dick Gregory on America's first world hunger run, yet another impressive success for the cause. Jack then moved to South Africa, where he worked as a Peace Corps director for five years. "At the end of my stay in Africa, I answered an ad," he explained. "It was in the back of some brochure, and from that I ended up the director of Amnesty for twelve years."

That was to be the little fork in the road that would change Jack's life. Shainee asked him what he was focusing his energy on today, twelve years after answering that ad.

"I'm working on a *people's* campaign for human rights," he began. "I want to use the fiftieth anniversary of the Universal Declaration of Human Rights, in 1998, as an opportunity to move the world toward nonviolence, so the next century is better than this one."

Shainee asked Jack to tell us about the Universal Declaration of Human Rights.

"The Universal Declaration of Human Rights was written in large part by Eleanor Roosevelt," Jack explained. "Eleanor saw poverty and pain, and she translated it into policy. It's a document that protects everybody on earth better than any other document in the world. And one of the primary reasons the Declaration was written was to be an antitoxin to the toxin of Nazi Germany. The Declaration was created in order to ensure that human rights violations like those did not occur again anywhere in the world.

"Since then, obviously, a lot of violence has occurred. People around the world should be using the Universal Declaration of Human Rights as a foundation, as something to move them forward, something to expand the thinking. If you give someone a document that has been agreed upon, like this one, it would be like Martin Luther King, Jr., when he used the U.S. Constitution in front of this building—'Equal Justice Under Law.' " Because we had to set up so far away from the building, the very inscription hovered just above Jack's head in my viewfinder.

"I view the United States as *one* of many countries in the world," Jack continued, "not the center of the universe. So what I'd like to do is create a universal celebration for the Declaration that was signed by nearly every nation in the world, although many of those countries violate that agreement today. Which is why public awareness of the document and the violations is crucial. The people's campaign would be a way of expressing to all countries that this is our international ethical code and contract, which we are all responsible for obeying. The next wave in the movement has to be local human rights organizations in each nation, big

Jack Healey

and small, because people everywhere need immediacy when filing grievances, and they need to be able to do it in their own languages. And I'd like to use that which is best in America—our creativity, technology, and imagination—and have other places in the world offer their talents so we can come together in a coalition that's equal and fair and democratic to everybody.''

There's a saying that some people have the vision and others quietly make things happen. Jack was definitely a big-picture visionary. To some, his ideas might seem idealistic or unrealistic, but just like Bill Siemering and Wes Jackson, Jack believed it was necessary to redefine the parameters of the discussion in order to push the envelope. Jack argued that as the global community continues to form and permeate our daily lives, it is impossible—even though *we* live in a liberated country—to ignore infringements upon a worldwide social contract that must evolve and be rooted in basic integrity and human decency.

Jack viewed the global community as siblings in a tight-knit family; he believed that people should look out for one another, help raise each other. Jack seems to take the statement—popularized in the title of Hillary Clinton's book *It Takes a Village*—one step further: If ''it takes a whole village to raise a child,'' then ''it takes a whole country to raise a village'' and, further, ''it takes a whole world to raise a country.''

We asked Jack what had inspired him to dedicate his life to ensuring and protecting other people's rights.

''My mother was raised when they brought in 'goon squads' to beat up the Irish miners,'' he explained, ''and she never forgot that. All of her brothers were poor miners. So justice to her meant battling for your rights. When I was growing up, she used to say, 'I didn't bring you here just to survive. I brought you here to get something done. . . .' She was like a quiet warrior who wanted her son—me—to jam the system and make it better for people, especially the poor.

''And there came a point when I was struggling with my mother about my own maturity,'' Jack continued. ''I kept buggin' her for answers, and she would just say, 'Grow up to be a man, Jack. Be a man.' It was just botherin' the hell out of me. So I finally said to her, 'What is it to be a man? What's the standard? How do I get this done so I can move on?' And she said, 'When you can walk the highways and byways of life and learn to listen to the weeping and the wailing of the poor, then you'll be a man.' ''

Suddenly, out of the corner of my eye, I saw a policeman coming toward us. I bristled a bit, anticipating a hassle. I was about to inform the officer that a guard had already said we could film on the sidewalk when I heard Jack ask, ''Doing all right, officer?''

''All right. How about you?'' the policeman responded, an uncommon amount of sincerity in his voice.

''Oh, I'm all right,'' Jack returned.

''You know,'' said the officer, ''if you move over some, you won't be in the sun so much.'' The policeman then directed his attention to me. ''He's in the sun. It's awfully hot.''

Caught off guard by the officer's helpful intentions, I didn't respond. But Jack took his advice and scooted a little to the left, out of the direct sunlight. "Yeah, that is better," he said. "Thanks."

"No problem," said the officer, continuing on his way down the street.

It was an interesting moment, especially set against the backdrop of the conversation we'd had at lunch about police brutality here and in other countries. As Michael Stipe had said, some people in America see *this* country as a brutal police state. Other people think it's the freest place on earth. It all depends on your perspective.

We asked Jack to describe what he thinks "human rights" mean to Americans. To answer, he clarified that his definition includes more than the right *not* to be tortured, which is how many people approach the subject.

Jack went on. "For the most part, human rights, to the West, has meant individual rights, where it should really mean collective rights, too—the right to a job, a roof over your head, the right *not* to starve to death. In America, you could have your rights and still starve to death. It's contradictory! What must happen is a broadening of the definition so that human rights includes the whole gamut of the Declaration, which encompasses the health and well-being of all persons. We don't want three percent of the world super rich, and ninety-seven percent starving, which is where we're headed. The goal of the Declaration is to close that gap and make it a little better for everybody."

Given that in the United States, most people are aware of their basic human rights, Shainee asked Jack to talk about the urgency of disseminating the information to other countries.

"Well," he began, "I went to Swaziland to get six kids out of jail who were being wrongfully held, and the government let them out before we got there, so they wouldn't get bad press. And the six kids were asking us, 'How did you know about me? Why are you here? Why would an organization somewhere on the other end of the world care about us?' And I think that's the power of believing in human rights—that some poor kid from Pittsburgh can go to Swaziland and help get political prisoners out of jail because . . . it's just a right. And I *know* that. And if you tell other people about it, they get the idea. It's like the idea of freedom. Once you got it, you never lose it.

"We can't trust governments with human rights," he declared. "There have been too many abuses, too many people killed, too many things ignored. So we gotta make it a people's movement."

Suddenly Jack looked as if he'd swallowed all of the suffering he'd been describing. His naturally flushed complexion went pale, and he slowly rubbed his belly in a repetitive circular motion, looking stunned.

"Are you okay?" I said.

"Do you have an antacid?" he asked.

Neither of us did. "But we can get one," I assured him. "Is your stomach burning?"

"No, it's just tightening up. Hiatal hernia," he muttered, still rubbing his stomach and breathing carefully. "All's I need is a . . . glass of water . . ."

As usual, we didn't have any water with us, but we spotted a hot dog cart about 200 yards away. I ran as fast as I could.

Relief

When I got back, he guzzled the soda water and was visibly relieved. After we sat for a few minutes, tourists moving around us, snapping photographs of this monument to justice to take home, Jack insisted that we continue the interview. Shainee and I didn't feel that we should. But when I looked back to Jack, I recognized that determined look in his eye and knew that "quitting" was just not an option. "Please just say the word if you need to stop for *any* reason," we insisted, knowing he probably never would.

Shainee asked Jack about his influences. "Dr. Martin Luther King!" he said without pause. "Because I was studying here in the sixties, at Catholic University up in northeast Washington, D.C., and we set up a vigil right here." Jack looked around him, remembering. "Right at this spot actually—a vigil for the passage of civil rights legislation in 1963. And I went to small discussions, where Dr. King gave speeches to organize the March on Washington, and we helped him do that—a number of us seminarians from local Protestant, Catholic, and Jewish schools. And hearing him in small and big groups and then in the final speech during the March was . . . I don't think a young person could have a better experience than that. Dr. King radiated goodness, and you felt it.

"And it was here in this city. I'm very proud of this city for having done that for me. Because as an American, you expect something from this city!" he exclaimed. "This is governmental leadership. These people are supposed to *excel* at decency. But oftentimes they fail us, and I don't like it one bit; and I want to go after them when they do."

We had an idea of what kind of civil and grassroots leaders had influenced Jack, but we were curious about what he thought of the American hero. "What is 'hero' to you?" Shainee asked.

"I think as life goes on—I'm now fifty-seven—" Jack revealed, "you get a sense that you need to be inspired. There's so many hard things in life. It's so hard to change a foreign policy that's gone wrong; it's so hard to change a community with lots of violence in it. How do you talk to young people who are on crack? And sometimes you find yourself overwhelmed with frustration. And so you hope that someone comes along and inspires you, teaches you a new way to look at these problems. To me, those people who step in and do that are heroes. And that's what's so incredible about this country—we have a lot of those people.''

Shainee asked Jack if he believed the American dream was alive and well. To answer, Jack redefined the American dream as one element of the ongoing American experiment.

''Oh, yeah! Oh golly!'' he exclaimed, in answer to the question. ''Absolutely. I think the American experiment of democracy is one of the finest human things that has ever happened in the world. I think we are a great experiment, and sometimes we do well, and sometimes we don't do well. But we're one of the great runs at what freedom can mean. At times, we can get hubristic about what we essentially took from the Indians: great land, great oil, great water. And we forget the cost of our conquest and setting up a system that was not fair to everybody, as it was purportedly intended. But it is a great run at it. And what we gotta remember is that we're not there yet. It's a goal out in front of us, and we need to keep running and chasing it. Just like this building—justice is a process, a searing process. Someone once said, 'God will judge us by how we treat the least of us.' Right now, I think we're learning a lot about the least of us.''

We asked Jack how he felt about America's future. ''I'm worried about the United States,'' he said frankly. ''Money does not make for a golden period; it's art, poetry, enlightened government, and decency. I think right now, we mostly have money. And when a country is restored to decency, it is always restored by the people, not a shift in political leadership. But I happen to be an optimist about this particular society, because I believe government and people *can* work together to make things better for everyone. People think the struggle is between the Democrats and the Republicans. It isn't. It's between the decent and indecent, the people who play it safe and the risk-takers, and between the gun barrel and dialogue.

''As an American,'' Jack continued, ''I want to go back to the Founding Fathers and ask, 'What did you *really* say? What was on Jefferson's mind in his *best* moments?' . . . I believe the Founding Fathers knew that democracy would be messy. I think it was Jefferson who said, 'Democracy is really made for the angels.' It is indeed a pursuit, because if you're in this process of democracy it will drive you crazy, but it's the only thing that's truly

great. I want that spirit back. I want the Eleanor Roosevelt spirit back. I want to bring back the spirits of the people who have made this country great and listen to them in the night like a spiritual growth, like a spiritual healing—hearing the best so we can pursue it. And I hope,'' Jack said, waving his hand around his ear as if drawing in these spirits toward him, ''that the whole nation is listening to those voices one by one, by one, by one.''

The sun had begun to set, draping Jack and the building behind him in shadows. I saw exhaustion on Shainee's and Jack's faces, and I felt it in my own. Jack helped us pack up our equipment, and we headed toward his house, leaving that view of the Supreme Court Building behind us as we turned the first corner.

We ended up continuing our conversation with Jack over dinner that night. A torrential rainstorm descended upon D.C. without warning. Soaked all the way through, our coats packed away deep in the car, we ducked into Jack's favorite Thai joint. Over lemongrass soup, we probed Jack, just out of our own personal curiosity, about his experiences in other countries. After dinner, he gave us Bruce Springsteen's contact number and wished us luck on our next interview with Chuck D.

Shainee drove and I rested my tired legs on the dashboard, lulled by the hypnotic rhythm of the windshield wipers. I thought about something Jack had said at lunch: that two out of every three people in the world still live under a government that tortures and kills its citizens.

A lot of people do extraordinary things to support decency, justice, and change—some give time, some give ideas, some write checks, and some set standards. To Jack, a poor kid from the coal mines, it seemed to be a simple fact that it is our job as human beings—no different than the responsibility of being a good parent or lawful citizen—to make this world more humane. Jack had said something to us while walking away from the Supreme Court, words that now rang in my head: ''A poet wants to write the perfect poem. A singer wants the perfect song. I want the perfect world, and it ain't no different or more silly than the poet who thinks he can write the perfect poem. It *should* be the goal of the poet to do that or the musician to write the perfect song. It *should* be the goal of the human being to make it a perfect world.''

Jack had reminded us of the necessity to continue to define and rearticulate the ideas and ideals set forth by our nation's founders more than two hundred years ago. I agreed with Jack that the minute we got comfortable and thought we'd ''arrived'' was the moment our ''great run at what freedom can mean'' would cease to exist.

CHUCK D

RAP ARTIST • LEADER OF PUBLIC ENEMY

ROOSEVELT, NEW YORK

(*Shainee*)

After our weekend in Washington, we went back to New York—again. We could have started our own D.C./NYC shuttle service at that point. But we were scheduled to stay put for a while; and we kicked off the first day with a visit to Long Island to meet with Chuck D of the rap band Public Enemy.

Kris and I had deliberated at the beginning of the trip about who to approach from the world of rap and hip-hop. Chuck has always spoken out in opposition to drugs and violence, never buying into the "gangsta" rap ethic that we see so much of now. He is also known for broadening the reach of rap and hip-hop to educate its listeners about the need to learn one's own history—specifically in the realm of racism and other forms of oppression. For example, he incorporated Malcom X's phrase "too black, too strong" into the single *Bring the Noise*, hoping it would capture people's attention and cause them to learn more about the man.

The requisite Internet search produced a bunch of quotes that sealed it for us. The president of Public Enemy's record label, Def Jam, once quipped that "Chuck's mouth is his gun, and words are his bullets." A Chicago newspaper reported, "What Bob Dylan did for rock in the 1960s, what George Clinton did for funk and Bob Marley did for reggae in the 1970s, Public Enemy's Chuck D has done for rap: given it legitimacy and authority far beyond its core following." We had found our man—a pioneer who seemed to be shaping the way Americans think, believe, and live. A friend of a friend made a call for us and put us in touch with Chuck's assistant, Crunch. Kris spoke to Crunch a few times and arranged a meeting.

The day didn't exactly go smoothly. We arrived at what we thought was Chuck's house in Roosevelt, Long Island, at around ten in the morning. We rang the doorbell several times and no one answered. Thinking we might be at the wrong place, we drove to the pay phone to try to call Crunch—twice. Unfortunately, Kristin couldn't remember whether his name was Crunch or Chunk and alternated between the two every time she left a message. When Crunch showed up at the end of the interview and we finally ascertained that that was indeed his name, I was mortified. He was not a small man.

On our second trip to the pay phone, we ran into a couple of teenage boys who live in Chuck's neighborhood. They were very curious about our cameras and actually approached us to ask if we were making a documentary or if we were with the news. When we told them we were making a film, they asked in stereo, "Can we be in it?"

"Sure," I said. "I'll put you in it right now," and turned the camera on them. One of them starting doing exuberant jumping jacks, like kids always do behind on-the-scene reporters, saying, "Do somethin' slick, man! The camera's on!" The other one actually got a little unnerved by the red light and moved out of the way, asking, "Does that thing really have film?" People's reactions to cameras, always fascinating. "You can stop filming. I might say something dumb. Then it'll be on TV and I'll look like a fool." This kid obviously had the Roger Zins complex. But the boys did confirm that we had the correct address for Chuck D. So we went back to try again.

We wandered around the house, trying every door. There was no sign of movement anywhere, until finally, we heard a telephone ring inside. We hoped it was Crunch calling to check on us. It sounded like someone answered and we knocked one more time before we heard a very deep male voice say, "Coming." The door swung open and on the other side stood a man in thick black sunglasses and a sweatsuit, rubbing his head. "I didn't know we had an interview today," he said. "Sorry I'm not ready. What's this for again?" We explained why we were there, and Chuck led us groggily into the living room. It was obvious that we had woken him up.

Nonetheless, he allowed us to set up the cameras beneath posters of Malcolm X, Martin Luther King, Jr., L. L. Cool J, and others. It didn't look like the home of a superstar but, rather, like a typical midsized postwar suburban house. In fact, Chuck told us that it was the house he'd grown up in and that he lived there with his own family now.

The interview was short; we didn't want to keep Chuck too long because we felt bad about waking him up and it was apparent from an overheard phone conversation that he had been working late the night before. We did ask a number of questions, and although Chuck was clearly exhausted, he answered every one thoughtfully.

I asked him if he had grown up in a political family or if his activism had grown out of his music. Chuck said that he was born in 1960 and saw what went down during the decade while he was growing up. His parents had sent him to a summer school run by former-Black Panther members who taught him about cultural pride and self-empowerment, the very ideas that would show up as the core of his lyrics. He explained, ''The family philosophy was: 'Whatever you do, try to be the best at it,' and they always gave me support. That was always helpful to me, and hopefully I can do the same with my children.''

Chuck originally went to school to study graphic design, then entered the world of rap with the intention of doing album covers and logo art. He said that he planned to continue to promote rap as a medium for communication by moving into multimedia. ''I'm going into the third cycle of my career,'' he explained. ''I figure I'll have five. My first was development—deejaying and the basics of rap and hip-hop music. The second was as an artist, starting the Public Enemy thing. The third is as a multimedia sparkplug juggernaut. Branching out and going into those areas that no one has gone to before in rap music and hip-hop.''

We talked a little bit about what Michael Stipe had said about being uncomfortable with the role of spokesperson. Chuck was the other breed of media figure—the kind who relishes that role.

''I'm comfortable with it,'' Chuck asserted. ''You have an avenue to reach a lot of people at the same time. It's one of the benefits of media in general. You can choose to do nothing or you can choose to say something. So I choose to say something. I try to use and exploit those avenues that will not only be beneficial to me but will be beneficial to those who pick up on it. So I feel very fortunate. But I guess the road to get to your goal is not a singular one. So I'm building more avenues and more highways to get to the ultimate goal, which is probably a general enhancing and enriching of mankind—or womankind.''

''What do you think defines 'hero' in America today?''

Chuck grinned for the first time since we had sat down and said with a low rumbling chuckle, ''A big Subway sandwich.'' We laughed too as he continued: ''What defines 'hero' in America? Someone who defies the odds and actually is out to help the masses of the people who are without. We have a lot of heroes out there that haven't even been tapped yet. So we have to watch how we use that word. Just because someone has media access does not merit them being called a hero. Hero status comes from—sometimes—the unseen, the unheard of. And we need to lend our credence to that.''

We talked a little bit about the people that Chuck considers to be heroes: Reverend Jesse Jackson and Dr. John Henry Clark. He has also been inspired by ''everyone from Nat Turner to Tina Turner,'' saying, ''I'm a big fan of black people because we've defied the odds.'' We talked a little bit about defying the odds in

order to access the American dream. Chuck's position on the notion of the dream was similar to Rita Dove's, although he wasn't quite as hopeful.

''I believe there is an American dream, but that dream hasn't been injected into everybody's consciousness. When you have fair opportunity and everyone can operate from equal footing, then the dream could become a reality,'' Chuck said. ''I think it all boils down to people recognizing society's control factors and taking more control over their own locale.''

I asked Chuck if he felt optimistic about the country as we head into the next millennium. He nodded his head, assuring us. ''I feel optimistic about life. Hopefully, we can understand it better. America is sort of irrelevant, when it comes down to life on this planet. If the planet goes down, you know, America's going down. You can't have people and their imaginary borderlines do whatever they want to, within their own lands. If you travel in the air and you look down, you don't see no lines. You see land, you see water.'' Strangely enough, Chuck was echoing pilot Rudy Engholme's words almost verbatim. He continued: ''If the earth was to be moved off its axis a million miles another way, the planet would go down. Suddenly you'd have people with a whole other concern other than America, or race issues, or financial matters. People would be trying to scramble to figure out how to save this place. I think we should have that idea now. Borderlines, imaginary boundaries, fiscal situations—these are only pawns in the game fighting each other. What we need to do is knock the heads off some kings and queens!'' Chuck laughed loudly, now fully awake. ''So that's where that's at.''

He went on to say that education is one of his primary focuses in the battle to get people to think in a more unified way. ''Education, you know, is not information. Education is sort of like bias, depends on what you're getting. So people are becoming more gifted on the computer but less gifted in the actual handling of physical capabilities," he opined. Chuck continued by saying that although he is working on multimedia projects himself, we have to seek balance between the information age and teaching actual skills.

I could hear Crunch milling around in the back room and saw Chuck's gaze wandering. They had work to do, so we had to finish up. I hadn't wanted to dwell on the subject, but Public Enemy has been scrutinized over the years by the press and various public-interest groups for disseminating militant images. I asked Chuck to talk about that criticism and where he drew his energy from.

"I draw from the inner self and I draw from studying the world. I like to travel, I like to see a lot of people, places, and things. I believe that for anyone to attack you, they must know you better than you know yourself . . . I've got a long ways to go to learn about myself, so I know everybody else is still far off."

We thanked Chuck and unmiked him. He seemed relieved and stretched his arms wide. He got up and went into the kitchen while we broke down the equipment, calling out to ask us, "Do you want some cranberry juice?" as he went back to waking up.

REBECCA WALKER

FOUNDER AND PRESIDENT OF THIRD WAVE • WRITER

BROOKLYN, NEW YORK

(Kristin)

During the trip, Shainee and I had stumbled upon a twenty-seven-year-old woman, Rebecca Walker, who has centered her attention on women's rights and helped to inspire a new generation of feminists.

We had first run into Rebecca's name in an article we had found in *Time* magazine on fifty future leaders of America. Subsequently, we heard her name mentioned in different circles and later learned that she is the daughter of novelist Alice Walker and the goddaughter of Gloria Steinem. So we already knew of two big influences. We found that Rebecca—at an early age and independent of the strong women in her family—became devoted to cultivating young women's leadership and activism. Third Wave, a non-profit national direct-action organization Rebecca co-founded, was designed to carry forward the unfinished work of feminism.

Third Wave tackles projects ranging from literacy programs to national voter-registration drives to linking up young women in cyberspace. In addition to her activism, Rebecca has been a contributing editor to *Ms.* magazine since 1989 and has been published in a number of journals, including *Ms.*, *Spin*, *The Black Scholar*, and *Harper's*. She recently published her first book, *To Be Real*, which addresses the complexities of female empowerment.

We made our way over the Brooklyn Bridge to Rebecca's apartment. As she opened the door, she held on to the collars of her two large guard dogs and welcomed us. She decided to let go of the dogs so they could get "used to us," but she warned us first: "One of them does bite people." That said, they were released. As they ran toward us, I chanted the "mean dog" mantra to myself: "No fear, no fear." I let them smell the camera, and without making any sudden moves, we went into another room to set up. Rebecca shuffled through papers on her desk. I watched her through my unobstructed left eye in color, and my right eye in black and white through the viewfinder of the camera. I had actually grown accustomed to observing life from a half-human, half-canine perspective.

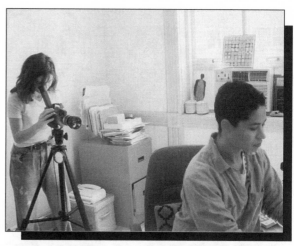

Rebecca is visually captivating, with perfect skin, cropped black hair that waves and curls in all directions, and beautiful deep brown eyes. She wore flowing white pants and a blue denim shirt; Indian jewelry adorned her arms. Sheer drapes hung on all the windows, filtering the light. It made the room feel tranquil and also happened to be great camera lighting.

As we described *Anthem* to Rebecca, she seemed most surprised that Shainee and I were still friends. We got that reaction a lot—about as often as people got

Rebecca Walker

Shainee's name wrong. But Rebecca spoke from experience about group travel; she explained that Third Wave's first project was a national voter-registration drive. "We registered twenty thousand people across the country," she explained, "in South Central L.A., in East St. Louis—some of the toughest neighborhoods in the country. We brought together a whole group of people from all different backgrounds on three buses. It was an incredible experience, because there were people who had been in drug rehab, and people who were living on the streets before they got on the bus, and people who had been community organizers for twenty years, and some who just graduated from college. And while there was often a lot of tension on the buses, it was ultimately an incredible learning experience on how to really allow for difference. And how, within a political organization, to stay focused on your goal and not get sidetracked by personal issues and dramas."

"Well," I said, "*that's* how Shainee and I are still speaking."

Rebecca went on to describe her childhood. She explained that her parents met during the civil rights movement and that she was born in Mississippi, in the midst of the movement, in 1969. Just then the phone rang. It was Rebecca's mother, whose ears must have been burning. Rebecca asked if she could call back later and then unplugged the phone.

Shainee asked Rebecca what had been the catalyst for the creation of Third Wave. "I was noticing that young women felt alienated from the idea of feminism, from the activism that has been visible and strong, and I thought someone needed to build some kind of bridge. I wondered if I could help create an organization that could encourage women's activism and facilitate different projects that would focus on women's issues but also show how multi-issued the women's movement is and has always been. When I say 'multi-issued,' I mean anything from welfare to housing to the environment to police brutality," she explained. Just then police

sirens screamed by outside. "Now my little sweet dogs are probably gonna start howling," she warned. "One of them really loves the sirens." We waited. The one who bites people just stared at the window, and the peaceful one's ears perked up, but neither emitted a peep. I guess it was a case of the "watched dog" theory.

Rebecca explained that she had published an article called *Becoming a Third Wave* that had initiated a lot of discussion. And she spoke to some friends her own age who were interested in creating an organization. "And," she concluded, "Third Wave was born. Now there are chapters sprouting up all over the country."

Shainee asked Rebecca if there had been a family philosophy that had significantly influenced her. She hearkened back to the civil rights movement; it was a model she could follow. "I got to see how people can work together to create radical change in the world. For example, I wouldn't have had access to an education if that struggle and that shift hadn't taken place. And that's a staggering thought to a generation who missed the integration era, even though there's so much more to do."

Shainee asked Rebecca if she believed there was such a thing as an American dream. "Well," she began, then paused. It seemed as though she was considering many possible answers. "Even within my own family, I've seen how wonderful the American dream can be and the price that it exacts on the other hand. My great-grandmother, who came here from Kiev, Russia, who fled the pogroms when she was eight years old, came here and married and had children, and she and my great-grandfather started a newsstand, and from that newsstand, they put their children through school, and then their grandchildren became doctors and lawyers. To her and that whole family, they lived the American dream—it was success, it was safety, it was freedom.

"But the flip side of my great Jewish Slavic grandmother's American dream," she continued, "represented by my mother's side of the family, which is Native American and African-American, is that my mother's ancestors were slaughtered. The Native American genocide in this country is the price of the American dream, and slavery built the American dream for my Slavic grandmother. My ancestry epitomizes the contradictions and ambivalence that America is built upon. So it also mirrors my own ambivalence about the American dream, because I know it has always been the case that for some people to have freedom in this country, other people have had to give theirs up. So the big question obviously becomes: What changes do we have to make to ensure that more and more people can have some version of the American dream, even if that's just safety, health, shelter, and personal freedom?''

Rebecca had managed to articulate the Declaration of Human Rights on the heels of the same assertion of the American dream made by Jack Healey.

As we packed up our equipment, Rebecca told us about her soon-to-open Cyber Café in Brooklyn and offered her support in anything she could do to help us. ''I know how hard these things can be,'' she sympathized, opening her front door for us. Her hairy best friends flanked on either side, we thanked Rebecca for meeting with us—and the dogs for not biting us.

ED TURNER

EXECUTIVE VICE PRESIDENT OF NEWS GATHERING, CNN

ATLANTA, GEORGIA

(Shainee)

Our next stop after New York City was Atlanta, where we had scheduled two interviews. During our visit with Hunter Thompson, he had promised to put us in touch with his fax pal, Ed Turner, making us promise that we would indeed interview "the rascally bastard" if given the chance. We readily agreed. The current role of the media in the ever-morphing American experiment was a topic that had come up in almost every interview. Many would cite the First Amendment as the backbone of the Constitution, then excoriate contemporary media in the same breath as the root of all evil in this country. Ironically, we entered the lion's den of international media, CNN, on one of the most frenzied days in the history of journalism—the day after the O.J. Simpson verdict was announced.

At first, we were concerned that our interview with Ed would be canceled because the CNN headquarters would be too chaotic. But Ed's assistant confirmed that morning. The sky was gloomy with torrential prehurricane rain as we drove to the Omni Hotel in downtown Atlanta—home of Ted Turner's Cable News Network and several other Turner stations. We found the sleek skyscraper and pulled into the parking garage under a CNN billboard that read O.J. IS FREE in blinking stadium lights.

The entrance to the headquarters is at the end of the hotel, through an atrium with glass-paneled walls that allow you to simultaneously witness fourteen floors' worth of CNN activity. As we waited at a security desk for passes, instructions, and an escort, we watched monitors showcasing a number of Turner's twelve networks. Ed met us at the doors to the anteroom and proved to be exactly what we had not pictured.

Sixtyish, about five-foot-nine, and slim, Ed has cut his thick brown hair in a style that lingers curiously close to one of the "Monkees." His glasses are large and round and his smile—devious. He gave us a hearty welcome and led us down a corridor to the newsroom floor, where we would conduct the interview.

The floor was bustling with activity; everyone was waiting for statements from O.J., the Brown family, and the Goldman family, the Pope was flying in to Newark, and a hurricane was heading up the East Coast. The newsroom is cavernous and clamorous, with row upon row of people and flickering computer screens. Everyone was on the phone, each trying to speak louder than the next. Words like "uplink," "wire," and "update" flew in every direction, creating a vortex of cacophony. The

Headline News set was at the front of the arena—separated by a pane of glass— with two cameras in position and commentators milling about.

We walked past a huge illuminated world map of every CNN bureau: nine domestic, twenty international, reaching 150 million households. As we moved farther into the epicenter of the commotion, the decibel level bordered on the intolerable. Ed played the role of CNN's Vanna White, yelling over the noise and waving his arms at various pieces of the news production puzzle. A balding man came sprinting up to us, stood in front of Ed with his hands at his side, clutching a single piece of paper, and said breathlessly, "Simpson's going to give a news conference at 11 A.M. in front of his house!" He waited expectantly for a reaction.

Ed's only question was "How much is admission?" The man giggled, said it was a buck fifty, and went back to his desk. Ed strolled past the wall of international clocks, surveying his domain with nonchalance, seemingly unfazed by the hubbub. Another man approached Ed, this one tall, in a tie and a Colonel Sanders mustache. Ed introduced us to Steve, saying, "Hunter Thompson sent them. In spite of that, they seem to be very decent, civilized people."

"And you let them in? Just 'cause you like Hunter Thompson doesn't mean the rest of us have to." Steve snickered.

"I don't like Hunter Thompson," Ed said mock-seriously. "He's a threat to the Republic! You see, our job is to deliver the news twenty-four hours a day, so it's in our best interest to keep him occupied. Alive and well, certainly, but agitated—always." Apparently, wit was a job requirement for those seeking a position under the aegis of Ed Turner. We left Ed to his minions while we scouted a good spot to set up; our only restriction was that we stay out of the background of the newscasts currently in progress. We found an empty chair in a row of bustling phones, bodies, and voices.

As we set up, a young man with a PUBLIC RELATIONS tag on his jacket approached and said he had been assigned to attend the interview and give us the full tour when we were finished. We asked him whether many people got confused, thinking Ed and Ted Turner were the same man or brothers. It was a question we had been asked several times since we had left Hunter's. Every time we'd say we were going to CNN to meet with Ed Turner, people would smile, embarrassed for us, and say, "*Ted*. His name is Ted with a *T*." In fact, I think Deborah, Hunter's assistant, had told us they *were* brothers. Ed walked up in the middle of the conversation.

O.J. Is Free

"For a little while, we were telling people that you were Ted's brother. We thought your parents had some wicked sense of humor and named you Ted and Ed," Kris kidded.

Ed twitched his neck and eye threateningly and said, "*Sister*. I had a sex change. I'm actually Susan, his crazy half-sister. I lived in the attic for about ten years." I watched the exchange, chuckling, thinking that Middle America might find the great Oz behind the CNN curtain a little bit frightening. However, we were delighted. We hadn't laughed so much since our visit with Hunter.

Ed took his seat and asked if he should take his coat off for the interview. "It's up to you," said Kris. "Sometimes people don't wear much of anything at all."

"Yeah, we do the nude news here too. You want to see? It's topless," Ed said with a grin. "That's our mission statement: something about a violation of good taste and civility, seven days a week, twenty-four hours a day." Hunter most certainly would have had a great comeback for that one. I clipped the microphone to Ed's striped tie and he giggled, saying, "I don't want to make you nervous, but if you shred the tie, you're out two hundred bucks." We were all set to go, Ed settling into his chair and straightening his torso, saying, "You are here on a great news day. Was O.J. guilty or not guilty? I keep forgetting."

"According to who?" a cameraman piped up as he walked by, wrapped in cords. I asked Ed if we could start and he said we would first have to tell him how much we were going to pay him. I said, "Two bucks, plus a piece of the back end," and asked him to tell us about his background.

"I was an armed terrorist in South Africa and, after ten years of prison here, they hired me to run CNN." Ed paused, took a breath, and continued without a bat of an eyelash, "I am a native Oklahoman, and I began in journalism in the fifth grade because I couldn't sing. In Bartlesville, Oklahoma, you had to work on the newspaper if you weren't in the chorus, and it's been all downhill from that point. When I graduated from the University of Oklahoma, I went to a station in Oklahoma City to learn political reporting. From Oklahoma, I went to Washington to set up a news operation for a large group of stations called Metro Media, which no longer exists—it's the Fox network today. Then I moved to New York to start a news operation worldwide for United Press International, and then went on to CBS News in New York as producer of the morning news program, and then down here, when Ted started the all-news operation in 1980. And I have been here for two million years."

Ed went on to explain that the network has two divisions—one is responsible for bringing in the news, the other for producing it in-house. His job is to oversee the former, which includes getting the news covered worldwide, in addition to overseeing all of the talk shows, except for *Larry King Live*, broadcast out of Washington. Ed's passion for what he does is evident, and I asked him if he knew exactly why he decided to be a journalist.

"Other than the fact that I couldn't sing in the fifth grade?" he asked. "I was around radio from a very early age, and I saw the newsrooms functioning then. At that time, 'cause I'm an old guy, World War II was a big story, and I was fascinated with it—the maps, the headlines, the radio reporting from Ed Murrow at CBS and from H. V. Kaltenborn at NBC. I was fortunate enough to be on hand as television dawned. In my years at Oklahoma, we were the laboratory—at the station I worked at—for CBS. So, out there in this small state, you had people five and ten years ahead of what was going on in New York, because we were experimenting. And that gave me a philosophical edge. I got the opportunity to learn in the very best possible place about television, film, news—how you put together a news story; how you tell it in documentary and long form."

I asked Ed what gave him joy about his work on a daily basis, now that CNN had given everyone such tremendous access to information. Ed was quick to correct me.

"Not information. News," he explained. "To me, information is a telephone book with all the numbers, the

Shainee with the day's news

names, and addresses. News is distilling that so that you can say, 'This year's phone book has fifteen more AIDS clinics than it did a year ago, and ten less escort services.' That's making something interesting and significant out of data. That, to me, is the news business. That's part of the joy of doing what I do; I love to explain stuff to people. I almost never met a news story I didn't like.''

Ed Turner

Ed continued to explain the difference between data and a story. ''David Brinkley once said, 'News is what we say it is,' which sounds arrogant, but it's really not, because not even with twenty-four hours a day can we show and tell everything. And so we're paid to have judgment to show and select and explain. We all enjoy the major breaking stories: the O.J. trial, the hurricane that's coming in today, the Pope's arrival. That's interesting, but the greater pleasure is in trying to find meaning in it. What does the O.J. verdict say in terms of race relations in the long run? Is there a lot of air there? Are we trying to make something out of nothing?

''We have such an open society in the United States, unlike anything the world has ever seen. With so much news, information, and opinion—on radio, in books, magazines, and television—there's no limitation, really, as to what you can see and hear and say. You have to be careful not to make too much of a bad thing or too little as well. And that's why I think we can do a service.''

I thought about what John Waters had said about the media's need to fill pages and pages of magazines with ''stories.'' Ed was saying he didn't have enough time, even with CNN's twenty-four hours, to tell all the *real* stories. I asked him to discuss the challenges of rapid distillation of information into news and the fact that many Americans would say that the emphasis on broadcasting the breaking story was diluting the overall usefulness of the journalism.

''One of the great problems in journalism—that sometimes is forgotten or overlooked—is that, after all, we are just presenting the first draft of history. It may be many years—it may be never—before the full truth is known. There are still debates going on about who started World War II and how it should have played out. Should we have known more about the slaughter of the Jews? And when we did, why did we not do anything about it? . . . So it isn't surprising that the events that happened this morning or yesterday evening are really kind of murky. Again, that's a great pleasure, though, to try and sort it out quickly and get it on the air.''

We took a break while Kris changed tapes. Then I asked Ed to discuss the progress of democracy in relationship to the progress of media.

''Of course we are not living up to the principles set forth in the Constitution, but this being the freest country ever, in the history of the earth, we're doing something right," he declared. Certainly, there are pockets of oppression. But what we live in now, I contend, is the golden time. When your grandchildren are asked to write about this period, they'll look back on the eighties and nineties as a remarkably free, open, vibrant time in the history of this country.

"As to your question about the media, no small part of a success of a democracy is dependent on the right of free speech. And that may be, at least according to Thomas Jefferson, the single most important aspect of a democracy if it is to function. And if the media is doing its job in this democracy, we are the watchdog. We're not a cheerleader; we're not someone to stand up and say, 'Hooray! Keep it up, Government!' That's not our function. There are plenty of people to do that in a political party. The watchdog is vital in keeping human beings as honest as they can possibly be in their endeavors. That's our role. I think we do it reasonably well. There's more journalists today than ever before, and with just volume alone, we can be effective.

"The head of the research laboratory for Emory University called me and asked, 'Why haven't you done a story on our substitution of journalists for rats in our laboratories?' And I said, 'I didn't know about that. Why are you using journalists instead of rats?' And he said, 'Three reasons. First off, there are more journalists than there are rats. Secondly, you can get attached to a rat. And thirdly, there are some things not even a rat will do.' That shows how the public looks at us, but it also emphasizes our role as watchdogs—in this case, watchrats."

So many of our interviewees had pointed to the media as being too big and all-pervasive. I thought about Ed's faxed prediction to Hunter about a big brother mechanism converting all media into cartoon form. I asked Ed if he thought a time would come when the media's supply would indeed overcome the demand.

He paused before responding, "Sure. Yes, there's always that danger, particularly if it's big and in the hands of a few. Right now, in spite of the moaning and groaning, that isn't a serious, real threat to this country. But there could come a time, as with totalitarian states, such as Germany, or Communist states, such as the Soviet Union, where you have a monolith in the news outlets. And what you get from that is *Pravda*, the Russian government's definition of news. You get a newspaper of lies and the people reading it knew they were lies, and all of that eventually led to the erosion of their government.

"I have spoken to many of the leaders of new countries in the world—Mandela, Yasir Arafat, the heads of government in the People's Republic of China, in Hong Kong, in Tunis, in Israel—as they fight to reestablish their own identities in this world. And the thing I say over and over to them is: 'Don't step on the press. Your greatest headache will be the press, but it will verify your legitimacy, so keep it clean, keep it healthy, keep it vibrant. There are a few dark places, but because of satellites, they won't stay too dark for very long. The truth really will come out these days and you're naive and foolish to think, Mr. Government, that you can hide it.'"

It was time for the inevitable question regarding the media's role in the creation and demolition of heroes—an idea that echoed repeatedly throughout our trip. Ed jumped right in. "Media creates celebrities, I fear. That's very different from heroes. Sadly, today there are too few serious heroes. I'm in my fifties. My heroes are Winston Churchill and Dwight Eisenhower and Maggie Thatcher, and some writers and poets. But today when I ask young people that question, they don't have much of an answer. I am sort of dismayed and depressed that there is little hero worship. And maybe those of us here in the news business must accept some of the blame because there is this demystification that goes on where we tell you more than you ever want to know about someone you may have really respected before we got through trashing him.

"On the other hand, the broadcast media should not be expected to carry all the water; we are, after all, the chroniclers of today. There is a far greater responsibility that the schools—and, most notably, history, English, sociology classes—should be teaching and carrying. And I look at what the schools are doing—or not doing—and it really offends me greatly. They are the ones, I contend, that need to implant the serious appetite for learning more about how this society functions . . . but I don't sense that it's giving that impetus, that thirst.

"So many kids don't read newspapers, much less books. And that's sad, and they will pay for it with shallow, thin lives—pale lives—that will leave them wondering, 'Is this all there is?' when they get to be my age. Of course there is more, but they don't have the eyes and ears to receive it, and that's really tragic."

"Do you believe there is an American dream?" I asked.

"Sure. And I think there's an English dream, and a Malta dream, and a Nigerian dream. No society can survive for any length of time and not inspire something within its boundaries to want to aspire to more. A great deal exists in this country.

"Journalists want to take what they see and explain it. And by explaining it, you inadvertently become an educator, even though you're a reporter. And so we contribute to or we help destroy the American dream, but that's what news is. News is that which goes wrong, and if you have a society where nothing stands out by virtue of not working properly, that means that your society is pretty rotten. I go back to the Russia of the seventies and eighties, where it was just so god-awful that anything was going to be better. Well, here we do have good and bad; we do have the contrast; and contrast is what goes to make news but also goes to make people's hopes and aspirations, and ambitions, and greed, and their dreams. You don't have a society without it, certainly no culture.

"There's nothing corny about dreaming. Show me someone who doesn't dream, and I'll show you a real dimwit."

Ed made a sweeping gesture with his arm, indicating the whole room. "What surrounds us here is not only an allegory for today but for tomorrow, too. The world has changed dramatically, and it won't be the way it was—ever again. We have seen a sea change that communications now blankets the earth, entertainment the same. There is going to be a commonality of experience caused by the

Internet and by the Cartoon Channel, and by the anchors from Atlanta, and London and Hong Kong that never existed before. The facts that got into Russia and into China stirred the revolutions—in Tiananmen Square, where it failed, in Moscow and elsewhere, where it succeeded. That's never happened before; you had tyrants who said, 'You will do this!' And it was done. Now it's much more difficult. And this, around you here, is sort of a symbol of it at CNN, because we are front-line players in these trenches, where we are shooting at each other—in an intellectual sense. And you have to begin to think in these terms to adjust to and enjoy that which is coming up.''

Our time was up. We felt that Ed had successfully countered the accusations and frustration about the media that had been cited all over the country. Ed's definition of the broadcast media as watchdog and its role in spreading freedom of speech globally echoed Bill Siemering's words of so many months before. His descriptions of tyrannical governments being hindered by the omniscience of media coverage as satellites are beaming news into the tents of Mongolia and the bush country of Africa reminded us of the power of the First Amendment. And even our mission, to provide a voice to the country as it approaches a millennium change, is an incarnation of the distillation of information and data that Ed had discussed.

Ed chatted with us a bit more and offered his services as an editor. He pointed to our cameras and said that CNN often uses the same ones. If an area they were covering was too dangerous, he said, they gave a local the camera and hoped it would come back with some footage. CNN had given away 500 in the last year. Even when the trenches were too perilous in Bosnia, Rwanda, or the Persian Gulf, the technology was there, sending back the information that became news to the rest of the world.

The wind was really picking up as we pulled out of the parking garage. Kris asked me if I knew what *pravda* actually means in Russian.

''Truth,'' I said, as we moved past the white bulbs of the billboard that were now announcing: O.J. NOT GUILTY!

DR. WILLIAM FOEGE, MD, MPH

EXECUTIVE DIRECTOR OF THE TASK FORCE FOR CHILD SURVIVAL AND DEVELOPMENT •

FELLOW FOR HEALTH POLICY AT THE CARTER CENTER

ATLANTA, GEORGIA

(Kristin)

Since *Anthem*'s inception, Shainee and I had intended to talk to a specialist in either science or medicine about the future of America and its place in the global community. We had been pursuing Dr. Mae Jemison, a physician, engineer, and former astronaut, but our schedules never seemed to mesh. Since we'd been in constant contact with Jimmy Carter's office, in hopes of interviewing him, Shainee and I had addressed the possibility of meeting with a leading scientist at the Carter Center. We were well aware of the fact that the center was breaking ground in the fields of public health, agriculture, and conflict resolution, as well as other disciplines. In explaining our dilemma to Doug Brinkley, during one of our monthly catch-up phone calls, he encouraged us to call Dr. William Foege. "He's doing *everything*," Doug had said. "If you could meet with him, your search would be over."

After some footwork, our search was indeed over. We followed Freedom Parkway Drive to Dr. Foege's office at the Carter Center and were greeted by his assistant, Louise. With Southern hospitality she invited us to come in and make ourselves comfortable. "Dr. Foege should be back soon," she assured us. "Would you like some juice?"

A man did soon appear at the door, the crown of his head nearly touching the top of the door frame. "Sorry I'm late," he said. "Someone was in my parking place." It dawned on me that Shainee and I had accidentally parked in his space.

"I think we probably took it," I said meekly. Dr. Foege laughed and moved toward us to introduce himself.

"You *are* a tall man," I observed out loud, unable to edit the words before they left my mouth.

"That's why I usually sit down for things like this," he said without missing a beat. I could tell we were going to get along just fine.

Dr. Foege was the living image of a white-haired Abe Lincoln—at least Lincoln as I imagine him—his manner, his voice, and his frame. Dr. Foege's humility was apparent in his handshake, which was offered, not asserted. A soft-spoken man, he still had a powerful presence. Best of all, his eyes seemed to shine at the marvels of the world, always on the verge of a wink—a quality I'd loved in Studs, Jimmy, Dorothy, and even Hunter.

"So I'd be happy to talk about anything in the realm of the information you sent to me," Dr. Foege declared, as he sat down.

"Well," I said, "we've done a lot of research on you, and you seem to be a very diversified human being, but I'm sure there are things about you we may not know. . . ."

Dr. Foege

"Let's hope so." He interrupted with a chuckle.

"Yeah," Shainee added, "there are still things about you that are *not* on the Internet."

"You know what I recently found out *is* on the Internet about me?" he asked. "Two weeks ago, someone sent me a copy of it—an NRA group had quoted me with a caption of: 'Here's what we're up against.' And I looked at the quote, and it *was* accurate; I had actually said it. We had a meeting at the Carter Center to discuss the unacceptable number of children who die of gunshot wounds. In closing the conference, I said, 'We have to figure out how to make handguns shift in view from symbols of sexy power to symbols of stupid impotence.' And the NRA apparently found that offensive."

I clipped the microphone to Dr. Foege's jacket. "Okay, you're all hooked up," I said, going back to the camera. "We are now magically capturing your voice inside this box over here."

"You know, that reminds me," he said, smiling to himself, "of when I was a kid, and I used to think about sending rockets out into space that would pick up sounds that had been made earlier. You know, rockets that go faster than the speed of sound?" he asked us with a childlike nod of enthusiasm, seeking confirmation.

We nodded back, more out of reflex than recognition of shared experience.

"I used to think," he further explained, " 'Wouldn't it be great to be able to send a rocket out and actually pick up Lincoln's Gettysburg Address?' Because technically, that is possible," Dr. Foege assured us. "I mean, it just keeps going forever, and so all you have to do is go fast enough to pick it up," he explained. He seemed to think that if he kept explaining it in different ways, we'd suddenly understand and say that we too had had that thought.

Shainee finally admitted, "That's definitely not something that most people can say was a common childhood wonderment."

"Yeah," I added. "You're pretty much on your own with that one, Dr. Foege."

And we all broke out in laughter. I was laughing because I had always come home after school, tuned into *The Brady Bunch*, eaten Ding Dongs, and performed elaborately costumed Cher concerts for a captive audience of kachina dolls. These were *my* childhood preoccupations. I was not contemplating the interstellar whereabouts of the Gettysburg Address. I think Dr. Foege, however, was laughing because the idea of capturing Lincoln's voice from space in the 1990s really tickled his physics-inclined mind and also because he clearly never took himself too seriously.

Shainee asked Dr. Foege to please give us a little of his personal background—where he grew up and how he was inspired to pursue the field of science and medicine. "I've actually led a very surprising life," he began. "Well, it surprises me," he qualified, "because I came from an average background from a less-than-average-size town—a hundred people, actually. And never for a moment did I think there would be a chance to get into medicine. And certainly no one was really thinking beyond the United States in those days. My family eventually moved to the state of Washington, and I eventually went to medical school.

"In school, I was very attracted to the writings of Albert Schweitzer and the fact that here was a person of enormous talent who was willing to go to Africa in order to use that talent. I always had this notion that one day I would meet Schweitzer in Africa. But I left for Africa the month he died in 1965. Nonetheless, that idea of Africa caught on with me, and I also had mentors along the way who described how much one could do in the area of public health. Putting those two together, international public health became a natural for me."

Dr. Foege continued by explaining that he had applied to the Harvard School of Public Health on the basis of a single article included in their literature. "It was called *Questions of Priority*. It was a commencement address by Thomas Weller, who had won the Nobel Prize for his work on tissue culture techniques that allowed people to grow the polio virus in the lab. And in that article, it was so telling as he described, 'You only live once and you only get a chance to use your talents once. You might as well use them *well*.' "

Dr. Foege's smile exuded reverence for Mr. Weller. "Thomas Weller later became a mentor of mine when I went to Harvard. The year he retired from the School of Public Health, I gave the commencement address at Harvard. I got that article out and read some of the sentences that had caused me to go there for my education, pointing out that you never know how you will affect what happens downstream with what you say and what you write. And as I read those passages, Thomas Weller got a standing ovation in the middle of that address, and it was a cycle completed."

He went on, describing a stint in Africa as director of a medical center in Nigeria. "I returned to the Center for Disease Control in Atlanta for what I thought was a temporary position, always intending, as soon as the war was over, to go back to Nigeria. I began working on smallpox eradication and when the war finally ended, much later than anyone anticipated, I was so obsessed with the cure that I felt I had to continue. Then I went to India to work on smallpox. Smallpox disappeared from the world in 1977—the first disease to ever disappear from the world by the hands of people. I continued at CDC and became its director between 1977 and 1983. And for the last ten years, I've been at the Carter Center.'' Dr. Foege had humbly glossed over the fact that he had been instrumental in that worldwide eradication of smallpox.

He went on to say that the Carters had established the center in an attempt to continue some of the work that they had been involved in at the White House and to address concerns raised by *The Global 2000 Report*, which was commissioned by Carter during his tenure as President. ''We started out not really knowing what such a center could do,'' Dr. Foege explained. ''In retrospect, I'm glad that we didn't draw up a strategic plan with objectives in the beginning, because the reality has far exceeded the vision.''

Dr. Foege explained what makes the Carter Center unique. ''It is supported by the academic strength of Emory University. And we operate with an activist inclination, which also exists in many other places. But the third thing—the access provided by President and Mrs. Carter—is unique,'' he declared. ''You put those three things together and it really is magic. You can do things in a short period of time that could not even be dreamed of otherwise.''

We told Dr. Foege that we were presently trying to get an interview with President Carter. He encouraged us, saying, ''He is such an unusual person. I don't know of anyone who has the self-discipline that he does. If he gets ten extra minutes in a day that he wasn't expecting to have, he uses it. It's a bit of a challenge to his staff—he can do so much that it sets a standard—which is a big reason for the productivity of the Carter Center.''

We started to talk about global medicine and America's role in it, and Dr. Foege discussed a disease that the center had worked on called river blindness. ''I'd like to call this a Polybius story,'' he began. ''Because I once gave a talk where I used the phrase 'global village,' and my son, who was a history major at the time, asked me if I knew who I was quoting when I said 'global village.' And I said, 'I think Marshall McLuhan.' He said, 'No, you're quoting Polybius.' And he went on to recite to me the Polybius quote from more than two thousand years ago, which addresses that it may have been possible in the past for things to have happened in isolation, but from this time forth, the world must be seen as an organic whole, where everything affects everything.

''Well, this is a Polybius story, because the cure for river blindness was developed from a soil sample taken from a golf course in Japan and worked on in a lab in the United States by a scientist from Bangladesh. And,'' he added, ''the drug is financially subsidized by the dogs of America.''

Dr. Foege went on to explain that the idea for the drug originally came from

Merck and Company as a cure for heartworm disease in dogs and that the company supplies the drug to the Carter Center at no cost. "The drug is now distributed in thirty-two countries," Dr. Foege continued, "with all of the ministries of health involved, the World Health Organization, UNICEF, countless nongovernment organizations, and mission groups of all kinds—all a part of the solution. Everything affects everything," he said, emphasizing his point.

We raised the idea of America's uniqueness and asked Dr. Foege if he had any thoughts on the subject of what currently sets America apart from other nations.

"I recently attended a conference where I had the opportunity to try and answer the question of what is unique about North America in the 1990s," he said. "And I tried to approach the question from the perspective of a historian in the year 3000, asking myself, 'What will historians say about us that will be similar to what India means to religion or China means to philosophy?' And I came up with only two things that are unique about this time in history in North America.

"It's incredible what has happened in this century in science in general. But if we make this a particular health question, I'd like to think of my father, who was destined to die, according to statistics, in the year 1954. He saw all of the 1950s, 1960s, 1970s, 1980s, and he's already seen the majority of the 1990s at this point. It means that during his lifetime, for every day he lived, science gave him an additional eleven hours. And for all Americans in general, we've been getting about eight hours a day extra as our life expectancy increases.

"So, first and foremost, this will be seen as the time of science, and America will be seen as the leader. Science has really flowed from the United States out. That was not true in the last century, but it's very true in this century.

"The second thing that I am sure that the historians will talk about is the fact that this is the first time we have collectively planned for a rational future, meaning that the majority of people can actually participate in democracy. In 1976, Norman Cousins wrote an article on the Bicentennial, asking the question: 'What is the most significant gift the United States has given the world?' And his answer was that the United States has shown that it is possible to plan a rational future, and in many ways our Constitution turns out to be the incarnation of that idea.

"But then you ask the question: 'Have we had two hundred years of democracy?' The answer is no. When democracy developed in Greece, about fifteen percent of the population actually could participate. Women didn't participate, the slaves, the poor, and so on. In this country, around the beginning of this century when my mother was born, the figure had gone from around fifteen percent to maybe thirty percent. Women couldn't vote, minorities didn't vote, the poor didn't vote. It's only in the last few decades that we actually have the ability for the majority of people to participate in democracy or in planning a rational future. I think that's going down in history as a legacy of this time and this place."

I thought of Ed Turner's declaration that we were indeed in the midst of a golden era. It may be that when you're in the midst of one, it's hard to recognize. But perhaps Ed Turner and Dr. Foege had a gift for seeing what others did not.

"There's actually a third thing," Dr. Foege continued, "that I would *like* to see, but I'm not sure that I will. I would like to see this be the time when we actually balance freedom and equality. If you ask Americans, 'Do we have freedom?' they say, 'Yes.' 'Do we have equality?' they say, 'In theory, yes.' But the two are incompatible; they cannot exist together, and if you give people absolute freedom, before long, twenty percent will own eighty percent of everything. If you insist on equality, you have to take away some freedom. The United States, I think, has done as good a job as any culture in balancing those two conflicting ideas, but it is not yet perfected.

"So we have to start with the free market system," Dr. Foege suggested, "and ask, 'How do we get the best balance of freedom and equality from a free market system and still maintain the best health for people?' I would hope that this could be seen as an age when that actually happens.

"This is also the age," Foege continued, "when we appreciate our dependence on the rest of the world, that we can no longer think nationally. A hundred and thirty years ago, here in Atlanta, if you were a Georgian, it was okay to shoot someone from New York. Not only okay, but you were *encouraged* to do that. And we've gotten over that so that it is now possible to be a good Georgian and a good American, and we don't see any paradox in that at all. We are now at a point in world history where we have to be able to see ourselves as good global citizens and good Americans and good Georgians, and see no paradox in that at all; what is good for the world is ultimately good for the United States.

"We don't have polio in this country, but the only way we are going to protect this country from polio is if we get rid of it in the rest of the world. We spend three hundred million dollars a year on polio here in America, even though we don't have the disease. If we had been willing, five years ago, to increase our budget from three hundred to four hundred million and spend the extra hundred million on the world, there would be no polio in the world today. We would already be recoup-ing our investment. So it also makes good financial sense to go global. We now have

The Peach State

a global economy. We have a global transportation system. We have a global communication system, but we don't have a global *ethic*."

Dr. Foege's statement reminded me of Jack Healey's mission to establish a global ethic in the realm of human rights. Many of the other people we'd interviewed were aware of this as a moment in which they needed to take their crusade from the national to the global arena. Was this America's new Manifest Destiny, as Doug had first speculated?

"I think one of the most awesome things in my own lifetime is to come from a town of one hundred people and now appreciate that you can not only no longer live in a single time zone, but you can also no longer live in a single time *period*. This global community, this global village, not only extends to all other countries, but it extends in the future as far as we can see. And when we live realizing that our current deeds have an impact on the world's future needs, that's when we will actually understand what it means to be a global *community*.

"My wife teaches four-year-olds," he continued, "and I go in once a year with a white coat and a stethoscope and talk about what happens when you get sick. Several years ago, a four-year-old girl asked me a question that was so surprising that I thought to myself, 'I would like to follow her career when she gets older, because it's not a question that you could ask accidentally.' She asked me, 'Do doctors have bosses?' Now, my answer was what I would like to be true. I said, 'Of course they do. Their patients are their bosses.' But I went to a UNICEF workshop several weeks after that and I used that comment and then asked, 'Who are the bosses for UNICEF?' The people immediately answered, 'All the children of the world.' And I pointed out that that's true *and* incomplete.

"The real bosses of UNICEF are all the children of the world, plus every child who will ever be born in the future. Therefore, UNICEF has to be thinking of not only immunizing children or saving them from diarrhea, but they have to be thinking about what kind of world is going to be left for the children born in the future. What do we have to do about population? What do we have to do about the ecology in the world? What do we have to do about the education of young females? All of those things become important to UNICEF. I believe that's the way the rest of us have to act—what is going to happen in the future is going to happen because of decisions that we now make every day."

We began to talk about the crisis-oriented sensibility of America which seemed to prevent us from addressing problems until we approached the brink of disaster.

"This is a cause-and-effect world," Dr. Foege said. "It's not an arbitrary world. It's not a mystery world. It's not a world of astrology. It's a cause-and-effect world. Health changes the ability to experience the quality of life, and we don't tend to value health until we lose it. It's just the way people are, which means the government's role has often been to address illness and disease once people are sick, rather than prevention. I can tell you the day someone is diagnosed with lung cancer, they would give every bit of money they have to be able to step back ten years and change their smoking habits. But a week before they get that diagnosis, you can't talk them into stopping.

"So it's been hard to get money funneled into public health. If we in public health changed our concept to think of health *outcomes*, I think there would be real change. For instance, we've gone through a very extended debate on health care reform in this country. I think one of the reasons we failed to come to a satisfactory solution is we started with the wrong premises. We debated access, quality, and cost. Access is not where we should have started. We should have debated health outcomes.

"People ask, 'What's the difference?' For example, we should put our emphasis not on what percentage of women have had pap smears but how many women have died of carcinoma of the cervix. No woman in this country should die of carcinoma of the cervix. We know how to test for it, we know how to prevent it, we know what to do. When a woman dies of carcinoma of the cervix, something went wrong with the system. And as long as our emphasis is on access measures rather than outcome measures, we're not going to correct the problem."

Dr. Foege went on to bemoan the lack of funds available for prevention from the institutions that dole out the money. "We want to focus on prevention, because it seems better to be alive and healthy than sick and dead," Dr. Foege expressed rather seriously. "That seems so obvious, and yet why is it that we have to argue it every year and end up with the droppings and not with the main resources?"

Dr. Foege was digging at the heart of our crisis-oriented nature—and one of our greatest cultural paradoxes. Did we inherit a sense of invincibility from the boldness of our pioneer fathers and mothers? Or were we just young, and like most young people, believe nothing tragic would ever befall us?

"I used to get so upset with politicians," he continued, "but now I tend to get upset with those of us in public health. Because if you go with the assumption that politicians are *trying* to make the right decisions, then when they don't, it must mean that we've not given them the right kind of information or the right arguments. And so we have to take responsibility for not being able to make a good case. So I've changed my feeling from one of being very hostile toward politicians to one of taking more of the blame."

This admission stunned me: that this man was able to step outside his profession enough to see this and then decide to take responsibility for it, expecting the same of his colleagues. Dr. Foege is someone I consider to be a modern hero—a civic leader—and the more time we spent with him, the more honored I felt simply to be in his presence.

Shainee asked Dr. Foege whether he believed in any incarnation of the American dream. "I have a context for the American dream, because I think I've lived it. I've had a chance, from what I consider quite humble origins . . . I mean, I went to a one-room schoolhouse. How many people do you know these days in the United States that actually went to a one-room schoolhouse—eight grades in one room?"

Well, there's you and then there's John Perry Barlow, I thought to myself.

Dr. Foege went on to say how remarkable it seemed to him to come from such a small-town perspective and then see the results of one's work *internationally*. It was indeed notable that both people we had met who had attended a one-room schoolhouse were influencing the *world* with their life's work.

"When I was taking my training in international health," he continued, "people did not expect to see results in one generation. People truly believed we were doing things to set the stage for a later generation, and suddenly everything changed. Infant mortality rates around the world are coming down so fast, faster even than at any time in U.S. history. Life expectancy is increasing faster in the world in some cultures than it ever increased in the United States. I mentioned the average American has seen an increase of eight hours a day. There are countries that, over the last two decades, have seen life expectancy increase twelve hours a day, which means the gap has been narrowing between the developing countries and the developed countries in terms of health statistics.

"Now, here's the problem. Simultaneously, life expectancy is improving, infant mortality is improving, diseases are improving, but the gap is widening between the poor and the rich. That's happening in this country, but it's also happening in the rest of the world. This, I think, is the product of a free market system without enough restraints." Dr. Foege paused. "I don't even remember the question. Sometimes I can go off on tangents," he admitted.

"It was about the American dream," Shainee reminded him.

"Oh, yes!" he exclaimed, picking right up. "Because I really feel that I had a chance to live that American dream, and I see lots of people still living the American dream. And, you know, I like the fact that the United Nations ended up in New York, for several reasons, but mostly because I think the way you introduce democracy to the rest of the world is you force leaders from other parts of the world to live in a democracy, even if only briefly. It spreads the dream.

"I think of the 1950s and the 1960s, 1970s, the Cold War and the one hundred and thirty or so countries sending some of their top representatives to New York—reading the U.S. newspapers every day, watching the United States government operate, and then getting together at the U.N., where they use democratic principles to communicate and implement. Now, how can you do that and then go home and say, 'Our system is better than a democratic approach'? Why did they use a democratic approach at the U.N.? Because no one could think of a better one!"

We officially finished the interview and started packing up, but then we got caught up in a conversation about how we all felt about the future of America. "I tend to be an optimist," admitted Dr. Foege. "I'm an optimist by experience, rather than a congenital optimist. There are things that keep happening."

"You mean, *reasons* for being an optimist?" I asked.

"Yeah," he agreed, "that's right. It's easy to be a pessimist. It's easy to be a cynic. I often quote Lily Tomlin for a lot of things, but particularly when she said, 'No matter how cynical you become, it's never enough to keep up.'

"Public health people in general," Dr. Foege continued, "are optimists because they start from the premise that they can change the world or they wouldn't be doing these things. Nonetheless, it's a challenge to *remain* an optimist. Some weeks ago, I was giving the final talk at a workshop on tuberculosis. During the workshop, what struck me was that half the people were really pessimistic. So in my closing remarks I said that my time with them reminded me of the person who went to a fortune-teller and was told, 'You will be very unhappy and very poor until you are forty-five.' And the man was shocked. Grasping at straws, he asked, 'What will happen when I'm forty-five?' And the fortune-teller said, 'You'll get used to it.' And, see, we can't let people get *used* to these things. We have to provide the optimism; we have to provide the vision that things don't have to be that way.''

I started feeling strangely guilty for having taken up any of this man's time. Just then Dr. Foege looked at his watch and jumped out of his chair, growing tall again. He grabbed his coat, apologizing for his need to run. ''I still don't understand why you wanted to interview *me*,'' he said, in movement, ''but I hope I said something in the vein of what you're looking for.'' I shook his hand good-bye with twice the appreciation as hello, and he was gone.

We asked Louise if we could use Dr. Foege's phone to make a quick call. Having dialed, I realized I needed a pen. I couldn't find one on Dr. Foege's desk, so I boldly cracked open his top drawer. Along with a few pens, the drawer contained, curiously enough, a number of unshucked peanuts—the good ol' American baseball kind. I couldn't help but wonder if it was a required allegiance to the name on the center plaque: ''I vow to keep an emergency handful of Georgia peanuts in my desk at all times.'' Dr. Foege had gone, so we'll never know.

ED RENDELL

MAYOR OF PHILADELPHIA

PHILADELPHIA, PENNSYLVANIA

(Shainee)

group of renegade patriots gathered at Independence Hall in my hometown of Philadelphia in 1776 and created a document, the Declaration of Independence, and a country, the United States of America, that changed the world. Ed Rendell, dubbed "America's Mayor" by Vice President Al Gore, is the 121st mayor of the first capital of the United States and is perpetuating the tradition of new ideas that began over two centuries ago. Mayor Rendell is a local hero. At the age of thirty-three, he was the youngest district attorney ever elected in the city of Philadelphia and, twenty years later, is currently serving his second term as mayor. Mayor Rendell was the first Democrat to run unopposed for reelection in almost forty years. He inherited the city on the verge of bankruptcy in 1992 and his economic reforms are credited with returning fiscal stability to the fifth-largest city in the country.

His commitment to the "reinvention of government" is visible all over Greater Philadelphia, in the form of aggressive revitalization plans and the forging of strong ties between the city and the private sector. With the help of hundreds of volunteer citizens and companies, the mayor successfully implemented several new programs that have brought the city out of enormous deficit, have begun to bolster some of Philadelphia's neglected neighborhoods, have created thousands of new jobs, and have stimulated small businesses. Philadelphia, due to its progress under Mayor Rendell, is being looked to by other urban areas all over the country, including Washington, D.C., as a model of metropolitan development.

Personally, every time I go home, I am stunned at the renaissance that has taken place. I've always loved Center City Philadelphia, with its colonial townhouses, cobblestone streets, iron horse posts and lanterns, and parks every few blocks. There is a palpable sense of history and patriotism on almost every block, a reminder of the birth of a nation and the creation of a historically unrivaled experiment in governing. However, when I was younger, there were also areas of the city that were scarred by burned-out buildings, plagued by crime and drugs—the usual. Now some of those areas have been restored to their original historical beauty *without* kicking out the people who were already living or working there. There are new theaters and dance stages sprouting up where there used to be only the danger of getting mugged. Mayor Rendell is the latest in a long legacy of Philadelphia leaders to be labeled ''maverick.''

We didn't realize *just* how maverick until we got a taste of his preferred location for interviews: in his car, while being driven from appointment to appointment. Rendell doesn't like to take time out from his taxpayers' day to deal with the media, so he invites reporters to sit in the back of his car as he commutes between mayoral commitments. We were told that things would move pretty fast and we should be prepared for uncontrolled conditions. So our appointment with the mayor turned into an adventure of sorts.

Scheduling any time with the mayor was difficult because the election was only a month away. (He won it, by the way.) We picked Columbus Day, a city holiday, thinking that maybe the mayor's schedule would be a little lighter than usual. (We were wrong.) When we arrived at City Hall—an eighteenth-century Beaux Arts building with a statue of William Penn, Pennsylvania's first leader, on its crown—all of the entrances were locked and marked CLOSED FOR COLUMBUS DAY. After milling around the courtyard at the center of the building and walking through archway after archway to various entrances, we found one that was unlocked and went up to the mayor's office.

The mayor's chief of security and his driver, Michael, were waiting for us in the reception area. They quizzed us on the film and asked if the mayor's driver would end up in it. We said there was a good chance and Michael smiled, saying he would do his Dean Martin impersonation for us if we could stop at a bar first. They told us that we would be attending a ceremony given by the Scandinavian community to officially declare Leif Ericsson Day, and then we would be heading to South Philadelphia to a luncheon being thrown by the Italian community commemorating Columbus Day. Ah, the life of the politician, honoring two different men from two different centuries and two different countries for ''discovering'' the same New World.

We waited for about ten minutes for the mayor to emerge. We asked Michael if we should run back to the car and get the rest of our equipment, because we had only one camera with us. We thought that one of us could shoot from the front seat and one from the back if the mayor would agree to sit in the backseat. They advised us to use only one camera and warned us about the reality of riding in the back of the mayor's car. ''He only sits in the front, so you'll have to scream. He always tries to cram too much in and always stays too long, because he won't say no to anyone. So we drive pretty fast. A girl from the *Inquirer* got carsick last week, so you really have to hang in there.''

The chief of security's walkie-talkie squawked and Michael was given his directions: "Put them in the car. He's getting ready to move." Michael threw his jacket on and ushered us out of the building and into the back of the mayor's black sedan. The car phone barked, "It's showtime, Michael." He was instructed to move "at warp speed," because the mayor was on the verge of late. Just as Michael placed his foot on the brake to put the car into gear, the mayor came flying into the car with perfectly timed synchronicity. He slammed the door, the siren went on, we lurched out onto the street and Mayor Rendell asked Michael if he had the "Leif Ericsson proc." (Short for proclamation?) Michael was prepared. Satisfied, the mayor said his hellos and took a breath. We asked Mayor Rendell how he was doing and he said, "Not pleased you're here. I know you have a timeline, but this is a very bad time for me. So anyway, what have you got? Shoot."

There was an awkward pause. Kris and I stared at the dark-haired man in disbelief while he tightened his tie and turned to look straight ahead as his driver raced toward Kennedy Parkway. We were dumbstruck. After our hesitation exceeded a second and a half, the mayor looked at us, and said kindly, "This is what you're going to get. This is cinema verité." And indeed it was. I anchored myself to the car's door handle, held the microphone as close to the mayor's mouth as I could, and began asking questions. The car swerved and veered and Kris got

Mayor Ed Rendell and Viking friends

knocked around on the other side of the seat trying to get a shot of the mayor, who was looking directly away from her. These were unusual conditions—even for us. Mayor Rendell was halfway through his first answer on how American cities were being forced to reinvent government as a result of the elimination of federal dollars when the car suddenly screeched to a halt. We had arrived at our first stop. The mayor opened the door and jumped out, saying he'd give us the second part of the answer when he got back.

There was a platform stage set up next to a statue of Leif Ericsson, overlooking the Schuylkill River. Live accordion music piped out over strategically placed loudspeakers. Several men sporting Viking costumes flanked the mayor on either side of the podium. They were in full regalia, with horned helmets and shields, shirtless beneath their breastplates. The accordions played both the American and Norwegian national anthems. Everyone sang out of tune. The mayor was in good spirits, having made his introduction on time, and he greeted the audience warmly. "Before I get started, I wanted to announce that I spoke to President Clinton this morning and he said that under the new crime bill, the Norsemen are going to be added to the streets of Philadelphia for patrol purposes." There was hearty laughter from the crowd, as well as the helmeted ones.

I talked to Michael for a bit while the mayor was speaking, and he filled me in on the day-to-day experience of working with Mayor Rendell. Michael enjoyed the mayor's breakneck pace and his informal style. "He don't much go in for the typical 'I'm the mayor. Bow down. Open the door for me' kind of thing. He understands that he's the mayor and he's here to do the work, which is great, I think." The mayor finished his five-minute speech with a city proclamation commemorating the wrong turn that Leif Ericsson made on his way to Greenland. Everyone clapped and we blasted off like the Batmobile.

The mayor didn't miss a beat, picking up exactly where he had left off. "I think it's probably true that cities are the best at reinventing government, because necessity forced us to do so. We had no choice. It's a little bit like the story about the little girl asking President Kennedy how he became a war hero and he said, 'Simple. They sunk my boat.' " The mayor finished his thought by stressing the fact that, in addition to economic restructuring through privatization and other means, American cities must begin to focus on the loss of jobs to technology.

One of the fundamentals of Mayor Rendell's renovation of the city's government is the utilization of volunteers. I asked the mayor to discuss his successes.

"The best example is that this past Saturday we opened all forty-nine branches of the public library six days a week for the first time in this city's history. Three years ago, I met with the library board and asked them to train volunteers to act as part-time library assistants. They were skeptical, but with the help of fourteen hundred volunteers, we did it. The advantage of using volunteers, in addition to the substantive benefit, is that the more people who participate in helping the goals of their city, the stronger we are as a city. It brings the mission to the grass roots of the neighborhoods. We often find that the people who live in our neighborhoods can sometimes answer questions and find solutions to problems better than their very skilled administrators at City Hall."

We hit some traffic heading down Broad Street, thanks to the mayor's plan to make one of the most forgotten boulevards of the city into an "Avenue of the arts." It gave us a little more time to ask questions and a little less need to hold on for dear life. I asked the mayor to talk about the reality of inalienable rights in the city that fostered them.

"The biggest of the goals that were set forth by our forefathers—that I don't think we've achieved yet—is equal opportunity for all, in terms of the economy. We still have to strive to make jobs available for city dwellers who don't have the benefit of a significant education or training."

"So do you believe the American dream is alive and well?" I probed.

"It's alive and well, but it's something that I would say is not universal. One thing that we need to stay aware of is not cutting education loans. One of the fundamental building blocks of the American dream has always been education, and we're not really saving any money by cutting these loans."

The Batmobile's brakes screeched again and we stopped abruptly, this time with Kris nearly clocking Michael on the head with the camera, as the mayor discussed his own political influences: President Kennedy, Adlai Stevenson, and Barry Goldwater. The mayor was scheduled to speak briefly at a lunch given by an Italian-American group celebrating their fellow expatriate Christopher Columbus. We rushed to keep up with Ed as the door swung open onto a large hall of people. The mayor was introduced as "the number-one citizen of the city of Philadelphia."

Kris and I hung out at the bar and sipped complimentary orange juice. The mayor seemed relaxed at his second podium of the day. There was no sign of stress or fatigue. He gave his thank-yous, shook hands all the way to the door, and tapped our elbows to follow him as he exited. Back in the car and heading north to City Hall for his two o'clock appointment, he asked if we were done. I asked him one more question: "Why politics?"

"I love government and public service. And the great part of this job is that the problems are so different. In one day I'll be dealing with criminal justice problems and the water department. And the next day I'll be dealing with economic development problems and arts and cultural problems. It's just a wonderful, diverse set of issues you deal with. And all of them have the bottom line of helping people and that's, again, an absolutely great thing. Absolutely great thing. I mean, it's never boring, it's always challenging. You know if you do your work well, people will benefit. That's just terrific, you know? So I'll keep doing it as long as I can keep it up."

The car phone rang. It was the mayor's wife, a federal judge, finishing a meeting at City Hall, wanting to know if he was close by and had time for lunch. The mayor squinted up at the feet of William Penn as the Batmobile rapidly approached City Hall, looked down at his watch, calculating her E.T.A., and said, "Meet you downstairs in about four minutes?"

GERALDINE FERRARO

CO-HOST OF CNN'S *CROSSFIRE* • 1984 VICE PRESIDENTIAL DEMOCRATIC CANDIDATE

NEW YORK CITY

(Kristin)

Geraldine Ferraro had been one of our most anticipated interviews. We had been looking forward to her insights regarding the place of women in America's pantheon of heroes and their role in the shifts of the political winds, as well as the redefinition of the American dream.

Many observers identify Ferraro as a linchpin in the slow process that has opened more doors for women in politics and business. In the way that Wes Jackson and Jack Healey have dedicated themselves to changing the ground rules for agricultural and social behavior, Ferraro has redefined the position of women in American society. Even though her vice presidential bid with Walter Mondale in 1984 was unsuccessful, her candidacy shattered taboos that had long lingered on the political landscape.

Though her public profile is significantly lower than in the mid-1980s, Ferraro continues to work behind the scenes in politics and human rights, and in front of the scenes, along with John Sununu, as a co-host of CNN's *Crossfire*.

It was an easy drive from Philly to Manhattan, where we met Ferraro in her office—a walk-up in SoHo that she shares with her realtor husband, John Zacarro. Ferraro looked as she had on my television set in 1984: self-confident, serious, strong. She talked so fast that three words often became one. As we sat down to get started, it was obvious that she was comfortable with the camera. Shainee, responding to Ferraro's "Let's get down to business" body language, asked her to describe how she had become the Democratic vice presidential candidate in 1984.

Ferraro spoke of a childhood in the South Bronx, where she had been raised by her mother, her father having died when Geraldine was five years old. "I didn't get involved in politics until I was in law school," she added. "I was teaching during the day, going to law school at night, and at that time it was very difficult for women to get jobs in law. I had tried to get a job down on Wall Street and that didn't work at all. One firm told me after five interviews that they weren't hiring women that year. When I was finally hired by an agency, the district attorney's office of Manhattan, and I told them I was getting married, they withdrew the offer because they felt as a Catholic, I would likely become pregnant, which would make me unable to fulfill my three-year contract. Those things were happening with great frequency. During that time, I had joined a local political club, figuring that if people got to know me—and I knew them—that it might help me get a job. I never really expected to become that personally interested in politics."

Geraldine Ferraro on the phone

After thirteen years of staying home to raise her children and five years as a teacher in the New York City public school system, Ferraro eventually joined the Queens County district attorney's office. She moved up quickly through the ranks and started the Special Victims Bureau, supervising the prosecution of sex crimes, child abuse, domestic violence, and violent crimes against senior citizens. "As an attorney," she continued, "I tried those cases, and I ended up feeling very convinced that the system wasn't working. I felt there had to be something we could do about it as a society.

"And so," Ferraro continued, "I decided I was going to run for office and try to effect legislation. I ran for Congress in 1978. It was a crazy time. I had no support from any political organizations. Thank God I had a big family, because they all helped me. It was an uphill battle, but I won. It kind of surprised everybody, including me. The paper the next day had the headline: 'Geraldine Who?' "

Geraldine described her first term in the House of Representatives. "It was an institution that was male-dominated," she said, aware that she was stating the obvious. "It is still male-dominated—but it was really male-dominated in 1979. And so, despite that, I had to figure out a way to become effective rather quickly. Seniority was a big thing, and I wasn't going to do it that way. And women were not commanding a tremendous number of votes, since there were so few of us."

Ferraro decided to run for secretary of the caucus, which was "a woman's job at the time." After she won, Speaker of the House Tip O'Neill decided to make the secretary of the caucus a member of the Steering and Policy Committee—a House leadership committee. "Once that happened," Ferraro commented, "the guys wanted the job, too, because then it got a little bit of power behind it.

"In addition to that," she continued, "those of us who were active in the Congresswomen's Caucus recognized that we weren't going to go too far with the numbers we had. So, we had to build up the membership. We couldn't elect more women to that office quickly enough to make it a good block of votes, so what we did, instead, was change the name to the Congressional Caucus on Women's Issues. And we reached out to the male members who were really worried about the gender gap and how women—who were starting to vote in larger numbers—were going to vote in their districts. And they only had to be with us on two nonnegotiable issues—the issue of choice and the Equal Rights Amendment. We ended up with a formidable caucus including a hundred men who were really anxious to become part of our group. And, of course, we were anxious to have them, because they had the clout that could make a difference."

Ferraro went on to explain that she served three terms in Congress and then decided she wanted to try and work with the Democratic convention in 1984 because she hoped to run for the Senate in 1986 and needed the exposure. "I reached out to the chair of the Democratic National Committee and said that I wanted a position for the campaign," she said. "I really wanted the platform chair, because it would allow me to travel around the country speaking on the issues that I really cared about; focusing attention on the Reagan policies, which I thought were horrendous. I ended up getting that platform chair and receiving more attention from that than I had expected. So when talk of a woman candidate began, I had already been on television a lot and people began noticing this third-term member of the Congress from Queens. That eventually led to my nomination."

Shainee asked Ferraro about the cultural shift that the vice presidential bid had unleashed. "There were two reasons why that window opened," she said. "One was Fritz Mondale, who truly, truly believed it was time. I don't know if it would have happened had it been anyone else running for the presidency. And the second reason was women across America who—some for the first time—involved themselves in the political process and gave tremendous support and voice to our campaign."

Shainee asked Ferraro if she felt what happened in 1984 has had a lasting impact for women in politics. "I think it has had a lasting impact for *women*," Ferraro answered, "not just women in politics. And I want to make it perfectly clear, I'm not talking about Geraldine Ferraro, I'm talking about the candidacy, because I think any number of women could have done precisely what I did with the exact same effect. I've been told by those people who keep statistics on this that the increase in the number of women who have run for office and have succeeded in winning office over the last eleven years can be traced back to the door that started opening in '84.

"But there are other things," she continued. "It is now thirteen years since that election, and I still have people coming up to me, saying, 'It made a difference in my life.' I've received letters saying, 'I went to medical school. I figured if you could do it, I could, too.' Others will write to say that they stayed home with their kids the way I did, and then said, 'It's my turn,' and went out to do something they always wanted to do. It's just seeing someone do it *publicly.*"

Listening to Geraldine talk about the cyclical aspect of inspiration and women stepping to the forefront of politics for the first time made me think of the Founding Mothers, whose contributions to the inception of the country have been largely overlooked and undocumented. Women came to this country, as men did, in pursuit of a better life for themselves and their families. I believe they too wanted to journey to a new land with the hopes of helping shape a more enlightened nation, even if their influence was—as dictated by the times—indirect. But I felt a vacuum when trying to think of the names of those women who came before us. I could conjure up only a few obvious figures, such as Betsy Ross, Susan B. Anthony, and Molly Pitcher. It wasn't as if we weren't aware of the historical oversight of the contributions made by women. But I suddenly became hyperaware of the fact that the threads of "herstory" have been mostly hidden from the "public" eye, Ferraro having made the point of how empowering it can be to *publicly* see a woman succeed.

Occasionally, people we met on the road would tease us, saying that our use of the term "founding parents" is too "politically correct." I believe it to simply be a *correction,* employing Studs Terkel's theory that quite often a "minority opinion" is more accurately a minority *expressed* opinion.

Shainee asked Ferraro how she felt about the probability of a woman being elected to the Executive Office. "I think the problem that we have right now," she explained, "is that the people who succeed in winning the presidency—for instance in the last fifty years—they've either been vice presidents, or they've been a United States senator, or they've been a governor; and the only one that has not been in this century was Dwight Eisenhower, who was the highest-ranking general of the military forces. Women are not prominent in those circles. A woman, obviously, has never been Vice President. There's never been a woman who's commanded a branch of the military. We do have women in the state houses and we do have women in the United States Senate. We have *one* woman governor. We have *eight* United States senators. Now, that's not a *huge* universe. And so we've got nine women who are in the universe in which these people run. And in addition to those nine, you have to have people who really want it. They have to come from the universe, *and* they have to really want it. We don't have that.

"I constantly work to elect Democratic women to office," Ferraro continued. "And I think it's great that the Republicans do it, too, because if they're going to elect a Republican, I want it to be a woman. At least girls are seeing role models of women who are capable of doing an important job. Once we get a larger universe of women who are willing and are credible candidates, we're going to have a woman run for office, and we're going to have a woman *win* office." Ferraro's delicate facial features and polished grace did not soften the determination and certainty in her stoic blue eyes.

We asked Geraldine if she had any role models as a young woman.

"Eleanor Roosevelt," she said easily. "She could have sat back and said, 'I'm the first lady. I just wanna hang out.' But, instead, she was very involved in the war effort. And then when her husband died, she became even more involved in human rights. She was one of the creators of the Human Rights Commission, and our first representative, and a woman who was really ahead of her time, as far as women's rights were concerned. I think if she were living today, she would be perceived differently. She may be living today in the form of Hillary Clinton!" Ferraro said, seeming to have just come to that conclusion. "They're both very active first ladies. And very much beaten up by the press and the public because of it. My own reaction to it is 'Thank God for both of them.' "

Geraldine went on to evoke the words spoken early on by George Stephanopoulos, acknowledging a current cultural inclination to lionize people only to later tear them down "almost for sport."

That said, we asked Geraldine what inspired her to continue fighting the good fight. "Well," she explained, "I think there is still more for me to do. I still feel very strongly that we're all put here for a reason other than for our own benefit. We're here, if we can, to make a difference."

During our trip, there were a few times when I felt we were coming face-to-face with the embodiment of a turning point in history—living history. Even though 1984 feels like a long time ago in the context of my short life, Ferraro's commitment and courage as a modern-day pioneer have fortified women everywhere. Shaking her hand felt different from most handshakes. Shainee and I struggled to find the words to thank her on behalf of women all over the world.

We left her office and walked outside, crisp fall air greeting us as we hit the pavement looking for a pay phone to check our voice mail. Shainee dialed, slowly shaking her head in disbelief as she listened to our one new message—the scheduler from Dr. Maya Angelou's office calling to cancel our long-awaited upcoming appointment with Dr. Angelou. "Her schedule has just filled up. I'm sorry," the secretary had apologized with a sugary drawl. Shainee and I took turns being angry, disappointed, frustrated, and then quietly sad, as we were reluctantly forced to face yet another shrunken universe.

JIM ADKISSON

OREGON CHAPTER STATE CHAIRMAN, CHRISTIAN COALITION • CEO OF CHROME DATA

OREGON CITY, OREGON

(Shainee)

After our Christian Coalition mishap in Washington, we followed up with their press office to schedule an interview with one of their regional leaders. One of Ralph Reed's greatest contributions to the Coalition, since taking over at the age of twenty-seven, was his organization of the grassroots effort. The Coalition runs leadership schools all over the country and their motto is: "Think like Jesus . . . Fight like David . . . Lead like Moses . . . Run like Lincoln." Through phone trees, fax and modem dissemination, letter-writing campaigns, and satellite uplinking, Dr. Reed keeps members plugged in. As a result, the coalition has created a rapid response network that can effectively spread the profamily gospel by deluging any congressional office with calls within minutes of a decision to take action.

The Coalition has made their presence felt by targeting local elections, which they've won in almost every state in the union. As we saw at the Road to Victory rally, they have also brought their weight to bear on national elections. *Time* magazine has suggested that not since the theocracies of the seventeenth century has a religious organization made such an impact on the secular world. As Dr. Reed had stated at the Road to Victory, months before, with a membership of almost 2 million, the conservative right has earned their place at the table in the conversation called democracy. We wanted to find out who had helped Dr. Reed get there.

Our research took us to Jim Adkisson, the president of the Oregon chapter of the Christian Coalition and the CEO of a small software company called Chrome Data. Jim had helped with the financing of the start-up and they were having great success with their first couple of product releases to the auto sales industry. Chrome Data had also been named one of the top twenty best companies to work for in Oregon, ranking right after Intel and in front of Nike. Jim is active in the local Republican Party, as well as being a husband and father. He's a busy guy, but when we called him to ask if he wanted to participate in our project, he said he "sure would."

We were still disappointed that the Coalition had canceled our interview with Ralph Reed, but Jim sounded committed to our proposed meeting. His only condition was that we fax him the list of questions in advance and sign a release restricting the uses of the interview. He was glad that we were coming, saying that the national media tends to focus on the Coalition's activities in Washington rather than at the grassroots level. In his opinion, the real news was being made in the hinterlands, where he was working. We agreed to drive *back* across the country and meet at Jim's office in Oregon City, twenty miles south

of Portland. What's another 3,000 miles when we had already clocked 21,000?

We stayed with a friend in Seattle on yet another shared futon. On the day of the interview, we drove the few hours to Portland, crossing the Columbia River and the Lewis and Clark Trail. The weather was stereotypically Northwestern, with thick fog and light rain. People left their porch lights on all day and they shone like fireflies in the thick, grounded clouds, providing the only light in the early afternoon.

Chrome Data's office is an open space in which approximately fifty employees are seated in designated areas divided by linoleum paths. There is a sky-blue 1956 Chevy Bel Air on display in the middle of the split-level showroom, a sauna and gym upstairs. The man who oversees the buzzing office of the successful company is not an obvious match with the M.O. of the Christian Coalition member, described by *The Washington Post* in the same sentence as the words "poor, uneducated, and easy to command."

Jim greeted us at the door, giving us each a hearty handshake. He is a tall, heavy-set, middle-aged man with large, dark, deeply set eyes. His hair, the same color as his eyes, is thinning. He led us to a fluorescent-lit conference room, where there was no natural light available because of the weather. So while Kris battled with our limited lighting choices, Jim gripped the list of questions we had faxed, skimming it and humming nervously. He was obviously uncomfortable and asked if we wanted him to answer the questions personally or from a social perspective. "There is a difference between what I think the American dream is to me versus what I think the American dream *should* be for most people," Jim said.

We tried to quell Jim's apprehension and told him that either perspective would be valid and welcomed. Jim was still concerned. "You see a camera and you want to send the right message," he said. "My inclination is to be open and honest

and not worry so much about spin control. The Christian Coalition has a media office and they always want you to call and get prepped. I called and they gave me the general social and political message that they want to put across. Yet my message is quite personal." Kris finished laying a halogen lamp across three chairs, pointing it toward Jim's face. She told Jim to answer however he felt most comfortable, that we had no intention of putting him in an awkward position.

Jim took several deep breaths, his foot almost tapping a hole in the floor as I tried to calm him further, realizing that since he'd seen our list of interviewees, he must be aware of his somewhat token conservative status among the group. "The point of the film is to give different voices a chance to be heard," I told him. "We set out to find a common thread between people no matter what their religious or political beliefs, what region they live in, or how old they are. And we've found that. People can be completely on opposite sides of everything—they think. Yet, deep down, most people do seem to want the same things. We've been very lucky. We've found a thread of faith and hope and people really feeling like they can make a difference. The idea is: 'This is how I did it' or 'This is why I did it.' So whatever is *you* is what we're most interested in."

Jim relaxed a little and explained that past interviewers had seemed to view him as "austere." "But when they see what I'm about or what I'm doing, they see I'm exactly the opposite. I think that there is a lot of humor in life." When I thought Jim was ready, and through with his awkward disclaimers, I asked him to tell us about his background.

Jim began, "My dad was in the military. So I was an army brat. I grew up pretty well all over the world. My formative years were spent in Japan, Germany, and France. And that had a pretty strong influence on my perspective of the United States. The military is very proud to be American. Especially when you are living in a foreign country, you draw your identity from that."

"My father came from the typical *Grapes of Wrath* family. They were Okies, coming from Oklahoma, and they moved to California in a pickup with twelve kids. And we didn't have a whole lot, either, my dad being a sergeant in the army. So I was raised to be fairly resourceful and independent. I went into the army at a very young age myself. I had moved from Texas to Northern California, and the school systems were entirely different. Everybody cursed at the teachers in California, there was no real homework—it was such a culture shock. So I just got frustrated, quit, and ended up going into the army. I was seventeen. I missed an awful lot of what people my age experienced in the United States. My perspective was always one step removed from what was going on here. When I came back from Vietnam, I still wasn't old enough to get a drink in a bar.''

I asked Jim what effect his time in Vietnam had had on him and his feelings about the country.

''In terms of the antiwar movement, I didn't necessarily object to it, but I didn't really feel a part of it. I was looking to belong, and I couldn't quite belong to the rebellion that was going on at the time. I did get a jaundiced eye about a lot of things, but it wasn't about the United States, it was about it needing some reformation. There needs to be some establishment of truth and honesty in government and dealing with people. My experience of Vietnam was challenging, but it didn't sour me from the United States, didn't sour me on life.'' Jim paused. ''So I didn't turn on the United States. I turned on what I saw as the things that needed to be fixed.

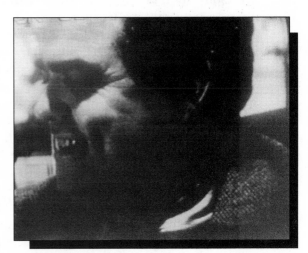

Jim Adkisson

''My experience in Vietnam certainly influenced me, but I think the thing that influenced me the most profoundly was when I became a Christian. Then I finally came into myself. That was about 1975. Up to that time I was in search of answers, in search of solutions, and purpose. My parents had been divorced. I didn't have a whole lot of support. I put myself through college and graduate school. When I got out of graduate school, my grades were good, but I couldn't find a job because I had no business experience. All the jobs I had, I took for pay—drilling wells, wherever the money was. I hadn't really paid attention to the value of having worked at an office. So I ended up coming back to Oregon with my wife and becoming a stockbroker and then helped start this business. And then I ended up taking over the position of state chairman of the Oregon chapter of the Christian Coalition.''

I asked Jim to tell us how he became the state chairman.

''It was sort of an accident,'' he replied. ''I am the type of person who always responds to a challenge. I hadn't even heard of the Christian Coalition, but there were some things going on here in the state that had gotten me politically involved. I was a foot soldier. I was getting petitions signed, raising money, going to rallies, and doing whatever the grassroots worker bee would do. Over the course of that period of time, Chrome Data became fairly successful, and I was approached by a fellow who asked me to get involved with the Christian Coalition—as sort of window dressing—on the board. They were trying to get a chapter going here in Oregon. The rest is history, as they say. This fellow resigned and there was no one there to pick up the slack, so I took the reins. One of my favorite sayings is that 'When it rains responsibility, people with broad shoulders get wet.' The Coalition has been around for three years. It's not really taking off here in this state.''

I asked Jim if he could get a little bit more specific about the politics that triggered his involvement. He seemed to get uncomfortable and started slowly. ''There had been several bills run in front of the state legislature here having to do with . . . with''—Jim paused to adjust the teetering halogen lamp. He kept his gaze on the suddenly fascinating lamp as his words rushed out—''having to do with this whole issue of minority status, homosexual rights, and things of that nature. And the bills had gone nowhere.'' Jim caught his breath and continued, ''The governor at that time, Neil Goldschmidt, on his own, issued an executive order, trying to establish in law what the legislature wouldn't do. Leaving aside any issues of a person's morality—or right or wrong—it was a complete circumvention of the legislative process. The bill had been debated and it was a Democratic legislature that turned it down. So the idea that by fiat, the governor was saying, 'This is the way things are gonna be, regardless of the will of people, regardless of the legislature,' felt wrong. That's how I ended up getting involved.''

Jim was referring to a bill that would have granted homosexual people the same rights against discrimination as any other minority. Jim and his wife, Christie, had been fighting advancements in gay rights and sex education for years. Governor Goldschmidt's efforts were ultimately defeated with the help of the conservative right. I asked Jim what other Christian Coalition accomplishments he was most proud of.

''Well, I think they've helped some people focus on an issue,'' Jim stated definitively. He leaned back in his chair and continued. ''There's an old saying that if you put a frog in water and turn the heat up slowly, you can boil the frog and he'll never even jump out. It's sort of a horrid analogy, but I guess it's true because I've heard it enough. Change is often like that—it's hard to identify what's really going on in a culture and what's happening. I think that the Christian Coalition has pointed out a subtle form of 'discrimination' that's been going on in our culture—political disenfranchisement, if you will.

''I'm not giving a conspiracy theory or anything, but if you are a conservative person of faith, somehow you are unacceptable. It's okay if you're a liberal person of faith—and we had a lot of that in the sixties. But the more traditional, orthodox, or more conservative people of faith—we're just persona non grata. When it came to political involvement, you had to check your faith at the door, and that's really just bigotry. The Christian Coalition has effectively pointed that out. When people who have an awful lot to offer no longer participate in the political process—because they've deemed it to be dirty or whatever—it's not good for the culture.''

I thought about Ralph Reed's reference to ''sitting in the back of the bus.''

Kris and I had had a visceral reaction to the metaphor, but it spoke to a commonality that made for strange bedfellows. Certainly, Jim was echoing frustration at being left out of the discussion, a feeling that had already been expressed by Wes Jackson, Chuck D, Winona Laduke, Jack Healey, and even Micah. Jim continued to explain the Coalition's contributions.

"The Coalition has done a lot of education in terms of our history. It's one of the most inspiring things that happened to me and I get pretty animated about it when I talk about it. How would you feel if you found out that you'd been lied to about the history of America?

"Studying the Founding Fathers, a lot of people say, 'Well, they're inspiring,' and they can usually quote a few verses out of the Declaration of Independence or whatever. But they really know very little of the founding of the country and what inspired the people who founded it. That has done a lot to shape my political involvement and a lot to straighten out my life too. They were people of principle, not because it was expedient but because they really did believe that if you find out what you believe, why you believe it, and you live consistently, it's the right thing to do. It's smart, it's good. It will bless you in life. The Founding Fathers—despite what a lot of visionaries want to say about them—were not perfect, but they were people of principle.

"Personally, I would really like to see the Christian Coalition accomplish one more thing—that people of faith are welcomed in government. I mean, when you go into the U.S. House of Representatives, and you look around the top at all the cameos, all the various lawgivers, Romans, etc., they're all in profile except for one that exhibits a full face, and that's the face of Moses, the chief lawgiver. Our heritage history is so interwoven with biblical concepts.

Kris stopped us because Jim's eyes were registering in the camera only as dark circles. "I've got a beetle brow, as they say," Jim apologized. We wrestled again with our jury-rigged lighting and Jim got on his knees to help us. When we got the problem straightened out, Jim continued, saying that there are whole sections of American history that are just not taught anymore. "You go back and read schoolbooks from a hundred years ago and the difference is amazing."

I told Jim that I was unaware of these missing holes and asked if he could give examples. He told us that his wife home-schools their children and uses books by Peter Marshall, who is the son of the former Senate chaplain. They also rely heavily on McGuffey's Readers, which are textbooks from the nineteenth century. "People back then really understood what they were doing when they set up the founding of this country and the three areas of government: the executive, the legislative, and the judicial. What people aren't told is that those are drawn right out of the Bible. And that's not me saying that—in their own words, the Founding Fathers say that. Faith and a belief in God had an awful lot more to do with the founding of this country than we are taught. You know how they say that the Pilgrims came here to escape religious persecution? We've always been taught that? It is totally and completely untrue. Not according to me, but according to their own words. They came here to propagate the Christian faith. They had religious freedom in whatever the country was that they came from.''

Jim paused for a second, trying to remember where the Pilgrims came from, and finally gave up, finishing, ''Well, they had it. If they really wanted religious freedom, they would have just stayed where they were at. They came here specifically, in their own words, to propagate the faith.''

He went on. ''James Madison, or George Washington, or one of them said that when they drafted the Constitution, it was drafted for a religious people, and it was wholly inadequate for anybody else. The reason they would say that is because all of the rights that we have in there and the privileges really do not work unless people have self-control. And what's going to give people self-control? Self-government,'' Jim declared emphatically. ''The population must be self-restrained. It all starts with fear of God. I don't want to give a sermon, but these people talked about this when they were setting up the government. To rip up the philosophy through historical revisionism, to take a lot of the facts away from the establishment of this country, really does an injustice to it.''

There was color in Jim's face as he reached for our list of questions to see what else he had missed. Then he remembered that he wanted to add to his last answer and the paper fluttered back to the ground as he continued, ''You know our first Supreme Court justice, a fellow by the name of John Jay—I think his name was—said something that would shock a lot of people. It was along the lines of that even if you're a person who doesn't believe in God at all, out of self-preservation, you should elect only Christians to office. Because if you have a person in office who doesn't fear God, in the dark of night, when no one's looking, who's going to control that person?

''I think that's part of the big problem we have in our culture—that governments are very rational in the way they behave—they follow whatever the prevailing philosophy is. All of the Lenins and Hitlers had a philosophy that they felt was very rational. But the Bible says, 'The beginning of wisdom is fear of God.' Flip it around and it means that you really can't have wisdom until you begin to fear God—fear, in terms of respect, not tremble. Know that there is a God, and you will be accountable; things do matter, whether anybody knows it or not.

''When leaders are alone and unaccountable, it means that you have to pass a whole ton of laws, because people can't be trusted when no one is looking. The thing I fear is if you look in modern history—I'm talking about the last hundred years—the greatest tragedies, in terms of a conscious loss of human life, would be the Holocaust in Germany, and the pogroms in Russia. Everyone needs to ask the question: 'How did that come about?' And I believe it came about because there was no fear of God in the prevailing philosophy. Nazi socialism started with this whole concept of Nietzsche is 'God is dead.'

"Look at the Japanese," Jim continued breathlessly. "They're a very civilized society and they're very cordial in terms of their etiquette, they have more cultural rules than we do; but they, as a people, have a very difficult time facing the war atrocities that their boys committed during the Second World War. 'How could it happen?' They couldn't quite figure it out, because it was unacceptable. But, you see, a Japanese mother will say to her child, 'Don't do that. People will laugh at you.' Whereas in the West you say, 'Don't do that. It's wrong.' There's a subtle difference there. One is that your behavior is enforced by the society and what the society thinks, and the other is that there's a right or wrong and you carry that with you.

"I think it has a lot to do with this concept of self-government. You go back to the McGuffey's Readers. All of the lessons were pulled right out of the Bible about the do's and don'ts. That has an influence on kids. Are they going to fear acting wrongly? Yes, they will. When someone's not looking, it will be in control of them.

"And I think that's particularly Western. You know, I'm not into ethnocentrism, but it is something that I think accounts for the rise of the West over the last couple hundred years. I think it's also going to account for its stagnation. That's something that I won't lay entirely at the left's feet, but I'm fearful about this country and the absence of God in government. Especially if it continues, through some mistaken doctrine of separation of church and state, that people of faith are asked not to participate in the political process. We're told, 'Keep it to yourself' or 'It has no place here.'

"There's a religious writer, he's dead now, he was popular in the late sixties and seventies, Dr. Francis Schaeffer. He taught in sort of a Socratic way, by asking a question that would cause you to learn. His question was: Would the average person today cut off their little finger if it would save a million people in China if no one would ever know? His point was that if you didn't believe in God, and you're going to be rational and you're going to be consistent, there is no reason to cut off your finger, because no one will know. And who is going to miss a million people in China? It sounds like one of those trick questions, but if you really begin to think about it, will a person in high office who doesn't believe in God, will they do the right thing? I don't think it's very hard to get to a point where you can justify just about anything. I fear that—where life is devalued.

"What other questions do you have?" Jim asked, resuming his humming and foot-tapping. He apologized for being long-winded. "It's sort of pompous to speak in such lofty terms." Kris consoled him, saying that most of our interviews take on the quality of those Thanksgiving Day conversations in which you talk about things you usually don't have time to discuss. Jim said it still felt kind of awkward and returned to perusing the list of questions. I said we'd pretty much covered everything, but he insisted on being thorough.

"How about what is my personal definition of the American dream?" Jim asked. "I thought about this question before work this morning. I can answer it two different ways. In terms of my social responsibilities, I would love to be found faithful, at the end of my life, to whatever the Lord has thrown my way—that I've done the right thing the best I could.

"The American dream to me has also meant that I could go as far as circumstance and talent would take me. And I didn't have to be born into the right group. Having grown up in the military and my father being an NCO, a noncommissioned officer, that was a class-based society. So I know what it's like to be viewed as a second-class citizen. The American dream to me is the opportunity to go as far as you can, given circumstance and opportunity and talent. It's not the guarantee, it's not a check that you can cash. It's merely the opportunity and you don't have to go and get someone's permission."

Jim was satisfied that we had reached the end of the list, except for the question of heroism. He said that his heroes in business are Sam Walton and Warren Buffett. Kris asked for his opinion on Dr. Reed. Jim sighed, saying "I don't know enough about him. I've read most of his stuff. He's very inspiring, a very sharp fellow. He's thinking down the road, a year, a year and a half, and Lord behold, you get down the road a year, and you turn around and, boy, this guy was really right. I don't know how Pat Robertson found him, but it was a very fortuitous sort of thing. Matter of fact, somebody who works here went to school with him and he used to be, I guess, a real cut-up and a real prankster and a real party animal.

"So Ralph Reed's an inspiration and I guess being in the Christian Coalition, I'm supposed to hold him up and all that. But he's just a regular sort of guy. He's disconcerting because he's so smart and yet so boyish. But he's pretty much exactly like he appears. There isn't a duality to him or anything like that. So I'm amazed by what Ralph has accomplished. The closest parallel that I can draw to the Christian Coalition is the old Walt Disney Company. Disney used to be just a crackerjack operation and whatever Ralph Reed and the Christian Coalition have gotten involved in has really been crackerjack. Matter of fact, they're always beating me up with memos about going out and getting more people involved and really educating, trying to get a little competition going from different states. One of the other nice things is that people that are not really supporters of the Christian Coalition are now supporting us financially—the key component of the vote is our constituency. And I think they're just underwriting success.

"But you didn't ask me who a hero is. I really dislike Richard Nixon. When I explain this, then you'll understand the flip side of who a hero is to me. When everybody listened to the Richard Nixon tapes and all of the foul, foul language, and the mean attitude he had about a lot of people and the way he looked at the world, you saw a very little man that was very much concerned about what history would say about him. A hero to me is someone that is willing to sacrifice in secret. Just common everyday folk, like a single mom, for instance. To me, they're heroes.''

We were finished and Jim heaved a sigh of relief, immediately launching into suggestions for restaurants and directions to the bed–and–breakfast he had kindly arranged for us to stay in. We asked him if he wanted us to sign the release he'd mentioned regarding the uses of his interview. He said no, that he had changed his mind, having spent time with us.

Everyone in the office had gone home hours before. It was dark and getting late. We thanked him for giving us his entire afternoon, noting that he was running a considerably large operation, and they had probably missed him that day. As he walked us to the car, telling us to drive carefully in the icy rain, he answered, ''Yeah. You know, with business being a success and the way things are going, it does look like I'm gonna be very very privileged in life. I already am in many ways. But I do pray that I'm humble and that I'm faithful when everything is said and done. It's hard, because I'm human and it's easy to be enticed. It's easy to get a swelled head. I'm talking with someone who is going to be running for Congress, and she would like my advice. I mean, that's nice. But it is vanity . . . and that's what I fear.''

TOM ROBBINS

AUTHOR OF *STILL LIFE WITH WOODPECKER, EVEN COWGIRLS GET THE BLUES,*
SKINNY LEGS AND ALL, ETC.

LE CONNER, WASHINGTON

(Kristin)

Over the past months, Shainee and I had watched the seasons change from the fishbowl of our car. I loved the feeling of moving through a season from one state to the next; driving through the Northwest had been like an extended scenic car wash. This particular gray Sunday offered up the kind of somber weather that made me think of lost love, a house I might someday build far away from a city, and growing old.

Just as Tom had promised, we passed a giant totem pole—with President Roosevelt's initials carved near its crown—before our last left turn into his tiny town. "It's a WPA totem pole," Tom had said while giving us directions over the phone.

We knocked on the front door of his office, a small house in a quaint neighborhood that he had converted into a workspace. Tom welcomed us in with few words. Pop and Eastern art co-mingled on the walls, and I could see his desk upstairs, planted under a skylight that filled the room with the grayish natural light.

Our initial exchange with Tom was somewhat awkward and strained. I felt intimidated by him, which was strange and unexpected, considering how few times that emotion had surfaced during any of our interviews. I was particularly surprised to find it creeping in near the *end* of the trip. Perhaps because his novels are so wild and quirky, I wondered if Tom would be equally unpredictable.

A Tom Robbins fan is usually a fanatic, and I have long believed everyone should read his work, for many reasons, but particularly for the sheer value of the way he explodes one paradigm after another. Which is, in essence, why we had hoped to interview him. Not to mention that his novels seem to reveal a deep appreciation and understanding of American culture.

358

Tom asked us if we wanted to follow him to his home and do the interview there. I thought it was a great idea, considering he had mentioned over the phone that he lived on the Swinomish Indian res- ervation and I was feeling claustrophobic. I figured the drive would soothe my sud- den anxiety spasm.

We followed him for miles as the ter- rain grew increasingly more lush, and I grew increasingly calmer as the space be- tween houses widened. We pulled up to Tom's home, which sits on the last piece of earth overlooking Puget Sound. As we followed him inside with our equipment, our camera knocked into a wooden plaque that read: WELCOME—WINDY CLIFF.

Inside, we were greeted by two Bud- dha figures anchored on either side of the door. Tom's place was not what I would call fancy or large, but it was decorated with an assortment of eclectic art, antiques, toys, and artifacts. He admitted that he had decorated the house himself, so I wasn't entirely surprised by the bold and competing colors—the cobalt-blue leather couch; the canary yellow fireplace; the orange toy chest; the circus posters and Asian art springing up in every other heroic color. It was a joyful place, in contrast to the gloominess outside. Rows of windows substituted for exterior walls in every room, so the house was also adorned with magnificent views of the Pacific Ocean.

We started to tell Tom more about *Anthem*, to prepare him for the interview. "I saw your materials and your list of people," he said. "I liked that you called Hunter Thompson a novelist, because I've never seen him referred to as anything besides a journalist. But I've always thought of him as a novelist."

"We were actually curious if you two had ever met," I said.

"No, we've never met," he answered, looking himself surprised. "But we had the same editor—a guy at Bantam Books who was fired but kept on retainer just to deal with me and Hunter. I guess the guys in New York thought we were a little too wild to deal with. So this guy would go out and spend time in Woody Creek with Hunter and then he'd come out and spend time with me. I got all the stories, but we've never met. I was invited to a Halloween party of his once—his Woody Creek Gun Club—but I couldn't go."

Talking more with Tom, I began to realize that our initial awkwardness in his office had been because he is shy. I hadn't expected that one. Sitting in his living room, our conversation became easy, the pauses naturally filled with laughter and more words, and I was relieved. "Do you mind if I sit on the alligator?" Shainee asked, pointing to a sturdy life-size wooden reptile bench.

"As long as you call it a crocodile," Tom corrected, and cleared his throat for a sound check: "Barrelhouse kings with feet unstable sagged and reeled and pounded on the table beat an empty barrel with a handle of a broom hard as they

were able, boom, boom, boom, with a silk umbrella and a handle of a broom, boome-lay, boomelay, boomelay, boom." Huh. Most people just count to ten or say their name. Shainee asked Tom to give us some background on himself. "I'm basically a hillbilly," he answered, adding that he grew up in Appalachia as the grandson of two Baptist preachers. "I spent my youth in the highest incorporated town east of the Rockies: Blowing Rock, North Caro-lina. And for nine months of the year, Blowing Rock was a little Dogpatch hill-billy town where the principal economic endeavor was taking empty beer bottles back to the store for the deposit.

"But, in the summer, it was a very swank summer resort. In the twenties, thirties and forties, it was a *Life Styles of the Rich and Famous* sort of place. So every year, around the first of June, a transformation would occur, and this hillbilly town would suddenly become pop-ulated with people in tennis whites, wearing lots of gold jewelry and driving fancy cars. There would be boutiques with the latest fashions and a movie theater that showed feature films as soon as they opened in L.A. or New York. In September, that all shut down. I think from that came the idea of transformation, which has really permeated my work. It also gave me an affinity for both sides of the tracks. I'm attracted to low life and high life."

Tom's attraction to low and high life was also revealed by his attire. He wore a colorful checkered shirt, blue polka-dot tie, a bomber jacket with the words CHINA DOLL embroidered across the back, mustard yellow high-tops, pink socks, and snake and moon rings on more fingers than not. Shainee asked Tom if there had been a specific American movement or philosophy that had captured his interest in a profound way.

"Well," he began, "I've always thought that movements were for Beethoven and the bowels, so I've stayed away from movements. But to answer your ques-tion, I was definitely a part of the antiwar movement during the sixties, until at one point it occurred to me that the people on the streets were just another army. Things started to get a little out of hand and I decided if you're for peace, then you should live peacefully.

"What I like about America is the haven it provides for individuality. See, I think one individual spirit can supersede and dismiss the entire machinery of history. An individual can overwhelm any one movement. Just the fact that America seems to foster individuals, although there is a great deal of pressure—and it seems to be growing daily, if not hourly—against individual expression and individual freedom in this county, still I think there is more individualism here than any other place on earth,'' he said, pausing.

''Say, if America were Swiss cheese and all of its faults were holes, there would hardly be enough left to make half a sandwich. *But* that sandwich has so much tang, the flavor of that sandwich is undeniable! For all of its faults, there's an edge here that you simply do not find in tired old Europe or fatalistic old Asia. And it's that edge, that roar, that flavors the sandwich, and that I find extremely nourishing!''

We started to talk about the current state of the American experiment, which evolved into a discussion about life in America as we enter the twenty-first century.

''See, I think,'' Tom said, ''we have to ask ourselves—and this is corny in a way—but what are we doing *here?* Not what are we doing in *America*, but what are we doing on this planet? What are we doing in this *world*, this *life?* And I've become convinced, after a lifetime of asking that question, that we are here to enlarge our souls, light up our brains, and liberate our spirits. And wherever I travel all over the United States, I find people who have a great longing to—it isn't always consciously expressed, in fact, it is seldom consciously expressed—to connect with what I call the 'Mystery,' for want of a better word. Mystery with a capital *M*. There's some kind of a cosmic connection that human beings seem to need and require and long for when they don't have it. This longing for ritual and celebration and—dare we use the word—magic. What surprises me continually is how few serious writers ever address that need.''

One of the most surprising commonalities that had surfaced among many of the people we met was an acknowledgment of that connectedness to a mystical aspect of life. And, ultimately, it was the longing to connect to that Mystery that is in both America and Americans that kept us on the road.

''In our months on the road, we've seen a lot of that,'' Shainee relected. ''And it's connected to something that we wanted to ask you about: the frontier spirit that is an integral part of your writing. We were wondering where that interest came from.''

''Well,'' Tom replied, ''it may still be the inbred, intrinsic part of all Americans to be on the road. I did a lot of hitchhiking when I was younger and I tried to never accept a ride if I knew where the driver was going. Because the adventure of the journey is what is important, and I think that can also apply to literature. When I begin a book, I do not have the remotest idea of where it's going. I have a sense of an overall effect that I want to create, I know some questions that I want to raise and maybe some answers I want to attempt, but I do not know where the plot is going, not even two or three pages down the road. And I think that's probably analogous to hitchhiking and this American penchant for travel and adventure.

"Out here on the Pacific Rim, we've gone as far, physically, as one can go, unless you count Hawaii. So when people land here, they either double back and retrace their steps, head east again, or they turn inward. And particularly here in the Northwest, where there is so much rain and inclement weather, there is a tendency to turn in on yourself and become introspective, which is also a part of the American character at a certain point of its development. Not generally true of society at large, which tends to be self-satisfied, money-crazed, and unreflective. But people who land out here on the Rim, on the edge, looking not back to Europe—from where most of our ancestors came—but toward Asia, do tend to turn inward. And for that reason, it's no surprise that many of the major developments or new trends have had their genesis here—from the psychedelic movement to Zen Buddhism and oriental systems of liberation."

We asked Tom if he believed in the American dream.

"I think the American dream is destroying the American dream," he declared without another word.

"Do you want to expand upon that?" Shainee asked.

"Not really," he said, covering his face shyly, then continued anyway.

A shyer side of Tom

"Well, you ask many people what they think of when they think of the American dream, and they think of a home of their own. Well, all these little single-family homes and all these little strip-mall one-story businesses are destroying the nation; they're destroying the land. It's urban sprawl coast to coast now. Americans know a lot about horizontals, because we're in such a large country with so many wide-open spaces. But we don't know much about verticals. I think we've got to start thinking vertically.

"My vision is for a vertical America— buildings that are two hundred miles high, not two hundred stories, but two hundred *miles* high. They would be so high that the top would be in orbit, which is what would actually hold them in place. Otherwise, they would be so heavy that the earth would tip on its axis. Now, they'll have to be made out of glass, because sand is the only raw material we have in enough abundance to support their manufacture. But you wouldn't need very many of them—maybe half a dozen in the whole country.

"Then the rest of the country can go back to agriculture and to wilderness. Buffalo will roam the plains again, vast herds of elk will migrate from New York to San Francisco, and we'll all be in these buildings two hundred miles high. You might be on one floor and your son or daughter is going to college on another floor, and you maybe see them at Christmas and Easter. And the elevators would be so big that you could have rock concerts in them. We have the technology to do that. So think vertical America.''

I chuckled to myself with the vision of a whole new landscape of vertical Manifest Destiny—thin air primed for the conquering.

''We read this thing on the Internet about you,'' Shainee said. ''An interview where you mentioned a Gary Snyder poem, and people living underground . . .''

''Yeah,'' Tom said, remembering. ''Gary Snyder has this wonderful vision of a future in which twenty-first-century tribes will spend six months of the year working underground with computers, the most advanced technology. And the other six months, spend roaming with migrating herds of elk, crossing the wilderness with great herds of migrating animals. So Gary's vision is to go underground, mine is to go up. But it doesn't matter. Whatever we do, we're going to have to do it hand in hand with wild nature or the human soul is going to diminish or possibly perish.''

Shainee asked Tom if he felt the ideals set forth by our founding parents, particularly liberty, the pursuit of happiness, and equality, were goals we were indeed approaching.

''Everything on earth, I suppose, has an upside and a downside,'' he qualified. ''And we are now living on the downside of democracy. Democracy, from its very inception in ancient Greece, had a built-in flaw, and that flaw has now become larger than the overall concept. And that flaw is that sooner or later, unless it were engendered with particular intelligence and sensitivity, democracy will come to be a matter of votes. Votes have become more important than ideas, than *ideals*, than people. Ninety-nine percent of politicians today are primarily interested in getting elected and being reelected. So that all the emphasis has switched off of the ideals, off of the ideas, off of a government, off of *governing*, really, to elections. Having said that, I still think that there's a greater possibility and greater potentiality for freedom here than anywhere in the world.''

Tom's comment reminded me of the story George McGovern had told us about the kid who had come to his office seeking McGovern's approval for his chosen curriculum of poll-taking, mass media, and advertising as a way to launch a career in politics.

''The trouble with democracy, too,'' Tom continued, ''is that it also runs the risk of becoming too egalitarian. I think that life—nature certainly—is elitist. But 'elite' has become a dirty word in the United States. Thomas Jefferson said that there is a false aristocracy based on wealth and title and property and family name. But that there is a *true* elite based on talent and intelligence and virtue. And in *that* particular elite I strongly believe, and I believe that will be the salvation for this nation—if there is a salvation.''

As I watched Tom through the viewfinder, the trees behind him bowed back and forth, parting themselves to offer us a glimpse of the stormy clouds and ocean beyond. Shainee asked Tom to tell us what the landscape means to him and what he loves about the physicality of his region.

"I'm here for the weather," he explained, his eyes glowing the same gray-blue as that weather. "The more it rains, the better I like it. My friends and acquaintances become suicidal after days and days of rain. I just get happier and happier. I think one reason why I came here was because I found in the Pacific Northwest an external climate that matched my internal climate; I think it's always been raining inside my head. There's something so intimate and romantic about this area, and I am, quite unabashedly and unashamedly, a romantic.

"So, this is my perfect environment. I spend most of my time in my work-room. I have a skylight over my desk and I sit there and look up while the rain drums its millions of fingers on the skylight and it's like an opening in the sky where all this energy can come through. That sounds pretty corny and mysterious—and it *is* kind of corny and mysterious—but it's very real. It is nourishing. A few raindrops on the brow keeps the soul green. Plus," he added, "I just love that this is where the frontier *stopped*. This here is the end of the road."

Knothole in a junkyard fence

I had almost forgotten until I heard Tom's last thought, that this place symbolized the end of the road for Shainee and me, too. After Tom, we would leave the Northwest and head to our final destination of New Orleans, where we had planned to begin the enormous task of editing our nearly 200 hours of footage. *Anthem* had taken us to almost every state and back again, and even though we were weary of borrowed couches and rented beds, fast food, and even each other, the thought of suddenly losing the newness of each day was terrifying.

Shainee's voice drew me from my daydream back to the moment as she asked Tom what motivated him—what gave him the temerity to get out of bed every day.

"Well," he began, "if you want to understand yourself, and understand your gender and your race, who you are and why you are here; if you want to look at life as a broad panoramic viewpoint, rather than through a knothole in a junkyard fence, then there is one place where you have to go and stand. And that place is where language and myth intersect at the imagination. It's a three-way street, and when I rise each morning, that's where I go to stand."

After the interview, Tom asked us if we wanted to take a walk to the edge of his property. We put on our jackets and wound down the path behind his house.

It did feel like the end of the earth, or at least America. I was caught up in shooting scenery and suddenly found myself alone—apparently Tom and Shainee had announced that they were heading back to the house, but the wind had swallowed their voices. I stood there for a while, just watching the elements spar.

Back in the quiet of his living room, Tom offered us his "special ginger ale," which was gladly accepted, our mouths dry from hours of talking. "I get this stuff shipped to me from South Carolina. Do you want spicy or super-hot?" he asked, sticking his head into the fridge.

"Uh, spicy?" I both asked and answered.

"Well, the original ginger ale was very spicy," he informed me, handing over a bottle. Shainee was in the bathroom, so Tom popped open a super-hot recipe for her and sat it on the counter to await her return.

The bottle felt cold, and I guzzled with thirsty relief. And then came the carbonated fire. "It's not hot until it goes down. Way down," I said to Tom, understanding for the first time what an ulcer must feel like. I calmly glanced around the kitchen looking for something soothing to swallow—like absorbent white bread or maybe a diaper—but saw nothing.

"Aren't you going to have one?" I asked, trying to keep my mind off the hole in my stomach. "No, I can't," he said, "because a while ago I thought I was having a heart attack. I had to spend four days in intensive care because I drank too many of these one day, and it touched off spasms in my esophagus. The emergency room doctors thought I was having a heart attack. I never told them it was caused by my favorite ginger ale."

"And now you're offering it to guests?" I asked, taking another swig without thinking.

"Are you okay?" he asked.

"I might be," I said, breathing invisible flames. "It's too soon to tell." Tom then told me that he used to drink about four a day, before the emergency room visit.

"The one good thing that came out of the scare is that the doctors who worked on me did tests and said, 'You have the heart of a twelve-year-old boy.'" This statement seemed too true; a vulnerable, hopeful, awkward twelve-year-old boy.

"That's great," I congratulated him.

"Yeah, but I told the doctors, 'I hope the kid doesn't want it back.'"

Just then Shainee came out of the bathroom and Tom nonchalantly handed her the drink. For the record, I determined that for Tom, offering the ginger ale was not, in fact, an amusing practical joke; he really did believe he was introducing us to the tastiest, most exciting drink on earth. I warned Shainee that it was a beverage unlike any other. "You might need a chaser," I suggested as she gulped. She winced a little, but it didn't seem to light her up the way it had me.

We heard the front door open, a gust of wind finding its way to the kitchen, followed by Tom's wife, Alexa. She was lovely, with a jet-black bob and knowing eyes.

"Oh, you went for the ginger ale," she said immediately, setting bags on the counter.

We all talked for about an hour in the kitchen, Shainee casually sipping her ginger ale and gaining more of my respect by the swallow.

Tom's letterhead

The afternoon fell away, gray becoming grayer, as Shainee and I eventually packed up to leave. "I wish you the luck I wish myself," Tom said with a sincerity that stopped Shainee and me in our tracks. We thanked him for his kind words and for inviting us into his home despite the fact that he didn't like on-camera interviews. Tom and Alexa stood next to their WELCOME—WINDY CLIFF sign, waving goodbye.

Shainee and I found ourselves missing Tom over the next few days, wishing we could pass him hitchhiking and promise *not* to tell him where we were going. A few weeks later, we got a call on our voice mail. It was Tom, asking if we'd gotten his note in the mail. We hadn't, so we called and he said he'd re-send it. Because getting mail while living on the road is not a science and finding an apartment in New Orleans took longer than we'd expected, we missed his note over and over again. He ended up sending it four times, and eventually all four found their way to us. The first page of the letter was a sweet thank-you note. The only other person who had sent us a thank-you note had been George McGovern.

The second page was an addendum to Tom's interview. Before we had left his windy cliff, Tom had bemoaned his lack of verbal ability. "If I can look at a blank sheet of paper," he had explained, "and I have that ballpoint pen in my hand, I can usually get it all out, but not when I have to say it." We told him that if he thought of anything he'd like to add, he could always pull out that ballpoint—or typewriter ribbon—and send it to us. We never thought he'd take us up on it, but he did. Four times.

TAKE 3

America is a nation of 250 million people. A 100 million of them are gangsters, another 100 million are hustlers, 50 million are complete lunatics, and every single one of us is secretly in show business. Isn't that fabulous? I mean, how could you fail to have a good time in a country like that? I could live literally anywhere in the world and do what I do, so, obviously, I live in America by choice—not for any patriotic or financial reasons but because it's so *interesting* here. America may be the least boring country on earth, and this despite the fact that the dullards on the religious right and the dullards on the academic left seem to be in competition to see who can do the most to promote compulsory homogenization and institutionalized mediocrity. It won't work. In America, the chronically wild, persistently haywire, strongly individualistic, surprisingly good-humored, flamboyant con-man sizzle is simply bigger than all of them.

—Tom Robbins

WILLIE NELSON

CO-FOUNDER OF FARM AID • SINGER/SONGWRITER

NEW ORLEANS, LOUISIANA

(Kristin)

Willie Nelson was at the top of our *Anthem* wish list. Republicans love him, Democrats love him, grandparents love him, farmers love him, women *love* him. And we love him, too.

We were particularly interested in Willie because of his work on behalf of the American farmer. He is a founder and continued supporter of Farm Aid, an organization that provides relief for family farmers in crisis and works to keep our nation's family farms intact. Like Amnesty International, Farm Aid is most famous for its benefit concerts, which bring together the talents and support of such artists as Neil Young, John Mellencamp, Bonnie Raitt, and, of course, Willie.

Arranging an interview with Willie was no easy task. He tours for months at a time and is rarely in the same city for more than twenty-four hours. At first the plan was to meet him in Kentucky during the tenth anniversary Farm Aid concert, but his publicist called at the last minute and told us we'd have to reschedule. As usual, things got down to the wire as Willie neared the end of his U.S. tour and was leaving immediately thereafter for the South Pacific for yet *another* tour. Finally we got everybody to agree to an interview after a private show in New Orleans on the very last night he would be in the country.

We had hoped to move into our new apartment in New Orleans a few days before the interview so we could get settled and begin to prepare for the edit, but we got hung up on the road and had to do a marathon drive just to make it to Willie in time—surprise, surprise.

When we finally wound down the trellis-lined balconies of the French Quarter it felt like a homecoming, minus the out-stretched arm greeters. I poked my head out the car's sunroof shooting *that* week's holiday decorations competing from balcony to balcony. (Every week in New Orleans is an excuse to have a holiday.) An eerie sense of conclusion hung in the air, but I think Shainee and I both believed that if we didn't discuss the fact that our trip was ending, it wouldn't actually be true. We were both excited to be moving to New Orleans—a city we had come to love during our initial visit— but the idea of a stationary life now felt foreign to us.

We arrived at the Hyatt Hotel and took the escalator up to the Regency Ballroom, where Willie was performing for a business association's private party. The men milling about the gigantic ballroom wore mostly black suits, accented with Willie-esque red bandannas, and the women were dressed in sequinned formals. Willie tunes were blaring through the surround-sound speakers as the attendees got more and more intoxicated with youthful giddiness and anticipation of the appearance of the braided one.

We searched around for Willie's road manager, Larry, and found him near the sound board. He bore an uncanny resemblance to Willie himself. We talked to Larry for a few minutes and made a plan for the interview after the show. Larry slowly rubbed his throat while he talked to us—too many cigarettes, I imagined.

Larry was just starting to get into juicy details of road life with Willie when the lights dimmed and people rushed to their seats. Larry disappeared, and Shainee and I moved to the front of the hall to shoot the concert. Then Willie took the stage and was greeted with enormous applause and whistles. He and the band moved easily through the classics: *Whiskey River*, *Georgia*, *All of Me*, *On the Road Again*, and *Mamas Don't Let Your Babies Grow Up to Be Cowboys*, this last song inspiring almost everyone in the audience to sing along. There was a woman in the front row with big blonde hair who swayed in her chair and mouthed the words to every song. On the first few chords of *You Were Always on My Mind*, she began to weep, her mascara going down with tears. On the second verse, Willie was joined by a surprise local guest, "Sheriff Harry," who shook slightly with nervousness while he sang the chorus with his long-haired idol.

Willie and his band turned out a two-hour-plus concert with four encores, treating it no differently than a big-venue

In concert

show like Farm Aid. It was an unusually intimate setting and Willie seemed so comfortable onstage, as if it were a concert for friends in his living room. After the fourth encore, the band left the stage and didn't return, except for Willie, who stayed to sign autographs.

I sat on the edge of the stage, about ten feet away from Willie's post-show "show," admiring this sixty-two-year-old man who smiled genuinely for each photo, kissing everyone on the cheek as they squealed with delight. I think ''saintly'' was the word that came to mind, knowing how exhausted Willie must have been. When he finally escaped, the concert equipment and the stage had already been broken down, except for a giant American flag and some naked scaffolding.

Kisses and autographs

Shainee and I followed a roadie out to the buses where they were loading the equipment. We were asked to wait outside Willie's tour bus, the Honeysuckle Rose, while Willie took a few minutes to unwind. Shainee and I stood next to the airbrush-painted bus, me thinking back to Willie's well-publicized love affair with Dyan Cannon and Shainee wishing we had a whiskey flask to pass between us to warm our bones. It was unusually cold in New Orleans, and wind was whipping through the passageway between the dumpster and the bus where we stood.

We observed the busy crew methodically packing hard cases, microphone stands, and speakers, and it dawned on me that *most* of the people who worked with Willie bore a striking resemblance to him. They all had his long hair, his jeans, his bandanna, and his placid aura—the only difference being that they were all a tiny bit more weathered than Willie, whose vitality belies both his age and tour schedule.

Larry waited with us—obviously feeling bad that we had to wait outside—and told us stories of his and Willie's concert exploits. Larry had been working with Willie since 1978, so neither had been home very much in the last twenty years. Shainee and I had gotten a taste of road life, but Willie and his crew had turned movement into a life*style*.

''You should get some footage of this bus,'' Larry encouraged, looking at the Honeysuckle Rose admiringly. ''It's not going to be around much longer.''

''Why?'' we asked.

''Well,'' he said, looking left and right for eavesdroppers. ''Don't tell nobody, but I think we're gonna get a new one. Probably around the springtime, I hope.''

We promised Larry his secret was safe with us until springtime, just as one of the other Willie look-alikes stuck his head out of the bus to welcome us aboard.

''Wow,'' I said, climbing in, unable to see the end of the bus from where I stood. ''Lots of smoke.'' Willie emerged from the haze at the back of the bus, drawing us forward with his soft-spoken voice.

"Hello, ladies," he said politely. "Sorry to keep ya'll waiting." He extended his hand out for a shake.

"No problem," we said in unison. "It's nice to meet you."

We set up our equipment as Willie began to braid his hair and ask us questions about our travels.

"How *is* Hunter?" he asked, upon hearing his name, becoming part of the motif of curiosity regarding the King of Fear and Loathing. Turns out Willie and Hunter have a long-distance respect for one another.

While I finished setting up, Shainee told Willie where we were from, and he did the same. "Well, I was born in 1933, and grew up in Abbott, Texas," he said, sipping his coffee from a tin camping cup. "Abbott is a small town, probably around

The bus

three hundred population. It's a great town. I still have a place there and I go back to spend time. Well, I try to."

I had a distinct feeling that Willie didn't spend too much time *anywhere*.

Shainee told Willie that we had read that he started writing songs when he was about ten years old and asked if he remembered what inspired him at that age to do that.

"I don't really know, because when I started writing there was no reason for me to be writing these poems about heartbreak and things I obviously had no experience with at that point in my life," he said, resting his chin on his hand. "But I was doing it, and soon after that I started writin' melodies and learnin' some chords on a guitar, and so it went from poems to songs."

Willie went on to explain that his parents had separated when he was very young and that he and his sister—who still performs in his band regularly—were raised by their grandparents from the age of six months. I wondered if Willie didn't know more about heartbreak as a young boy than he let on.

"Did your grandparents instill a philosophy that influenced your life and work?" Shainee asked.

Willie smiled before responding. "My grandparents were very involved in singing and gospel music, and we attended the Methodist church there in Abbott. So I grew up in the church, really. And we would go to Hillsboro, which was only ten miles away, an' on Wednesday nights they'd have singing conventions. People would get together and sing gospel and sing out of these songbooks."

Willie explained that shortly after he married his first wife, he sold his first song, *Family Bible*, for fifty dollars, so he could feed his family. During those early years, he sold encyclopedias and Bibles door-to-door, worked as a plumber's ap-

prentice, janitor, and disc jockey while continuing to write and perform in local Texas bars and clubs. We knew that Willie still kept his permanent residence in Texas, and we asked him if there was something specific about the region that made him want to stay there.

"What I like about Texas is there's no one in control," he said as we all started to laugh at its truth. "It keeps me going back. It's just a great place to live. The people are good, the land is good. It's difficult to describe because when you start talking about it, it sorta destroys it in a way. What I would want to say could never capture the place. You have to *experience* it. Texas is just a special place."

Willie and Shainee

"We read that at Farm Aid's tenth anniversary show," Shainee explained, "you said that when you started Farm Aid, you had hoped there would not still be a need for the benefit concerts ten years later. Do you think what's going on with the family farmer mirrors what is going on with the country in any way?" she asked.

"It mirrors what's going on with the *planet*," Willie said, emphatically. "What's happening to the farmer here is happening to the farmer in China, it's happening to the farmer in Russia, it's happening to the farmer everywhere. The backbone of the planet is sorta in bad shape. So, yeah, it's a serious problem for the earth, but more of a problem for the *people* than for the earth, because earth will survive. All she has to do is cough a couple of times and a million people are dead. So it's to our advantage to take care of the earth, because the earth might not care if we stick around," he said with a nervous laugh.

"What do you think about the American dream as it relates to the farmer?" I asked.

"Well, I think now is a very important time in the history of our country," Willie said, "because when the farmer has problems, everyone has problems. There are numbers that back this up: when five farmers in this community go under, one business goes under. And then it all starts snowballing. It goes to the hospitals, the schools—entire towns become ghost towns, and the people move on, only to become a problem to the next town, because they're unemployed and they're homeless. Until we can put a young couple back on a couple hundred acres of land and they can make enough plowing it and milking cows to make a living, we're gonna have a problem.

"Corporate farming is not what this country needs," Willie declared. "Everyone who eats needs to ask themselves, 'Do I want my food grown by families or factories?'

"We need to make sure that we take care of the farmer, because when he goes under the whole country will go under. The fight to save family farms isn't just about farmers, even though they are a valuable part of our heritage, it's also about making sure that there is a safe and healthy food supply for *all* of us. It's about jobs from Main Street to Wall Street. And the soil itself is suffering. Every civilization that's gone under in the past has gone because of soil erosion and the inability to feed its people. And people say, 'Well, how can that affect us?' But a few years back, the state of Iowa lost over fifty percent of its topsoil. It is a real problem, and  we could be facing a famine—not only in this country but all over the world—if we don't take care of the soil."

Willie's words reminded us of Wes Jackson's. Willie hadn't heard of The Land Institute, but we promised to send him some literature.

"I think the focus in America has been on the bottom line," he said, continuing his thought. "Money, money, money, money, money. And as long as this is the focus, then we're headed for Hell in a handbasket. As we all know, flowers and things that grow naturally, if taken care of, do better, and the soil itself is no different. This is something that has slid by corporations' interests. They don't care for the land. They drain every acre of resource they can get from it, and then they move on to the next acre. We have to get small family farmers and small businesses back into the countryside."

"Driving around the country," Shainee explained, "it *seemed* like all we saw were small, family-owned farms. It's very sad to find out that many are an illusion, that many of them don't belong to *farmers*."

"Yeah," Willie responded. "You drive through these small country towns and there's maybe one store still open; everything else is boarded up. We're still losing five hundred farmers a week—last week, this week, next week."

"That's the rate?" I asked in disbelief.

"Yes," Willie said resolutely. "We started out with over eight million small family farmers, and now we're down to less than two million."

"And what role is Farm Aid playing in helping the farmer to keep his farm?" I asked, still stunned by the staggering number Willie had quoted.

"Farm Aid can only do so much," he explained. "It can only inform as to what's happening out there, and what little money that it takes in, it distributes as best it can.'' Willie went on, ''The American farmer should be part of the American dream. The American dream was born from the humble traditions of the American farmer, and as a culture, we've turned our back on that part of our history. The rehabilitation of this country has to start with the farmer, where the country began. It's naive to think that it could ever start any other way than with the soil itself and the people who care for it.''

It was almost 2 A.M., but Willie was just getting his second wind. Shainee brought the conversation back to center, asking Willie if he believed the American dream was still alive, despite its apparently damaged state.

''Oh, yeah,'' he said, becoming more animated. ''I don't think you can give up on the dream. We can see there are problems, there is a serious illness to the dream, but this is something that *can* be cured and healed,'' he said, adding, ''by us.''

I asked Willie how he saw us progressing as a nation. ''What direction do you see us going in?''

''Well, I love the line about the light at the end of the tunnel being a freight train,'' Willie said, laughing. ''But I believe that somewhere out there, there is a light that's not a freight train. Hopefully, it will come . . . sooner than later. There's a whole lotta positive things that are happening in the world, that are also creating a lot of havoc, because any time you start rattling the cages around you, you're going to upset the people who have locked you in.''

''Growing pains,'' Shainee added to Willie's comment.

''Growing pains,'' he repeated, smiling.

When asked for his thoughts on America's uniqueness, Willie's response was short and to the point. ''We're in an unusual position right now,'' he said, ''where the rest of the world is watching us. So I would believe it wise to, in turn, watch the rest of the world.''

Sitting with Willie, I was reminded of Micah, who in his infinite teenage wisdom had said, ''Knowing who you are is more important than knowing where you're going.'' Willie was someone who through his hard-earned years, seemed to know both. We started talking about traveling and movement and whether or not Willie had always loved the road or if it just grew on him.

''There's a whole lotta Gypsy in me,'' he answered, ''and I guess in all these other people that travel with me. We've always enjoyed traveling. It's addictive.''

''Yeah, we've grown attached to it as well,'' Shainee said. ''There's something very peaceful about moving.''

''And waking up in a different town every day is nice,'' Willie added.

''Yeah, we find that just about everyone we've met has wanted to come with us,'' Shainee offered. Willie laughed, having had the same experience. I imagined Honeysuckle Rose had had her fair share of stowaways.

''A friend of mine, Billy Joe Schaffer, has a saying that 'moving is the closest thing to being free,' '' Willie said, taking another sip of his coffee and swallowing with a heavy sigh. ''I think he's right.''

We chatted about Willie's upcoming tour in the South Pacific while we packed up our equipment. "You should come see me again," Willie said finally, still sitting in his tiny kitchen nook. "And please let me know how you're doin'. You're asking good questions; I'm curious to see how this will turn out."

"We'll certainly let you know as soon as we know," I assured him as Shainee and I heaved our bags over our shoulders.

"Drive careful," he added as he stood up, stretching his arms and legs. He watched us struggle a bit with our many bags and tripod. You could tell he'd known a lot of women who insisted on doing things themselves and thought it wiser not to intervene for fear of insulting us. We successfully maneuvered everything to the front of the bus, and I could tell our Abbott and Costello routine amused him. Willie swayed forward, stretching while he held on to the walls of his kitchen. "Ya'll need a roadie," he said, not able to hold back from stating the obvious any longer.

"Yes," I agreed. "Can you lend us one of yours?"

Before Willie could decline, we stepped out of the warm cocoon of the bus and back into the windy Southern night. Shainee and I stood still for a minute, staring at the bus. I thought about how fun it would be to buy the old Honeysuckle Rose when it got sent out to pasture. Maybe we could use it for an *Anthem 2* tour.

We started our trek back toward our car, which was parked about a mile away. "Those teeth!" I screamed, once we were out of earshot. "My God, that smile!"

"I know. He's *so* sexy," Shainee agreed, both of us surprised that Willie was even more alluring up close than he had been from afar. The Honeysuckle Rose passed us as we searched for our parked car, loudly singing the words to *Angel Flying Too Close to the Ground.* As the bus barreled by, we hoped our off-key crooning hadn't been heard through open windows.

We drove away from the Hyatt, past the familiar Dixie Mill Supply and New Orleans Copper Works, and into the French Quarter. We stopped for a drink at the Blacksmiths Shop, which leans drastically to one side, and has a piano player who plays only requests but can't remember the lyrics to *any* song. Having been away for more than six months, it was nice to find that some things never change. After our drink, we had to meet our date at Café du Monde.

Doug had suggested a late-night rendezvous for a "Welcome back to New Orleans" meal of coffee and *beignets*. As we sat down, the very same waiter we'd had on our first visit those months ago walked over to take our order, which seemed rather miraculous considering Café du Monde employs probably a hundred waiters. Doug walked in and ordered a large latté in preparation for the night's work. He always worked while other people slept—I think Hunter taught him that trick. It was good to see him, and it was comforting to know that we already knew one of our new neighbors.

I looked down at my watch, exhaustion creeping in from the long drive and our late-night encounter with Willie Nelson. The hands on my watch marked 3 A.M. sharp, and I realized that it was the exact hour at which we'd first arrived at Café du Monde, those many months ago. We had literally come full circle: New Orleans, Doug, the waiter, the hour, and a double order of *beignets*. I looked over at Shainee, who with powdered sugar covering her face, was recounting our night for Doug. And I felt, for the very first time, a sense of peace about planting ourselves in this one place, which we would, for now, call "home."

ROBERT REDFORD

FOUNDER/PRESIDENT OF THE SUNDANCE INSTITUTE • ACTOR/DIRECTOR/PRODUCER

SUNDANCE, UTAH

(Shainee)

Robert Redford had been the elusive Holy Grail throughout our trip. Personally, I'd become a little obsessed with putting one of my own heroes—and the man who was partially responsible for me believing I could make a film—in the film.

For the prior three years, attending the Sundance Film Festival had been part of my job responsibility. I'd also had the privilege of working closely with key festival staff, which influenced me greatly. Although I was already living in Los Angeles and working in the independent film community, it wasn't until I got to Sundance that I really understood what independent film meant.

Best known for its festival, the Sundance Institute was started in 1981 by Redford and some colleagues who wanted to "enhance the artistic vitality of American film." One of the first orders of business was to take over the U.S.A. Festival in nearby Park City, which ultimately became the internationally renowned Sundance Film Festival. A fair representation of the festival's annual programming is also shown at satellite Sundance festivals in Tokyo and Beijing. The institute sponsors "labs" in screenwriting, playwriting, directing, and producing. They workshop emerging American playwrights and have a children's theater program. They also sponsor filmmaking labs in Mexico, Brazil, Cuba, and Chile, with plans to include Hungary and Scotland soon. And the Sundance Channel appeared on American cable boxes recently, featuring independent films as the main portion of its programming.

Sundance began with a mountain. In 1969, Robert Redford purchased the Timphaven Ski Resort and much of its surrounding lands outside of Provo, Utah. He renamed it partially after one of his most famous roles, the Sundance Kid, and partially after its own raw beauty. Sundance is nestled in the Wasatch Mountains, a range of the greater Rockies. Unlike the red-rock cliff country of Zion and Bryce Canyon farther south, Sundance is a snowy wonderland in the winter and a pastoral paradise in the early summer, with riots of wildflowers blanketing alpine meadows and aspen groves. There are waterfalls and creeks, hiking and fly-fishing, a huge outdoor amphitheater with a mountain-crested backdrop, a couple of great restaurants—including the restored 1890s Owl Bar, which was frequented by Butch Cassidy's Hole-in-the-Wall gang—and, of course, a screening room with ongoing film programs for visitors. Guests stay in snug wooden cottages with cushy linens and stone hearths and the entire resort is run eco-consciously. It's—well—perfect.

Perfection is not necessarily surprising coming from one of America's favorite sons. Robert Redford's résumé reads like the "dream" American dream: actor, filmmaker, political advocate, and champion of the arts. And given how often Hollywood and the media had been cited as bad guys in our interviews, as the catalyst for the demise of the American hero, it seemed important to hear from a venerable Hollywood voice.

So I took it upon myself to send "the" venerable Hollywood voice a letter every couple of months for a year. It wasn't until we were settled in New Orleans and had begun editing our movie that I got the call from Redford's assistant, Wendy. Wendy was always prompt about returning our chain of calls, letters, and faxes. And she was always very nice and patient when letting us down. So when I heard her voice on the other end of the line while doing the dishes one day in our French Quarter apartment, I didn't get excited. The conversation began the same way it always did: "Hi, Shainee. It's Wendy Hopkins from Sundance. I spoke to Bob about your latest request . . ." (I found myself mouthing the expected ". . . and I'm sorry, but . . .") This time, however, she completed her sentence differently: ". . . and he wants to try to set something up in the next month." I was struck speechless. I mean, we were done. The cameras were already gathering dust under my bed, and we'd given up hope long ago of interviewing Redford. Now we'd be heading west—one last time.

Actually, scheduling the interview caused some of the most difficult maneuvering of the entire project. Bob, as we were instructed to call him, was crazy busy prepping a film in Montana and wasn't spending much time at the resort, but they thought it would be easier for us to meet in Utah than in Montana. So every weekend—for several weekends—Kristin and I were "on call" for the trip. Once we even got scheduled and were on our way to the airport when word came that the Sundance administrative building had burned down—and our long-awaited meeting would again have to be postponed.

When the day actually came, we didn't have much warning, so we had to grab a 6 A.M. flight with a nightmare layover in Houston. The day paid testament to the cruelty of Murphy's law: the flight was delayed on the ground, our luggage was lost, and our rental car was delivered only after an hour spent in a line that refused to move. We knew that Bob was flying in from Montana that afternoon specifically to meet with us, so our interview window was inflexible. By the time we hit I-15 out of Salt Lake City, we were already late and super stressed. We drove past the same boys hawking beef jerky out of a pickup truck three times, before we found the sign to the resort, which was, of course, hidden by construction. Wendy later told us she'd thought we'd been in a car accident.

When we finally checked in, we called Wendy at her office, hoping she would grant us half an hour to take a shower after our twelve-hour trek. She couldn't; Bob had to meet with the summer theater people right after us. The good news was that Wendy had set us up in a junior suite, so we had a generous supply of fluffy unbleached towels and colorful glycerine soaps with which to take a quick sponge bath. Of course we had eaten nothing—not wanting to break our record so late in the trip—but Wendy had thought of everything and ordered us box lunches that were waiting for us at the interview site.

We met Wendy in the Sundance offices. All of the buildings were designed to blend into the landscape and not detract from it, so the office was a cabin set back in the forest with big windows, light-colored woods, skylights, and solid inviting chairs in front of the fireplace. She was glad to see us and hurried us down a path, over a wooden bridge, to a wide lawn that rose from the back of the recreation hall. We picked a spot that was flanked by trees on one side and a brook babbling noisily on the other.

The staff at Sundance were all disarmingly helpful and pleasant. Wendy left to find Bob, but made sure we were taken care of, assigning two very cute young (too young for us) college boys to help us set up. We began to relax, the chaos of the journey melting away in the serenity of this place. There was a wedding about to begin on the other side of the bridge, and we could hear a quartet warming up as we munched on egg salad and potato chips while trying to steady the tripod on the steep slope of the hill.

Twenty minutes later we were ready, replenished, and calm. Gone was my anxiety about finally meeting this man that we had pursued and admired for so long. Suddenly it all felt very natural—the mountain air mixed with the smell of the restaurant's outdoor grill, the sound of water rushing past us toward the nearby Deer Creek reservoir, an intimate celebration of love happening a hundred feet away, hikers heading past us up to the waterfalls, and Robert Redford walking up the hill to meet us. Holy shit! Robert Redford is walking up the hill to meet *us!*

It was similar, I guess, to one of those moments that people experience when they think they're going to die or are about to say, "I do." Our whole trip flashed before my eyes as I watched the man in jeans, sunglasses, and that unmistakable golden hair climb the hill with his hand outstretched to shake ours. It had been a full year since we left Los Angeles to pick up that car in Tampa, and the people and places that had come into our lives all swirled into one happy, peaceful moment when I took the hand of our very last interviewee. I heard Wendy say, "Shainee, Kristin, this is Bob."

Bob had just gotten in and Wendy went to grab him a welcoming cup of coffee while we got him set up. He pointed to the chair that one of the fresh-faced boys had brought up the hill for us and smiled at its positioning under a tree. "So what have we here? You're going to frame me in my element, like I'm coming right out of the leaves," he teased. But Bob was glad we wanted him in the shade. He had also been operating on no sleep and apologized if he seemed sluggish. He didn't. At all. We explained that we had been up late editing the night before, and had been awake since 4 A.M., so we were all in the same boat. Wendy came back with a steaming cup of stimulant and we all settled in.

"So, *Anthem*. It seems like a really great project. It's a good idea. You might find the truth about the country this way," Bob stated simply, taking a sip.

"We hope so" and "We're looking," we answered simultaneously, as Bob checked our camera angles for us and began to give us his background.

"I was born in Los Angeles in 1937, during the transition between depression and war. So I had a wonderful beginning. I came into the world facing issues like rationing, heavy propaganda, and heavy patriotic jingoism, that I took all for granted and accepted because I was a child. It was a time that fewer and fewer people can now remember except through pictures, when there was still space in Los Angeles. But I do. I came from a relatively poor background; my father delivered milk, my mother was supporting the family. So there wasn't a lot of means, but there was space, and there was a good feeling in the air.

"Los Angeles in those days . . . Maybe it's revisionist, but I think it had a kind of provinciality to it. I really think Los Angeles changed after the war. It became such an incredible place of opportunity. The figures were staggering. They were coming fifteen hundred a day into Los Angeles County, without any abatement. So it was like Gold Rush, covered wagon time into the Los Angeles basin, and it finally backed up into itself and the trouble began. The air went bad, concrete began to replace grass and the natural setting that I grew up in. The influence was primarily Hispanic, because they were the pioneering cultural group, and I thought that was wonderful. Then that all changed and became this sort of hodge-podge of styles, everything related to opportunity and money. For me, it lost its root system, the one that I liked, and so I left."

We hadn't realized that Bob actually grew up in Los Angeles. I asked if his career in film began in L.A. as a consequence of growing up there.

"No. I left Los Angeles when I was seventeen. I went to the University of Colorado for a short, undistinguished time—I wasn't ready for school. Strict academic education and I were not meant for each other. I have a lot of respect for education. It's important. But the L.A. school system was pretty poor in those days, so I was never inspired in a classroom. It was a different kind of education that I was after and was to benefit from.

"I shifted my gears when I was eighteen and went to Europe to study art. For me, that's when my growth really began, my education started. And it was when I came back from Europe a year and a half later—and got kind of sidetracked in New York City—that acting came into it. My acting career started in theater in New York. It had nothing to do with Los Angeles."

The music was getting pretty loud in the background. Bob stopped to ask if it would pose a problem for our sound. "It's not great, but it's the wedding, right?" I asked.

"Well, no, it's my theme song. It goes around with me as I travel. I can dial it down for you," he kidded, flashing that killer smile. I felt so at ease with him that I was almost loath to bring his megastature into the conversation by asking about the generational change in the American hero. But it was now or never, so I asked.

"Well, heroes. Yes, it has changed." Bob thought for a second. "Let's see if I can put this in a frame here. It has to do with mythology. I share Joseph Campbell's view that every culture, every society should have mythology. Without it,

you die, eventually. When I was a kid, you were inspired to read. Radio was the only other form of communication to the masses, and film of course. There was no television. I went to the library, because my family couldn't afford to do anything except go to a movie once a week, and go to the library once a week. But, that was okay. And I read mythology. It was the most interesting to me, because it was the most entertaining. It showed larger-than-life situations, which is really attractive to a kid. I'm sure it influenced me a lot.

"But now I feel that this culture has lost its mythology and it's been replaced by this bogus one because of the Information Age, which has changed things pretty drastically. So the whole idea of heroes is a

Balm break

little bit different. It's so distorted, and it's so much in a cartoon area. Probably starting with Reagan and what he represented to the public, which was for me, personally, a bit on the cartoon side of reality. But it was licensed, it was 'Okay.' Then we had movies that reflected that, movies that were literally seventy-five-million-dollar cartoons. So I feel that evidence is part of the change.

"Whereas the mythology that I grew up with was different. It had something to do with some fundamental truth. The only truth that I can see from the heroics of today is money. The root for that in film is you have heroic figures doing absolutely ludicrous or impossible things, largely through technological abilities. It's got very little to do with the person or their character. And then sometimes heroes are villains. Right now, I think they are. They either have to be such extreme, ludicrous characters that we can almost laugh at, or they're villains because we like to champion villains as well. But that's what we're given.

"So young people, I suspect—as I did when I was a kid—take what is available to them in terms of heroics. For me, it's such a wild distortion that I don't know about heroes. The real hero is a more complex character that doesn't very often have a happy ending. In fact, in history, the real heroes very often are the ones who are sacrificed for their heroics, like some revolutionaries. I think Campbell describes it in his book *The Hero With a Thousand Faces*. I think he describes a hero as somebody that's just plucked out of the masses, who sees something or who reaches for something that lifts him above those that he is with. And he touches something and brings it back as a gift and is usually destroyed for the effort."

I asked Bob if he himself had been inspired by anyone as a child. He said that Ted Williams, the baseball player, was inspirational but that no one person in particular had influenced him. He continued: "For me, the greater inspiration—I think the great*est* inspiration—has come through nature. As I became more and more attached and connected to nature, the more I understood it, the more I became inspired by it. Outside of that, I don't think there were figures, other than a teacher here, a coach there, a conversation I've had here or there. It's been a string of moments for me that have been my inspiration.

"As far as the influence of the so-called anthem of the country, the axioms I was given as a kid, being largely false, largely mythological, have kind of informed my work as an artist. The slogans you were given as a kid that you tried to adhere to: 'It's not whether you win or lose but how you play the game.' That's just not true. That is not the truth of this country and certainly hasn't been for a long time—if it ever was.

"And images and portraits of people—whether it's George Washington or whoever—as being these sort of saintly white creatures without a flaw was simply not true. So as you grow up—and if you're paying attention—you slowly come to realize that you've been given propaganda and myth as a child, because that's part of the heritage as well. And then you start dealing with the truth, and the truth is quite something else."

The wedding march swelled in the background, melodically scoring my next question to Bob about our inalienable rights of "life, liberty, and the pursuit of happiness," and his own attempts to provide opportunities to young people through the institute. The timing of the music made him smile, and he answered, "I think that any generation will produce its own opportunity. The space for opportunity seems to be drastically reduced by what previous generations have done with the planet. If we looked at it in just the short view, it would be almost apocalyptic. But life has a funny way of retrieving itself just before it goes over the edge. If something is about to become extinct—or even if it does become extinct—it's replaced by something else. Or just before it goes extinct, it saves itself. America is great at going right up to the brink and saving itself. So I guess, optimistically, I'm assuming something may happen.

"At the same time, the resources are shrinking in this country and the population is increasing, so opportunities are narrowing, at least in this era. And you say, 'Well, what is that going to do for young people? What are they being given for any kind of guidance or opportunity?' In terms of heroes, or models, there are few, if any. And that's largely due, in my opinion, to the Information Age, which gives us every single fact we don't need and some we do. Nothing is left to the imagination, or little is left to the imagination. We're just assaulted with images and information, so it doesn't allow you anyplace to dream. It doesn't allow you anyplace to imagine.

"When I'm looking at someone young today, I say they just don't look at the same world that I did, because there just isn't enough space anymore. There's nothing as sacred as it was when I was a kid. Most of it is gone. And it's gone because the generations that have come along before this one have usually passed the baton to the next one by saying, 'I'm sacrificing so that you can have a better life.' My parents said it to me, theirs said it to them, and it was true. Each generation—with some exceptions, I guess—was a little better off than the last, because of the space and real opportunities available. But now it's been so squandered, for the most part, there's little left. So I don't think it's something so easily said today, 'We're sacrificing so that you can have a better life.'

"First of all, is it? Can it be? It's somewhat doubtful. We just came out of two generations that were inspired not to sacrifice. They were inspired to greed, to get what you can and as much as you can." Bob paused to catch his breath and continued, "Somebody like myself, I'm trying to do what I can about it, but I'm just one person. I feel like what I should do is apologize. My generation so squandered its assets that we leave you so little that you're going to have to generate your own, or rebuild for yourself, or build from scratch for yourself. I don't think there is a lot of *opportunity* as we have come to know the meaning of the word. It has to be redefined."

He seemed so genuinely sad and concerned. I wanted to tell him that he was succeeding every day—that Kris and I were living proof of his efforts. But I had another question for Bob, a man who had created his own paradise in the mountainous West. It was the question of the frontier. ''Are we at the end of our possibilities?''

He replied, ''The whole business about the last frontier, that's been myth for quite a while. There's no frontier left, physically. The only frontier left is one of the mind: what you're willing to stay open to, what you're willing to change to preserve our imagination, to preserve our brain and our hearts and therefore our souls, is gonna have to now be more reliant on the mind than striking out into the boondocks and conquering space and staking your claim and building a homestead with a family, and so forth.''

I moved on to the question about the American dream.

''Yes, I believe there's an American dream, but I don't think it exists as the same dream that I knew. When I was a kid, there was more variety to the word. You aspired to a kind of dream that incorporated figures who were worth aspiring to. As soon as we start championing Trump, Simpson—you know, people whose darker sides we may tend to not want to look at—then you get a different kind of dream. So I don't know what young people dream about today, other than trying to get into moneymaking enterprises, chiefly my business. I've never seen so many people flocking to film schools who want to get into the business because of, I think, the financial opportunities that come with it and the personal glories that come with it. Not so much the art of it, sadly.''

We talked a little bit about how Bob has reached out in so many different ways as a political and environmental advocate. I asked Bob if he had always envisioned himself speaking out on those issues, and he replied that his own dream was always to be a good artist and that global citizenry came as a by-product of the art. I asked Bob what he dreams about now.

''I still aspire to the same dream of some incorporation of nature and art, putting them together through my eyes, through the lens of my work or who I am as a person. And humanity, as it relates to social issues and art and nature—and the grand design of nature that I don't think we could ever come close to surpassing, no matter how much we try to compete or conquer it.

''I'm always happy when nature demonstrates that it can't be dominated, like Mount St. Helens or some big fire or earthquake. As sad as that is, there's something kind of revivifying about it. It's a reminder that there's this great architect that has put a scheme and an order to things that is so miraculous and so fabulous that we are genuinely stupid to not pay attention to it.''

I asked Bob if, in spite of the Information Age and the bombardment of images, he still believed that people are indeed encouraged to dream and to believe that there is do-it-yourself opportunity.

''Do it yourself—D.I.Y.—was the spirit of independence, and yet independence has been taken away from us. It's not so encouraged. We're encouraged to have a herd mentality: 'Let's all turn on the computer, let's all turn on the television, let's all watch this show.' You say, 'Do it yourself,' and that's a wonderful concept—but how can you do it for yourself when the culture has built a new age around not doing it?

"Yes, you can punch a button. But to really do something yourself, for me, feels like something you should do manually. We're getting further and further away from our ability to touch something with our hands and therefore feel the symbiosis between the object and your own body. Personally, that bothers me. Because I think we're not able to know what the consequence of that is going to be.

"Just like the consequence of the age that I grew up in, essentially the Industrial Age. Everybody was so busy diving into the age itself for all of its financial benefits. No one stopped to think about the negative side of it—what was going to be the shadow that would come with it. So as a result, there was this huge age of opportunity that came just after the war. 'We can build and develop anything we want.' No one stopped to say, 'Wait a minute. We should preserve, and we should be careful to look at the cost.' No one did that." Bob paused for a second, seeming to have gotten ahead of his own words.

He finished, "Not asking those questions produced negative side effects that now make you wonder how beneficial the age was to begin with, despite all of its wonderful breakthroughs: transistor radios, television, flying to the moon. Those are all amazing achievements with very positive effects, but there have been so many negative effects that have come with them: pollution, we can't breathe, chemicals in water. We have to practically walk around in bubbles, because of our not looking at the other side of it.

"So now here's another age, the Information Age, and is anybody looking at the issues relating to the human being? The humanistic side of it, like privacy? What happens when you lose the right of privacy? What happens when you're not encouraged to have any space to reflect? It seems to me you're moving toward a shallower culture. A culture that doesn't think or reflect or digest or process or question is bound to become shallow. And it feels to me like that's what's happening."

I asked our final question, one we had asked many times before. "So, on the opposite side of that, is there something specifically that you value most about being an American—anything that sets us apart or makes us unique?"

Bob's entire face changed when I asked that question. A softness took over and a smile spread sheepishly across his face. He did not want us to go away with the wrong impression. "I sure do. I do. I'm extremely patriotic, I really am, but on a very, very deep, almost spiritual level. This is the best country to be in, despite its frustrations. I still say there's no greater place physically. And the fact is we still can, for the moment, boast the one ingredient that would make me say always this is the best place to be—and why I like to be here—and that's freedom."

Bob's views, like so many others, echoed dismay and worry about the country's current direction. But when confronted with the question of the value of being an American, of the United States' unique offering to its people, Bob's answer unanimously recalled the country's original foundation—"Freedom."

And with that we were done. We had completed our schedule and a year of our lives.

It somehow seemed fitting that the man who most personally inspired the making of the film had completed the circle of our journey. The sun hung low— just nudging the snowy peaks—and the sight was exactly how we would have scripted the scene, if we'd been able: the "perfect ending." As Bob unhooked his microphone, he suggested we relax with a hike up to the waterfalls and a nice dinner at the resort's restaurant that night. He was off to his next meeting and then back to Montana that night. We shook hands, thanking him perhaps too profusely, and the Sundance Kid jogged off into the sunset, disappearing into the trees.

THE END OF
THE ROAD

ABOUT ONE MONTH AFTER OUR ARRIVAL IN THE CITY
OF NEW ORLEANS, LOUISIANA 1/5

(Kristin)

I have chosen this day, and this quaint New Orleans spot, to write about the end of our journey. I'm sitting in a café that's kitty-corner to Jackson Square; if you blindfolded people and brought them here, they'd swear you'd dropped them in a corner of Paris. The smells of chicory coffee and the clippity-clop of horses' hooves over cobblestones find their way in and out of the often-opened door. There is a man outside the café's picture window. He is pointing. Standing very still. He seems to be barely breathing.

The man is a mime—the statue-still-on-a-milk-crate kind, not the trapped-in-the-box kind. His face is painted white and is crowned by a faded red, white, and blue shag wig, reminiscent of my childhood bedroom carpet. A class of about twenty unchaperoned junior high school students are gathered around him. They're hitting him with balloons, screaming in his face, kicking him—though not hard enough to inflict real pain—and laughing obnoxiously, all in an attempt to make him flinch. After about five long minutes of this torture, which I witness in agony, the mime's unwavering patience wins out. The children move on, like a passing tidal wave, having gotten no satisfaction from the man's still, stone face. His tip can remains empty.

There is something tragic about the mime's worn-out wig, but something gloriously reassuring about his resilience, as he stands so still, so vulnerably silent. I assume he's always known that he will be ridiculed by some who pass, but I imagine it is the complex web of choices he's made that led him to stand there, that gives him his power. I love that quality in Americans—that we take so seriously our freedom to do what we want—even if what we want to do is stand stockstill on a street corner. There is a palpable American spirit. As a result, everything imaginable will be done by someone in this country, every niche filled, spreading like warm icing over a just-baked cake. Someone will want to mime—just as someone will want to cure cancer, someone will want to build houses, and someone will want to tell stories about all the things that people are doing. And though there's no guarantee we'll be good at it, no one can stop us from getting on the milk crate and dreaming of being the best mime in the whole damn world.

Traveling across the country, my own notions of life's possibilities were expanded, as we singled out and observed people living their dreams, pursuing their passions, and fighting to ensure the same for others. If I was pressed to say what makes Americans unique, I would say it is our *potential* for tandem dreaming. As Americans, we are given—in our founding documents—the freedom and encouragement to dream, and to ''spot'' each other as we walk in succession across life's tightrope. But we so often don't. I can't help but wonder why more of us—in a nation founded by people who fought for the right to dream and live freely—aren't working more closely together today to sustain and pursue those ideals. Not just for ourselves, but for others, and those who will follow. Does our innate decency struggle uphill against the inclination to taunt each other, just waiting for the other to flinch? Why do we so often get in the way of each other's dreaming?

There seem to be two main forces at work in our nation—two forces that are conflicting by definition, but ultimately dependent upon one another. Obviously, the impulse toward freedom and individuality is strong; we are a nation of people who expect to go their own way, do their own thing. And yet, we are also a nation in which our gravitation toward community is strong—we recognize it as the civilizing force that will allow our society to continue to flourish, the society that bestows those very freedoms we so value. It is, after all, our shared experiences, cultural memories, and common morality that give our individuality contextual meaning, and vice versa. The driving force of our patriotism has become our collective identity as a nation defined by individualism. It seems imperative, therefore, that our impulse toward freedom and our impulse toward community be balanced, if we are to continue to grow and prosper *collectively*, instead of merely surviving in isolated pockets.

Jack Healey's mother had said to him, "When you can walk the highways and byways of life, and learn to listen to the weeping and wailing of the poor, then you'll be a man." I think this is what our founding parents had in mind for this country in their most enlightened moments. That it is not enough to succeed; we must uplift, we must contribute, we must bring others along with us. As individuals, as Americans, that is our inherited responsibility. Shainee and I saw this spirit exemplified in so many of the people we encountered, people whose passions—often articulated as a "mission"—were so integrated into their daily lives that flying to Bosnia to mediate peace talks, or curing an internationally debilitating disease, or starting public radio in North America and South Africa, or inspiring millions of people was, in their minds, no different from the mailman delivering the mail on time. "It should be the goal of the human being to make it a perfect world," Healey had urged. And so many of his fellow interviewees, like him, were using their unique freedom to do so, to forge a stronger sense of self, and ultimately, a stronger community.

Before we left in search of America, Shainee and I had wondered if there was anything that tangibly binds us as Americans, other than the geography that we share. We were curious if we would find traces of a common identity, a shared dream, a heroic pursuit of ideas and ideals, and crossover reflections on America spoken by diverse voices. It was a tall order, and one that we didn't *count* on finding. But what our search revealed is that the landscape, individual inspiration, the American dream, and American heroism are indeed woven tightly together. Almost everyone we met spoke of having inherited inspiration from the work, struggles, and successes of other people as well as the land that sustains us. Those same individuals spoke of that inspiration as something that encourages them to dream, and through the dream, pursue happiness. The pursuit, in turn, unfolds combined efforts—often heroic—which shape the character of a nation called ''America.''

Shainee and I were relieved to find that we seem to be among a majority of people searching for more—more meaning, more understanding, a fortified community, a shared past, new friendships. As two young women traversing the country, we were taken care of, protected, fed, and encouraged by people everywhere we went—many of them unlikely caretakers. What we found was not a fearful, suspicious America, but an ambitious people, desirous of growth, change, movement, connection, and a voice in the future of this country. And surprisingly, we encountered an almost unanimous rejection of cynicism, which usually resulted in a commitment to be a *part* of this free society, instead of being acted upon *by* it.

We could have continued on the *Anthem* road for the next fifty years and still not have talked to all the people who should, or could, have been included. The trip and the viewpoints to which we were exposed have now become so integrated into our lives that a day does not go by when we don't think about one or more of the individuals we met. I find myself quoting them regularly, or silently consulting them when faced with a challenge. In the collective voices of these people—the anthem that Shainee and I have recorded—I now hear a constant reminder to stay aware and stay courageously engaged in the world around me. Inspired by what I have witnessed in others, I feel I must, for my duration on earth, stand up and be counted—hoping to live up to Jack's mother's creed to listen, always listen, and, in whatever way I can, steady the tightrope for anyone else who might be crossing after us.

NEW ORLEANS, OUR APARTMENT ON ROYAL ST.   4/29

(Shainee)

Next week we leave this wondrous city. It's hard to believe that one year ago we were frantically preparing to embark on the journey of a lifetime, and now that journey is ending in the same place it began. We put together a trailer of the movie and wrote a proposal for a book and—voilà—someone cares: we have sold a book that we didn't know we were going to write and it looks like we have a distributor for the film as well. So now we are heading to the city that will put every post-production need at our fingertips—New York. About as far away as we can get from the balm of the Louisiana bayou.

Our stomachs begin to churn every time Kris and I discuss the demands of reducing hundreds of hours of footage and a year's worth of experiences into a mere two-hour film. The prospect of a book gives us a little more latitude, but both are daunting in their current state as blank canvases. In some ways, the expectations of a publisher and distributor for a finished product feel invasive. Up until now, our trip has been intimate, circumscribed within the island of our car and our own minds. We lost track of time in that car. The traditional language of the calendar—months and days—fell away, and for a while, we measured out our lives by states and interviews. Now we must make the transition to begin measuring by pages of transcripts and hours of footage. But faced with the prospect of translating the experience for an audience, the voices of those we have met seem only to ring in our ears, an unruly cacophony. That—*and* leaving our beloved New Orleans—is overwhelming to say the least.

I have grown to love this city, the city that first enchanted us and gave us Doug, our guardian angel. I have come to cherish its dark centuries-old mysteries, the languid vernacular, the smells of generations of restaurants, and a color of light that I swear comes only from the New Orleans sun. I've come to welcome being awoken each morning by the sound of a riverboat's foghorn, followed by the pipe organ's music, every day, just as it sounds right now.

You see now that we have decided to leave this city it seems to be revealing its most secret hues to us in all their splendor and intrigue. Which brings me to today . . .

I woke up feeling crotchety and unrested due to a surprisingly fierce spring sunburn and the anxiety of our impending departure. I cursed the sultry caress of the climate reaching through my open window—usually one of the most alluring features of this city, but today only taunting. Desperately in need of a Café du Monde iced café au lait pick-me-up and some aloe for my crispy shoulders, I ventured out alone into a misty rain.

All of my senses peaked. Everything seemed sharper, more acute. Walking by the renovation of the eighteenth-century shotgun house next door, the painter's sanded dust seemed redder than usual; across the street, the alcoholic's eyes seemed glassier than they normally do when he emerges from the corner market with the morning's first brown bag; and the scent of the night-blooming jasmine drifting from third-floor flowerboxes seemed to pierce my nose. New Orleans was making its mark on me so that I will never forget it.

My futile hope for the usual quiet of a weekday morning at Café du Monde was met with a swamp of Jazz Fest tourists who had taken over the city earlier this week. I begrudgingly took my place in line. The women behind me spoke in a quintessentially sharp Texas drawl, debating the souvenir possibilities of the cafe's gift boxes. The couple next to me were obviously recently engaged and already looking bored with each other. The girls in front of me were nineteen-year-old ex-Deadheads, displaced in the wake of Jerry Garcia's death. One had pink hair and only one shoe on. When the waiter came over to tell her she'd have to leave—"Bare feet are a health hazard young lady"—she began to hop on her solely shoed foot. In spite of my torpor, I cracked the first smile of the day and got my coffee.

Crossing the street to Jackson Square, giving myself my standard pep talk about change being the only thing we can count on and therefore deserving of embrace, I began to feel a little better. I moved toward St. Peter's Cathedral, opting to take the long way home. The light rain felt cool against my shoulders as the chicory elixir began to provide its full healing effect. As I rounded the corner in front of the church, the buzz of the Decatur Street tourist traffic began to diminish, and the faint, sweet notes of a saxophone came drifting toward me. I looked around for the source of the music and spotted a man, playing alone. He had no audience but a few pigeons—I guess all the tourists were at the festival—and there was no instrument case lying in front of him to receive pitched change. It was only him, playing a soft, lilting lament that matched the pattern of the rain, the kind of song that makes you gulp. I have never seen the square so empty.

My hazy morning eyes focused in on his face and I felt a sharp pang of recognition—it was Leonard, the saxophonist we interviewed almost one year ago. Leonard, who brought us to Joe's Cozy Corner in the Tremé and laughed and gyrated and flirted with us. Leonard, who invited us into his world, intoxicated us with it, and then sent us along with a wonderful memory, one of our first. Now we have layered an entire year's worth of memories onto that first unexpected delight—a series of moments that could have occurred only once, on one given trip, during one given summer, seen through the eyes of two particular young women. I sat down to watch him, far enough away so as not to disturb him. I didn't want to say hello; I just wanted to hear him play again.

As Leonard's song took over the stillness in the air, my muddled thoughts gave way to realization: Kris and I are at a pivotal juncture in our journey. This is not merely the end of our trip, but the beginning of something just as significant, the telling of the story. Soon we will be reliving every encounter over and over in hopes of distilling the tale into a version worthy of sharing with others. Kris and I set out to record the country's ideas about itself and its dreams; in the process, we have lived our own. We have been given the precious gift of experience. We have come to understand the difference between simply knowing and actually seeing and hearing for ourselves. It began with our visit to Kent State and continued from Dollywood to Oklahoma City; from the back roads of Woody Creek, Colorado, to the dark wall of the Vietnam Veterans Memorial; from the wave of an Amish man to the wreath hanging on the railing of the Lorraine Motel.

I began to see the moments as they were and still are—indelible moments imprinted forever in the collective consciousness of Kristin and me: Stud's Terkel singing opera and Ida's apple juice, Bill Siemering reciting Whitman from a crumpled piece of paper, John Waters's Buick, and George McGovern's grandchildren; a coquette's wink of Dorothy Betts' eye, tomatoes from Wes Jackson's garden, and homemade tortillas with Jimmy Baca's family; and finally the sight of Robert Redford's smile taking over his entire face as he uttered the word that has been echoed over and over, "freedom." Kris and I were reminded everywhere of what the gift of freedom means in this country simply by making a decision last year to exercise our right to it.

Slowly the voices of *Anthem*—the cacophony that has sounded so intimidating these past weeks—seemed to hush. My mind cleared and for the first time I began to hear them as one, a few perfect notes from this man's saxophone, composing one melody on a gray New Orleans morning—an anthem. One could choose to hear the whole country as a cacophony, a meaningless schizophrenic frenzy that feels hollow and instills only fear and confusion. That's the sound Kris and I heard when we fled Los Angeles. But I truly believe that we have spent the last year hearing something else. I think what we've heard is that Americans—perhaps in spite of themselves—do absorb a piece of the dream. That regardless of its definition, of what is truth and what is myth, it has seeped into our psyche. Somehow. I think we found that we have more in common than we might think and that "the American" does indeed exist. What do we have in common? The freedom to dream.

Leonard's song finished, and I got up to leave before he noticed me. I silently thanked him for reminding me that memories can become stories and that our journey can continue as long as we want it to. Then I came home to resume the all-too-familiar rite of passage: packing up and moving on.